Defense of the West

Transatlantic security from Truman to Trump

Second edition

Stanley R. Sloan

Manchester University Press

The right of Stanley R. Sloan to be identified as the author of this work has been asserted
by him in accordance with the Copyright, Designs and Patents Act 1988.

Published by Manchester University Press
Altrincham Street, Manchester M1 7JA, UK

www.manchesteruniversitypress.co.uk

British Library Cataloguing-in-Publication Data is available
First edition published by Manchester University Press in 2016

This edition first published 2020

ISBN   978 1 5261 4622 9 hardback

ISBN   978 1 5261 4623 6 paperback

The publisher has no responsibility for the persistence or accuracy of URLs for any external or
third-party internet websites referred to in this book, and does not guarantee that any content
on such websites is, or will remain, accurate or appropriate.

Typeset by Newgen Publishing UK
Printed by TJ International Ltd, Padstow

Defense of the West

MANCHESTER
1824

Manchester University Press

Contents

Lists of figures, boxes, and tables *page* vi
Foreword by Lawrence Freedman viii
Acknowledgments xi
List of abbreviations xiv
Maps xviii

Part I: Cold War alliance 1

1 The transatlantic bargain and defense of the West 3
2 Genesis of the bargain 20
3 The transatlantic bargain revised 37
4 The bargain through the Cold War, 1954–1989 50
5 The United States and Europe at the end of the Cold War:
  some fundamental factors 83

Part II: Post-Cold War alliance 101

6 The 1990s: transitions and challenges 103
7 The 2000s: turbulent transatlantic ties 182
8 The 2010s: new tasks, new traumas 253

Part III: Defense of the West 315

9 External threats and internal challenges 317
10 Can the West survive? 339

Appendix 1: The North Atlantic Treaty: Washington D.C.—April 4,
 1949 347
Appendix 2: Active Engagement, Modern Defence, NATO Strategic
 Concept, November 20, 2010 351
Select bibliography 362
About the author 369
Index 371

Figures, boxes, and tables

Figures

2.1 President Truman watches while Secretary of State Acheson
signs the North Atlantic Treaty. Source: NATO Photos.   23

2.2 General Dwight D. Eisenhower, NATO's First Supreme Allied
Commander. Source: NATO Photos.   30

3.1 October 23, 1954 Signature of Paris Agreements, inviting the
Federal Republic of Germany to join NATO. Source: NATO
Photos.   46

4.1 UK and US delegations at 1973 opening of Mutual and Balanced
Force Reduction negotiations in Vienna (author is seen
immediately behind US Ambassador Jonathan Dean). Source:
US Delegation to Mutual and Balanced Force Reductions.   60

5.1 This promotion for the *Atlantic Community Quarterly* suggested
the transatlantic allies should see the Atlantic Ocean as a river,
implying that shared values and interests could overcome
geography. Reproduced by permission of the Atlantic Council
of the United States.   86

6.1 The fall of the Berlin Wall, November 1, 1989, with the
Brandenburg Gate in the background. Source: NATO Photos.   105

6.2 Secretary General Manfred Woerner played a key role in NATO's
transformation to post-Cold War institution. Source: NATO
Photos.   109

6.3 Opening of the 1999 Washington 50th Anniversary Summit.
Source: NATO Photos.   146

7.1 'NATO Team'. Copyright © Kevin Kallaugher. Reproduced
by permission.   191

7.2 Secretary General George Robertson and Russian President
Vladimir Putin meeting in Brussels after Putin's reaction to
the 9/11 attacks had led to one of the few high points in
Russia–NATO relations. Source: NATO Photos.   224

7.3 EU High Representative for the Common Foreign and Security
     Policy (and former NATO Secretary General 1995–1999), Javier
     Solana and NATO Secretary General, Jaap de Hoop Scheffer, meet
     in October 2008 in the context of a joint session of NATO's North
     Atlantic Council and the EU's Political and Security Committee.
     Source: NATO Photos.   239
8.1 NATO leaders at 2009 Strasbourg/Kehl 60th Anniversary
     Summit (British Prime Minister Brown, US President Obama,
     NATO Secretary General Jaap de Hoop Scheffer, German
     Chancellor Merkel, French President Sarkozy).
     Source: NATO Photos.   255
8.2 President Obama greets NATO Secretary General Stoltenberg in
     May 2015 on Stoltenberg's first official visit to Washington as
     Secretary General. Source: NATO Photos.   286

Boxes

2.1 Some key developments (June 1947–May 1952).   33
3.1 Some key developments (January 1953–May 1955).   44
4.1 Some key developments (March 1957–November 1989).   79
6.1 Some key developments (November 1989–April 1999).   173
7.1 Some key developments (January 2001–April 2009).   242
8.1 North Atlantic Treaty, Articles 4 and 5.   259

Tables

8.1 Participation in Euro-Atlantic Security Institutions (2020). 272
8.2 Some key developments (January 2009–May 2020).   303

Foreword

by Lawrence Freedman

The principle behind an alliance is simple: states lacking the strength to cope with a powerful adversary on their own have a better chance of doing so when acting together. Yet historically, alliances are often tentative and temporary. This is why the North Atlantic Alliance, established by the Washington Treaty of April 1949, is quite unique. It has not only outlived the conflict that brought it into being, but it has managed to acquire new members. NATO is now a familiar part of the strategic landscape and, until recently, its existence has remained unquestioned, with neither its present value nor future durability under threat.

That changed with the election of Donald Trump. His view was that NATO represented a poor deal for the United States, since compared with the European members of NATO, the US committed a far larger share of its GDP to military expenditure and made a greater contribution of forces to the alliance. At the same time, Trump did not share the same security concerns as Europeans and was keen to repair relations with President Vladimir Putin, despite the ongoing conflict over Ukraine. In Europe, many look to the EU as an alternative source of security policies; however, President Emmanuel Macron has wondered whether NATO is 'brain dead'. Meanwhile critics on the left have argued that such a powerful alliance is provocative and encourages the militarization of foreign policy. The issues of whether NATO should continue to exist and what its role should be are becoming more pressing and urgent.

Why has the NATO alliance lasted as long as it has? First, the alliance was based on common values, as well as a shared threat. In 1949, the Soviet Union represented a different form of totalitarianism to Nazi Germany, which though illiberal and anti-democratic, was opposed to free markets. NATO also contained undemocratic states at times—Portugal until the mid-1970s and the military regime in Greece from 1967 to 1974—but they were treated as outliers and eventually became democracies. The second factor in the alliance's longevity is that its strategy was essentially deterrent. Since the conflict that brought it into being was ideological as well as geopolitical, it could not be resolved by political concessions. Yet it was also too dangerous to attempt to resolve by war, a fact that became progressively truer as both sides built up their nuclear arsenals. The foundational conflict therefore remained in place for forty years.

The third factor is that the deterrent effect of an alliance depends as much on its cohesion as the armed forces at its disposal. NATO only became a military organization in 1950. In 1949, the formation of an alliance was supposed to be a deterrent in itself. The European democracies believed that they had suffered badly in two world wars while waiting for the United States to join the fight. All the belligerents might have been spared much grief if the Germans had known for sure in 1914 and 1939 that should they opt for war, they would face the full weight of American power. With the Washington Treaty, there would be no doubt about the US commitment to defeating aggression. The corollary to that commitment was that without the alliance there would be no deterrent. During the Cold War a great effort was therefore put into keeping the alliance together, enduring tensions related to burden-sharing, strategy, and nuclear weapons, as well as differences over how seriously to take the Cold War outside of Europe. American presidents were irritated by the lack of support for their world-wide efforts to contain communist advances, while European governments were wary of being drawn into unnecessary conflicts.

The fourth factor that has ensured the alliance's continued existence is that while the United States was the indispensable contributor to NATO, with capabilities far exceeding those of other members, it also had potentially less at stake than those more vulnerable to Soviet aggression. Just as the United States had hoped the Atlantic Ocean would help it to stay out of European conflicts prior to the two world wars, there was always the suspicion in Europe that this might be its default position. Within American politics, there was always an isolationist tendency ready to pull the US away from all international entanglements. The importance of US nuclear threats to NATO strategy led to worries about whether these really could be credible, when implementing them would mean probable Soviet nuclear retaliation against US territory. One way to reduce dependence on incredible nuclear threats was to build up conventional forces; however, the Europeans were reluctant to raise their defense budgets, and made the comforting assumption that the Soviet Union was as keen as they were to avoid a third world war. The US was thus expected to accept nuclear danger in part because the allies wanted to keep their military costs down. The *quid pro quo* for this was that the United States had to be leader of the alliance and exercise the supreme command of the collective military effort.

These four factors—shared values, a preference for deterrence over appeasement or conquest, member states overcoming differences to stick together, and the dominant power and leadership of the United States—were all in place as the Cold War came to an end. Having in effect 'won' the Cold War, there was no incentive for the alliance to disband. It could now guard against a resurgent Russian threat, while looking beyond its traditional missions. As one of the core institutions of the West, there was a clamor from the post-communist states of Central and Eastern Europe to join. These issues of expanding ambition and growing membership would continue to dominate NATO debates.

The first notable shift in missions was the intervention in the conflicts associated with the breakup of the former Yugoslavia. Following al-Qaeda's attacks on the United States in September 2001, NATO entered Afghanistan, while also supporting rebels to overthrow the Libyan leader Colonel Gaddafi. While the interventions in Bosnia and Kosovo came to an end, it was hard to be satisfied with the experiences in Afghanistan or Libya. This led to pressure to scale back to the core mission in Europe, while the question of how to deal with Russian aggression became bound up with issues of NATO expansion.

NATO initially adopted a more flexible approach to work with former members of the Warsaw Pact, and the 'Partnership for Peace' allowed for close relations short of full membership; however, countries that were still wary of Moscow wanted a full alliance commitment. Thus the expansion of NATO membership led to a growing anxiety in Russia, especially when it appeared that Georgia and Ukraine might join. This was part of the backdrop to Russia's conflict with Ukraine, which reached a head with the annexation of Crimea in March 2014 and active support of separatists in Eastern Ukraine. The Russian campaign of menace and intimidation, designed to discourage NATO countries from supporting Ukraine, helped NATO regain its old sense of purpose. Nonetheless, in an expanded NATO, there were tensions between those concerned about an assertive Russia and those worried about instability to the South, notably in North Africa. These tensions placed a greater premium on US leadership, but even under the Obama administration there was evidence of a declining American readiness to play this role. With Trump this tendency became even more pronounced.

This is why NATO's future appears fragile, and this is why Stanley Sloan's book is so timely and vital. He has a unique perspective on the history of the alliance, having been following it closely through his career. When I first got to know him in the late 1970s, he was already established as one of America's leading 'NATO-watchers'. This is a role he still plays and it's why he writes with such authority, knowledge, and lucidity. Sloan is uniquely aware of the past challenges overcome, the disagreements calmed, and the problems the alliance faces in a tense international environment. This book is not only an essential history of the alliance in the context of global developments, but it is also a compelling description of the value of NATO as an instrument of diplomacy, crisis management, and defense. NATO serves a purpose simply by existing, for in doing so it precludes other forms of destabilizing, competitive alliance formation in Europe and offers a forum in which all security issues can be addressed. Its durability and familiarity is part of its strength. If NATO did not exist now, it would be desirable to create it—but extremely hard to do so.

Sir Lawrence Freedman

Acknowledgments

Thinkers, researchers, writers all stand on the shoulders of those who have come before us. We learn from our predecessors and contemporaries alike and try to add something worthwhile to the foundations already established. When in 1985 I published the first in a series of books on NATO, I adopted the term "transatlantic bargain" from the man who first developed the concept. Ambassador Harlan Cleveland passed away in 2008, but the idea that the transatlantic bargain is a deal among the Europeans and between Europe and North America, remains a helpful prism through which to see Euro-Atlantic relations.

In 1985, I suggested that there was another partner to the bargain: the US Congress. From the beginning, the powerful American legislative body has played a major role in shaping, as well as critiquing, the deal. The roles played by the US House and Senate are indicative of the fact that the bargain is one made among states with democratic systems that respect individual liberty and the rule of law. As a result, the bargain is by no means static. Changes in the deal over the years have been validated by successive generations of leaders in the United States, Canada, and Europe, and will continue to require such validation. Recently, President Donald Trump has made this validation even more challenging and, at the same time, more critical.

The twists and turns of transatlantic relations have been traced and dissected by many commentators, historians, and political scientists. However, for me and many other scholars in the field, the late Lawrence S. Kaplan stood head and shoulders above the rest. Larry was widely regarded as NATO's leading historian, and I am privileged to have known him as a friend and to have benefitted greatly from his guidance and encouragement over the years.

The 24 years that I spent at the Congressional Research Service of the Library of Congress introduced me to another contingent of experts with broad shoulders, whose peer reviews of my work always required that I think more deeply and effectively. A few of my former colleagues still work at this marvelous institution, and they have been joined by new analysts who continue to produce the best objective and non-partisan research around. Fortunately for scholars, CRS reports are now more readily available to the public.

For almost 30 years now, I have been fortunate to have been invited regularly to lecture on transatlantic relations at the NATO Defense College in Rome. This little-known institution makes an important contribution to spreading awareness of what NATO is, and what it isn't, to military officers and civilian defense and foreign policy officials of NATO countries, and now of partner countries from Europe, North Africa, the Middle East, and Asia. I appreciate the decisions of the College's many commandants, deans, and their staffs over the years to allow me to share in and learn from this experience.

Since leaving government service, my work has particularly been stimulated by many bright and capable students at Middlebury College, where I have had the privilege of teaching in the winter term for some 16 years. The challenge of trying to contribute to the education and world views of these bright young people has, for me, been an invaluable learning experience. Guest lecturers and friends who have enriched the sessions for me and my students include Lawrence R. Chalmer, Marten van Heuven, and Leo G. Michel.

I was immensely fortunate for the 2016 edition of this volume to have benefitted from the research assistance of four Middlebury College students who had previously taken my course on Euro-Atlantic Relations and were therefore very familiar with the previous edition of this book. Conor Maxwell, Nathanial Crenner, Lukas Marble, and Courtney Cano all made important contributions to research for this book and provided perceptive critiques of the chapters as we revised old ones and created new ones.

This revised edition was informed in part by the book I was asked to write for publication by Manchester University Press in 2018 titled *Transatlantic traumas: has illiberalism brought the West to the brink of collapse?* That volume benefitted from the creative and supportive work of three additional Middlebury students, all of whom had previously taken my course on transatlantic relations. Rowen Price, Travis Sanderson, and Grace Vedock volunteered to serve as research assistants and became full-fledged collaborators.

Finally, I was fortunate with this edition to have been supported by Ideal Dowling, who produced the best final paper in my most recent transatlantic relations course at Middlebury and graciously accepted my invitation to work with me on this volume. Ideal is a talented writer and editor as well as a young lady any parent would be proud to have as their daughter. As a bonus, Ideal is a star performer on Middlebury's intercollegiate women's squash team.

The endorsement offered by the renowned strategic thinker Sir Lawrence Freedman in the foreword to this volume is greatly appreciated. Lawry has provided an important perspective to help frame my interpretation of the history of transatlantic relations security relations from Truman to Trump.

I am pleased to have been welcomed into the stable of writers for the Manchester University Press. This well-respected publisher took over projects previously in the hands of Bloomsbury Publishing when that press decided to go out of the international security business. My thanks to the publishing team at Manchester as well as to the anonymous reviewers of the proposal and manuscript who were so supportive of the effort and offered some excellent suggestions to enhance the book's value.

While I appreciate all the sources of assistance with this project, responsibility for any mistakes or roads not taken in this book is, of course, mine.

Finally, I wish to acknowledge most importantly my in-house critic, copyeditor, supporter, and loving wife Monika. My everlasting love and gratitude go out to the better half of our own "transatlantic bargain."

Stanley R. Sloan
Lake Groton and Richmond, Vermont

Abbreviations

ABM	Anti-Ballistic Missile Treaty
ACLANT	Allied Command Atlantic
ACO	Allied Command Operations [NATO]
ACT	Allied Command Transformation [NATO]
AFSOUTH	Allied Forces Southern Europe [NATO]
ANA	Afghan National Army
ANAAC	Afghan National Army Air Corps
ANP	Afghan National Police
ANSF	Afghan National Security Forces
ASOP	Afghan Social Outreach Program
AWACS	Airborne Warning and Control System
BENELUX	Belgium, the Netherlands, and Luxembourg
Brexit	British exit from EU membership
CAP	Common Agricultural Policy [EU]
CARD	Coordinated Annual Review on Defence [EU]
CBRN	Chemical, Biological, Radiological and Nuclear Defence Battalion [NATO]
CDE	Conference on Security and Confidence Building Measures and Disarmament in Europe
CDP	Capability Development Plan [EU]
CEE	Central and East European countries
CFE	Conventional Forces in Europe Treaty
CFSP	Common Foreign and Security Policy [EU]
CIS	Commonwealth of Independent States
CJTF	Combined Joint Task Force [NATO]
COMECON	Council for Mutual Economic Assistance
COPS(I)	(Interim) Political and Security Committee [EU] (French acronym)
CSCE	Conference on Security and Cooperation in Europe
CSDP	Common Security and Defence Policy [EU]

CSTO	Collective Security Treaty Organization
DAESH	Also: ISIS/ISIL—Islamic State in Syria (in Iraq and Levant)
DCI	Defense Capabilities Initiative [NATO]
DDPR	Deterrence and Defense Posture Review [NATO]
DPC	Defense Planning Committee [NATO]
DSACEUR	Deputy Supreme Allied Commander in Europe [NATO]
EAPC	Euro-Atlantic Partnership Council [NATO]
EC	European Communit(y)(ies)
ECSC	European Coal and Steel Community
EDA	European Defence Agency
EDC	European Defence Community
EDF	European Defence Fund [EU]
EEC	European Economic Community
EFTA	European Free Trade Area
EMS	European Monetary System [EU]
EMU	European Monetary Unit [EU]
EPC	European Political Cooperation [EU]
ESDI	European Security and Defence Identity [WEU/EU]
ESDP	European Security and Defence Policy [EU]
ETT	Embedded Training Team [NATO, ISAF]
EU	European Union
EUFOR	European Force [EU-Bosnia]
EUMC	European Union Military Committee [EU]
EUMS	European Union Military Staff [EU]
EUPOL	European Union Police [EU]
EURATOM	European Atomic Energy Community
Euro	European Union currency unit
EUROCORPS	European Rapid Reaction Force [EU]
Eurogroup	Informal grouping of NATO European defense ministers dissolved in 1993
FATA	Federally Administered Tribal Areas [Pakistan]
FSU	Former Soviet Union
FYROM	Former Yugoslav Republic of Macedonia
GATT	General Agreement on Tariffs and Trade
GDP	Gross Domestic Product
GWOT	Global War on Terror
ICS	Integrated Command Structure
IED	Improvised Explosive Device
IEPG	Independent European Programme Group
IFOR	Implementation Force (for Bosnia) [NATO]
IGC	Intergovernmental Conference [EU]
IMS	International Military Staff [NATO]
INF	Intermediate-Range Nuclear Forces

ISAF	International Security Assistance Force [NATO]
ISIS/ISIL	Islamic State in Syria (in Iraq and Levant)
JCPOA	Joint Comprehensive Plan of Action [Iran accord]
KFOR	Kosovo Force [NATO]
LANDCENT	Allied Land Forces Central Europe [NATO]
LTDP	Long Term Defense Plan [NATO]
MAP	Membership Action Plan [NATO]
MBFR	Mutual and Balanced Force Reductions
MC	Military Committee [NATO]
MLF	Multilateral Force [NATO]
MPCC	Military Planning and Conduct Capability [EU]
NAC	North Atlantic Council [NATO]
NACC	North Atlantic Cooperation Council [NATO]
NAFTA	North American Free Trade Area
NATO	North Atlantic Treaty Organization
NGO	non-governmental organization
NPA	NATO Parliamentary Assembly (formerly NAA, North Atlantic Assembly)
NPG	Nuclear Planning Group [NATO]
NPT	[Nuclear] Non-Proliferation Treaty
NRF	NATO Response Force [NATO]
NSC	US National Security Council
OECD	Organization for Economic Cooperation and Development
OEF	Operation Enduring Freedom
OMLT	Operational Mentoring and Liaison Team [NATO, ISAF]
OSCE	Organization for Security and Cooperation in Europe
PARP	[Partnership for Peace] Planning and Review Process [NATO]
PCC	Prague Capabilities Commitment [NATO]
PESCO	Permanent Structured Cooperation [EU]
PfP	Partnership for Peace
PJC	NATO–Russia Permanent Joint Council [NATO]
PRT	Provincial Reconstruction Team
PSC	Political and Security Committee [EU]
RMA	Revolution in Military Affairs
SACEUR	Supreme Allied Commander, Europe [NATO]
SACLANT	Supreme Allied Commander, Atlantic [NATO]
SDI	Strategic Defense Initiative
SFOR	Bosnia Stabilization Force [NATO]
SHAPE	Supreme Headquarters Allied Powers, Europe [NATO]
SNF	Short-Range Nuclear Forces
STANAVFORMED	Standing Naval Force Mediterranean [NATO]
START	Strategic Arms Reduction Talks

TEU	Treaty on European Union, "The Maastricht Treaty" [EU]
T-JIOC	Tripartite Joint Intelligence Operations Center [NATO-ISAF]
TTIP	Transatlantic Trade and Investment Partnership [EU-US]
UK	United Kingdom
UN	United Nations
UNDP	United Nations Development Program
UNPROFOR	United Nations Protection Force (in Bosnia)
UNSC	United Nations Security Council
UNSCR	United Nations Security Council Resolution
US	United States of America
USSR	Union of Soviet Socialist Republics
VJTF	Very High Readiness Joint Task Force [NATO]
WEAG	Western European Armaments Group
WEU	Western European Union
WMD	weapons of mass destruction

Map 1 Current membership of NATO

Map 2 Current membership of the European Union

Part I

Cold War alliance

Part I

Cold War alliance

1

The transatlantic bargain and defense of the West

> The glue that has held the allies more or less together is a large, complex and dynamic bargain—partly an understanding among the Europeans, but mostly a deal between them and the United States of America. (Harlan Cleveland, *NATO: The Transatlantic Bargain*)[1]

Crafted in the late 1960s, Harlan Cleveland's description of the North Atlantic Treaty Organization (NATO) as a "transatlantic bargain" remains, in the early years of the twenty-first century, a helpful prism through which to analyze the North Atlantic alliance. Cleveland, a former US permanent representative to NATO, knew the alliance was far more than the sort of deal struck between business partners. Although the transatlantic bargain is based firmly on unsentimental calculations of national self-interest on both sides of the Atlantic, it also depends on some amorphous but vital shared ideas about man, government, and society. It is a "bargain," to be sure, but a bargain with roots in the hearts (and values) as well as in the minds (and interests) of the partners. Because this alliance serves both values and interests, it has come to represent the primary framework for defense of "the West."

The United Kingdom's Lord Palmerston, a nineteenth-century British statesman, famously declared that "Nations have no permanent friends or allies, they only have permanent interests." Palmerston's observation stood up well through the mid-twentieth century. However, the persistence of NATO—the leading component of the transatlantic bargain—seems to be challenging Palmerston's assertion.

Following George Washington's warning in his farewell address that the United States should avoid permanent foreign alliances, particularly with European states, the United States took his advice—until April 1949, when the North Atlantic Treaty was signed. As Lawrence S. Kaplan has observed, "The Europeans may have initiated the process, but bipartisan U.S. advocates brought it to a conclusion and terminated America's 149-year tradition of political and military non-entanglement with Europe."[2] Superficially, the treaty certainly looked like what Washington had warned against. However, both the circumstances and the alliance were in fact quite different than what Washington had considered.

This volume examines the origins and development of the transatlantic alliance with an eye on the major factors that have influenced its evolution, and may offer clues about its future. Throughout NATO's history, the alliance has been said to be moving from one "crisis" to another, and its demise has frequently been projected by scholars and officials alike. So far, they have been wrong. The question is: will they continue to be wrong, or will intra-Western divisions on both interests and values bring down the West's main alliance?

NATO and alliance theory

Before opening our historical examination of the transatlantic bargain, it might be useful to reflect briefly on some of the work that political scientists and international relations theorists have done on alliances: why they happen, what they do, and how they end.

The traditional international relations concept of alliances is that they are agreements among nation states to work together to achieve a specific purpose. Hans J. Morgenthau, considered the father of twentieth-century realist theory, regarded alliances as arrangements between states based on shared interests. According to Morgenthau, "Whether or not a nation shall pursue a policy of alliances is, then, a matter not of principle but of expediency."[3] Nations make alliances with others when they "need" to, and avoid them when their interests do not require them. Morgenthau's formulation leads to the logical conclusion that when the need no longer exists, an alliance will be disbanded, or will simply fall into disuse.

The North Atlantic Treaty was designed to help organize the United States and its European democratic allies to defend against the perceived threat posed by the Soviet Union and communism. This goal satisfied the requirement that Morgenthau set for "common interests" to undergird the alliance. However, the drafters of the North Atlantic Treaty importantly layered an ideological commitment on top of the pragmatic heart of the transatlantic alliance. The preamble to the treaty declares that the signatories "are determined to safeguard the freedom, common heritage and civilisation of their peoples, founded on the principles of democracy, individual liberty and the rule of law."

Morgenthau judged that "A purely ideological alliance, unrelated to material interests, cannot but be stillborn." On the other hand, he recognized that ideological elements can play a role in alliances, and "can lend strength to the alliance by marshaling moral convictions and emotional preferences to its support." The danger, however, is that the ideological components could "obscure the nature and limits of the common interests" and raise expectations about "concerted policies and actions."[4] He went on to warn that alliances that don't deliver more-or-less equal benefits to the participating states can seriously weaken the relationship—a warning that is evidenced in the long history of burden-sharing trials and tribulations over the persistent burden-sharing issue, which has weakened, but not so far destroyed, the transatlantic alliance.

Morgenthau saw alliances mainly as devices to ensure that power is balanced in the international system. During the Cold War—beginning in the late 1940s and ending in the early 1990s—NATO effectively balanced the power of the Soviet Union and its alliance, the Warsaw Pact. The character of these two "balancing partners" could not have been more different. Membership in NATO was a voluntary choice, and the alliance in fact was stimulated by requests from European democracies for American support. But membership in the Warsaw Pact was required by the Soviet Union for its "allied" states, all governed by communist regimes installed under Moscow's control. The bottom line was that the two-alliance structure tended to keep the international system "balanced" and relatively stable, although the countries of Eastern and Central Europe forced to remain in the Warsaw Pact could be forgiven if they asked whether they were the ones paying the greatest price for this stability.

At the end of the Cold War, when the Warsaw Pact was disbanded and the Soviet Union disintegrated (see discussion in Chapter 6), the logical question from a realist perspective was why NATO should continue when its balancing partner had disappeared. But, not only did the United States and its allies decide that NATO should stay in business, it found new challenges in dealing with the conflict in former Yugoslavia, the desire of former Warsaw Pact members and Soviet republics to join the alliance, and the need for a constructive relationship with the diminished but still-important Russian Federation.

In fact, the decisions made by the allies in the 1990s lie behind the debate that has accompanied the 2014 Russian seizure of Crimea and support for separatists in the former Soviet republic of Ukraine. NATO enlargement was supported by the "liberal internationalists" of the Bill Clinton administration (1993–2000), motivated by the desire to enlarge the community of states sharing American values, and by the "neo-conservatives" of the George W. Bush administration (2001–2008), who wanted to enlarge the area of American power and influence.[5] Today, "neo-realists" argue it was a big mistake. According to this perspective, argued strenuously by academic commentators John Mearsheimer[6] and Stephen Walt,[7] the process of enlargement overlooked important power considerations, stimulating a reaction from Russia that arguably has led to a "new Cold War" between Russia and the West (discussed in Chapter 8).

Ironically, no matter how one looks at the debate over "who lost Russia" at the beginning of the twenty-first century, Vladimir Putin's more aggressive, expansionist approach to European security has given new life to NATO as a potential balancer against Russian power. Even before this development, however, one international relations scholar had offered a strong argument as to why NATO had survived beyond the end of the Cold War. Wallace J. Thies argued in 2009[8] that NATO is different from previous alliances in at least two key ways. First, it was established not just to meet a specific threat or serve a narrow purpose, but was designed to have much more lasting utility. Second, NATO was an alliance among liberal democracies, with a value foundation that previous alliances had lacked. Perhaps the big question now is whether that value foundation is still strong enough to resist some of the value-based threats that have emerged from within the alliance, as well as those that have appeared from outside.

What was the original bargain?

The original transatlantic bargain, described in Chapter 2 of this book, was a bargain between the United States and its original European partners[9] with the militarily modest but politically important participation of Canada.[10] The first half of the deal was that the United States would support Europe's economic recovery from the war if the Europeans would coordinate their efforts to use the assistance most effectively. The second half pledged that the United States would contribute to the defense of Europe if the Europeans would organize themselves to help defend against the Soviet threat.

The European allies were quite successful in developing the first half of the bargain. In 1948, the Organization for European Economic Cooperation was created to coordinate utilization of Marshall Plan assistance from the United States and to promote European economic cooperation. The Europeans constructed a European Coal and Steel Community (ECSC, 1951) and then, through the 1957 Rome Treaties, the European Economic Community (EEC) and the European Atomic Energy Community, the precursors of today's European Union.

The allies were not nearly so successful in the security area. As discussed in Chapter 2, France had proposed the creation of a European Defense Community (EDC) to organize Europe's military contribution to the bargain. When that initiative failed in 1954, the arrangements adopted in place of the EDC, considered in Chapter 3, left the transatlantic bargain highly dependent on US nuclear weapons and a substantial US force presence in Europe to give credibility to NATO's defense against the Soviet threat.

Throughout the Cold War, the alliance lived with the 1954 "revised" bargain and a persistent burden-sharing debate between the United States and its European allies, as well as between successive US administrations and the US Congress.

Congress, given the crucial constitutional roles of the Senate in the process of ratifying treaties and the House of Representatives in legislating funding for government programs, participated actively in shaping and overseeing the US side of the transatlantic bargain. The involvement of Congress, judiciously sought by President Harry Truman's administration in the late 1940s, ensured a solid foundation for US participation in the transatlantic bargain. But it also guaranteed that senators and representatives would, for the life of the deal, closely inspect its terms and conditions. From the beginning, this inspection process has focused particularly on whether the costs of the deal were being fairly shared. For most of the history, they have found the sharing process lacking; this continues to be the case today, even under much-changed conditions.

In addition to the important congressional "clause" in the transatlantic bargain, there were many subordinate bargains that were more important to individual allies than to the United States. For example, France wanted the deal to ensure that it would not have to face a resurgence of German power on its own. The United Kingdom wanted US participation in European defense to provide an effective deterrent to Soviet expansionism so that some British military assets would be available to maintain its position as a global power. Canada wanted the bargain not only to be about military power, of which it had little, but more about political values, which it held high. When the Federal Republic of Germany joined in the bargain, it accepted constraints on its military capabilities in return for sovereignty over its internal affairs.

Every addition to the membership of the alliance brought new subordinate bargains as European states sought specific benefits from the alliance. Recent candidates for membership, starting with the Czech Republic, Hungary, and Poland in the 1990s, have seen belonging to NATO and the European Union as the two key tokens of acceptance in the Western community of nations and as protection against external domination by Russia or any other power.

Factors that emerged in the transatlantic relationship over the course of the Cold War still resonate in relations among the allies today, as discussed in Chapters 4 and 5. The period of transition and new missions from 1989 through the first decade of the twenty-first century is examined in Chapter 6, which looks at the challenges posed by the conflict in former Yugoslavia, the process of NATO outreach and enlargement, NATO and Russia, and the attempt to find a balance between transatlantic and European defense cooperation. Chapter 7 then examines the alliance in the 2000s, with a focus on the alliance after the September 11, 2001 attacks on the United States, the disruptions caused by the US-led invasion of Iraq, NATO's role in Afghanistan, deteriorating relations with Russia and the blossoming of European separatist thinking in attempts to create an "autonomous" European security and defense policy. In Chapter 8, the Obama presidency provides the starting point, featuring a new strategic concept for NATO, decisions to end US combat roles in Iraq and Afghanistan, the new threats posed by Islamic radicals, and the crisis in relations with Russia over Ukraine.

Chapter 9 looks at the external threats and internal challenges confronting the transatlantic bargain. The external threats range from those posed by Russian policies and radical Islamic actors like al-Qaeda and the Islamic State (ISIL, ISIS, or Daesh) to terrorism and the proliferation of weapons of mass destruction. Then we ask whether the alliance might be rotting out from the inside, as American President Donald Trump has challenged the US commitment to the alliance while questions remain about whether the European allies are capable of producing serious defense efforts, and internal political and economic conditions weaken commitments to the liberal principles that have undergirded both the European Union and NATO.

Chapter 10 concludes by asking whether an effective defense of the West can be constructed in response to the external threats and in spite of the internal challenges. Transatlantic security in the twenty-first century calls for the use of a wide variety of policy instruments extending well beyond the military cooperation that is part and parcel of NATO's mandate. Does the mandate need to be enhanced or do the allies need a new framework for cooperation on the non-military aspects of security? We conclude by addressing the question of whether or not the transatlantic alliance is becoming "permanent," or if it is on its last legs, as predicted by some observers.

What has NATO become?

NATO provides the starting point for any examination of transatlantic and broader Western defense, so it is important to consider where NATO's evolution has brought the alliance early in the twenty-first century. Today, more than 30 years after the fall of the Berlin Wall, many diverse views about what NATO is—or should become—remain. The discussion of NATO's essence recalls the Indian fable about the king who asked a group of blind men to feel various parts of an elephant and describe the elephant on the basis of the part they had touched.[11] Naturally, each blind man produced a different description of the elephant. This analysis starts from the premise that an objective assessment of NATO's purpose and mission can be based on several sources: on the provisions of the 1949 North Atlantic Treaty;[12] on the declared goals and intentions of its members; and on the fact that an organization is in many respects defined by its activities.

NATO has always been more than simply a defensive alliance. The North Atlantic Treaty provides a broad and flexible mandate through which to defend and promote allied interests and security. Moreover, preserving the attributes of a collective defense system—including a military command structure, a vital defense planning process, and thoroughgoing political and military consultations—strengthens NATO's ability to play new roles and assume new missions that respond to the post-Cold War challenges to the values and interests of the members.

NATO is a community of values

The North Atlantic Treaty was designed to counter Soviet expansion and military power. But the treaty itself was based on common values, identified no enemy, protected the sovereign decision-making rights of all members, and was written in sufficiently flexible language to facilitate adjustments to accommodate changing international circumstances. British Foreign Secretary Ernest Bevin, one of NATO's "founding fathers," urged the creation of a "Western Union" in a speech to the British Parliament on January 22, 1948. He asserted that "our sacrifices during the war, our hatred of injustice and oppression, our party democracy, our striving for economic rights and our conception and love of liberty are common among us all." During the negotiation of the treaty, the government of Canada argued the need to reflect "the ideological unity of the North Atlantic powers." US Secretary of State Dean Acheson subsequently maintained that "the central idea of the treaty is not a static one" and that "the North Atlantic Treaty is far more than a defensive arrangement. It is an affirmation of the moral and spiritual values which we hold in common." During the 1949 Senate hearings on the treaty, Acheson and other Truman administration witnesses argued that what they were proposing was very different from previous military alliance systems.[13]

What made NATO different from previous military alliances was that the treaty's preamble clearly articulated allied support for "democracy, individual liberty, and the rule of law." It is true that, during the Cold War, these values occasionally took second place when authoritarian regimes in NATO were tolerated in the interest of maintaining a militarily strong alliance. But NATO's survival beyond the end of the Cold War suggests that its value foundation and the inherent logic of Euro-Atlantic cooperation remain important ingredients in the glue that holds the alliance together. These same factors combined with the perceived need for a security link to the United States have made NATO membership attractive to new European democracies. The question is whether these values are still shared among NATO and European Union members sufficiently to provide a strong foundation for the future defense of the West.

NATO is based on a broad and flexible mandate

The North Atlantic Treaty's relatively simple language does not spell out in great detail how its objectives should be implemented. There is no specified military strategy, and no requirement for any particular organization or even military arrangements beyond the creation of a North Atlantic Council and a defense committee. This suggests substantial latitude for adaptation and adjustment to changing circumstances. The only limits on such changes are imposed by national interests, values, inertia, and other human and institutional factors, not by the treaty.

NATO's flexibility was demonstrated, for example, by the military build-up and elaboration of a military command structure in the early 1950s that had not been anticipated when the treaty was signed and that was judged necessary only after North Korea invaded South Korea. The alliance was adjusted again following the failure of the EDC in 1954. In the mid-1960s, NATO was forced to adapt to France's departure from the military command structure. In 1967, the allies revamped NATO's strategy with the doctrine of "flexible response" to a possible Warsaw Pact attack. That same year, they approved the "Harmel Report," which gave the alliance the mission of promoting détente as well as sustaining deterrence and defense. And, in the 1990s, the allies reoriented NATO's goals and activities to take into account the peaceful revolutions that brought democracy to Eastern and Central Europe and gave Russia, Ukraine, and other former Soviet republics the opportunity for independence and democratic reform.

NATO is a collective defense system

At its founding, the most prominent aspect of the treaty was its requirement for individual and collective actions for defense against armed attack. Article 3 of the treaty provides that the allies "separately and jointly, by means of continuous and effective self-help and mutual aid, will maintain and develop their individual and collective capacity to resist armed attack." In Article 5, the treaty's collective defense provision, the parties agreed that "an armed attack against one or more of them in Europe or North America shall be considered an attack against them all." They specifically agreed that each party to the treaty would "assist the Party or Parties so attacked by taking forthwith, individually and in concert with other Parties, such action as it deems necessary, including the use of armed force, to restore and maintain the security of the North Atlantic area."

During the Cold War, NATO's strategy and the way in which the United States, Canada, and the United Kingdom deployed their forces on the continent gave Article 5 more substance in practice than suggested by the words in the treaty. Beginning in the early 1950s, the United States deployed its military forces and nuclear weapons forward in Europe, mainly in Germany, in a fashion ensuring that a Soviet attack on the West would, in its early stages, engage US forces, thereby constituting an attack on the United States as well as on the host nation. In the mid-1950s, the United States threatened massive nuclear retaliation against the Soviet Union should it attack a NATO country. After massive retaliation's credibility was undermined by Soviet acquisition of long-range nuclear weapons, NATO adopted its "flexible response" strategy.

Flexible response suggested that battlefield nuclear weapons might be used early in any European conflict. Such weapons were deployed well forward in West Germany to ensure that they were seen as part of NATO's first line of defense.

Today, the collective defense commitment still endows the North Atlantic Treaty with special meaning. It is a potential deterrent against would-be enemies of the allies and a source of reassurance should future threats develop. With no imminent Soviet-style threat currently facing the allies, they have been adapting NATO strategy and force deployments to fundamentally new circumstances. For several years, most activities of the alliance have turned toward purposes of defense cooperation that lie beyond collective defense, even though the institutions and processes developed to implement collective defense, including the military command structure, remain critically important to NATO's future. Article 5 still provides a continuing rationale for maintaining the military command structure, and the day-to-day political and military consultation and planning that make NATO a unique facilitator of defense cooperation among the member states. The allies have been seeking to translate their commitment to cooperate against threats posed by terrorist operations and weapons of mass destruction into NATO strategy, force planning, capabilities, and operations. But now Russia has forced the allies to think once again more seriously about their collective defense commitment. Will Russia continue its attempt to gather in Russian-origin populations from around its borders? If so, will this include political, military, and economic moves that threaten the territorial integrity and security of NATO allies? How should the alliance prepare to deal with such attempts while at the same time keeping the door open for a more constructive relationship with Russia in the future?

NATO is a cooperative defense organization

NATO has been and always will be a political as well as a military alliance. Following the end of the Cold War, it was popular for observers to say that NATO would have to adapt to new circumstances by becoming "more political." In 2002, following the initial US failure to use NATO military structures to organize military operations in Afghanistan, and the decision to intensify cooperation with Russia, many said that NATO was clearly in the process of becoming, for all intents and purposes, a political organization. But NATO's activities in the past and today make clear that its unique role is as an instrument of both political and military cooperation among member and partner states. The process involves consultations in the North Atlantic Council and its many subordinate bodies, practical coordination developed in the work of the Military Committee, and day-to-day collaboration in the military command structure. In the 1990s, consultation and cooperation with partners, including Russia and Ukraine, became a critical part of NATO's role. The goals of such cooperation today, however, are more diverse and complex than during the Cold War.

NATO creates policy options for crisis management

At the end of the Cold War, the allies questioned whether they still needed an elaborate system of political and military cooperation at a time when the Soviet threat had all but vanished. Their answer, in the November 1991 "new Strategic Concept," was that political consultation and defense cooperation, so essential in the Cold War, could be broadened to include other purposes. NATO cooperation was widely accepted as having facilitated an effective US-led coalition response to Iraq's invasion of Kuwait, and the experience had a significant influence on the directions taken in the 1991 Strategic Concept. Since that time, most of NATO's military activities have been focused on "non-Article 5" requirements, starting in the Balkans and continuing in Afghanistan and Iraq. The mandate for such activities is found primarily in Article 4 of the North Atlantic Treaty, which authorizes cooperation to deal with circumstances that threaten the security of one or more NATO members.

NATO remains an organization of sovereign nation-states in which no member can be compelled to participate in a military operation that it does not support. There is, as a consequence, no guarantee that the allies will respond to any given political or military challenge. But NATO can be used to build political consensus and create military options to implement political goals. The allies would have fewer credible military options if their military leaders and forces were not working together on a day-to-day basis, developing interoperability of those forces, planning for contingency operations, and exercising their military capabilities. This day-to-day routine develops political and military habits of cooperation that underpin the ability to work together under pressure and, more importantly, under fire.

The interests of the allies clearly will require the application of military force in defense of US, Canadian, and European interests for the foreseeable future. The political/military cooperation that is unique to NATO gives the allies the option of facing such circumstances as an effective coalition rather than as individual nation-states.

NATO defense cooperation is a burden-sharing tool

NATO can also be seen as a way to ensure that allies carry a fair share of the burdens of maintaining international peace. This is a role that can be seen as a glass half full or half empty. During the Cold War, some Americans saw NATO as a creator of burdens for the United States rather than as an instrument for sharing them. Some may still hold this view, particularly in light of the growing gap between US and European military capabilities, and the large gap between North American and continental European military contributions in Afghanistan. On the one hand, the US military presence in Europe, down to well under 100,000 troops on shore, had become more oriented toward force projection and peace operations rather than toward defense of European territory. The NATO framework provides the United States with leverage to push for additional European defense efforts, presuming that the Europeans want the United States to remain involved in European security, which they apparently do. On the other hand, it could be argued that the habit of European security dependence on the United States is perpetuated by NATO, and that new means of cooperation, for example by giving the European Union a home-grown role in defense, are needed to increase European self-reliance and reduce US burdens.

NATO defense cooperation is an instrument to promote political change

NATO defense cooperation is now being used more prominently for political goals beyond its members' borders as well. Perhaps for this reason, some see NATO as becoming "more political." The Partnership for Peace (PfP) was established at the Brussels Summit in January 1994 to develop cooperation with non-NATO states. Through the PfP, Europe's new democracies have been learning how to develop systems of democratically controlled armed forces as well as habits of cooperation with NATO nations and neighboring partners. The partnership approach helped the Czech Republic, Hungary, and Poland meet the requirements for NATO membership in 1999 and remains the principal path through which other nations have prepared to enter the alliance. Countries that had been neutral during the Cold War are using the PfP to participate in NATO's efforts to promote stability in and around Europe.

Since the end of the Cold War, the allies had tried to use political/military cooperation with Russia to attempt to change Russian perceptions of the alliance and, it was hoped, to change the political relationship between Moscow and NATO by gradually integrating Russia into a cooperative Euro-Atlantic security system. In a sense, the 1997 Founding Act with Russia, creating a NATO-Russia Permanent Joint Council, updated NATO's attempt to promote improved relations with Russia, a goal that was prominently advanced in the 1967 Harmel Report. The strengthening of that tie in 2002 sought to continue the process. However, most of the more optimistic projections for this relationship were dashed by Russian President Vladimir Putin's decision to challenge the post-Cold War European security system. From Putin's perspective, the enlargement of NATO and the European Union to include former allies and even republics of the Soviet Union took advantage of Russian weakness and diminished Russian security. The hope is gone that defense cooperation with Russia could move from a relationship governed by arms control to one characterized by the transparent, predictable, and confidence-building nature of defense cooperation. Such a change would have marked a sea change in the European security system. But the emergence of an authoritarian regime in Moscow and Russia's self-definition as a dissatisfied power, wanting to change the European security status quo, has led to what looks more like a new Cold War than a new era of peace.

NATO is an open organization

The drafters of the North Atlantic Treaty made it clear in Article 10 that accession to the treaty would remain open to "any other European state in a position to further the principles of this Treaty and to contribute to the security of the North Atlantic area." This "open door" policy led to the membership of Greece and Turkey in 1952, Germany in 1955, and Spain in 1982. After the countries of Central and Eastern Europe freed themselves from communism and began establishing democratic systems of government, NATO's rejection of their desire for membership in the alliance would have repudiated everything the North Atlantic Treaty stands for. Acceptance by the allies of the Czech Republic, Hungary, and Poland in 1999, Bulgaria, Estonia, Latvia, Lithuania, Romania, Slovakia, and Slovenia in 2004, Albania and Croatia in 2009, Montenegro in 2017, and North Macedonia in 2019 highlights the fact that NATO is organized around transcendent values and goals that do not require an enemy to validate their continuing relevance. Now, however, the so-called "open door" has been effectively shut to Georgia and Ukraine, as the result of Russia's seizure of parts of both of these countries and assertion of rights over their futures.

NATO is a source of stability

It is clear that NATO serves a variety of purposes for individual member states beyond these broadly stated goals. Many such secondary agendas help explain why current members of NATO want the alliance to continue and why the new Central and East European democracies sought to join. Former members of the Warsaw Pact still see NATO as a guarantee against falling once again into the Russian sphere of influence, as well as an insurance policy against resurgence of a Russian threat, which seems to have begun emerging in 2014. Most European governments hope that the process of European unification will lead to more intensive security and defense cooperation among European states. But they continue to see the transatlantic link as essential to their security.

Further, many Europeans believe that the US role in Europe, particularly as translated through NATO, provides an important ingredient of stability that facilitates cooperation among European states. For example, even though Germany is not seen as a threat by its neighbors, both Germany and its neighbors feel more comfortable with Germany's role in Europe thoroughly integrated within the framework of both the European Union and the transatlantic alliance. From the US point of view, NATO cooperation is a way to seek equitable sharing of the burdens of maintaining international stability with like-minded states.

NATO is at the center of a cooperative European security system

Finally, it is necessary to address the somewhat academic but politically important question of whether NATO is a collective security organization. The term "collective security" is widely and loosely used in today's discussion of NATO's future role. According to its classic definition, collective security is a system of interstate relations designed to maintain a balance of power and interests among the members that ensure peaceful relationships within that system. The League of Nations, established after World War I without US participation, is usually regarded as such a system.

From the outset, NATO was designed as a system of cooperation among member states to deal with challenges and problems originating outside that system, not within it. Granted, NATO has to some extent tried to promote peaceful settlement of problems within the system in support of its mission of defending against external threats. It is credited with having helped heal World War II wounds inflicted by Nazi Germany on its neighbors. NATO has served to mitigate conflicts between Greece and Turkey. Indeed, the requirements of collective defense promoted a degree of cooperation between these two NATO members that might not have been realized in NATO's absence. In recent years, several NATO activities sought to support the goal of collective security. Russia–NATO cooperation, the PfP, and the Euro-Atlantic Partnership Council, for example, were designed to help maintain peaceful and cooperative relations among all states in Europe. However, Russia now contends that the only way toward a cooperative European security system would be to replace NATO with another organization in which it had a leading role.

When the allies began preparing for NATO's post-Cold War enlargement, they made clear to potential applicants that they must resolve differences with their neighbors in order to be seriously considered for NATO membership. The NATO countries insisted that new members leave their old baggage of bilateral and ethnic differences with their neighbors by the wayside when they join NATO. So far, not all issues related to ethnic nationals residing in neighboring Central and East European states have been "resolved." However, the NATO commitment helps keep such differences within bounds and promotes peaceful resolution.

From a legal perspective, NATO does not have principal responsibility for collective security in Europe—the North Atlantic Treaty does not suggest such a role. In fact, the Conference on (now Organization for) Security and Cooperation in Europe (OSCE) was designed to promote peaceful relations among states "from the Atlantic to the Urals." The 1975 Helsinki Final Act of the OSCE established a series of agreed principles, or "rules of the road," to govern relations among states in Europe. The OSCE member states (all European states plus the United States and Canada) have adopted further agreements and principles, have given the organization some diplomatic tools for conflict prevention, and convene regular meetings under OSCE auspices to try to address problems before they develop more serious proportions. So far, however, cooperation in the OSCE has largely been unsuccessful in preventing the slide toward a new Cold War in Europe.

The future of the transatlantic bargain

In the fable of the blind men and the elephant, the king finally observes, "Well is it known that some Samanas and Brahmanas cling to such views, sink down into them, and attain not to Nirvana." An "ideal" NATO is probably beyond the reach of member governments today. And participants in the debate on the future of the transatlantic bargain may well continue to "fight among themselves with their fists," as in the fable, declaring that "such is an elephant, such is not an elephant." The future of the bargain most likely must be built on a foundation that accommodates all these perceptions to one degree or another.

In sum, the North Atlantic Treaty still accurately represents the values and goals articulated by the United States and its allies despite persistent differences among them concerning how best to promote those values and defend their interests. The collective defense commitment in the North Atlantic Treaty is an obligation assumed by all current and future members, even though Article 5 leaves much room for nations to decide collectively and individually what to do under any given crisis scenario. This was clearly demonstrated when NATO invoked Article 5 following the September 11, 2001, terrorist attacks on the United States. Continuing defense cooperation in NATO keeps alive the potential to mount collective responses to aggression against alliance members. Defense cooperation also creates policy options, though no obligation, for responses to crises beyond NATO's borders, and serves as a tool for changing political relationships between NATO countries and other nations, most importantly Russia. NATO is not a collective security organization; it is designed primarily not to keep peace among its members but rather to protect and advance the interests of the members in dealing with the world around them. But some of NATO's activities contribute to the goal of collective security, helping maintain peaceful and cooperative relations among all states in Europe.

These attributes of NATO bear witness to the continuing relevance of the North Atlantic Treaty and the importance of continued US–European security cooperation. However, over two decades have passed since the dramatic changes at the end of the Cold War. Over that time, the transatlantic allies have sought to understand and relate effectively to a fundamentally new international system. The alliance has recently been shaken by an American president who, for the first time since the United States in 1953 threatened an "agonizing reappraisal" of its participation in transatlantic defense arrangements, suggested the United States might renege on its North Atlantic Treaty commitment. Now the time may be approaching for the United States, Canada, and the European allies to decide whether their thoroughly intertwined interests and still-potent shared political values remain valid. Does NATO require serious reform? Do the allies need a broader framework for cooperation than provided by NATO and other bilateral and multilateral Euro-Atlantic institutions? Can the alliance move from crisis to creation of even stronger cooperation, giving renewed meaning to the concept of an "Atlantic Community"?

US unilateralist tendencies and their counterpart in some European countries have threatened commitments to the alliance on both sides of the Atlantic. But as the United States and its allies focus on the newly framed threats of terrorism and weapons of mass destruction, and on the new challenges thrown up by Russia, it may now be the hour in which a serious reconsideration is warranted to ensure that this historic transatlantic bond survives into the uncertain future. Without a strong new commitment to the indivisibility of security and well-being in the Euro-Atlantic area, the transatlantic bargain could well begin to come undone.

The way of life represented by the societies of NATO and European Union member states faces a great variety of challenges. Rising powers such as China, India, and Brazil will, over time, rebalance international power relationships. Demographic decline in traditional European populations may threaten the very fabric of those societies. In this setting, a renewed commitment to the importance of transatlantic ties could give rise to the speculation that this alliance is indeed becoming "permanent." NATO—the organization that symbolizes and operationalizes transatlantic security ties—may not last forever. But the transatlantic community is much more than NATO, and the members of the transatlantic community may have to make serious decisions in the years ahead about what values and interests they are defending and if they still need to do so together.

Questions for discussion

1. What did you know about NATO before opening this book? Which of your opinions regarding NATO do you expect to change after reading it?
2. Based on your reading of this chapter, what has set NATO apart from other military alliance systems? In what ways is NATO more than a military alliance?
3. What kind of international systems do the terms "collective security" and "collective defense" describe? How are these terms most accurately applied, particularly with regard to NATO?
4. When you think about American foreign and defense policy, does NATO come immediately to mind, or are other institutions, concepts, or regions more important for defending and promoting American interests abroad? From a European perspective, how does NATO fit into the framework for defending the interests of European members of the alliance?

Notes

1 Harlan Cleveland, *NATO: The Transatlantic Bargain* (New York: Harper & Row, 1970).
2 Lawrence S. Kaplan, *NATO 1948: The Birth of the Transatlantic Alliance* (Lanham, Md.: Rowman & Littlefield, 2007), 223. Professor Kaplan, widely recognized as NATO's premier historian, has produced a number of books that chronicle in detail NATO's evolution from its origins through the Cold War. In addition to *NATO 1948*, they include *The United States and NATO: The Formative Years* (Lexington: University Press of Kentucky, 1984) and *NATO and the United States: The Enduring Alliance* (New York: Twayne, 1988).
3 Hans J. Morgenthau, *Politics Among Nations* (New York: Alfred A. Knopf, 1960), 181.
4 Morgenthau, *Politics Among Nations*, 184.
5 For a detailed critique of the relationship between the liberal and neo-conservative approaches to American foreign policy since the end of the Cold War see: Sean Kay, *America's Search for Security: The Triumph of Idealism and the Return of Realism* (Lanham, Md.: Rowman & Littlefield, 2014).
6 John J. Mearsheimer, "Why the Ukraine Crisis is the West's Fault: The Liberal Delusions That Provoked Putin," *Foreign Affairs*, September/October 2014.
7 Stephen M. Walt, "Why Arming Ukraine is a Really, Really Bad Idea," *Foreign Policy*, February 9, 2015.
8 Wallace J. Thies, *Why NATO Endures* (New York: Cambridge University Press, 2009).
9 The Treaty of Washington was signed on April 4, 1949 by the governments of Belgium, Canada, Denmark, France, Iceland, Italy, Luxembourg, the Netherlands, Norway, Portugal, the United Kingdom, and the United States.
10 Canadian priorities and diplomacy resulted in the Treaty's Article 2: "The Parties will contribute toward the further development of peaceful and friendly international relations by strengthening their free institutions, by bringing about a better understanding of the principles upon which these institutions are founded, and by promoting conditions of stability and well-being. They will seek to eliminate conflict in their international economic policies and will encourage economic collaboration between any or all of them." For discussion of the Canadian role in shaping the treaty, see Sean Kay, *NATO and the Future of European Security* (Lanham, Md.: Rowman & Littlefield, 1998), 21–31.
11 According to The Udana, or the Solemn Utterances of the Buddha, the story goes something like this:

>   And the King went to where the blind men were, and drawing near said to them: "Do you now know what an elephant is like?" And those blind men who had felt the head of the elephant said: "An elephant, Sir, is like a large round jar."
>   Those who had felt its ears said: "it is like a winnowing basket."
>   Those who had felt its tusks said: "it is like a plough-share."
>   Those who had felt its trunk said: "it is like a plough."
>   Those who had felt its body said: "it is like a granary."
>   Those who had felt its feet said: "it is like a pillar."
>   Those who had felt its back said: "it is like a mortar."

> Those who had felt its tail said: "it is like a pestle."
> Those who had felt the tuft of its tail said: "it is like a broom."
> And they fought amongst themselves with their fists, declaring, "such is an elephant, such is not an elephant, an elephant is not like that, it is like this."

12 The text of the Treaty of Washington of 1949 (North Atlantic Treaty) can be found at Appendix 1.

13 US Senate Committee on Foreign Relations, North Atlantic Treaty, Hearings before the Committee on Foreign Relations, 81st Cong., 1st sess., April 27–29 and May 2–3, 1949.

2

Genesis of the bargain

The transatlantic bargain finds its origins in a series of political decisions and diplomatic events in the mid-to-late 1940s. As the end of World War II neared, US President Franklin D. Roosevelt was particularly sensitive to the fact that President Woodrow Wilson's failure at the end of World War I to engage the United States in the League of Nations had been a contributing factor to the rise of Adolf Hitler in Germany and the events leading to World War II. Roosevelt wanted to ensure that the United States played a leading role in constructing a new international system under the auspices of a United Nations organization. Unlike Wilson, Roosevelt carefully engaged leading members of Congress in the process, including the influential and pre-war isolationist Senator Arthur H. Vandenberg, to increase the chances that the United States would commit to the venture.

Meanwhile, wartime ally the United Kingdom, led by Prime Minister Winston Churchill, was naturally focused on how post-war Europe could be organized to protect British interests, and particularly on how to keep German power contained and prevent further Soviet advances into Western Europe. Roosevelt died in 1945, just before the end of the war in Europe and the signature of the UN Charter in San Francisco. In the United Kingdom the Labour Party, led by Clement R. Attlee, defeated Churchill's Conservatives, putting the post-war conclusion and reconstruction in the hands of successors in both countries.

The United States, under President Harry Truman, moved into a debate on how best to deal with the Soviet Union, as it increasingly appeared that the wartime cooperation between Roosevelt and Soviet leader Joseph Stalin was turning toward a more competitive and even hostile relationship. British Foreign Secretary Ernest Bevin set out to convince the United States to lend its power and influence to a post-war system in Europe that would prevent further Soviet political and military advances. Out of office, Winston Churchill, speaking in Fulton, Missouri, warned of the expansionist tendencies of the Soviet Union, saying, "From Stettin in the Baltic to Trieste in the Adriatic an iron curtain has descended across the Continent."

Responding to the growing perception of a Soviet threat, in March 1947, President Truman promulgated what became known as the Truman Doctrine, urging the United States "to support free peoples who are resisting attempted subjugation by armed minorities or by outside pressure." A few days later, the United Kingdom and France, demonstrating that they worried not just about the Soviet threat but also about the possibility of a resurgent German challenge, signed the Treaty of Dunkirk, agreeing to give mutual support to each other in the event of renewed German aggression. The process of shaping the transatlantic bargain had begun in earnest.

In a speech on June 5, 1947 by Secretary of State George C. Marshall, the Truman administration proposed what became known as the Marshall Plan to provide funds for economic reconstruction to war-ravaged nations in western and southern Europe. The plan was warmly welcomed by the United Kingdom and other European countries, not only because it would provide much-needed assistance but also because it was a sign of US commitment to Europe's future. Then, speaking before the British House of Commons on January 22, 1948, Foreign Secretary Bevin proposed creation of a Western Union comprising the United Kingdom, France, and the Benelux countries (Belgium, the Netherlands, and Luxembourg). As one author has observed, this step "launched the making of the Atlantic Alliance."[1]

Over the course of the next two years, three formative steps shaped the transatlantic bargain: the Brussels Treaty (1948), which resulted from the Bevin initiative; the Vandenberg Resolution (1948); and the North Atlantic Treaty, also known as the Washington Treaty (1949; the text of the treaty is given in Appendix 1). These events outlined the objectives of the bargain, identified the partners in the deal, and suggested some of the reciprocal obligations to be borne by the participants.

In the Brussels Treaty of Economic, Social and Cultural Collaboration and Collective Self-Defence of March 17, 1948, the governments of France, the United Kingdom, Belgium, the Netherlands, and Luxembourg provided the initial framework for post-war West European cooperation. More important, these five countries signaled to the United States their intent to structure post-war intra-European relations to encourage internal stability and defense against external threats. The treaty stated the basic European commitment to the transatlantic bargain-to-be. To make sure that the signal would be heard loudly and clearly where it needed to be heard the most—in the halls of the US Congress—President Truman, coincident with the Brussels Treaty signing, told a special joint session of Congress that he was "sure the determination of the free countries of Europe to protect themselves will be matched by an equal determination on our part to help them protect themselves." And so the first part of the bargain was in place, and the foundation had been laid for the next act of alliance construction.

The second part of the bargain was America's response to the European signal. The basic structure of the bargain was being hammered out behind the scenes, primarily by officials of American and European governments. But these officials recognized that the bargain's political viability ultimately depended on its acceptance by Congress. They were keenly aware, as had been Franklin Roosevelt, that Woodrow Wilson's plan for US engagement and leadership in the League of Nations had failed because it lacked the essential support of Congress. Mid-century statesmen were determined not to ignore history only to pay the price of repeating it. On the US side, Congress had to be a partner in the deal.

Vital congressional acceptance of the bargain was given political life in the so-called Vandenberg Resolution, personalized, as are many important congressional actions, to acknowledge the role of the principal congressional architect, Senator Arthur Vandenberg, the sponsor and chairman of the Senate Committee on Foreign Relations. The Truman administration went to great lengths to encourage Vandenberg's post-war conversion from isolationism to a more "internationalist" inclination. Christopher S. Raj, in *American Military in Europe*, relates, "The Administration had skillfully placated Vandenberg by including him in US delegations, and the State Department cultivated him assiduously by consulting him often on European affairs."[2]

Following signature of the Brussels Treaty, the State Department asked Vandenberg to prepare a resolution that would express congressional support for the administration's desire to affiliate the United States with the European self-help project. Vandenberg complied and crafted a resolution that, in part, suggested that the United States should support "the progressive development of regional and other collective self-defense in accordance with the purposes, principles, and provisions of the [United Nations] charter." The resolution was approved by the Senate on June 11, 1948, with overwhelming bipartisan support, providing political sustenance, in principle, for the emerging bargain. The Soviet Union infused the project with added urgency by imposing a blockade of Berlin late in June 1948. After six more months of debate and negotiation among the founding partners in the bargain, the deal was consummated. By the spring of 1949, ten European governments, the United States, and Canada were prepared to sign the North Atlantic Treaty. The document, finally signed on April 4, 1949, reflected a compromise between the European desire for explicit US commitments to provide military assistance to prospective NATO allies, and the American desire, strongly expressed in Congress, for more general, less specific assistance provisions. In this fundamental aspect of the bargain, the Europeans had to settle for a general commitment that was more consistent with the mood in Congress.

Between Congress and the Europeans, the Truman administration practiced a form of diplomatic footwork that subsequently became a standard part of the repertoire of every American administration from Truman to Obama. In the 1949 context, the Truman administration was challenged "to convince Western Europe that the American commitment through the North Atlantic Treaty was a strong one, and ... to assure Congress that the treaty did not involve the United States in an 'entangling' military alliance."[3] Since that time—until Donald Trump became president—subsequent administrations of both parties continued to reassure the Europeans of the validity of the American defense commitments to Western Europe while justifying to Congress the price tag for the "entangling alliance" that NATO became.

Consequently, when the Senate approved ratification of the treaty in 1949, it did so despite some strong concerns about the potential long-term costs of a US commitment to defense of Europe—misgivings that then-opponents of the treaty might today well believe to have been justified.[4] On the other hand, most of those senators who voted for ratification based on the strategic arguments for the alliance would probably today see their action as having been legitimized by history, particularly in light of NATO's contributions to deterrence during the Cold War and the alliance's role promoting stability and cooperation in post-Cold War Europe. Some of the issues debated in the halls of Congress in recent decades over NATO enlargement—burden-sharing, Bosnia, Kosovo, Afghanistan, and Iraq—echo those heard in the ratification debate of 1949.

At the end of the day, as Lawrence S. Kaplan has observed, it took "an awareness of America's new weight in the world combined with the weakness of Europe and the power of Soviet Communism to win over the Senate and the nation."[5] Importantly, the Senate's close involvement in the treaty's develop-

Figure 2.1 President Truman watches while Secretary of State Acheson signs the North Atlantic Treaty.

ment and its approval implied that the bargain was not a simple partnership. It was a deal struck among governments, to be sure, but with the clear implication that two branches of the American government were parties to the deal and that management of the bargain would be a shared responsibility as long as the alliance endured.

Unresolved issues

With signature and subsequent ratification of the North Atlantic Treaty in 1949, NATO's founding fathers had shaped the basic deal: the United States had pledged its continued involvement in European security arrangements in return for a European commitment to organize itself for both external defense and internal stability.

But two central and intimately related issues were left unresolved by these formative steps. The first was how the US commitment would be implemented. The Treaty neither suggested the institutional framework for US involvement nor specified whether the US military contribution would consist primarily of strategic bombing and naval capabilities or whether it would also include substantial US ground forces in Europe—issues regularly raised throughout most of NATO's history.

The second issue was how West Germany would fit into this Euro-Atlantic framework of defense obligations. The treaty did not clarify Germany's status vis-à-vis its West European neighbors, leaving open the question of whether West Germany would be permitted to rearm and, if so, under what circumstances.

In 1949, there was no consensus among the allies or between the Truman administration and Congress concerning how best to deal with these two issues. The national security priorities of the United States, Britain, and France were sharply in contrast. These three leading powers agreed that the Euro-Atlantic partnership, in its broadest form, was designed for the dual purpose of balancing Soviet power and providing an acceptable way to integrate West Germany into the Western community of nations. But it was by no means self-evident how this would be accomplished.

The basic conflict was between French and American priorities—another underlying factor that has affected Euro-Atlantic relations through most of the alliance's history. The French government, not without good cause, was obsessed with preventing Germany from acquiring any substantial independent military capabilities, and placing political constraints on Germany in both the European and the Atlantic frameworks.

In 1949, the French government, doubting the US willingness to remain involved in any European power balance, was not confident it could provide, on its own, the economic or military counterweight to a Germany already demonstrating its potential for industrial recovery and resurgence. Timothy

P. Ireland has observed that "As it became apparent to the allies that (1) the defense of Europe would have to begin with the Federal Republic and that (2) West Germany's industrial strength was necessary for a successful rearmament program, traditional French apprehensions vis-à-vis Germany became more and more manifest."[6]

The United States was not unsympathetic to France's preoccupation but was fixed on its own priority—balancing the power of the Soviet Union in Central Europe. From the American perspective, German industrial capabilities and manpower were assets that could not be overlooked, particularly given Germany's geographic position in the center of Europe. Furthermore, Secretary of State Dean Acheson, sensitive to the fact that the North Atlantic Treaty might not win Senate approval if it appeared to commit the United States to a large military build-up in Europe, had assured the Senate Committee on Foreign Relations that the United States would not, as a consequence of treaty ratification, be required to send large numbers of troops to Europe.[7] Thus Congress, one of the important partners in the bargain, had signed on to the deal with the tacit understanding that the US contribution to the alliance would consist largely of strategic bombing (the nuclear guarantee) and sea control.

To complicate the problem further, the British absolutely opposed any suggestion that they maintain a substantial presence on the continent to help balance potential German power. The reluctance of the British to play a large military role in the Central European balancing act reflected London's own priorities. Even though the United Kingdom remained strongly committed to a transatlantic alliance, the British Labour government of the time viewed a major political and military commitment on the continent as less important to British interests than its Commonwealth ties and global responsibilities. Britain's eyes were still turned away from the continent, across the Atlantic toward the "special relationship" with the United States and around the world to its vast colonial holdings.

In retrospect, this British orientation was as unfortunate for the post-war alliance as the French paranoia concerning Germany was troublesome for the United States. More than two decades would pass before Britain even tentatively acknowledged that its future world role and internal well-being were intimately dependent on the United Kingdom's relationship with its neighbors across the English Channel. But in the meantime, the British attitude denied the post-war allies the potential for a more coherent and effective European pillar for the Atlantic partnership. (Subsequently, of course, the UK did join the European Community (EC). Then, following a referendum that narrowly favored exiting the EC's successor, the EU, the "Brexit" process ironically began unraveling the ties.)

The contrasting French and American preoccupations, combined with the British orientation away from continental involvement, produced two distinctly different sets of preferences for the way Euro-Atlantic relations should be structured to serve the "agreed" purposes of the alliance. The American preference was to help balance Soviet power in Central Europe by rearming West Germany. To ensure that Germany's rearmament took place within a stabilized framework, the United States envisioned West Germany's membership in NATO as well as its cooperation in a multilateral European framework growing out of the Brussels Treaty. From the American perspective, German, French, and other continental nations should provide the bulk of ground force manpower in Central Europe, with less substantial, primarily symbolic, contributions by the United States, the United Kingdom, and Canada. West German membership in NATO would legitimize German participation in the military effort, and the European cooperative arrangements would provide France a means of monitoring and controlling German power.

The French preference was, first and foremost, to avoid German rearmament. France also opposed German entry into NATO, viewing such entry as validation of a rearmament program, eventually permitting Germany to escape from any control provisions established in a European framework. Second, the French hoped to convince the United States to commit substantial forces to forward defense of Western Europe in Germany. Third, Paris wanted to weave a web of political and economic relationships within Western Europe that would reinforce German self-interest in cooperation and deter any possible future hegemonic or aggressive behavior.

In fact, the French National Assembly authorized ratification of the North Atlantic Treaty with the understanding that the pact would not lead to Germany's rearmament. Foreign Minister Robert Schuman reassured French parliamentarians prior to the Assembly's vote for the treaty, saying, "Germany has no army and should not have one. It has no arms and will not have any... . It is therefore unthinkable, for France and her allies, that Germany could be allowed to adhere to the Atlantic pact as a nation capable of defending itself or of aiding in the defense of other nations."[8]

The conflict between French and American priorities could not have been sharper. While the United States had refocused its policies toward confronting the threat posed by the Soviet Union, French vision remained fixed on the "German problem," which it hoped to solve once and for all by denying Germany the armed forces with which it could once again threaten France.

The Korean catalyst

On June 25, 1950, North Korean troops attacked the Republic of South Korea. This aggression, almost halfway around the world from Western Europe, proved to be the catalyst for shaping post-war Euro-Atlantic relations and resolving the Franco-American impasse on German rearmament. The Korean War, seen as demonstrating the global threat of communist aggression, provided the political momentum required to overcome congressional resistance to a substantial deployment of US ground forces in Europe. Such an

American commitment undoubtedly was essential in helping to ease French concerns about the potential of a resurgent German neighbor.

For more than a year, the State Department and the Pentagon had argued the issue of German rearmament. The Pentagon, and particularly the Joint Chiefs of Staff, contended that German armed forces would be required if the West hoped to balance Soviet power in Central Europe. But the Department of State resisted any formal discussion of German rearmament with the allies, believing that the political costs of such an initiative would be greater than the military benefits. Secretary of State Acheson "feared that any plans to associate Germany with the Atlantic alliance would undermine the whole structure of western defense by running the risk of alienating France."[9]

The Pentagon was not anxious to take on what appeared to be a massive and potentially open-ended commitment in Europe without parallel development of West European defense forces. Given the British reluctance to play a major role on the continent and the fact that France, with forces tied down in Indochina, would not provide sufficient ground forces to balance the Soviet Union in Central Europe, German rearmament seemed an inescapable prerequisite for any major US commitment to continental defense. This position was considerably strengthened by the reasonable expectation that Congress too would not approve a build-up of US forces in Europe without a parallel European effort.

And so, stimulated by the Korean War, a most significant elaboration of the original bargain began to take shape. The United States would deploy substantial ground forces to Western Europe and place them within an integrated NATO command structure. This structure would serve the practical role of coordinating Western defense efforts in Europe as well as providing the crucial Atlantic framework for bringing German military forces into the Western defense against the Soviet Union.

President Truman announced his decision to send a substantial number of American troops to Europe on September 9, 1950, after difficult negotiations during the preceding summer had forged a common Defense and State Department position on the question. The decision marked a momentous change in US policy toward Europe, declaring that the United States would commit combat troops to peacetime defense forces in Western Europe. Truman's declaration linked this commitment to the efforts expected from the European allies, without specifically raising the issue of German rearmament, even though reconstituting the German military had become a principal goal of US policy:

On the basis of recommendation of the Joint Chiefs of Staff, concurred in by the Secretaries of State and Defense, I have today approved substantial increases in the strength of the United States forces to be stationed in Western Europe in the interest of the defense of that area. The extent of these increases and the timing thereof will be worked out in close coordination with our North Atlantic Treaty partners. *A basic element in the implementation of the decision is the degree to which our friends match our action in this regard.* Firm programs for the development of their forces will be expected to keep full step with the dispatch of additional United States forces to Europe. *Our plans are based on the sincere expectation that our efforts will be met with similar action on their part* (emphasis added).[10]

The Truman administration recognized that it would first have to get the French government to move away from its strong opposition to German rearmament in order to make the deployment of US troops to Europe acceptable to Congress. American pressure on the French government throughout the summer of 1950 intensified in September. Truman's statement of September 9 added a sense of even greater urgency, and the French understood that they would have to respond to the US action. The United States, after all, had now expressed its willingness to deploy combat troops in Europe, just as Paris had desired.

But the French acceptance of the need to act did not mean that Paris was yet prepared to contemplate German rearmament within the NATO framework. The French still hoped to win acceptance for some European organization within which future governments in Paris would be able to control German military efforts.

The French responded to their apparent dilemma by proposing the creation of a European Defense Community. The so-called Pleven Plan, proposed by economist Jean Monnet and named for French Premier René Pleven, envisioned the eventual creation of a European army within which token German units would be included. The army would not be formed until a European decision-making framework had been established, with a European defense minister and a European parliament to approve funds for the operation. The French National Assembly initially approved the plan on October 24, 1950.

The Pleven Plan did not respond fully to the American requirement for German rearmament, and American officials were skeptical concerning the motives of the French (to put off German rearmament indefinitely?). They also questioned whether it would be wise to allow the French to exercise the greatest influence of any European nation over the future role of Germany.[11] Nonetheless, the Pleven Plan moved the French one step closer to the American position and helped prepare the way for compromise at the NATO meetings of foreign and defense ministers scheduled for December.

The compromise and Congress

As the allies prepared for the regular end-of-year meetings of NATO foreign ministers, both Secretary of State Acheson and French Foreign Minister Schuman signaled their interest in reaching a compromise on the German rearmament issue. Encouraged by signs of flexibility from Paris, US Deputy Representative to the North Atlantic Council Charles Spofford crafted a compromise proposal that suggested that the United States endorse the long-term concept of an integrated European defense force in return for French acceptance of short-term measures to start bringing German manpower into use "under strong provisional controls" until a more permanent system of European cooperation could be developed.[12] Under the Spofford Compromise, the United States would appoint a Supreme Allied Commander and begin deploying US forces to Europe without waiting for German troops to materialize.

A number of factors convinced Acheson that moving too rapidly on the rearmament issue could be destabilizing in Germany as well as in France. The opposition Social Democrats in Germany were not at all enthusiastic about the prospect of integration into a Euro-Atlantic framework, believing that it would destroy chances for eventual German reunification. In response to domestic criticism, Chancellor Konrad Adenauer felt compelled to press for equal treatment for Germany in return for Germany's willingness to join in the economic and military enterprises that were being designed mainly in Paris, London, and Washington. Adenauer had his own agenda: independent state-hood for Germany. But Acheson apparently was convinced that the French government might lose a vote of confidence in the National Assembly should it be forced to move too far too fast on the rearmament issue.

Acheson communicated to Schuman his willingness to compromise in a letter sent to Paris on November 29; the American secretary of state tried to reassure Schuman of the US intent to appoint a supreme commander and, by implication, to begin deployment of American troops to Europe. Acheson argued that the United States had already demonstrated "the depth and per-manence of its interests in Europe, its support for closer European association, its willingness to cooperate with Europe." He told Schuman that cooperation between France and the United States in NATO was "an essential corollary to an orderly progression from German cooperation in defense, to European inte-gration, and thus final solution of the problem of relations with Germany."[13]

On December 17, 1950, the North Atlantic Council—NATO's decision-making body—approved the package Spofford had designed and the French and American governments had ultimately accepted. The council approved the French plan for creating a European Defense Force on the condition that the plan not delay the availability of German manpower for Western defenses, and it authorized the establishment of a supreme headquarters with the expectation that a US officer would be appointed supreme commander. At the meeting, Secretary of State Acheson announced that President Truman had appointed General Dwight D. Eisenhower as supreme commander and that the number of US forces in Europe would be increased in the near future.

The bottom line, according to Timothy Ireland's study of this period, was that the compromise satisfied the principal objectives of the French government and the US administration: "The United States had gained French adherence to at least the idea of German rearmament. The French gained an immediate American military commitment to the defense of Europe while delaying the rearming of Germany."[14] The deal, however, had not yet been approved by another party to the original bargain: the US Congress. While

Figure 2.2 General Dwight D. Eisenhower, NATO's First Supreme Allied Commander.

the path for approval of the original North Atlantic Treaty had been care-fully prepared in the Senate, Congress had not been formally involved in the steps leading to the Franco-American compromise. As the subsequent "Great Debate" in Congress would demonstrate, Congress had no intention of relin-quishing its role in helping manage the transatlantic bargain.

Congress was in recess following the mid-term elections when the NATO meetings concluded, but when the legislators returned to session in January 1951, the new American commitment moved rapidly to the top of the con-gressional agenda. Troop deployment was most severely questioned by con-servatives among the Republican majority in the Senate. They were supported by some influential conservative spokesmen outside Congress, most notably former President Herbert Hoover. On December 19, 1950, Hoover, reacting to the appointment of General Eisenhower as Supreme Allied Commander, Europe (SACEUR), had commented the next day that "the prime obligation of defense of Western continental Europe rests upon the nations of Europe. The test is whether they have the spiritual force, the will and acceptance of unity among them by their own volition. America cannot create their spiritual forces; we cannot buy them with money."[15]

The conservative Republicans focused on two principal issues: whether it was appropriate for the United States to deploy substantial ground forces to Europe as part of an integrated Atlantic defense structure, and whether the president could, without congressional authorization, deploy American troops overseas—the "war powers" question that later returned to prominence with the Vietnam War and has remained a sticking point between subsequent US administrations and Congress. The war powers issue was pointedly raised by Senator Robert Taft, who argued, "The President has no power to send American troops to fight in Europe in a war between the members of the Atlantic Pact and Soviet Russia. Without authority he involved us in the Korean War. Without authority, he apparently is now adopting a similar policy in Europe."[16] The administration and its supporters in Congress argued that the president did not need specific congressional approval to make such a deployment. The argument, however, was not convincing for those senators who questioned not only the constitutional validity of the action but also the defense and foreign policy rationale underlying the troop deployment and par-ticipation in a military command structure in NATO.

Following Truman's January 8 State of the Union Address, in which he strongly defended American involvement in the defense of Western Europe, the debate was joined in Congress. Senator Kenneth Wherry, the Republican floor leader, introduced Senate Resolution 8, which asked the Senate to resolve "that it is the sense of the Senate that no ground forces of the United States should be assigned to duty in the European area for the purposes of the North Atlantic Treaty pending the formulation of a policy thereto by the Congress."[17] The Wherry resolution was referred to the Foreign Relations and Armed Services Committees, which then held joint hearings on the troop deployment issue. During these hearings, the Truman administration sought to avoid a direct conflict with Congress on the central war powers issue raised by Wherry's resolution. Administration strategy apparently was to defend the president's constitutional right to deploy US forces while at the same time not attacking directly the congressional prerogatives in this area. The administration carefully avoided any acceptance of the idea that it needed congressional approval to do what it had already told the allies it would do.

After extensive hearings, in which a wide range of constitutional, strategic, and economic aspects of the issue were aired, the committees submitted a joint report to the full Senate. Senator Tom Connally, chairman of the Senate Committee on Foreign Relations, then introduced Senate Resolution 99 on behalf of the committees. With Senate Resolution 99, the committees attempted to deal with concerns that had been raised by Senator Taft and others while, at the same time, supporting the appointment of General Eisenhower as SACEUR and the deployment of four US Army divisions to Europe.

Senate Resolution 99 was approved by the Senate on April 4, 1951, by a vote of 69 to 21. Senator Taft, who had so severely questioned the commitment, voted with the majority, apparently believing that his concerns were reflected in the bill.

And so the Truman administration's decision was vindicated in the Senate vote, but not without qualification. The resolution endorsed General Eisenhower's appointment and approved the four-division Army deployment. The Senate also declared, however, that the Joint Chiefs of Staff should certify that the European allies were making a realistic effort on behalf of European defense, that the European allies should make the major contribution to allied ground forces, and that provisions should be made to utilize the military resources of Italy, West Germany, and Spain.

The form of the congressional action—a "sense of the Senate" resolution—did not insist on congressional authority over the president's decision, but the Senate did not give up its claim to exercise such control in the future. Incorporated in the final version of the resolution was an amendment offered by Senator John McClellan that expressed the Senate's desire that "no ground troops in addition to such four divisions should be sent to Western Europe in implementation of Article 3 of the North Atlantic Treaty without further Congressional approval."

The Senate once again had made clear that it wanted to be regarded as an active partner in the transatlantic bargain. It remained reluctant to contemplate an extensive, open-ended US commitment to the defense of Europe, and it expected Europe to carry the bulk of responsibilities, particularly in ground forces, for the continent's defense. The Senate sought the rearmament of Germany as central to the success of the NATO effort, and it pointedly reminded the administration that it retained the right to involve itself more decisively in US policy toward the alliance should its wishes be overlooked.

Box 2.1   Some key developments (June 1947–May 1952)

June 1947   Marshall Plan proposed
March 1948   Brussels Treaty signed
April 1949   North Atlantic Treaty signed
May 1950   French Foreign Minister Schuman proposed France
and Germany and others pool coal and steel resources
(Schuman Plan)
Sept 1950   President Truman announced decision to send substantial US troops to Europe under NATO command
Oct 1950   French Premier Pleven proposed European Defense
Community
Dec 1950   Eisenhower named as first NATO Supreme Allied
Commander
April 1951   European Coal and Steel Community treaty signed
Feb 1952   Lisbon ministerial meeting set force goals, established
North Atlantic Council as NATO's deliberative body
March 1952   Britain's Lord Ismay named first NATO Secretary General

---

Wrapping up the package in Lisbon

With the requisite congressional mandate in hand, the Truman administration could move toward firming up the deal with the allies. Throughout the remainder of 1951, administration officials worked with allied counterparts on plans for NATO's future organization and force posture, developed the outline for a European Defense Community, and planned for the relationship between NATO and the defense community. The significant progress made in these discussions was confirmed at a meeting of NATO foreign, defense, and finance ministers in Lisbon, Portugal, in February 1952.

The Lisbon meeting is perhaps remembered best for the fact that it set force goals for NATO that remained elusive for the alliance until they no longer needed them at the end of the Cold War. A report adopted by the ministers set the goal of deploying 50 allied divisions, 4,000 aircraft, and listed substantial additional targets for future years. The allies never reached these so-called Lisbon Goals. The failure of the European members of NATO to build up their conventional military forces to balance those of the Warsaw Pact created the burden-sharing issue that, in one way or another, dominated congressional consideration of the US role in NATO throughout the Cold War.

The NATO ministers also reorganized the civilian management of NATO, making the North Atlantic Council a permanent body, with member governments represented by senior officials and supporting delegations at NATO headquarters in Paris. This organizational change established NATO as a permanent forum for diplomatic exchanges and foreign policy consultations among the allies.

The allies also took note of NATO's further expansion into the Mediterranean region, welcoming the accession of Greece and Turkey to the alliance. Both countries, in advance of the Lisbon meeting, had signed and ratified the North Atlantic Treaty. The addition of these two countries was seen as a critical move to block expansion of communist influence in south-eastern Europe. But it also brought subsequent problems to the alliance. Greece and Turkey's bilateral disputes over the control of Cyprus and the territorial waters between them frequently disrupted internal alliance cohesion and, from time to time, verged on war between the two allies. (In the twenty-first century, Greek/Turkish issues continued to block much-needed cooperation between NATO and the European Union.)

In diplomatic exchanges prior to the Lisbon session, some of the most intensive negotiations among the allies had dealt with the question of West Germany's future role in the Western alliance. The Franco-American compromise formally endorsed in Lisbon had taken shape over the two previous years. A year prior to the Lisbon gathering, France had hosted the first session of the Conference for the Organization of a European Defense Community (EDC). The early meetings of the conference were attended by representatives of West Germany, Belgium, Italy, Luxembourg, and the host government, France. The Netherlands had joined the project in October 1951. In Lisbon, these countries presented a report on their progress to the NATO ministers.

The conference report on the EDC described in detail the considerable technical progress that had been made toward establishing a defense community. The participants were, in fact, able to report that they had begun preparation of a draft treaty and associated protocols. In the conclusion of the report, they reaffirmed the purpose of their work:

> To create a European Defense Community which can fulfill the imperative requirements of military effectiveness; to give the Western World a guarantee against the rebirth of conflicts which have divided it in the past; and to give an impetus to the achievement of a closer association between the Member countries on a federal or confederate basis.[18]

When the Lisbon session adjourned on February 25, the ministers announced they had concluded that the principles underlying the treaty to establish an EDC conformed to the interests of the parties to the North Atlantic Treaty. They also said they had agreed on the principles that would govern the relationship between the proposed community and NATO. And so, when the 35 foreign, defense, and finance ministers and their delegations completed the intensive round of meetings in Lisbon, they had seen the bargain through another significant stage of development. NATO now had an integrated military command structure with a Supreme Allied Commander. The NATO countries had agreed to make substantial ground, air, and naval commitments to the integrated command. Greece and Turkey had been welcomed into the alliance. Progress had been recorded toward the establishment of an EDC, designed to reassure France against future German power and to provide a constructive framework for the creation of a united Europe.

The stage was set for Secretary of State Acheson to travel to Bonn to negotiate and sign, on May 26, 1952, the Convention on General Relations among the Federal Republic of Germany, France, the United Kingdom, and the United States. Acheson then flew to Paris to participate in the May 27 signing of the treaty establishing an EDC and the various associated agreements specifying the intended relationship between that community and NATO. Not too long after these historic ceremonies, however, the package started to come undone.

Questions for discussion

1. What did the Brussels Treaty (1948) and the Treaty of Washington (1949) contribute to the shaping of the transatlantic bargain?
2. How was the Truman administration able to overcome isolationist tendencies in the United States to establish an internationalist strategy after World War II?
3. What role did the US Senate play in the genesis of the transatlantic bargain? Why was it important, constitutionally and politically?
4. In the beginning, the Euro-Atlantic alliance was intended variously to balance Soviet power in Europe, help integrate West Germany into the West, and keep the United States engaged in European security. How have those goals been affected by subsequent events, including the end of the Cold War and, more recently, Russian attempts to reassert influence in previously Soviet-dominated areas?
5. How have the original rationales for NATO evolved over time? How has the process affected the alliance's missions and commitments?

Notes

1 Don Cook, *Forging the Alliance* (New York: Arbor House, 1989), 114.
2 Christopher S. Raj, *American Military in Europe* (New Delhi: ABC Publishing House, 1983), 8.
3 Timothy P. Ireland, *Creating the Entangling Alliance: The Origins of the North Atlantic Treaty Organization* (Westport, Conn.: Greenwood, 1981), 119.
4 For a discussion of the concerns raised by senators and administration efforts to deal with those concerns, see Phil Williams, *The Senate and U.S. Troops in Europe* (London: Macmillan, 1985), 12–27.

5 Lawrence S. Kaplan, "The United States and NATO: The Relevance of History," in *NATO After Fifty Years*, ed. S. Victor Papacosma, Sean Kay, and Mark R. Rubin (Wilmington, Del.: Scholarly Resources, 2001), 246.

6 Ireland, *Creating the Entangling Alliance*, 177.

7 US Senate Committee on Foreign Relations, *Executive Sessions of the Senate Foreign Relations Committee*, vol. 4, 82d Cong., 2d sess., 1952. Historical Series, 1976.

8 Journal Officiale, July 25, 1949, p. 5277, as cited in Michael M. Harrison, *The Reluctant Ally: France and Atlantic Security* (Baltimore, Md.: The Johns Hopkins University Press, 1981), 14.

9 Ireland, *Creating the Entangling Alliance*, 186. This discussion of events in 1950–1951 benefited substantially from Ireland's account, which is based largely on the US State Department's Foreign Relations of the United States series covering this period (hereafter cited as FRUS).

10 *The New York Times*, September 10, 1950, as cited in Raj, *American Military in Europe*, 22.

11 Such reactions are found in detail in diplomatic exchanges recorded in FRUS, 1950, vol. 3, *Western Europe*.

12 FRUS, 1950, vol. 3, *Western Europe*, 480.

13 FRUS, 1950, vol. 3, *Western Europe*, 498.

14 Ireland, *Creating the Entangling Alliance*, 207.

15 *The New York Times*, December 21, 1950, as cited in Raj, *American Military in Europe*, 26–7.

16 *The New York Times*, January 6, 1951, as cited in Raj, *American Military in Europe*, 27.

17 US Senate Committee on Foreign Relations, *Executive Sessions of the Senate Foreign Relations Committee*, vol. 3, pt. 1, 82d Cong., 1st sess., 1951, Historical Series, 1976, 559.

18 FRUS, 1952–1954, vol. 5, *Western European Security*, 246.

3

The transatlantic bargain revised

The ink was barely dry on the European Defense Community (EDC) treaty when the Lisbon package started to come apart. The force goals so bravely adopted in Lisbon soon appeared unreasonably optimistic. Neither the British nor the French government could fit substantial troop increases into budgets already stretched thin by non-European military commitments—the French bogged down in Indochina, and the British struggling to keep a global role intact. Rumors spread around Europe that the United States was reducing its aid to the NATO countries. Press sources speculated that the entire NATO structure was on the verge of total breakdown (a prediction heard many times since).

The long road from Lisbon to Paris

The State Department, alarmed by the emerging trends in US as well as European public opinion, drafted a message to send to the embassies in London and Paris. The cable expressed Washington's concern with all-too-common suggestions in the press that "(1) [the] NATO force plan has already been revised unilaterally; (2) Sov[iet] tension has diminished; (3) [the] entire NATO defense program is facing collapse."[1]

The secret cable noted that it apparently was becoming popular in Europe to blame cutbacks in American assistance for French and British inability to meet force goals. The cable suggested that should such misleading information continue to be so prominent in the European press, the US government would be forced to point out some facts—"US defense expenditures [are] four times [the] total [of] all other NATO countries combined; [the] US with smaller population has more men under arms than all other NATO countries combined; [the] percentage of GNP spent by [the] US is above all others and twice [the] NATO average; US per capita defense expenditures are six time[s the] NATO average." Noting the potential impact on US domestic opinion, the cable argued that placing the blame on the United States for European shortfalls would "infuriate Amer[icans] and cause them [to] recall with indignation vast US contributions to Eur[opean] recovery and defense." The message continued with the warning that such duplicity reinforces the arguments of NATO critics who assert that Europe is a "'bottomless pit' and will 'do nothing for itself.'"[2]

After making the State Department's concerns so clear, the cable instructed the embassies in London and Paris to encourage the British and French governments to "find opportunities" to clarify the situation to the public, especially making these tersely worded points:

a.   There has been no revision NATO targets adopted at Lisbon; cannot be revised unilaterally. What we face is possible shortfall in meeting targets.
b.   US is fulfilling aid commitments and has not reduced them.
c.   There is no evidence easing of Soviet threat, and NATO defenses remain inadequate.
d.   Prospective shortfall, while increasing and prolonging security risks, should not be interpreted as NATO "breakdown." Defense build-up will continue forward as rapidly as possible.[3]

The NATO ministers met in December 1952, following the elections in the United States in which NATO's first Supreme Allied Commander, Europe (SACEUR), General Dwight David Eisenhower, had won his Republican Party campaign for the White House. Perhaps with little anticipation of how crucial events in Indochina could be for the NATO alliance, the ministers issued a communiqué proclaiming that the campaign being waged in Indochina by the forces of the French Union deserved the support of the NATO governments.[4]

When the new secretary of state, John Foster Dulles, returned from his first NATO ministerial meetings in April 1953, he reported that the allies had accepted, though with some qualms, the new administration's inclination to concentrate on the quality rather than the quantity of assistance to the NATO allies. The Eisenhower administration was working toward a "new look" at American defense policy. The administration, while seriously concerned about the Soviet challenge, was equally intent on rationalizing US commitments abroad as part of an overall program of economic austerity. The Truman administration had not been able to decide to what extent US strategy should depend on nuclear weapons, but the Eisenhower administration was inclined virtually from the outset to use nuclear weapons deployments to meet national security objectives while pursuing fiscal solvency. Dulles had attempted to reassure the allies that rationalization in no way suggested a US tendency toward isolationism.

At the same time, the new administration clearly hoped that closer cooperation among the NATO European allies would eventually relieve the United States of some of its European defense burdens—a theme of US policy that has persisted until today. In his 1953 New Year's message to Chancellor Konrad Adenauer, Eisenhower made a special point of saying that the development of an EDC "would contribute much to promote peace and the security of the free world."[5] At a meeting at the Pentagon a few weeks later, Eisenhower argued strongly for support of the EDC, saying, "The real problem is that of getting German participation. Anything which does not accomplish that doesn't mean very much." The general-turned-president went on to recall, "In hearings before the Congress, I have always had to face the question as to when we were going to get German help in defending Europe. It would be difficult to justify Congressional appropriations for Europe if there were no such prospect."[6]

It is therefore no surprise that Dulles was concerned, as had been the previous administration, by the slow progress toward implementation of the EDC plan. On his return from Europe, he reported to a meeting of the National Security Council that his "one great worry in retrospect ... was the delay and failure to ratify the EDC treaties and to secure the desired German contribution."[7] Dulles felt that the political steam had gone out of the drive toward an EDC. The post-Stalin leadership in the Soviet Union, through its first "peace campaign," had already managed to dispel some of the sense of urgency that had earlier helped motivate work toward an EDC.

As 1953 passed without any of the six EDC signatories having ratified the treaty, the dilemmas inherent in European security arrangements became increasingly apparent to US officials. At a meeting of the National Security Council on December 10, 1953, preparatory to a scheduled NATO ministerial meeting in Paris, Secretary of Defense Charles Wilson expressed his "distress" that the United States seemed "hopelessly caught between the fear of the Europeans as to the use of atomic weapons, and our own desire to bring our forces home."[8]

Responding to Wilson's concerns, President Eisenhower explained, "Our one great objective at the moment was to secure the ratification of EDC." Eisenhower said that the United States could not afford "to take any steps toward redeployment, or even to talk about redeployment [of troops in Europe to the United States], until these objectives have been reached." To buttress his point, the president added, "The French have an almost hysterical fear that we and the British will one day pull out of Western Europe and leave them to face a superior German armed force."[9]

When Secretary of State Dulles left for the Paris meetings, he apparently hoped to provoke some new movement toward realization of the EDC, which had become key to the US goal of German integration in Western defenses and eventual withdrawal of some US forces from Europe. At a press conference held during the NATO meetings on December 14, Dulles administered shock treatment in an attempt to resuscitate the defense community project when he said:

> We also understand that action [creating a united Europe to prevent future Franco-German antagonism] will be taken within the framework of the North Atlantic Treaty, which will bring into association with the European Defense Community (E.D.C.) this strength which lies around the periphery of E.D.C.
>
> It is that policy, in regard to Europe, to which the United States is committed. In essence that is the European policy which we are trying to cooperate with, and we earnestly hope that policy will be brought to a successful conclusion.

If, contrary to our hopes and beliefs, it should not happen that way, it would force from the United States *an agonizing reappraisal* of its foreign policy (emphasis added).[10]

The implication that the United States would reconsider its commitment to European defense should the EDC not be approved appeared reasonable from Washington's perspective. The US Defense Department, impatient with the slow progress toward ratification of the EDC, had already considered some contingency plans for incorporating German forces in Western defenses in the absence of an EDC. But in Paris, the Dulles statement probably looked like a strong-arm tactic, raising the hackles of the consistently nationalistic and sensitive French.

The well-respected US minister in France at the time, Theodore Achilles, observed in a memorandum to Dulles that "it is too soon to tell whether your press conference has arrested [an] unfavorable trend [in France against the EDC], but it has certainly provided food for thought and again posed clearly the issue and the urgency."[11] But Achilles also recorded the prophetic reaction of one French Foreign Ministry official who reportedly said that the press conference had finished the EDC, that it must have been deliberate, that the problem now was to save the Atlantic Alliance, that some new way would have to be found to tie Germany to the West, perhaps through NATO, and finally that France would now have to do some painful rethinking of its own policies.[12]

In the first half of 1954, US policy struggled to shore up the transatlantic bargain with constant reassurances to France and its prospective EDC partners that the United States remained supportive of the EDC concept and committed to European defense. The United States was unable to dispel a lingering concern in France that once the EDC was in place, the United States would take its leave of Europe, exposing France to German power. There was, of course, some cause for this concern. The Eisenhower administration did see the EDC as a potential source of relief, though not an escape, from the burdens of European defense. Many in Congress, however, hoped that the EDC would in fact provide the escape route many Europeans feared the United States would take all too quickly once the EDC was set up.

Congress had demonstrated clearly its desire to see the EDC ratified. The Mutual Security Act of 1953, governing military assistance to the NATO allies, required the administration to withhold portions of the aid intended for EDC nations that had not ratified the treaty. In the spring of 1954, a modified form of the provision was incorporated in the Mutual Security Act of 1954, effectively preventing future deliveries of military equipment to the two countries that had not yet ratified the EDC: Italy and France. The Eisenhower administration had originally opposed the prohibition but supported the version incorporated in the 1954 legislation, apparently believing that it might add pressure to the campaign for EDC ratification.

At the same time, however, the administration's nuclear weapons policies may have undermined the credibility of its case for French ratification of the EDC. The administration's intent to increase substantially US and consequently NATO reliance on nuclear weapons, tactical as well as strategic, suggested the United States had given up hope of mounting a credible non-nuclear defense against the Soviet Union in Central Europe, even if West German forces were incorporated in Western defenses via the EDC. Under such circumstances, why should France be willing to risk sacrificing substantial national sovereignty for the sake of participation in a European army that US nuclear weapons policy was making increasingly less relevant?

Despite the potentially counterproductive interaction between the new-look strategy, which emerged full blown in 1954, and the EDC goal, the United States moved assertively on both fronts. At the NATO ministerial meetings in April 1954 (by then the Netherlands, Belgium, Luxembourg, and the Federal Republic of Germany had ratified the EDC treaty), Secretary of State Dulles cautioned the gathered ministers:

> Without the availability for use of atomic weapons, the security of all NATO forces in Europe would be in grave jeopardy in the event of a surprise Soviet attack. The United States considers that the ability to use atomic weapons is essential for the defense of the NATO area in the face of the present threat.

Then Dulles summarized his argument with a judgment undoubtedly not accepted by all his colleagues around the table: "In short, such weapons must now be treated as in fact having become 'conventional.'"[13]

The defeat of the EDC

As Secretary of State Dulles was preaching the gospel of nuclear dependence, the EDC story was moving toward a dramatic conclusion. The French government formed by Pierre Mendes-France in June 1954, the latest in a succession of politically vulnerable Fourth Republic regimes, was preparing a ratification vote on the EDC treaty in the French National Assembly. Mendes-France suspected that the treaty's supranational nature could lead to its defeat in the Assembly or that it might be approved by such a slim margin as to undermine the entire program of his government.

Apparently hoping to generate a more substantial majority for the treaty, Mendes-France asked the other EDC signatories to approve a package of modifications in the treaty. The foreign ministers of the six nations met in Brussels from August 19 to 22 to consider the French proposals. The Belgian foreign minister, Paul-Henri Spaak, submitted a set of compromise proposals that was accepted by all the other countries except France. The conference adjourned without agreeing on modifications to the EDC plan, and Mendes-France prepared with little enthusiasm to move toward a vote in the National Assembly. It is still not clear whether Mendes-France, had he obtained the changes he requested, could have won ratification of the accord. In any case, with an unenthusiastic governmental advocacy of the EDC case, the treaty failed on an August 19, 1954, procedural vote by a margin of 264 deputies for and 319 against.

According to a post-mortem on the ratification vote, drafted by the American embassy in Paris early in September 1954, changes in French perceptions of the threat influenced the outcome. Although the French remained concerned about the potential German threat, they had become more relaxed about the Soviet threat and somewhat more wary of American intentions. The embassy's analysis suggested that:

> in 1954, the fear of Russia was less than in 1953, when it was less than in 1952 and much less than in 1951 and 1950. Correspondingly, there existed, perhaps not only in France, a greater fear of some future action or reaction on the part of the US which might lead to world war; and in the specific case of EDC a greater fear that the US might in some way back the irredentist aspirations of Germany in a manner detrimental to French security interests.[14]

French perceptions of the threat had changed, but a number of other factors also influenced the mood in Paris. The French had been freed from their Indochinese dilemma by the July 1954 Geneva accords, but only in the wake of military defeat. This defeat, combined with the prospect of a long struggle against an independence movement in France's North African Algerian colony, presumably made more than a few French deputies wary of taking on additional military commitments. Furthermore, the structure of the Fourth Republic consistently produced weak governments, and as the embassy post-mortem pointed out, "No French government ever dared to challenge the opponents of EDC and carry the battle to them. Indeed, they could not have done so without breaking up the governing coalition."[15]

History has yielded no single explanation for France's defeat of a French idea that had been adopted in principle by the entire Western alliance. Some analysts have speculated that a deal had been cut between Mendes-France and Soviet Foreign Minister V. M. Molotov. According to this theory, in return for Soviet cooperation in the Geneva negotiations in July 1954 bringing an end to the war in Indochina, Mendes-France chose not to compromise at Brussels, thereby guaranteeing defeat of the treaty in the National Assembly. Moscow was strongly opposed to the EDC, and its active peace campaign of 1953–1954 bore witness to the depth of Soviet concern. But there is still no firm evidence of any deal between Moscow and Paris to receive a graceful exit from Indochina in return for defeat of the EDC.

The Soviet campaign certainly contributed to the delay and indecision that characterized the French approach to EDC ratification between 1952 and

1954, and French Communist Party deputies, closely following the Moscow line, were unalterably opposed to the treaty. The Soviet campaign's main influence, however, was probably on the large number of French Socialist deputies, many of whom could have gone either way on the treaty.

The Indochina episode had a profound effect on French attitudes toward the United States. As France was being pushed out of the region, the United States was moving in, creating the Southeast Asia Treaty Organization with the mission of containing communist expansion in Asia and tasked specifically with protecting South Vietnam. According to Lawrence S. Kaplan, "The Indochina trauma poisoned Franco-American relations in the Fourth Republic and provided a major justification for Charles de Gaulle's treatment of NATO in the next decade. For France, the Indochina humiliation at the hands of the United States was replicated at Suez in 1956."[16]

In the final analysis, France's fear of a resurgent Germany remains the most prominent factor in the rejection of the EDC. Had France been in an optimistic frame of mind, perhaps the nation would have been able to suppress its sense of insecurity toward the Germans and take on the challenge. But the economic outlook was gloomy, France had lost the war in Indochina, and the French governmental system was weak and ineffective. As a result, "the whole debate took place in an atmosphere of a tremendous national inferiority feeling." And noting this mind-set, the embassy commented further, "One of the most important, though usually unspoken arguments against EDC had long been the belief that in any community including France and Germany the latter would inevitably gain the upper hand because the Germans are more capable soldiers, organizers, businessmen and politicians."[17]

More than 60 years later, concerns about Germany's potential political and economic domination of Europe still haunt many French politicians and influence French attitudes toward European integration and transatlantic relations—plus ça change, plus c'est la même chose! (the more things change, the more they remain the same). However, French concerns about Germany today relate more to the studied pacifism that influences Germany's contemporary approach to security challenges and Berlin's economic power, rather than fear of German militarism.

The decision against the EDC was a tragic chapter in the history of Western post-war alliance construction. Ironically, it was France, the original author of the EDC plan, which had become uncertain about its work and had finally torn up the script. The embassy concluded, "This deep pessimism, it must be recognized, is perhaps justified," awkwardly adding the phrase "at least in part" to the end of the sentence, seemingly trying to take some of the edge off this dark assessment of the French national psyche. The phrase perhaps also reflected some acknowledgment that the policies of the Eisenhower administration had helped undermine the EDC project by intensifying French fears of being seduced into the defense community with Germany and then abandoned by the United States.

Box 3.1	Some key developments (January 1953–May 1955)
Jan 1953	Dwight Eisenhower entered office as President of the United States
Dec 1953	US Secretary of State John Foster Dulles warned NATO allies that failure to establish a European Defense Community would result in an "agonizing reappraisal" of US support for European defense
Aug 1954	European Defense Community treaty rejected by the French National Assembly
Sept 1954	Four-Power and Nine-Power Conferences held in London
Dec 1954	NATO adopted the strategy of "massive retaliation," agreeing to use nuclear weapons in response to an attack by the Soviet Union
May 1955	The Federal Republic of Germany became a NATO member

Picking up the pieces

France's rejection of the EDC removed what had been intended as a vital link between the post-war Western alliance arrangements and the goal of a sovereign and rearmed West Germany. While the action destroyed the intended framework for Germany's integration into the Western community as a sovereign and equal participant, it by no means meant that such a link would be impossible.

The United States had quietly been considering possible alternatives to the EDC for more than a year and had discussed such options with the British early in 1954. All along, the United States had viewed the EDC principally as a means to an end: the rearming of West Germany as part of the Western alliance against the Soviet Union. Secretary of State Dulles affirmed this priority in a statement issued just two days after the vote in the National Assembly. Expressing regret that France had turned "away from her own historic proposal," Dulles stated that the United States would now be required to "reappraise its foreign policies, particularly those in relation to Europe," as he had promised eight months earlier. At the heart of this reappraisal would be the place of the Federal Republic of Germany in the Western alliance:

The Western nations now owe it to the Federal Republic of Germany to do quickly all that lies in their power to restore sovereignty to that Republic and to enable it to contribute to international peace and security. The existing Treaty to restore sovereignty is by its terms contingent upon the coming into force of EDC. It would be unconscionable if the failure to realize EDC through no fault of

Germany's should now be used as an excuse for penalizing Germany. The Federal German Republic should take its place as a free and equal member of the society of nations. That was the purport of the resolution which the United States Senate adopted unanimously last July, and the United States will act accordingly.[18]

Officials in the United States did in fact move very quickly, as Dulles wished, to develop alternative arrangements. Interagency discussions, although revealing somewhat different (and natural) priorities among the State and Defense Department officials involved, nonetheless produced agreement on the general objectives. By mid-September, Dulles had met with Chancellor Adenauer in Bonn and British Foreign Secretary Anthony Eden in London, and a strategy had been agreed on. The goal was a four-power meeting among the United States, the United Kingdom, the Federal Republic of Germany, and France to obtain French agreement on three points:

1. Further progress toward European unity by expansion of the Brussels Pact so as to admit Germany and Italy.
2. Admission of Germany to NATO.
3. The working out of "accompanying arrangements" by the Federal Republic and the occupying Powers, who should at the same time declare their intentions with regards to restoration of sovereignty.[19]

This agenda, based on a British initiative, stimulated a flurry of diplomatic activity in September that culminated in the Nine-Power and Four-Power Conferences at London from September 28 to October 3. The Four-Power Conference meetings involved foreign ministers from the United States, the United Kingdom, France, and West Germany, and the Nine-Power Conference added foreign ministers from Belgium, Canada, Italy, Luxembourg, and the Netherlands. Those present decided to end the occupation of Germany, to allow West Germany to join NATO, and to strengthen and expand the Brussels Treaty with the membership of West Germany and Italy.

The foreign ministers of the same countries reconvened in Paris on October 20 and were joined by those of the remaining NATO countries: Denmark, Norway, Iceland, Greece, and Turkey. The formal decisions were confirmed on October 23 at three different levels. First, the foreign ministers of the United States, the United Kingdom, France, and the Federal Republic of Germany signed the Protocol on the Termination of the Occupation Regime in the Federal Republic of Germany, the Convention on the Presence of Foreign Forces in the Federal Republic of Germany, and the Tripartite Agreement on the Exercise of Retained Rights in Germany.

Next, the foreign ministers of the United Kingdom, France, Belgium, the Netherlands, and Luxembourg signed the Declaration Inviting Italy and the Federal Republic of Germany to accede to the Brussels Treaty and its four protocols. (Italy was an original signatory of the North Atlantic Treaty but not of the Brussels Treaty.) Finally, the 14 NATO foreign ministers signed the Protocol to the North Atlantic Treaty on the Accession of the Federal Republic of Germany.

With these agreements, the three occupying powers had recognized the Federal Republic of Germany as a sovereign state and ended their occupation. In return, the Federal Republic agreed to authorize the stationing on its territory of foreign forces at least equal to the strength existing at the date the agreements came into force. West Germany and Italy joined the Brussels Treaty, and the "Western Union" became the Western European Union (WEU). West German military capabilities would be monitored within the WEU framework, but Germany would become a member of NATO. The United States and the United Kingdom agreed to station forces on the European continent for as long as necessary.

Figure 3.1 October 23, 1954 Signature of Paris Agreements, inviting the Federal Republic of Germany to join NATO.

The French National Assembly voted in favor of the London/Paris agree-ments on December 30, 1954, and the bargain was put back together again—but not according to the original plan. West Germany became a NATO member on May 5, 1955, and nine days later the Soviet Union concluded the Warsaw Pact with the governments of Albania, Bulgaria, Czechoslovakia, East Germany, Hungary, Poland, and Romania, with whom Moscow had earlier negotiated bilateral defense pacts.

Meanwhile, the US campaign for allied approval of the new-look strat-egy had also moved to a conclusion. The NATO ministers, meeting in mid-December 1954, adopted a report prepared by the NATO military committee designated "MC 48," modestly titled "The Most Effective Pattern of NATO Military Strength for the Next Few Years." In a memorandum to President Eisenhower in November 1954, the presidential staff secretary, Colonel Andrew J. Goodpaster (a future SACEUR) summarized the proposed change in NATO strategy by writing, "An effective atomic capability is indispensable to a maximum deterrent and essential to defense in Western Europe." Goodpaster continued:

> [The first] element of proposed action is to secure NATO-wide approval of the concept of the capability to use A-weapons as a major element of military operations in event of hostilities. For this purpose, the US should be prepared, if required subject to constitutional limitations, to give assurances that A-weapons would be available in the hands of US forces for such operations.[20]

On his return from the NATO sessions, Secretary of State Dulles reported to the National Security Council that a number of allies were concerned that the new policy might take vital crisis decisions out of the hands of civilian leaders of allied countries. Dulles had met with British Foreign Secretary Anthony Eden and Canadian Secretary for External Affairs Lester Pearson prior to the NATO meetings, and the three worked out a formula whereby the new strat-egy would be adopted under the condition that "there was to be no delegation by the NATO governments of their right as the civilian leaders to give the signal for bringing the atomic defense into action."[21] With this reassurance and the belief that any crisis would allow time for allied consultation prior to the use of nuclear weapons, NATO Secretary General Lord Ismay formally put the proposal before the ministerial session of the North Atlantic Council. Dulles reported that the resolution occasioned "virtually no discussion or debate, and was unanimously approved by the Council."[22]

And so, apparently with little controversy, the alliance quietly mortgaged its future strategy to nuclear weapons. The mortgage came with relatively small payments in the early years, a consideration that, at the time, seemed more important than any foreseeable future costs. By the end of 1954, there-fore, the alliance had assumed its basic shape, with the way cleared for the admission of the Federal Republic of Germany. Alliance strategy had evolved toward heavy dependence on nuclear weapons and a continuing US ground force presence in Europe.

But this formative period for the Western alliance had left two fundamental desires unfulfilled. First, the plan to coordinate European contributions to the alliance through an EDC had failed to materialize. This failure meant that Germany would not remain a military midget within a French-controlled EDC; it also frustrated American hopes that such a community would eventually make it possible for the United States to withdraw most of its ground forces from Europe.

Second, even at this early stage of alliance development, it became clear that the United States and its allies would not match the quantitative force levels fielded by the Soviet Union and its allies. Despite a continued substantial American troop presence and the rearming of West Germany, the Lisbon force goals had become little more than paper promises, even though the alliance was not as yet willing to backtrack formally on the commitments made at the Lisbon ministerial meetings.

As a result of these two changes in the goals agreed on at Lisbon, the military strategy of the alliance came to rest heavily on the threat of the United States to use nuclear weapons against the Soviet Union should Soviet forces attack Western Europe. At the same time, the credibility of that threat depended on a continuing and substantial American military presence in Europe. These two changes in the original bargain bequeathed a legacy that troubled the alliance throughout the Cold War. The fact that NATO's military credibility was so dependent on the US force presence in Europe ensured that burden-sharing would remain an issue between the United States and Europe as well as between successive US administrations and Congress.

Questions for discussion

1. What were the prime influences leading to the defeat of the European Defense Community initiative in the French National Assembly? Should the failure be blamed entirely on French politics or were the actions of other countries, including the United States, partly to blame?

2. Throughout the Cold War history of the alliance, differing perceptions of "the Soviet threat" influenced relations among the allies. What impact did those differences have in the early 1950s? How important a role is played by such differences over the threat posed by Russia today?

3. In the early years of the alliance, NATO was quite reliant on US nuclear weapons to deter a Soviet attack on Europe. Do you think this was warranted? What role do you think nuclear weapons should play in NATO's deterrence strategy today and why?

Notes

1 US State Department, Foreign Relations of the United States (hereafter cited as FRUS), 1953–1954, vol. 5, Western European Security, 313.
2 FRUS, *Western European Security*, 314.
3 FRUS, *Western European Security*, 314.
4 NATO *Facts and Figures* (Brussels: NATO Information Service, 1981), 32.
5 *The New York Times*, January 7, 1953, A1.
6 FRUS, *Western European Security*, 711–12.
7 FRUS, *Western European Security*, 398.
8 FRUS, *Western European Security*, 451.
9 FRUS, *Western European Security*, 451.
10 FRUS, *Western European Security*, 468.
11 FRUS, *Western European Security*, 868.
12 FRUS, *Western European Security*, 469.
13 FRUS, *Western European Security*, 511–12.
14 FRUS, *Western European Security*, 1112.
15 FRUS, *Western European Security*, 1112.
16 Lawrence S. Kaplan, *NATO Divided, NATO United: The Evolution of an Alliance* (Westport, Conn.: Praeger 2004), 24.
17 FRUS, *Western European Security*, 1113.
18 FRUS, *Western European Security*, 1121.
19 FRUS, *Western European Security*, 1121.
20 FRUS, *Western European Security*, 534–5.
21 FRUS, *Western European Security*, 561.
22 FRUS, *Western European Security*, 561.

4

The bargain through the Cold War, 1954–1989

It is difficult to look at the roots of the original transatlantic bargain without being impressed by the persistence of some factors, and the significance of change in some others. After more than 70 years, US policy toward the alliance is influenced by many of the same issues, with an enduring focus on better burden-sharing. Presidential administrations have not always been comfortable with the bargain but, except during the first term in office of President George W. Bush and more recently and dramatically by President Trump, have consistently defended it in the face of congressional skepticism. The United States and France continued through much of the alliance's first 70 years to pursue different visions for the future of transatlantic relations, but into the second decade of the twenty-first century new leaders in Washington (President Barack Obama) and Paris (Presidents Nicolas Sarkozy and then François Hollande) narrowed the gap between American and French attitudes. In Europe, France still worries about Germany, but now it is a reunited Germany's "soft" power and its pacifistic tendencies that trouble Paris the most.

In this mix of continuity and change, the bargain has constantly evolved. More dramatic change came after the Cold War ended, but even in the 35 years between 1954 and 1989, a number of things changed. The allies, acting unilaterally in some cases and in concert in others, made conscious changes in and amendments to the bargain. Some of these changes were inspired by developments over which the allies had little control (such as the Soviet Union's drive toward nuclear parity with the United States, calling into question NATO's nuclear strategy), while political and economic trends rooted primarily within the alliance spawned other changes.

Identifying certain events or developments as representing significant changes in the bargain, while leaving some others aside, is in itself a subjective exercise. With that in mind, the following alterations in the bargain before the end of the Cold War are suggested as having produced changes that were important in their time and relevant to the Atlantic Community's future:

1. France's development of an independent security policy under President Charles de Gaulle, culminating in withdrawal from NATO's integrated military command structure;
2. NATO's adoption of the "Harmel Doctrine," giving the alliance a dual defense and détente role in East–West relations;
3. NATO's approval of the military strategy of "flexible response" and the efforts to keep the strategy viable with deployment of intermediate-range nuclear forces in Europe;
4. British acceptance of an active role in continental Europe's future through membership in the European Community (now European Union);
5. Political maturation of the Federal Republic of Germany;
6. Emergence of European Political Cooperation as a forum for shaping common European positions on foreign policy issues and as a foundation for a European "pillar" in the alliance.

All these developments represented fundamental changes in the nature of the transatlantic bargain. There were other shifts, to be sure, such as the wavering commitments of some allies (e.g., Greece) and the admission of Spain to NATO. There were attempted shifts that failed, such as Secretary of State Henry Kissinger's "Year of Europe" initiative in 1973, designed to convince the European allies that the transatlantic bargain should take into account "out of area" challenges to Western interests and redress the balance between economic costs and benefits of the transatlantic bargain for the United States.[1] Enthusiasm about and policies toward the alliance fluctuated over time in most alliance countries. But the factors discussed in this chapter arguably are the ones that most fundamentally influenced the core of the transatlantic bargain during the Cold War.

The French rebellion

When President Charles de Gaulle withdrew France from NATO's integrated military command structure in 1966, he unilaterally altered the transatlantic bargain with a flair befitting this most French of modern French leaders. The general's move, however, was not so much a break from Fourth Republic policies as it was the culmination of attitudes and frustrations that had roots in a uniquely French mixture of historical doubts about the reliability of the United States and concerns about US domination. France had never been comfortable with the way the original bargain turned out. De Gaulle's strong will and unique leadership ability, combined with the powers that he had insisted be built into the constitution of the Fifth Republic, simply provided the means for translating French displeasure into political action.

From the beginning, France had substantially different objectives for and interests in the transatlantic alliance than did the United States. The earliest

French proposals for tripartite French, British, and US management of the alliance emanated from Fourth Republic governments, even though this approach may best be remembered as a "Gaullist" line. The directorate concept was an expression of the French image of itself as the leading continental European power as well as of the French desire to be acknowledged clearly as having rights and powers superior to those available to the Federal Republic of Germany. The structure of the alliance favored by the United States, granting in theory equal rights to all members, provided a framework for the American superpower to exercise a primus inter pares role within the alliance, subordinating France to a position, in this sense, no more privileged than that of West Germany.

Fourth Republic governments had already decided that France, in order to obtain the status they thought essential to French security and national independence, would be required to take unilateral measures. One route available to France but denied to Germany was to become a nuclear power. When the Fourth Republic gave way to de Gaulle and the Fifth in 1958, development of a French nuclear weapons capability was well under way. It remained only for de Gaulle to articulate a political philosophy and develop a military strategy to give the force de frappe a major role in projecting French independence.

Perhaps from a French perspective, de Gaulle's stunning unilateral change in the transatlantic bargain was not totally unprovoked. France had hoped, indeed expected, from the early days of the alliance that its role as a global power would be acknowledged as an asset to the Western alliance and that the rhetorical support that the NATO countries accorded the French role in Indochina in the December 1952 ministerial communiqué would be followed by more substantive assistance. Seen from Paris, however, the United States not only failed to provide that assistance but also eventually turned against French interests in the Third World. The disenchantment in this regard perhaps began with the French defeat in Indochina, when the United States was faulted by Paris for not providing crucial military assistance to besieged French forces at Dien Bien Phu. The "lesson" of Indochina for Paris was bitterly repeated with American failure to support France's struggle in Algeria and, in 1956, with active American opposition to France and the United Kingdom in the Suez crisis. French leaders could be forgiven for seeing the United States as having made the first unilateral change in the original bargain. Michael Harrison, in his book *The Reluctant Ally*, reaches this conclusion: "NATO's value to France never recovered from the allied failure to support her cause in Africa, from the American reaction to Suez, and from the conviction that the United States had morally and materially turned against France and violated the Alliance tie."[2]

Whether or not one is sympathetic to the French case, it remains clear that the experiences of the Fourth Republic governments had set the stage for de Gaulle's rebellion against the Western "order." This is not to say that de Gaulle was simply following through on Fourth Republic initiatives. De Gaulle's wartime experiences had galvanized his doubts that the United States could be counted on to defend French interests. This skepticism eventually was reinforced by post-war-era nuclear politics, which led him to believe that France (or any other country for that matter) could not expect the United States to risk nuclear destruction of an American city to defend that of any ally. Only if France had an autonomous nuclear deterrent could it truly be independent. And de Gaulle believed strongly that a nation, once robbed of its independence, would soon lose its spirit and eventually die. These beliefs made de Gaulle suspicious of American plans for nuclear sharing with Europe, as manifested by the US/UK Nassau Agreement of December 1962, which made modernization of British nuclear capabilities dependent on American assistance, and by the abortive multilateral nuclear force plan of the early 1960s. His concerns about French independence were heightened by what appeared to be a growing tendency toward US–Soviet condominium in the wake of the Cuban Missile Crisis and by the signature of the Test Ban Treaty in July 1963, which de Gaulle saw as symbolizing a US–Soviet collaboration to monopolize the nuclear arena and eventually squeeze France into a non-nuclear status.

Just prior to de Gaulle's ascent to the presidency of France in 1958, the Rome Treaties had taken effect, establishing the European Economic Community (EEC), precursor of the European Community (EC) and now the European Union (EU). De Gaulle, believing as strongly as he did in the nation-state as the heart of the international system, hoped to lead his European partners away from the supranational inspiration of the Rome Treaties and toward a *Europe des patries*, a European unity based on sovereignty of the nation-states and led, of course, by France. An important part of the French plan was the so-called Fouchet initiative for political cooperation among the EC members, conceived to build the foundation for an independent European coalition positioned between the American and Soviet superpowers.

When the uncompromising Gaullist approach to European unity proved unacceptable to the other five Community members, de Gaulle became convinced that only unilateral French action, within Europe as well as toward the United States and in East–West relations, could effectively promote French interests. In 1963, de Gaulle vetoed the British application to join the EEC, seeing the United Kingdom as still too Atlanticist to be a committed "European" partner. De Gaulle also provoked an internal crisis within the Community in order to block a scheduled transition to qualified majority voting on certain Community policy decisions. The move had been intended to subordinate national interests in specified policy area to broader "community" interests, as well as to make Community decision-making more effective.

Then, in 1966, de Gaulle took his boldest step, announcing France's decision to leave NATO's integrated military command and asking NATO to remove its headquarters, forces, and facilities from French territory by April 1, 1967. De Gaulle made it clear that France would continue as a participant in the political aspects of NATO and would remain true to its treaty obligations. But from that point forward, France would declare itself independent of American leadership as symbolized and, to a certain extent, operationalized by NATO's military command structure.

What could have been a devastating event for NATO actually was turned into a positive stimulus for the alliance. The 14 other allies carefully avoided emotional responses to the French action and concentrated on the practical challenges that the withdrawal posed. Harlan Cleveland, US ambassador to NATO at the time, recalls, "President Johnson, whose private references to General de Gaulle stretched his considerable talent for colorful language, imposed an icy correctness on those who had reason to discuss French policy in public."[3] The allies quickly relocated NATO headquarters to Brussels, Belgium, and went on with the business of the alliance almost as if nothing had happened.

In fact, the French move appeared to have had so inconsequential an impact on the alliance that some observers questioned whether it had any importance at all other than producing domestic political points for de Gaulle. One such observer, a NATO diplomat, described the action as "a cheap anti-American gesture, which changed almost nothing militarily, certainly did no harm to French security, yet enabled the general to crow that he had 'withdrawn from NATO'—for home consumption."[4]

In retrospect, however, de Gaulle's withdrawal from the alliance did have some long-term consequences, some of them quite detrimental to the transatlantic bargain despite the admirable fashion in which the 14 other allies adjusted to the French action.

Militarily, the French move weakened NATO's lines of supply and communications. Even if the allies could, in theory, have counted on France to join in the battle should Warsaw Pact forces have attacked Western Europe, the infrastructure for supporting NATO's front lines and for bringing in new supplies and reinforcements would be closer to the front and more vulnerable to enemy interdiction. Some of the negative effects were mitigated by continued French participation in certain NATO infrastructure projects and by the fairly extensive but low-key military cooperation that developed between France and the other allies in subsequent years. But the benefits to allied defense plans, which full access to French territory would have offered, were lost.

The political costs to the alliance, however, may have been far more important than the military consequences. The French withdrawal substantially altered the political balance within the alliance. With France conferring on itself an "independent" status, the alliance became even more dependent on American leadership than it was before. This strengthening of American preeminence in the alliance ironically came at a time when Western Europe was moving toward a more powerful position in the Atlantic relationship as a result of its economic strength, the increasingly important role of West German forces in the alliance, and the growing strategic importance of French and British nuclear forces.

It was also ironic that one consequence of the French move was to enhance the importance of the German role within the alliance. The withdrawal virtually guaranteed that the Federal Republic, even without nuclear weapons of its own, would become the most influential continental European member of NATO and perhaps even more important to the alliance than the United Kingdom, given its position on the front lines opposite Warsaw Pact forces. Even though France remained a participant in all aspects of the alliance not directly associated with the integrated military command structure, its voice in alliance councils became less influential as a consequence of its decision to limit its formal military participation in the alliance.

The French withdrawal also raised serious political and structural obstacles to the chances for European defense cooperation within the alliance. In the years following the withdrawal, the allies actively tried to develop ways to expand cooperation with the French. The West Germans sought to exploit the avenue of bilateral Franco-German military cooperation, which de Gaulle saw as preferable to such cooperation within the NATO framework. The West Germans walked a fine line in such cooperation, attempting to expand the relationship in every way possible without jeopardizing in any fashion Germany's NATO obligations and its relations with the United States. But the political conditions imposed by France's qualified participation in NATO severely limited the options available for closer defense cooperation among the European allies.

It is difficult, in retrospect, to see any unequivocal gains for France as a consequence of the withdrawal. French security may not have been damaged, but it also was not appreciably enhanced by the move. Perhaps it could be said that an "independent" French position resulted in more political energy and financial resources being devoted to defense than if France had remained in the integrated military structure, but this is hard to prove. Furthermore, France did not become a more valued interlocutor with the Soviet Union, because the United States and the Federal Republic of Germany held the cards of greatest interest to Moscow. An independent position might have seemed of some tactical value to the Soviet Union from time to time, but in the end Moscow sought to deal principally with the two Western countries that could most benefit or harm Soviet interests.

The alliance may, however, have benefited in one regard from the French withdrawal. The establishment of a truly independent alternative Western nuclear decision-making center produced additional complications for Soviet strategy. Whatever uncertainty French nuclear forces and strategies created for Moscow may have enhanced Western deterrence. This was in fact recognized in Washington and officially by NATO. As Pascal Boniface has written:

> Once the French force de frappe became a reality ... the United States was obliged to accept it. Washington eventually made a virtue out of necessity—by acknowledging in the Ottawa Declaration of 1974 that France's nuclear capability was in fact useful for the defense of the West and for greater European security.[5]

On balance, however, the French rebellion was to the detriment of the long-term viability of the Western alliance. Most important, the withdrawal made it more difficult for the alliance to translate increased European strength into a more substantial European role in the alliance. This alteration in the bargain, therefore, was one of the most important factors that had to be accommodated when the allies turned to the business of building a European pillar for the alliance after the end of the Cold War.

NATO's role in defense and détente

The French rebellion had shaken the foundations of the alliance. But another fundamental challenge lay at hand. The North Atlantic Treaty was approaching its twentieth anniversary, auspicious primarily because the treaty's escape clause gave members the opportunity to leave the alliance after 20 years. As the alliance closed in on the 1969 opportunity for desertion, the greatest challenge to its political viability was not the French challenge. Rather, it was the question of whether this alliance, constructed in the chilly atmosphere of the Cold War, could survive in the warming climate of East–West détente.

In Germany, Social Democrat Willy Brandt had come into government as foreign minister in a "grand coalition" with the Christian Democrats, assuming the position on December 6, 1966. He believed that the Federal Republic's policy of non-recognition of East Germany and of existing European borders stood in the way of improving human conditions in Europe and particularly in the German Democratic Republic. Brandt's concept of "Ostpolitik" represented a major shift from Germany's orientation under Chancellor Konrad Adenauer, and he brought this new philosophy to his first NATO foreign ministerial meeting in Paris later that month.[6] Brandt's Belgian counterpart, Foreign Minister Pierre Harmel, felt strongly that the alliance would have to respond to critics who charged that NATO had become irrelevant under the changed international conditions. On the basis of Harmel's initiative, at least partly inspired by Brandt's philosophy that NATO defense and East–West détente could be compatible, the December 1966 meeting of NATO foreign ministers commissioned a yearlong study of "The Future Tasks of the Alliance." According to Harlan Cleveland, even the title of the study took on special meaning in the context of the mid-1960s. Cleveland, who represented the United States in the North Atlantic Council in the period before, during, and after the study, recalled that "if the 'Future of the alliance' had been studied, that would have implied doubt about continuation of the Alliance beyond 1969. 'Future tasks' assumed that NATO would survive its twentieth birthday, and called only its functions and priorities into question."[7]

The critique of NATO that inspired the Harmel exercise suggested that NATO's emphasis on the military aspects of security tended to undermine prospects for political solutions to East–West problems. The alliance had, of course, focused primarily on ways to maintain and improve Western defenses. It had not, however, been totally blind to the political aspects of security. Already by the mid-1950s, the allies had recognized that a narrowly focused Western military approach to the Soviet threat would not be sufficient to serve the broad range of allied political and economic as well as security objectives. The communiqué issued by the NATO foreign ministerial meeting in Paris in December 1955 marked the first formal alliance initiative broadening its perspectives on security, taking the Soviet Union to task for Moscow's refusal to consider intrusive systems of arms control verification, such as President Eisenhower's "Open Skies" proposal.[8]

In 1956, the allies began developing the rationale and mandate for arms control consultations in the alliance. The spring ministerial of that year appointed a "Committee of Three on Non-military Cooperation" to study ways in which NATO non-military cooperation could be expanded. The "three wise men"—Foreign Minister Gaetano Martino of Italy, Halvard Lange of Norway, and Lester Pearson of Canada—reaffirmed the necessity for collective defense efforts but strongly emphasized the need for better political consultation among the members. In particular, their report, approved by the North Atlantic Council in December 1956, observed that consultation "means more than letting the NATO Council know about national decisions that have already been taken; or trying to enlist support for those decisions. It means the discussion of problems collectively, in the early stages of policy formation, and before national positions become fixed."[9]

"The habit of consultation," strongly advocated by the three wise men, became an important part of alliance rhetoric, almost approaching theological heights. Even before the report—and ever since—NATO problems, to one extent or another, have been blamed on the failure of one or more allies to consult adequately. Virtually no report or commentary on the alliance can reach its conclusion without recommending "improved consultations."

The Harmel Report appropriately commended the virtues of improved consultation. The report's most important contribution, however, was its conclusion that "military security and the policy of détente are not contradictory but complementary." The report, the product of a prestigious committee led by Harmel, asserted that the alliance had two main functions. The first function, and the one with which the alliance had become most closely identified, was "to maintain adequate military strength and political solidarity to deter aggression and other forms of pressure and to defend the territory of member countries if aggression should occur." The second, newly assigned function of the alliance, was "to pursue the search for progress towards a more stable relationship [with the East] in which the underlying political issues can be solved." Approved by all the allies, including de Gaulle's France, the report offered this summary perspective:

Collective defense is a stabilizing factor in world politics. It is a necessary condition for effective policies directed towards a greater relaxation of tensions. The
way to peace and stability in Europe rests in particular on the use of the Alliance
constructively in the interest of détente. The participation of the USSR and
the USA will be necessary to achieve a settlement of the political problems in
Europe.[10]

The allies adopted the Harmel Report at their ministerial meeting in
December 1967 and, in this bold stroke, fundamentally altered the objectives,
image, and "future tasks" of the alliance. The report's "defense and détente"
combination provided an intellectual and political framework for NATO policies that accommodated the growing split in the alliance between left and
right. By bridging two different views of how best to ameliorate East–West
tensions, it broadened the potential base of political support for NATO in
European countries and in the United States. Subsequently, instead of polar-
izing Western politicians, policy elites, and publics, the alliance could serve
as a fulcrum for balancing divergent perspectives on the requirements for the
West's security policy in Europe. Not inconsequentially, this critical addition to
NATO's role provided the foundation for NATO to become an important political instrument following the end of the Cold War, when its military relevance
appeared open for debate following disappearance of the Soviet threat.

Acceptance of the Harmel Report also provided a way to deal with another
problem that had been brewing between the United States and the European
allies. The United States had become actively involved in bilateral arms control
discussions with the Soviet Union, and these discussions occasionally left the
allies wondering whether their interests would be protected by their American
ally. At the same time, American officials had become increasingly concerned
that the European allies would become "infected" by the Soviet peace campaign, with individual allies drifting off to cut their own deals with Moscow.
The Harmel Report implied that NATO consultations could serve to coordinate
Western approaches to the East. This coordination function would help allevi-
ate European concerns about US–Soviet bilateralism while providing a brake
on any European tendencies toward excessive détente fever.

In a very practical sense, the Harmel exercise created a whole new set of
responsibilities for NATO. A few weeks after the Harmel Report had been
approved, the allies agreed to strengthen the political institutions of the
alliance by establishing a "Senior Political Committee." This step could be
regarded as an institutional sleight of hand because the new box on the organizational chart simply referred to meetings of the NATO Political Committee,
with the allies represented by the deputy permanent representatives (instead
of the lower-ranking political counselors). Nonetheless, to the extent that
bureaucratic structures can be manipulated to send political signals, the alliance in this way marked the increased importance of the political side of alliance activities. A further institutional signal was sent later in 1968, when a

new section in the NATO international staff was created to deal with disarmament and arms control issues.

The allies wasted no time translating the Harmel mandate into alliance policy. When the North Atlantic Council met in Reykjavik, Iceland, in June 1968, the allies issued a "Declaration on Mutual and Balanced Force Reductions." The so-called Reykjavik signal announced allied agreement that "it was desirable that a process leading to mutual force reductions should be initiated." They agreed "to make all necessary preparations for discussions on this subject with the Soviet Union and other countries of Eastern Europe," and they urged the Warsaw Pact countries "to join in this search for progress toward peace."[11]

The Reykjavik signal echoed NATO's June 1967 expression of interest in mutual force reductions. However, the Reykjavik declaration was notable in that it not only expressed interest but also voiced NATO's intention to prepare for discussions that the East was invited to join. The Reykjavik signal, therefore, marked NATO's formal entry into the world of arms control initiatives, putting into action the recommendations adopted in the Harmel Report six months before.

The Harmel exercise revitalized the foundations of the alliance. It reiterated NATO's commitment to maintain a strong defense, but broadened substantially the goals of the alliance. This amendment to the original transatlantic bargain provided a political framework more relevant to the challenges posed by the East–West environment of the 1960s. It also responded to the evolving relationships between the United States and its West European allies. The Harmel formula gave the alliance a new lease on life and a renewed sense of purpose.

Perhaps the most lasting contribution of the Harmel exercise was the change in NATO's mission that would become so relevant at the end of the Cold War. For many years, NATO's search for the fruits of détente appeared unproductive and to some perhaps even counterproductive. Negotiations on Mutual and Balanced Force Reductions (MBFR)[12] opened in 1973, and some of us involved in the talks were hopeful that this first serious East–West negotiation on the military confrontation in Europe could reduce the danger of war breaking out there. In spite of this hope, the talks in a sense became a victim of the East–West competition, and droned on for more than a decade before being converted into negotiations on Conventional Armed Forces in Europe in the mid-1980s. The latter negotiations finally produced a deal, largely because the fading Cold War finally made it possible. That deal not only provided the framework for dramatic cuts in military forces and equipment across Europe but also established an intensive, cooperative monitoring system that would eventually help ease the transition from Cold War confrontation to a more cooperative security system in Europe.[13]

In addition, in 1975, NATO's initiatives helped turn Moscow's propagandistic proposals for a "Conference on European Security" into the Conference

Figure 4.1 UK and US delegations at 1973 opening of Mutual and Balanced Force Reduction negotiations in Vienna (author is seen immediately behind US Ambassador Jonathan Dean).

on Security and Cooperation in Europe (CSCE), a meaningful East–West forum on a broad spectrum of issues.[14] The East–West dialogue in the CSCE may well have contributed to undermining the control of communist regimes in the East and to the unraveling of the East–West conflict.[15]

Despite the opening of MBFR talks and the beginning of the CSCE process, many Americans saw little in the way of demonstrable benefits for NATO's pursuit of détente. When President Gerald Ford (in 1974 Ford succeeded President Richard Nixon, who had stepped down after the Watergate scandal) suggested that the term "détente" should be removed from the West's political vocabulary, many Europeans winced but hoped that the comment would not be prophetic. Ford's declaration, inspired by some deeper trends in American thinking, in fact did project accurately the future course of American policy.

The administration of President Jimmy Carter (1977–1980) was unsure in its early years what it would do about the growing disenchantment, particularly among American conservatives, with the era of détente. The administration revealed a split personality in its approach to the Soviets. On the one hand, it wanted—and negotiated—a strategic arms control accord with Moscow. On the other hand, the administration's fixation on human rights issues produced a strong critique of the Soviet Union's treatment of its own citizens, criticism that cohabited very uncomfortably with the administration's attempts to sell a US–Soviet arms control deal to the US Congress.

While the Strategic Arms Limitation Talks (SALT II) treaty was languishing in the US Senate, the Soviet Union provided the stimulus for resolution of the dilemma in Carter administration policy. In the closing days of 1979, Moscow sent troops into neighboring Afghanistan, collapsing whatever was left of US–Soviet détente. A US Atlantic Council report in 1983 noted, "The death of détente was sounded when the Soviets invaded Afghanistan in 1979. President Carter imposed sanctions, withdrew the SALT II agreement from Senate ratification, and recommended substantial increases in US defense spending which were further enlarged under the Reagan Administration."[16] Washington's unilateral declaration of the death of détente, however, was never fully accepted in Europe. The Soviet invasion of Afghanistan was seen as distasteful evidence of Soviet insecurity and interventionism but not as a direct threat to Europe, and certainly not as a sufficient rationale for jeopardizing the fruits of détente in Europe. As Josef Joffe put it, "For the United States, détente did not 'work,' for the Europeans it did—hence their almost obsessive attempts to snatch as many pieces as possible from the jaws of the rattled giants."[17]

Even before the invasion of Afghanistan, Henry Kissinger had argued that the Harmel formula was inappropriate for the circumstances of the late 1970s. Addressing a conference on the future of NATO in Brussels in September 1979, Kissinger dismissed NATO's détente role as an intrusion on the real business of the alliance.

European (and some American) participants in the conference shook their heads in amazement that Kissinger could so lightly dismiss a political aspect of NATO that had been so important to the credibility of the alliance for more than a decade. Kissinger's approach, however, was a clear warning that the critique from the political right in the United States was increasingly affecting American perspectives on the alliance and its policies.[18]

In the late 1970s and into the 1980s, the United States and the European allies struggled with the great variety of issues raised by their differing perspectives on the importance of détente and whether détente was "divisible," applicable to Europe but not the Third World. The debate intensified with the advent in 1981 of the Reagan administration which was determined to implement a tough new American policy toward the Soviet Union, backed by a substantial defense build-up.

The allies managed to work out compromises on many of the specific issues raised by the differing American and European perspectives. But European governments never accepted the American contention that détente was dead or that the alliance should jettison its mandate for pursuing improved relations and arms control agreements with the Soviet Union.

Ironically, the Reagan administration, whose hard line toward Moscow had troubled the Europeans so much, managed to initiate the end-game negotiations on both intermediate range nuclear missile cuts and conventional force reduction negotiations in Europe. In subsequent years, supporters of President Reagan claimed that his tough policies toward the Soviet Union had helped bring about its collapse. Critics of the American president suggested that Soviet leader Mikhail Gorbachev should be given most of the credit for opening both the Soviet Union and the Warsaw Pact for change. Looking back, it would appear that both factors played a role and that, to some extent, the outcomes that unraveled the Warsaw Pact and dissolved the Soviet Union were unexpected consequences of Soviet and American policies. In any case, the relevance and importance of the Harmel doctrine appear in historical perspective to have been borne out by the end of the Cold War and the need for NATO to adapt its role further to accommodate the dramatically new international realities.

NATO's nuclear strategy

From massive retaliation to flexible response

NATO's reliance on the threat of a massive nuclear attack on the Soviet Union had been suspect virtually from the day MC 48 was approved in December 1954. NATO's first nuclear strategy was not quite as simple as implied by the image of "massive retaliation" most frequently used to describe the essence of MC 48. The strategy spelled out in this document did not exclude the possibility that nuclear weapons might be used only within the confines of the battlefield. Despite US deployment in the 1950s of a variety of nonstrategic nuclear weapons in Western Europe, alliance strategy remained at least implicitly reliant on the suggestion that the Soviet Union would risk a massive nuclear strike on its territory should its forces attack Western Europe.

This nuclear strategy, driven principally by the austerity program of the Eisenhower administration, and the failure of the allies to meet the Lisbon conventional force goals, did not sufficiently anticipate the implications of Soviet nuclear force deployments. The Soviet Union had successfully tested an atomic device in 1949 and a hydrogen bomb in 1953, but when MC 48 was approved, the Soviet Union had only limited means for delivering its few weapons on Western targets, and virtually no credible means for threatening American territory. The United States, meanwhile, had surrounded Soviet territory with a bomber force capable of devastating strikes on the Soviet Union. This situation was, for obvious reasons, intolerable for the Soviets and, even as the NATO ministers were approving MC 48, Moscow was developing its own long-range bomber force and planning to deploy medium- and intermediate-range ballistic missiles targeted on Western Europe. The launch of the Sputnik satellite in 1957 symbolized the dramatic progress the Soviet Union had made in a very few years toward developing its own strategic nuclear weapons force capable of holding both European and American cities hostage to a nuclear threat, calling into question the US policy of massive retaliation.

The NATO allies struggled from the mid-1950s with attempts to adjust NATO's strategy and force posture to the evolving strategic environment. In 1959, the Eisenhower administration deployed US medium-range ballistic missiles to Europe: 60 Thor missiles to England and 90 Jupiter missiles divided evenly between Italy and Turkey. The missile deployments were intended to help offset the Soviet deployment of SS-4 and SS-5 missiles that had begun in the late 1950s and to bolster the confidence of European governments in the ability of the United States to implement its nuclear guarantee.

The alliance was at the same time grappling with some internal political dynamics that had begun to undermine its nuclear weapons strategy. European fretting about civilian control of nuclear weapons, so much in evidence when the United States had first attempted to sell the new-look strategy to the alliance in 1954, developed into a more specific European desire to have a say in Western nuclear decision-making. By the late 1950s, the British had an independent nuclear capability, and the French were on the way toward nuclear power status. The United States was by no means anxious to encourage the proliferation of nuclear weapons states and would have preferred that neither France nor the United Kingdom develop nuclear forces.

Between 1959 and 1963, a number of schemes emerged for some form of nuclear sharing among the NATO allies. These schemes were motivated to varying degrees by Soviet nuclear weapons advances and by the tension within the alliance about the American monopoly in nuclear decision-making. Of these proposals, only the Multilateral Force (MLF) made any headway. The MLF would have been a force of 25 surface ships, each carrying eight Polaris nuclear missiles, manned by multinational crews, funded jointly by participating allies and assigned to the NATO Supreme Allied Commander. The United States would have retained ultimate veto power over the use of the MLF weapons.

The MLF proposal, ingenious as it might have been, never had much chance of political acceptance. President de Gaulle interpreted the scheme simply as a means for the United States to retain control over Western nuclear policies while appearing to share it. He saw his suspicions confirmed when the British, seeking to modernize their nuclear forces, chose to purchase Polaris missiles from the United States. According to de Gaulle, British Prime Minister Harold Macmillan "mortgaged" Britain's future nuclear capability to the United States in the Nassau Agreement with President John F. Kennedy in December 1962, when he agreed to buy Polaris submarine-launched ballistic missiles from the United States. After further NATO discussions of various MLF variants that continued into the administration of Lyndon B. Johnson, MLF was consigned to the closet of historic curiosities.

The MLF failure left unresolved the issues it had been designed to address, in particular the political requirement for broader allied participation in nuclear decision-making. Even if France and the United Kingdom were determined to maintain their own nuclear forces, US officials remained convinced that West

Germany would have to be given a more acceptable role in nuclear decision-making given Bonn's increasingly central role in the alliance.

By the early 1960s, the United States had positioned in Western Europe a wide array of nuclear weapons, ranging from intermediate-range systems to short-range weapons intended for use on the battlefield. However, it kept either full control over the weapons or joint control by retaining one of two keys necessary to release them. This massive infusion of US nuclear weapons in NATO defenses, combined with the desire of some West European allies for a more influential role in NATO nuclear planning, led to the creation of the Nuclear Planning Group (NPG) in 1966. The NPG was designed to allow alliance members to influence planning for the potential use of nuclear weapons and to give them a role in nuclear decision-making in a crisis. The United States also agreed to assign 64 Polaris submarine-launched ballistic missiles directly to NATO along with the British Polaris force, both of which would be responsive to requirements of the Supreme Allied Commander, Europe.[19]

The abortive MLF project and the subsequent creation of the NPG were responses largely to developments within the alliance. During the same period, the alliance was also moving toward a substantial shift in its nuclear strategy. Although massive retaliation had died years before, it had never been formally buried; the United States started pushing for a proper interment in the early 1960s.

From an American perspective, the steady growth of Soviet nuclear capabilities clearly necessitated a more flexible set of guidelines for the use of nuclear weapons. It was no longer credible simply to threaten attacks on the Soviet heartland with nuclear weapons in response to a Warsaw Pact offensive in Western Europe—the American heartland had become vulnerable to a response in kind. The need for change had been signaled by Secretary of Defense Robert McNamara in 1962.

Such a momentous change in nuclear strategy, however, met with skepticism in Western Europe, largely from fear that the credibility of the nuclear guarantee would be destroyed by a strategy that foresaw the possibility of limited or controlled nuclear exchanges. The concepts that lay behind MC 48 had been of American origin, but they had been embraced by the European allies, and in the 1960s the threat of a massive nuclear strike still seemed a needed deterrent to Soviet aggression in Europe, as well as an affordable substitute for adequate non-nuclear forces.

In 1967, following France's departure from NATO's integrated military command structure, and after several wrenching years of discussion and debate among the allies, NATO adopted the doctrine of flexible response. According to the new strategy, NATO would be prepared to meet any level of aggression with equivalent force, conventional or nuclear, and would increase the level of force, if necessary, to end the conflict. The doctrine attempted to accommodate the American desire for more flexible nuclear options and West European concerns about the nuclear umbrella. Under the doctrine, Chicago might not be put at risk in the early stages of a conflict, but the possibility of escalation supposedly "coupled" the fate of Chicago to that of Paris, Hamburg, or London.

The new strategy, substantially altering the original transatlantic bargain, compromised conflicting US and European perspectives on the requirements of deterrence. As Simon Lunn wrote, "While theoretically sound, it [flexible response] left considerable latitude for differences concerning the levels of forces necessary at each stage to insure credible deterrence. This ambiguity permitted the accommodation of conflicting American and European interests, but it did not represent their reconciliation."[20]

While the new nuclear doctrine did not reconcile American and European differences on nuclear strategy, it did provide a formula that was sufficiently ambiguous to achieve political credibility on both sides of the Atlantic—at least for a while. The strategy, combined with the advent of allied consultations on NATO's nuclear policy in the NPG, formally accorded nuclear weapons, from the smallest yield battlefield systems to the strategic forces of the United States, their own unique places in NATO military strategy. Not only would nuclear weapons serve as a deterrent against a Warsaw Pact attack, but, under flexible response, the entire range of nuclear weapons had a potential role to play in wartime scenarios. Furthermore, the United States had acknowledged the legitimate interests of the allies in shaping NATO nuclear doctrine and sharing the responsibilities of decision-making in a crisis. The United States provided no iron-clad guarantee about how extensive consultations might be in a crisis, but at least the NPG provided the ways and means for such consultations.

The decision also recalled the long-standing but unfulfilled NATO objective of mounting a credible non-nuclear defense against the Warsaw Pact. A more substantial conventional capability would fit comfortably within the flexible response framework. In this regard, the new strategy was at least superficially consistent with the original bargain, in which substantial European non-nuclear forces were to be a key support for NATO strategy. Under the circumstances of conventional insufficiency, however, the new doctrine implied greater reliance on the possible use of short-range nuclear weapons, as well as the possibility that a nuclear exchange might be limited to the battlefield or to the European continent.

Flexible response, in this sense, was a double-edged sword. Reliance on a wide range of battlefield nuclear weapons implied an even more permanent US commitment to its force presence in Europe because virtually all of NATO's nuclear weapons were under exclusive US control or subject to US veto. NATO's defense options, as well as its deterrent strategy, had become more dependent on the US troop presence. The October 1954 American commitment to maintain troops in Europe for "as long as is necessary" therefore became longer and more necessary under the flexible response strategy.

At the same time, whether or not the US intent was to provide a greater buffer between its homeland and a possible war in Europe, the new doctrine clearly left open the possibility that the United States would place a higher value on avoiding nuclear strikes on the United States than it would on protect-ing West European territory. Although the first edge of the sword committed the United States even more firmly to participate in the defense of Europe, the second edge of the sword cut away some of the credibility of that commitment.

In fact, the Soviet Union's drive, first to obtain the means to threaten the United States directly and then to achieve nuclear parity, changed one of the most important conditioning factors for the original transatlantic bargain. The American homeland became dangerously exposed for the first time since the young upstart of a nation had chased the European powers from the Western Hemisphere. Technological advances had given the Soviet Union the potential to threaten all of the United States with its nuclear weapons. But the Atlantic Ocean still separated the United States from its European allies. It therefore remained possible, at least in theory, for the United States to limit its involve-ment in a war in Europe in order to save the American homeland, and, given the emerging Soviet nuclear capabilities, it had much more reason to do so.

Flexible response undermined

With the advent of flexible response and the development of limited nuclear options, the certainty implied by massive retaliation was replaced by the elusive goal of "escalation control." That NATO "advantage" was countered in the 1970s by Soviet nuclear force improvements, including deployment of the SS-20, a mobile, accurate missile system capable of carrying three indepen-dently targeted warheads on each missile.

For many West Europeans, the nuclear deterrent had remained cred-ible throughout the perturbations in the nuclear balance and adjustments in Western nuclear policy. There was no certain guarantee that the American president would push the button for Europe, but no iron-clad commitment could be expected. The Soviet Union had not risked an attack on Western Europe and did not seem likely to do so. A qualified guarantee, therefore, appeared sufficient for deterrence. For many nuclear strategists, however, there was no such confidence.

In the 1970s, West German Chancellor Helmut Schmidt became the single most influential European commentator on alliance strategy and force posture. By the mid-1970s, Schmidt had become convinced that Soviet con-ventional force advantages over NATO, combined with its superiority in theater nuclear forces, put Europe at risk. Schmidt was concerned that the codification of a US–Soviet balance of strategic weapons in the SALT process could make these weapons of "last resort," weaken extended deterrence, and leave Europe exposed to Soviet power. He highlighted such concerns in a major address to the London International Institute for Strategic Studies in October 1977. Although Schmidt's comments did not refer to theater nuclear forces, they "focused public attention on the concept that a gap was appearing in NATO's deterrent capability."[21]

In the fall of 1979, Henry Kissinger, having served earlier as national security adviser and then secretary of state under Presidents Nixon and Ford, strongly criticized European and American governments for permitting the fate of their nations to rest on such a foundation of hope rather than on adequate deterrence forces. Kissinger "confessed" to a Brussels meeting of American and European defense experts and officials that he had "sat around the NATO council table in Brussels and elsewhere and uttered the magic words [promising extended deterrence for Western Europe] which had a profoundly reassuring effect and which permitted [allied] ministers to return home with a rationale for not increasing defense expenditures." Then Kissinger stunned much of his audience with his conclusion:

> If my analysis is correct, these words cannot be true. And we must face the fact that it is absurd to base the strategy of the West on the credibility of the threat of mutual suicide. Therefore, I would say—which I might not say in office—the European allies should not keep asking us to multiply strategic assurances that we cannot possibly mean, or, if we do mean, we should not want to execute, because if we execute we risk the destruction of civilization.[22]

Kissinger urged that NATO modernize its European-based nuclear forces (an action the alliance was already preparing to take three months later) and encouraged the allies to strengthen conventional defense, an objective sought with limited enthusiasm since the alliance was founded. In other words, Kissinger argued primarily for more "credible" nuclear options combined with a stronger conventional defense to deal with NATO's nuclear dilemma. His analysis suggested that extended deterrence had been invalidated by the advent of Soviet strategic nuclear parity and that the expansion of Soviet theater nuclear forces, particularly deployment of the SS-20 missiles capable of striking targets throughout Western Europe, had checkmated NATO's adoption of the flexible response strategy and deployment of thousands of short-range nuclear weapons in Europe. Kissinger's argument, framed by a politically conservative analysis and a pessimistic perspective on trends in the East–West military balance, represented the conventional wisdom that justified NATO's December 1979 decision to deploy new long-range theater nuclear forces.

Kissinger's message, while compelling, gave short shrift to some additional requirements of Western policy. First, NATO's political viability had come to depend on a fine balance between allied defense efforts and Western attempts to reach mutually acceptable accommodations with the East. Second, any unilateral NATO efforts to improve its nuclear force posture would likely produce a countervailing response from the Soviet Union. As a consequence of the first requirement, NATO's plan for dealing with the perceived deterioration in the nuclear deterrent would have to make sense to European and American publics. In order to gain public confidence, the allies would have to make a serious arms control proposal to the East. Furthermore, the only way to reduce the threat posed by Soviet SS-20 missiles and to forestall a countervailing Soviet response would be to negotiate limits on such systems with the Soviet Union.

And so, in December 1979, led by the US administration of President Carter, the NATO allies decided to modernize its theater nuclear forces while seeking to negotiate limits on such forces with the Soviet Union.[23] This decision came despite growing public opposition in several West European countries to new missile deployments, particularly on their soil.

The debate between East and West and within the Western community that preceded the initial deployments tended to obscure rather than illuminate the rationale of the original decision. The debate between East and West became a contest for the "hearts and minds" of the Europeans. Within the West, the issue became part of a larger struggle between competing concepts of how best to deal with the Soviet Union. The 1979 decision therefore became a surrogate for the discussion of much broader aspects of East–West relations. The initial deployments, marking as they did a "victory" for one side of the debate, perhaps opened the way for a more reflective look at the fate of the 1979 decision and its implications for the future of NATO.

The 1979 "dual-track" decision was, after all, perfectly consistent with the stated objectives and strategies of the alliance. The decision attempted to deal with conflicting American and European perspectives on deterrence by providing more flexible nuclear systems—in response to the American requirement for credible nuclear options—which, nonetheless in their ability to strike Soviet territory, could be seen as strengthening the link between the European theater and the strategic nuclear standoff—in response to the European requirement for extended deterrence.

According to the decision's rationale, deterrence for Europe would be strengthened because the Soviet Union, in contemplating any attack on Western Europe, would be forced to calculate that the West might respond by striking Soviet territory with the new systems. And, in using the systems, the West would know that the Soviet Union might respond by striking American, not just European, targets. Therefore, both sides would be aware that hostilities initiated in Europe might escalate rapidly to a strategic exchange.

This logic was no foolproof guarantee of extended deterrence. The American president could, in theory, decide not to use the new systems in case of a Soviet attack and could even choose to "lose" them rather than invite strategic retaliation. That decision, however, would have to be made much earlier in the conflict than might previously have been the case. The new deployments, therefore, compressed the time in which the Soviet Union could advance through Western Europe without risking a nuclear strike on Soviet territory. The new missiles were not principally intended as a means for physically targeting the Soviet SS-20 missiles, as some observers mistakenly thought, but rather for deterring any attack from the East. Because of this linkage rationale for deploying the new weapons, there was no magic number of missiles that had to be deployed. The deployment would have to be sufficiently large to guarantee (in combination with other factors, such as mobility) survival of enough weapons to remain a serious option in a crisis. Beyond this pragmatic rationale, the final number of 572 missiles was also influenced by the desire to deploy systems in a number of allied countries to "share" the risks and responsibilities of the decision.

The arms control "track" of the dual-track decision also had a very specific purpose. It brought the decision in line with the Harmel formula, which the allies had developed in 1967 to give NATO a role in promoting détente with the East as well as sustaining defense and deterrence. It undoubtedly was clear to the allies that they might need to demonstrate their interest in arms control in order to defend the deployment decision before their publics. The arms control initiative, however, could do something that the deployment would not accomplish on its own. Only if there were an arms control agreement with the Soviet Union to limit intermediate-range nuclear systems could the West restrict the extent of the SS-20 threat to Western Europe.

Why, when the decision on intermediate-range nuclear forces seemed so well designed to serve the strategy of extended deterrence, did it ultimately provoke in Europe fear of nuclear war rather than produce increased confidence that war would be deterred? The answer lies in the fact that the viability of extended deterrence rested on three pillars: the weapons themselves, a credible strategy relating the weapons to the purpose of the alliance, and political confidence that the weapons and the strategy would make it less rather than more likely that war would occur. Historically, the United States has tended to place greater emphasis on the weapons and the strategy for their use than on the political context for their deployment. Europeans, on the other hand, have tended to place greater emphasis on the political context, believing that wars usually are "about something," the product of political disagreements rather than spontaneous unexplainable events. Critiquing the 1979 decision, one European analyst suggested:

> The historical record since World War II demonstrates that the faith of Europeans in Washington's ability to use its power in a measured and prompt way to defend Western interests, whether inside or outside the NATO area, is a far more important determinant of their confidence in the reliability of the US nuclear umbrella and of their acceptance of nuclear defence than is the nuclear balance between the Superpowers.[24]

Even under the best of circumstances, it would not have been easy to negotiate an arms control agreement limiting intermediate-range nuclear systems. As it happened, the negotiations began under a dark cloud because of the general deterioration in US–Soviet relations that had begun in the years immediately prior to the NATO decision and that quickened in its wake.

The Soviet invasion of Afghanistan, only two weeks after the NATO 1979 decision, provided a rallying point for the critique of Soviet global intervention that had been building in the United States for a number of years. The critique had already been a major factor in the failure of the Senate to ratify the SALT II treaty. The invasion brought consideration of the treaty to a full stop.

Ronald Reagan, after trouncing Jimmy Carter in the 1980 elections, set American foreign policy on a new course. President Carter had already begun a defense build-up that the Reagan administration promptly accelerated. Just as important, the Reagan administration came to office infused with great skepticism about arms control based on a perception of unrelenting Soviet antagonism toward US interests. The administration put arms control on a back burner and concentrated on developing its defense program.

The Reagan administration's approach to the 1979 decision was based on its dominant philosophy that the Soviet Union—the "evil empire"—would not act seriously in arms control negotiations until Moscow saw that an expensive arms race was the alternative to arms control agreements. It took six months for the administration even to announce that it intended to open arms control negotiations on intermediate-range nuclear weapons. That decision came only after urgent pleading from the allies and a contentious decision-making process within the administration, in which officials argued whether arms control negotiations would undermine deployment plans or, on the other hand, make it easier to deploy the missiles.

Almost another six months passed before the administration set its goal for the negotiations. The famous "zero-option" proposal, announced by President Reagan on November 18, 1981, called for the total elimination of all Soviet intermediate-range nuclear weapons in return for cancellation of NATO deployment plans. The plan was received with skepticism by many experts. Some suspected that the far-reaching nature of the approach was designed to produce a Soviet rejection, allowing deployment to proceed.

The initial Soviet response was negative, as was to be expected. Tough negotiations stretched out over several years, seemingly destined to become an arms control failure. Meanwhile, however, other factors were working on the Soviet Union. At home, the Soviet system was proving increasingly incapable of providing basic necessities. As a consequence, Soviet President Gorbachev judged that the Soviet Union could not afford to engage in an open-ended arms competition with the United States. He decided to cut a deal.

On December 8, 1987, the United States and the Soviet Union signed the Intermediate-Range Nuclear Forces (INF) Treaty designed to eliminate two categories of their intermediate-range nuclear missiles: long-range INF, with a range between 600 and 3,400 miles, and short-range INF, with a range between 300 and 600 miles. The treaty did not cover short-range (under 300 miles) nuclear force missiles. In this shorter-range category, NATO countries still had the aging LANCE missile system with approximately 700 warheads. The United States deployed some 36 LANCE missile launchers in Western Europe. Belgium, the Netherlands, West Germany, Italy, and the United Kingdom deployed around 60 LANCE launchers with nuclear warheads available under dual-key arrangements with the United States. These missiles could not reach Soviet targets from their launch sites in Europe and therefore were not of great concern to Moscow and did not accomplish the same strategic objectives originally intended through deployment of the INF missiles.

Although European as well as American public opinion strongly supported the INF Treaty, some observers judged that elimination of the missiles would undermine the credibility of flexible response and argued that the alliance would have to compensate for the loss of the INF missiles to keep its strategy intact. Others argued, however, that the United States still committed a small but strategically significant portion of its relatively invulnerable sea-launched ballistic missile force for use by NATO's Supreme Allied Commander, and that this force, plus nuclear weapons carried on FB-111 and B-52 bombers based in the United States, preserved a strategic strike potential for NATO. They also argued that a continuing US troop presence in Europe served as a "trip wire" and thus ensured linkage to US strategic nuclear forces.

In addition, British and French strategic capabilities, capable of hitting targets in the Soviet Union, which were not included in the INF negotiations or in US–Soviet strategic arms talks, were being modernized and expanded.

In the event, implementation of the INF Treaty became part of the process of winding down the Cold War, a circumstance anticipated by no one when the treaty was signed in 1987. The intensive inspection regime associated with provisions for dismantling the missiles created a vehicle for testing the possibilities for US–Russian cooperation in the post-Cold War era.

With the end of the Cold War and the dissolution of the Soviet Union, NATO's struggles with nuclear doctrine and extended deterrence promised to enter a new phase. The aspect of the transatlantic relationship that, in many ways, had been the most difficult for the allies to sustain in capabilities and public support was suddenly overtaken by welcome events. But changed relations with Russia in the mid-2010s threatened to raise new questions about the necessity for nuclear deterrence.

Britain joins Europe

The original transatlantic bargain had been seriously flawed by the British refusal to become more closely involved in post-war continental European affairs. The United Kingdom had been centrally involved in shaping the Western alliance and had promised to maintain forces on the continent, at least as long as the troop presence in Europe did not conflict with British global commitments. But the British commitment to Europe was highly qualified and purposefully distant. The United Kingdom had wanted no role in a European Defense Community and could not see itself as any part of a European unity movement. The United Kingdom's European role in the 1950s was, in effect, an extension of its special relationship with the United States and a distraction from British global political and military involvements. Furthermore, British foreign trade with the Commonwealth was more substantial than that with continental Europe.

The United States valued the special relationship and appreciated the important role that the United Kingdom had played in the formative years of the alliance. Only in retrospect, perhaps, is it possible to see so clearly how the United Kingdom's distance from the continent handicapped efforts to organize a more coherent European pillar for the alliance. Had the United Kingdom been willing to join in the European Defense Community or to make a stronger commitment to European defense, perhaps French concerns about balancing Germany on its own would have been allayed. Of course, such speculation serves very little purpose other than to suggest how much the alliance needs British involvement on the European side of the bargain. It would have been unreasonable to expect this global power to acknowledge in the early years of its decline that its future would have to be more intimately linked to that of its neighbors across the English Channel. Luigi Barzini captured the British attitude with this colorful portrait:

> Most of the men who at the beginning rejected the European idea had had responsible roles in World War II. They kept on considering their country what it had been indisputably only a few years before, one of the three great powers ... . Such men naturally found it unthinkable to join a condominium of defeated, weak, frightened, and impecunious second-rank nations... . Were they not still better than any continental in every—well, practically every—field that really counted? Didn't the ordinary inferior humans still begin at Calais? To be sure, some individual continentals could be brilliant and sometimes admirable, but most of them were bizarre, slippery, and often incomprehensible. They ate inedible things such as octopuses, frogs, and snails. "Only foreigners waltz backward," Englishmen said contemptuously in the past, when the waltz was still fashionable.[25]

A new generation of British politicians in the 1960s decided the United Kingdom should join the EEC, but the commitment to Europe remained highly qualified. When the British finally joined the Community in 1973, they did so, according to Barzini's interpretation, "reluctantly and somewhat squeamishly, though politely concealing their feelings, like decayed aristocrats obliged by adverse circumstances to eat in a soup kitchen for the needy."[26]

Britain's first tentative approach to Europe, of course, ran into General de Gaulle's veto in 1963. De Gaulle accurately perceived the United Kingdom's commitment to Europe as still prejudiced by its Commonwealth ties and, most important, by its special relationship with the United States. Seeing the United Kingdom as an "Atlanticist" Trojan horse, de Gaulle explained his action by saying that with Britain in the Community, European cohesion would not last for long, and "in the end there would appear a colossal Atlantic Community under American dependence and leadership which would completely swallow up the European Community."[27]

By the time Britain made its second attempt to join the Community, much had changed. De Gaulle had been replaced by a Gaullist but more pragmatic leader, President Georges Pompidou, whose prestige was not at issue over British membership in the EC. More important, the United Kingdom's circumstances had substantially altered. British defense policy had become more Eurocentric with the withdrawal of its forces east of Suez. British trade with the Commonwealth had declined in the 1960s as a share of total British foreign trade, while commerce with continental Europe had steadily increased. The special relationship with the United States had become less and less of an equal partnership as symbolized by the British withdrawal from a far-flung global presence.

The British, as a people, still had not fully accepted their place as a "European" country. Even in later years, some Brits still talked of "going to Europe" when they crossed the Channel. But by the early 1970s, it was already more than clear to objective observers that Britain's strategic interests could be served only as a European power, "waltzing backwards," following Barzini's image, as a member of the EC even while perhaps resisting the temptation to eat snails.

The British turn toward Europe represented a fundamental change in the transatlantic bargain. British membership in the EC could not change the fact that the bargain might have been a far different deal had the United Kingdom joined Europe 20 years earlier. It nonetheless enhanced the potential for Europe to become a true second pillar for the alliance, and this became a crucial factor as the Europeans—not only including the United Kingdom but also with British leadership—began trying to construct a new transatlantic bargain at the end of the twentieth century. The Brexit debate over England's place in Europe, however, extended well into the next century, keeping open questions about the future of the European project.

West Germany's ascendance

When the original transatlantic bargain was struck, it was principally a deal between the United States and France. The British actively participated as facilitators, negotiators, and mediators. The Germans were actively involved but more like lobbyists, trying to protect German interests from just outside the formal negotiating process rather than as full-fledged participants. After all, the bargain was partly about Germany's future, about how German power could be contained as well as utilized within the Western alliance.

Luigi Barzini observed, in mock-Germanic style, "The future of Europe appears largely to depend today once again, for good or evil, whether we like it or not, as it did for many centuries, on the future of Germany."[28] Germany was a central issue when the alliance was formed. Throughout the Cold War,

Germany remained at the heart of Europe's future, and the Federal Republic gained in strength, stature, and influence within and outside the alliance.

By the late 1980s, Germany had become a key player in the Western alliance. Only because it was not a nuclear weapons state did Germany rank second in power to any other European country. German armed forces provided the backbone of NATO active-duty forces in Central Europe, as well as a large reserve component. The German economy, even as it struggled in the recession of the early 1980s, had become more vibrant than that of either France or the United Kingdom. The fact that the German question remained at the core of intra-Western as well as of East–West relations granted the Federal Republic substantial political influence in both Western and Eastern capitals. In the late 1960s and early 1970s, Foreign Minister and then Chancellor Willy Brandt's Ostpolitik exercised a major influence on Western alliance policy by seeking to overcome East–West divisions with contacts and cooperation rather than confrontation.

West Germany, however, remained constrained in unique ways—the residue of World War II and the post-war division of Europe. The Western powers continued to exercise certain rights with regard to Germany, and some of the constraints that were wrapped up in the 1954 London and Paris accords remained in effect. Most of the limitations on non-nuclear West German military operations and arms production had been removed or liberalized, but there were still legal constraints on the production or possession of chemical or nuclear weapons. And the Soviet Union still held effective veto power over the future of relations between the two Germanys, with Berlin's hostage status the leading symbol of Moscow's line of influence to the West German government in Bonn.

The Germans accepted the constraints placed on them by the Western post-war security framework as a price of the war and a ticket to independent statehood and renewed respectability. Over time, those constraints were woven into the fabric of West German political life. One close observer of German–American relations, Gebhard Schweigler, has observed that the outside constraints on Germany became progressively irrelevant as West German policies and political behavior were shaped according to the preferences of Bonn's Western allies. Once West Germany had "internalized" those constraints, Schweigler maintained, many policy differences with the United States grew out of the fact that West Germany was not willing to change from directions originally taken at the insistence or urging of its Western allies.[29] In the early years of the twenty-first century, Germany's "lessons learned" from the World War II victors have remained a source of differences with the United States and other allies due to a united Germany's political constraints on the use of its military forces in combat roles beyond German borders. This problem persisted even during Germany's commendable commitment of forces to the 2000s war in Afghanistan against al-Qaeda terrorists and the Taliban.

Despite these external and internalized limitations, in the Cold War confrontation with the Soviet Union, West Germany became America's most important

NATO ally. The fact that West Germany's development as an independent power included its emergence as a potent military ally, at least within the confines of Western Europe, represented a major geostrategic gain for the United States.

The progress of West German national growth can be observed in many aspects of US–German relations. One of the best examples, perhaps, is the evolution in the financial aspects of the relationship. In the early 1950s, the United States was still providing substantial financial assistance to support West German rearmament. As the US balance of payments weakened in the late 1950s and the German economy accelerated, the United States looked for ways to retrieve some of the costs of its military presence in Europe. In 1961, the United States and West Germany agreed to an offset program whereby West Germany would purchase military equipment in the United States to compensate for US military expenditures in West Germany. These agreements were renewed and expanded during the Johnson and Nixon presidencies to include German purchases of US Treasury bonds and, in the 1970s, the repair of barracks used by US forces in Germany.

By the early 1970s, however, the Germans had grown uncomfortable with the idea of paying the United States to maintain troops in Germany. Bonn (West Germany's capital during the Cold War) did not like the idea of paying for American "mercenaries" and preferred to concentrate its resources on improving German military capabilities. The United States accepted German arguments for a more "normal" relationship between the two allies, and the offset agreement was allowed to expire in 1975. As the German "White Paper 1983" on defense recalled, "The changes that had meanwhile taken place in the international monetary structure and the extensive contribution made by the Federal Republic of Germany to common defense no longer justified these additional burdens on the Federal budget."[30]

By the mid-1980s, some Germans were arguing that US economic policy was effectively making Germany (and other countries as well) pay for the US defense build-up. The logic of the argument ran something like this: continuing deficits in the United States kept US interest rates high, attracting investment capital to the United States and artificially elevating the value of the dollar on international exchange markets; the investment capital attracted to the United States was therefore not available to help prime a German economic recovery while the elevated value of the dollar kept energy prices high in Germany (because oil is traded in dollars), also restricting German economic recovery. Although the argument certainly does not tell the whole story of Germany's economic problems, it does illustrate how substantially the defense economics of US–German relations had changed since the early 1950s.

The German assertion that the United States was making Germany pay for the American defense build-up suggested that Germany's maturation had brought with it some changes that have been difficult for the United States to accept. Over the years, a number of the factors that guaranteed the United

States substantial influence over West German policies had eroded. The United States no longer served as the model of society and government it once did for many Germans. West Germans might not have been fully satisfied with their own political and social institutions, but they no longer felt burdened with a sense of systemic inferiority toward the United States. As a consequence, the West Germans no longer believed it was necessary to look to Washington to define West German security interests. The Federal Republic, with greater confidence than ever since World War II, began basing its foreign and defense policies more and more on home-grown assessments of German interests.

The process of German maturation could have been viewed as one result of the then-perceived deterioration in the US position of international leadership. Alternatively, it could be seen as a logical consequence of the Federal Republic's development into a more normal participant in the international system and in the Western alliance.

The emergence of West Germany as a more independent participant in international relations produced a fundamental change in the transatlantic bargain. In many ways, Germany filled the vacuum that France created when it abandoned NATO's integrated commands in search of a defense policy more independent of the United States.

Virtually no one expected that Germany's situation would change even more radically with the end of the Cold War. West Germany's evolution during the Cold War helped prepare German leaders and citizens to face the consequences of what they had long hoped for but dared not expect: a peaceful and sudden reunification of the two Germanys. The emergence of self-identified interests in West Germany accelerated after reunification, whose advent initially owed much to the support of its Washington ally, overcoming resistance in Moscow and in West European capitals as well.

Foreign and defense policy in the process of European unification

A central feature of the original transatlantic bargain had been the pledge of the European allies to work toward greater unity among their separate nations. The United States, in fact, had made Marshall Plan assistance contingent on the development of coordinated European approaches to the use of that aid. While the Europeans were unable to translate their unification efforts into a European Defense Community, they did expand economic cooperation through a community approach.

The cooperative West European efforts encouraged by the Marshall Plan were transformed into the European Coal and Steel Community in the early 1950s. The scope of West European cooperation was dramatically expanded when, on March 25, 1957, the governments of France, West Germany, Italy, Belgium, the Netherlands, and Luxembourg signed the Rome Treaties. These six original Community members agreed in Rome to establish the EEC and the European Atomic Energy Community as sister organizations to the Coal and Steel Community. The treaties sought progressively to eliminate obstacles to trade among the six countries while building up common policies among them. A common agricultural policy was the original centerpiece, designed in particular to benefit French farmers. Over the years, these three communities, with their decision-making processes and civil servants, were combined under one institutional roof. By the mid-1980s, the European acronymic stew was most accurately referred to as the "European Community," capturing in one simple phrase most of the activities and institutions that formed the core of a uniting Europe, today known as the "European Union (EU)."

Even though de Gaulle's rebellion had frustrated plans for expansion of the membership and powers of the Community, Europe's healthy economic growth in the 1960s provided the economic margins for steady integration in the near term and lofty dreams of full economic union in the not-too-distant future. But the oil price-induced recessions of the 1970s, carrying into the early 1980s, combined with strong nationalistic approaches among the members, slowed the integrative process to an almost imperceptible crawl and dashed hopes for early progress toward full economic and monetary union.

Nevertheless, the "six" became "nine" in 1973 when the United Kingdom, Ireland, and Denmark became EC members and "ten" when Greece joined in 1981. The Community became "twelve" with the accession of Spain and Portugal in 1986. This expansion of the Community, however, brought with it additional economic problems, and the integration process stalled in the mid-1980s, waiting for renewed economic growth to provide the financial margins to underwrite further integration.

While the process of European unification was struggling through the bad economic weather, the EC members moved forward on the political front. The foundations of the Community remained firmly planted in the economic integration process established in the Rome Treaties. Advocates of European unity nonetheless always recognized that the economic heart of the Community would eventually need to be guided by a political soul.

For many years, the search for greater political unity was caught up in debates over the purposes and methods of cooperation—between advocates of a supranational Europe and partisans of a Europe of nation-states, between the Gaullists and the "Communitarians," and between the "Europeanists" and the "Atlanticists." Finally, in December 1969, the leaders of the original six EC members, meeting in The Hague, bypassed these traditional conflicts and instructed their foreign ministers "to study the best way of achieving progress in the matter of political unification, within the context of enlargement" of the Community.

When the foreign ministers reported back to the heads of state and government on October 27, 1970, they recommended that the EC members initiate a process of European Political Cooperation. The report was accepted, recording agreement of the six countries to ensure through regular exchanges of information and consultations a better mutual understanding on important international problems and to strengthen their solidarity by promoting the harmonization of their views and the coordination of their positions and, where it appears possible and desirable, common actions.

Over the years, the members of the EC expanded the scope and content of their consultations to the point where, by the end of the Cold War, European Political Cooperation had become a regular and accepted part of the process of foreign policy formulation in the 12 EC countries. One result of this process of foreign policy coordination was a proliferation of foreign policy issues on which there was a European consensus or a record of previous joint actions. Political cooperation produced a number of results (many of which could also be called "successes"): coordinated positions in a variety of international forums, including the CSCE and the United Nations; various declarations on the Middle East; agreement on a package of sanctions in response to the declaration of martial law in Poland; and a coordinated reaction to Argentina's occupation of the Falkland Islands.

This expansion of topics and problems covered by the political consultations inevitably led the EC in the direction of "security policy." The EC members consciously stopped short of what could be considered "military policy," an area that until the late 1990s remained reserved almost exclusively for NATO cooperation. But even though the EC members were careful to steer clear of actions that would conflict with NATO's prerogatives, EC consultations by the mid-1980s regularly included issues that were on NATO's consultative agenda as well.

In 1987, the European allies took some significant steps toward European defense cooperation. France and Germany agreed to form a "European brigade," and in September of that year, the two countries conducted a major joint military exercise in Germany with combined French and German forces operating under French command.[31] Perhaps most notably, the Western European Union (WEU) countries in October 1987 issued a "Platform on European Security Interests" that constituted the most explicit and far-reaching European statement to date on common approaches to European security issues. The document emphasized the continuing importance for Western security interests of both nuclear weapons and American involvement in European defense. The West Europeans also used WEU consultative and decision-making procedures to coordinate their enhanced naval contributions to the Western presence in the Persian Gulf in 1987.[32]

The political consultations in the EC and the revival of activity in the WEU remained exercises of coordination among the member states rather than a process of political integration. They nonetheless established the foundation for much more dramatic developments during the 1990s— the fall of the Berlin Wall in 1989, the end of the Cold War, and the dissolution of the Warsaw Pact and Soviet Union—creating an entirely new set of international, transatlantic, and European circumstances.

Box 4.1   Some key developments (March 1957–November 1989)

March 1957   Rome Treaties signed

Jan 1963   French President Charles de Gaulle vetoed the United
             Kingdom's application to join the European Economic
             Community

June 1966   France withdrew from NATO's integrated military
             command structure

Dec 1966   NATO's Nuclear Planning Group created

Dec 1967   Policy of "flexible response" and Harmel Report adopted
             by NATO

June 1968   "Declaration on Mutual and Balanced Force Reductions"
             issued by the North Atlantic Council

Jan 1973   Britain joined the European Community

Oct 1973   Negotiations on Mutual and Balanced Force Reductions
             opened in Vienna

Dec 1979   "Dual track" decision made to modernize NATO's nuclear
             forces while seeking to negotiate limits with the Soviet
             Union

Dec 1979   The Soviet Union invaded Afghanistan

Jan 1981   Ronald Reagan entered office as President of the United
             States

Oct 1987   Western European Union countries issued "Platform on
             European Security Interests"

Dec 1987   United States and Soviet Union signed the Intermediate-
             Range Nuclear Forces Treaty

Nov 1989   Berlin Wall fell

Lessons from Cold War history

Judged by the outcome of the Cold War, the North Atlantic Alliance had served the allies well despite the failure of the European allies to deploy the non-nuclear forces they had promised at Lisbon in 1952. The hallmark of the alliance was its adaptability. The transatlantic bargain was revised and reshaped almost constantly from 1949 to 1989 as the central organization for the defense of the West. Some of the internal battles were bitter and left scars. But, on balance, there was much more success than failure and much of which NATO's founding fathers would be proud. The next period of history would bring with it even more dramatic changes. The way in which the NATO allies would deal with those changes was influenced by their experiences and interactions during the Cold War. The next chapter turns to some observations about the transatlantic bargain drawn from the Cold War years.

Questions for discussion

1. This chapter discusses disparities amongst the viewpoints and objectives of several NATO countries. What were, in your judgment, the most fundamental disagreements and sources of conflict within the alliance during the Cold War?
2. Trace the evolution of the European Economic Community of 1958 through the European Community all the way to the European Union today. What features and characteristics of the modern EU can you link to its historical foundations as outlined in this chapter?
3. France's departure from the military command structure was a dramatic expression of French "independence." What benefits did France derive from the decision? What were the costs, if any, to French interests? How did it affect NATO's ability to function as the key institution in the defense of the West?
4. Why was the Harmel Report a critical contribution to NATO's political viability? What are its lingering effects?
5. How did the policy of "flexible response" generate an ambiguous shift in US commitment in Europe? Hint: look for the passage about flexible response having a "double-edged sword" effect and explain that phenomenon with regard to the content of the new policy.
6. Consider the list of changes to the bargain during the Cold War discussed in this chapter. Which of these changes do you think have had the greatest impact on today's alliance and why?
7. This chapter highlights the ways that Germany, France, and the United Kingdom responded to the Cold War and subsequently altered the transatlantic bargain with the United States. How did the United States most radically change the bargain with its actions during this same time?

Notes

1 Kissinger's so-called Year of Europe in US foreign policy heightened European suspicions of US intentions and laid bare a number of conflicting interests, particularly regarding how to deal with Western vulnerability to a disruption of Middle East oil supplies. The exercise yielded a "Declaration on Atlantic Relations," approved by the NATO foreign ministers in Ottawa in June 1974. The document reflected no fundamental change in the transatlantic bargain, but the difficulties encountered in producing the declaration perhaps provided a foretaste of things to come.

2 Michael M. Harrison, *The Reluctant Ally: France and Atlantic Security* (Baltimore, Md.: The Johns Hopkins University Press, 1981), 48.

3 Harlan Cleveland, *NATO: The Transatlantic Bargain* (New York: Harper & Row, 1970), 106.

4   Unnamed diplomat as cited in Cleveland, *NATO*, 104.

5   Pascal Boniface, "The Specter of Unilateralism," *Washington Quarterly* 24(3) (Summer 2001): 161.

6   Anthony Glees, *Reinventing Germany: German Political Development Since 1945* (Oxford: Berg, 1996), 154–6.

7   Cleveland, *NATO*, 144.

8   In 1955, President Eisenhower proposed that the United States and the Soviet Union exchange maps detailing the locations of their military facilities, followed by mutual aerial inspection of the sites to confirm compliance with future arms control accords. It is unlikely that the Eisenhower administration expected Soviet agreement to the proposal, and it was predictably rejected by Soviet President Nikita Khrushchev as an "espionage plot."

9   Report of the Committee of Three, NATO Online Library www.nato.int/cps/en/natohq/official_texts_17481.htm [accessed March 16, 2015].

10 NATO Online Library, www.nato.int/cps/en/natohq/official_texts_26700.htm [accessed March 16, 2015].

11 NATO Online Library, www.nato.int/docu/comm/49-95/c680624b.htm [accessed March 16, 2015].

12 MBFR was the Western term for their initiative, emphasizing the word "balanced" to imply the need for larger Warsaw Pact than NATO reductions to overcome Pact numerical advantages. Moscow, of course, objected to this term, and the agreed title of the negotiations was Mutual Reduction of Forces and Armaments in Central Europe.

13 At a summit meeting of the Conference on Security and Cooperation in Europe in Paris on November 19, 1990, the 22 member states of NATO and the Warsaw Treaty Organization signed a major Treaty on Conventional Armed Forces in Europe and published a joint declaration on non-aggression. The treaty included major reductions of military manpower and equipment in Europe as well as a wide array of cooperative inspection and compliance measures.

14 On August 1, 1975, the heads of state and government of 33 European states, Canada, and the United States signed the Helsinki Final Act establishing the CSCE.

15 John Fry, *The Helsinki Process: Negotiating Security and Cooperation in Europe* (Washington, D.C.: National Defense University Press, 1993), 165–73.

16 Atlantic Council of the United States, "Arms Control, East–West Relations and the Atlantic Alliance: Closing the Gaps," Washington, D.C., March 1983, 62.

17 Josef Joffe, "European–American Relations: The Enduring Crisis," *Foreign Affairs* 59 (Spring 1981): 840.

18 The September 1979 gathering in Brussels received its greatest notoriety for Kissinger's warning to the European allies that they could no longer count on the American nuclear guarantee against the Soviets. Kissinger's observations were substantially edited and revised before publication, taking some of the rhetorical edge off the more dramatic statements made in the conference session (based on author's notes taken at the session). Kissinger's (revised) speech and other major statements to this conference can be found in Kenneth A. Myers, ed., *NATO—The Next Thirty Years: The Changing Political, Economic, and Military Setting* (Boulder, Col.: Westview, 1980).

19 The Nassau agreement had included a British pledge that its Polaris force would be assigned to the alliance and withdrawn only when "supreme national interests are at stake."

20 US House of Representatives, *The Modernization of NATO's Long-Range Theater Nuclear Forces* (report prepared for the Committee on Foreign Affairs by the Congressional Research Service, Library of Congress, by Simon Lunn, Washington, D.C., 1981), 11.

21 US House of Representatives, *The Modernization of NATO's Long-Range Theater Nuclear Forces*, 16.

22 Joseph Fitchett, "Kissinger Cites Gaps in US Nuclear Role," *International Herald Tribune*, September 3, 1979, 2.

23 NATO members agreed to modernize the Europe-based US nuclear arsenal by deploying a total of 572 new ground-launched systems capable of reaching Soviet territory from West European sites. The deployment would consist of 108 Pershing II ballistic missiles and 464 ground-launched cruise missiles, all with single nuclear warheads. The missiles would be deployed in five European countries: P-IIs and cruise missiles in West Germany and cruise missiles only in the United Kingdom, Italy, the Netherlands, and Belgium. The allies also agreed to attempt to negotiate with the Soviet Union East–West limitations on theater nuclear forces in the context of SALT. For a detailed discussion of the decision, see US House of Representatives, *The Modernization of NATO's Long-Range Theater Nuclear Forces*.

24 Simon May, "On the Problems and Prerequisites of Public Support for the Defence of Western Europe" (paper presented at the annual conference of the Centre for European Policy Studies, Brussels, November 23–26, 1983), 2.

25 Luigi Barzini, *The Europeans* (New York: Simon & Schuster, 1983), 58, 59.

26 Barzini, *The Europeans*, 60–1.

27 Press conference, Ambassade de France, *Major Addresses, 1958–1964*, January 14, 1963, 214.

28 Barzini, *The Europeans*, 70.

29 Gebhard Schweigler, *West German Foreign Policy: The Domestic Setting*, Washington Papers no. 106 (New York: Praeger, 1984), 6–24.

30 Federal Republic of Germany, Federal Minister of Defence, *White Paper 1983, The Security of the Federal Republic of Germany* (Bonn, 1983), 126.

31 "Manoeuvres," *Atlantic News*, no. 1951 (September 25, 1987), 3.

32 "Allies End Week of Hesitation by Sending Ships to Gulf Region," *NATO Report 2*, no. 45 (September 21, 1987), 8.

5

The United States and Europe at the end of the Cold War: some fundamental factors

When, in sudden historical succession, the Berlin Wall was breached, communist regimes were swept from office throughout Eastern Europe, the Warsaw Pact was dissolved, and the Soviet Union disintegrated, the NATO allies could not believe their good fortune. These events raised concerns in Washington and in West European capitals about potential instability growing out of so much change in such a short time. But a 40-year struggle had been resolved in their favor without a shot fired in anger. The Cold War had never turned hot, deterrence had worked, and the values on which the transatlantic alliance was founded had triumphed.

The time for celebration, however, was short. The allies almost immediately found themselves dealing with the consequences of their victory and asking questions as fundamental as "Do we still need NATO if there is no more Soviet threat?"

The chapters that follow in Part II of this book discuss how the allies responded to this challenge, and how international events shaped the post-Cold War alliance. This chapter, however, reflects on some of the fundamental factors in transatlantic relations as seen in the Cold War experience. It is, in a sense, an assessment of the assets and liabilities that the transatlantic bargain brought to the table at the end of the Cold War. Such an assessment may seem particularly timely as the allies face new challenges from radical Islamic terrorism, a Russia seeking to expand its influence and control in Europe, as well as political and economic developments inside NATO and the European Union that raise questions about whether or not the West can defend itself effectively against these new threats.

NATO: more than a military alliance

Had the transatlantic bargain been inspired by no more than the desire to balance Soviet power in Central Europe and to control Germany, it might have survived through the Cold War and beyond, but it certainly would not have prospered. The founding of NATO reflected hopes as well as fears, and those were recorded in the North Atlantic Treaty. The treaty's preamble declared that the parties to the treaty were "determined to safeguard the freedom, common heritage and civilizations of their peoples, founded on the principles of democracy, individual liberty and the rule of law." With an economy of language that characterized most of the treaty, the allies described the alliance as more than a traditional arrangement among nations to preserve a favorable balance of power. The treaty recorded fundamental beliefs and interests shared by the allies that might have drawn them together even in the absence of a common threat to their security.

The allies also agreed that their belief in democracy and individual liberty should be translated into some common goals in their relations with other nations. They pledged to "contribute toward the further development of peaceful and friendly international relations by strengthening their free institutions, by bringing about a better understanding of the principles upon which these institutions are founded, and by promoting conditions of stability and well-being."

After recognizing their common political heritage and ideals, the allies noted the importance of economic factors in their relationship. Fully aware that economic factors had played a major role in provoking both wars of the twentieth century, the allies pledged in Article 2 of the treaty that they would "seek to eliminate conflict in their international economic policies" and would "encourage economic collaboration between any or all of them."

These political and economic statements of purpose have been inscribed so frequently in books about the alliance that their repetition is now regarded as an obligatory part of the NATO analyst's ritual. These phrases usually are read over quickly in order to get to the meat of the matter. Do these motherhood and apple pie declarations perhaps deserve more attention? From a cynical perspective, it would be quite easy to dismiss such exhortations as little more than treaty niceties, paid only lip service in practice. After all, the treaty, one among believers in "the principles of democracy, individual liberty and the rule of law," was originally signed by a Portuguese regime that fell far short of democratic standards. In subsequent years, military regimes in Greece and Turkey were allowed to continue full participation in the alliance because of their geostrategic significance despite protests heard from some northern European quarters. Furthermore, the international economic policies of the allies were anything but free of conflict.

A measured dose of skepticism may indeed have been warranted by the Cold War experience. The alliance has not always lived up to its own standards. The Treaty drafters understood that the alliance would work most effectively if the policies of the member states fully reflected their shared political beliefs and intertwined economic destinies. What made the treaty special was the allies' belief that they were defending a way of life and a means of governing that were most likely to benefit the well-being of their citizens as well as enhance the stability of the international system.

From the signing of the treaty in 1949 until the end of the Cold War, troubles in the alliance were provoked primarily by nuclear and East–West issues, but the degree to which they threatened the solidarity of the alliance was undoubtedly influenced by the quality of relations within the West.

The alliance, like any partnership, depended on the willingness of the partners to understand and respect what is motivating the others. Each had to walk a mile in the other's shoes in order to make the arrangement work. Eventually, through compromises, the partners developed sufficient common ground to provide the basis for joint action. The beginning resided, however, in understanding.

We are here, and they are there

Perhaps the most basic differences between European and American approaches to East–West relations during the Cold War could be traced to the fact that the Atlantic Ocean and many miles separate the United States from Europe, and that Western Europe occupies the same land mass as did the Soviet Union and its Warsaw Pact allies. It is less than 1,000 air miles from Moscow to Berlin, about the same distance as between Washington and New Orleans. It is approximately the same distance from Moscow to Paris or London as it is from New York to Denver. But Washington is almost 5,000 miles from Moscow.

Many Americans wondered during the Cold War why Europeans, much closer to the Soviet Union, appeared far less concerned about the "Soviet threat." The short answer, "We are here, and they are there," identified the puzzle but did not resolve it. Proximity to Soviet military power should have led to greater concern, according to the logic of the American question. But it clearly did not, suggesting that even in an age of instantaneous communications and space travel, the Atlantic Ocean divided us more than it united us.

Western Europe's proximity to Soviet power, in fact, made Europeans particularly concerned about the consequences of war and, therefore, quite determined to avoid them. For Americans, the European "theater" could be separated, at least intellectually, from their homeland; for Europeans, the homeland was the potential battlefield, whether or not nuclear weapons were used by either side. As a result, Americans and Europeans placed different emphases on deterrence versus war-fighting capabilities, on conventional versus nuclear weapons, and on arms control versus defense improvements.

These geographically based differences asserted themselves strongly in the early 1980s. One of the principal themes of the anti-nuclear movement in Europe was that the United States was moving toward a nuclear war-fighting posture in Europe, and the installation of new long-range theater nuclear

Figure 5.1 This promotion for the *Atlantic Community Quarterly* suggested the transatlantic allies should see the Atlantic Ocean as a river, implying that shared values and interests could overcome geography.

weapons was evidence of that tendency. This charge was set against the enunciation by the Carter administration of a more flexible nuclear employment strategy (PD-59) in 1980 and the decision of the Reagan administration to construct (but not deploy) enhanced-radiation warheads—the "neutron bomb"—that would have killed people but left inanimate objects standing. For many Europeans the final proof of American willingness to contemplate "limited" nuclear war in Europe came on October 16, 1981, when President Reagan remarked that he "could see where you could have the exchange of tactical [nuclear] weapons against troops in the field without it bringing either one of the major powers to pushing the button."

When geography is married with history and related to the implications of war, the "European" perspective as opposed to the "American" view takes on special meaning. As one observer noted in the early 1980s, "Nobody in Europe, West or East, imagines that war means only fighting overseas. For all Europeans, the question of war is the question of survival, not just of superiority."[1]

But geography is a complex factor. How would you explain that Canadians, in the same relative geographic position as the United States, display some very "European" traits when it comes to defense efforts and arms control? With regard to defense spending, the Canadians have never been among NATO's big spenders by any measure. In the Canadian case, the reason (or excuse) for not doing more may have been the geographic proximity to the United States. In other words, Canada relies on the fact that the United States must regard Canada's defense as vital to its own security. (When it came to the role of the Canadian military after 9/11, however, the Canadians joined their Anglo-Saxon allies in taking on the most dangerous assignments in Afghanistan.)

This is simply to say that the end of the Cold War did not change the geography of the Atlantic alliance, and it did not erase some of the instincts and strategic predispositions that developed on either side of the Atlantic during the Cold War. The same can be said of the profound influence of history on transatlantic attitudes.

The different lessons of history

It is an objective fact that the United States and Europe have passed through their own unique historical experiences and naturally have drawn somewhat different lessons from those experiences. Europe was the site of two devastating wars in the twentieth century and was the principal host to the Cold War as well. Most continental European countries, at one time or another in the past century, have been defeated and occupied by foreign forces. From a European perspective, the desire to avoid war remains an immediate and meaningful imperative. Fritz Stern, an American historian, describes the effects of these differing experiences with war:

The Europeans cherish a different historic memory from ours. To Europeans the increase in overkill capacity is an irrational art, an absurdity: they know that we have enough to kill and be killed a hundred times over again. Their historic experience in this century—unlike America's until Vietnam—has not been the triumphant use of power but the experience of brute and futile power, blindly spent and blindly worshiped. Even an unhistorical generation in Europe remembers World War I as the epitome of the mindless worship of force; they remember the guardians of morality sanctifying violence. For the Europeans, this [twentieth] century has been the experience of the absurd, first as an intuition of artists, then as drama produced by history. Having lost their preeminence in repeated wars, the Europeans today seek alternatives to force.[2]

Americans also want to avoid war. But no major hostilities have been fought on American soil since the Civil War, over 150 years ago. The United States emerged from both world wars "victorious," suffering neither occupation nor the ravages of war on its territory, save Pearl Harbor. The most popular American historical perspective on World Wars I and II is that the United States was forced to join the hostilities because Europe had not dealt effectively with threats to the peace. One consequence, particularly growing out of the World War II experience, is that Americans tend to view appeasement of an antagonistic power as the greatest danger for their interests.

Many Americans would say that European nations, in seeking alternatives to the use of force throughout the Cold War, opted out of responsibility to their citizens as well as to their alliance. The European starting point appeared to be the possible rather than the desirable. History, on the other hand, left Americans with an expectation of virtually unlimited possibilities—a theme that has helped to elect more than one American president.

The United States emerged from World War II wearing a "white hat." America had come to the rescue of democracy and freedom and had provided the additional force needed to defeat fascism. After the war, Americans saw themselves as the main barrier to the spread of communism. America's involvement in Vietnam called into question its moral posture and raised issues about the role that the United States should play in the world—issues that are still unresolved and perhaps were even more pointed at the opening of the twenty-first century than they were in the 1980s. But Americans still see themselves mostly as reluctant warriors who, when called into action, fight to win.

An even longer-term factor reinforces the American tendency to seek the desirable rather than to work within limits. The United States matured with one frontier after another to cross and with a record of sustained accomplishment and growth. Throughout most of its history, this country had seemingly unlimited resources to call on to support its national objectives. Analysts and politicians have argued at many times since the end of World War II that the United States must begin to shape its world role in ways more compatible with finite resources. But the American psychology has reliably inclined Americans to reach beyond their grasp and to regard limits as new frontiers to be crossed rather than as boundaries to be observed. Thus, in the Cold War competition with the Soviet Union, the United States was inclined to push beyond limits that the European allies found more judicious to accept.

Europeans are more willing to accept limits in part as a consequence of painfully bumping into each other for hundreds of years. Innumerable attempts to change national boundaries—to alter political realities by the use of force—have produced unimaginable death and destruction. The Germans, in particular, were forced to accept limits on their sovereignty as well as on their freedom of international maneuver. Economic and geostrategic factors, not legal limits, have constrained France and the United Kingdom. Most other European countries are so small and relatively weak that their ability to influence international events is effective only in the context of their participation in larger groups, such as the European Union, NATO, and the United Nations. Limits, therefore, tend to be accepted facts of life for most Europeans rather than the frustrations they are for most Americans.

In the twenty-first century, such divergent perspectives play out, for example, in attitudes toward the question of what to do about Iran possibly becoming a nuclear weapons state. No European government wants Iran to go nuclear. However, if diplomacy and other incentives fail to convince Iran not to develop nuclear weapons and their delivery systems, most European governments will regret the outcome and move on, prepared to face the new circumstances created. This choice would appear unacceptable to most Americans, who appear much more willing to use force to prevent Iran going nuclear than most Europeans.

American scorn for the ways of the "old world" remains well engrained in US national history, and American national attitudes result in part from rejection of those ways. As Louis J. Halle wrote:

> We have to recall that the American nation had its beginnings in the seventeenth century, as a nation of refugees from the tyrannies, the persecutions and the power-politics of the Old World. ... In our American mythology, the refugees and their children had established in their God-given land a new and entirely different kind of society in which all men were free and equal, in which all men were brothers, in which the wicked devices of the Old World ... were happily unknown. ... Not only had God given us a virgin continent, replete with all goods, on which to establish our society, he had given us the great oceans to protect it. Part of our American mythology, then, was that we were beyond the reach of the wicked.[3]

Europeans, including Russians, were of course never beyond the "reach of the wicked." And in another marriage of geography and history, West Europeans generally viewed Russian behavior as conditioned by the numerous times that marauding armies have marched across Russia's naturally exposed frontiers. Americans tended to see the Soviet Union as an expansionist power attempting to spread communism across the world. In 2015, as Americans watched Russia try to re-establish its European power base by calling on some instincts drawn from the Soviet period, these differing American and European perspectives on how to deal with Russia still came into play.

Debates between Americans and Europeans over East–West relations during the Cold War often turned toward what Stanley Hoffman called the "game of historical analogies." As with most historical analogies, those used in this debate could be turned to favor either side of the argument. Both Europeans and Americans hearkened back to the beginning of World War I to prove the validity of their approach to the Soviet Union. Americans likened Soviet Russia to imperial Germany, while Europeans compared the competing Cold War alliances with those of 1914. Hoffman described the scenario:

> To the Europeans, Washington's view of 1914 suggests that war is the only way to curb Moscow, just as it was the only way to cut down German expansionism. To the Americans, the Europeans' view of 1914 means that—as in the Thirties—they are in effect willing to appease Moscow's expansionism. ... To the Americans, if the Europeans failed to react strongly to as clear-cut an aggression as the recent one [the Soviet invasion of Afghanistan in 1979], what are the chances of their standing up in cases that may well be more ambiguous. ... To the Europeans, if Americans overreact in this instance, aren't they going to push the Soviets onto a collision course that could still be averted by a wider policy?[4]

Hoffman's perceptive analysis may be as relevant today as it was during the Cold War.

One measure commonly applied to analysis of differing US and European attitudes toward East–West relations was the (false) dichotomy between being "red or dead." During the Cold War, Europeans appeared more willing to opt for the "red" option than did Americans. It seems clear that differing historical experiences help explain the contrast between American and European perspectives on this issue. Most European countries have, at one time or another, been occupied by foreign powers or subjugated by domestic authoritarian regimes. Their more recent political freedom and relative economic well-being tell many Europeans that a condition of occupation or subjugation is not necessarily permanent and that resistance and recovery are possible; death is quite permanent. On the other side of the Atlantic, since chasing British colonialists from the continent, Americans have experienced neither authoritarian subjugation nor foreign occupation and find the prospect essentially intolerable.

Importantly, US and European historical experiences have produced differences in transatlantic attitudes toward vulnerability. The United States never came to terms with its vulnerability in the nuclear age and continued to long for a return to its historic invulnerability to direct external threats. This psychological orientation lay behind the Reagan administration's search for a ballistic missile defense shield, dubbed the "Star Wars Program" by its critics. This focus of US policy moved into the background in the early years of the post-Cold War period but never left American minds. The American unwillingness to tolerate vulnerability may be just as potent a motivation for US national security policy as was the Soviet Union's deep security paranoia for its military programs and policies. It helps explain the deep shock and surprise of Americans in response to the September 11, 2001, terrorist attacks on US targets.

On the other hand, Europeans have tended to accept vulnerability as a fact of life. From an American perspective, the European allies are much too willing to tolerate vulnerability. Europeans, meanwhile, find the American search for invulnerability verging on the incomprehensible. Witness the quite different European and American reactions to the 9/11 attacks. This is not, however, a question of right or wrong but rather one of differing historical experiences and contemporary capabilities. Nevertheless, different American and European attitudes toward vulnerability create sharply differing standards for judging the requirements of a viable security policy for an ever-changing global environment.

Finally, one important exception must be noted to this discussion of historical sources of divergent transatlantic perceptions. The exception is the United Kingdom, whose experience in the two world wars of the past century created a perspective distinct from, but perhaps in fact a blend of, the American and the continental points of view. The United Kingdom suffered substantial military casualties in both wars and took heavy bombardment of its homeland in World War II. But, like the United States, it emerged from both wars victorious, never having been occupied.

A mixed ideological heritage

Americans and Europeans are united in their desire to protect individual rights, defend their democratic political systems, and sustain equitable and strong social and economic systems. Common ideological objectives are, in fact, explicitly expressed in the North Atlantic Treaty. But despite a wide area of shared ideological commitments, there are some fundamental differences between the European and American ideological experiences and cultures—differences that were highlighted during the Cold War and that remained in the background of transatlantic relations in the post-Cold War world.

The Marxist critique of capitalism has deep historical and political roots in Europe. A number of European countries had large communist parties during the Cold War (most of which were transformed or marginalized in the post-Cold War period). Many Europeans regard Marxist ideals as a source of inspiration even if they reject the systems that were spawned by the Russian Revolution. All European countries have important Socialist or Social Democratic parties, all of which support intervention of the government in the social and economic realm to allocate more equitably the costs and benefits of life within the country. In the continental European NATO countries, such programs are so thoroughly a part of the fabric of society that even conservative parties in government embrace a much more extensive social safety net than that acceptable to American conservatives.

The Marxist critique of capitalism has virtually no roots in the United States. The Democratic Party could by no stretch of the imagination be described as having a socialist program by European standards. The very term "socialism" still attracts a visceral negative reaction in the United States, and is often used by some politicians to smear their opponents. Even though the United States has, over the years, developed extensive social programs, they were adopted and developed within a pragmatic rather than an ideological framework.

During the Cold War, these differing ideological perspectives contributed to divergent outlooks on East–West relations. Americans viewed the Soviet Union's communist system as more threatening than did many Europeans and saw it as the main threat to American democracy. The end of the Cold War and the dissolution of the main enemy, the Soviet Union, were seen by many Americans as a huge "victory" for the United States and its system of government.

The perspective from Europe was somewhat different. The ideology that motivated the Soviet system was unacceptable to the vast majority of West Europeans. The end of the Cold War was seen as a victory of sorts, but not one to be celebrated at the expense of the citizens of the former Soviet Union and by no means as a rejection of the more generous social services safety net deployed by European nations.

On balance, Americans at the end of the Cold War still saw most Europeans as having been too "soft" on communism, and most Europeans viewed the United States as having been too hard. The contrast in images is sharpest when the United States is being governed by a conservative Republican presidency, as it was during the Reagan-Bush years and more recently under Presidents George W. Bush and Donald Trump. Socially conservative US governments usually find themselves with few soul mates among the European allies.

Roles and capabilities

It is a simple fact that, at the end of the Cold War, the United States was a global power with global military capabilities, while the European nations were, with the exception of France and to a lesser extent the United Kingdom, regional powers with military capabilities limited to Europe. It was not always so, and the reversal of world roles has much to do with disagreements between the United States and Europe concerning how best to deal with the Soviet challenge in the Third World in the closing years of the Cold War.

Slowly but surely, following World War II, European nations retreated from extensive Third World military involvement. The international consensus favoring the process of decolonization was the prime political factor behind Europe's withdrawal; the economic impetus was provided by Europe's need to reconstruct its devastated industrial capacity, and its desire to concentrate resources on economic recovery and the process of regional economic integration. France retained a military intervention capability in Africa and an impressive naval presence in the Mediterranean and the Indian Ocean. But for the most part, Europe's ability to influence global events with military forces was steadily shrinking. The United States attempted to fill vacuums left by the European withdrawal to ensure Western interests by limiting territorial or political gains for the Soviet Union and protecting access to Third World markets and sources of vital natural resources.

The decline in Europe's ability to influence events in the Third World was accompanied by an evolution in European strategies toward Third World problems. European policies became increasingly dependent on political and economic instruments to influence events in the Third World. The American experience in Vietnam confirmed for many Europeans their skepticism regarding the utility of military force beyond Europe's borders. And the fact that the former colonial powers retained or re-established close ties with their former colonies, based in many cases primarily on the strength of political, economic, cultural, and linguistic links, reinforced the faith of our allies in these policy tools.

As the end of the Cold War approached, the United States and the European allies carried forward fundamentally different attitudes toward the use of force in international relations. European leaders believed, for the most part, that diplomacy, development aid, and trade policies should be the weapons of first resort in dealing with Third World instability. Many Europeans feared what they saw as an American tendency to concentrate too narrowly on military responses to security challenges, believing that other approaches might be more productive and less costly in terms of Western interests. They were at least equally, if not more, interested in developing economic ties and political bonds that would both ensure cooperative relations with less developed states and discourage adventurism by the Soviet Union or potential rogue states. The 1980 British White Paper on defense, the product of a Conservative government, put the European perspective quite clearly:

> The best answer is to try to remove the sources of regional instability which create opportunities for outside intervention. In some circumstances, military measures will not be appropriate at all; in others, they may form only one component of the total response. Diplomacy, development aid and trade policies will usually have a greater contribution to make.[5]

Furthermore, Europe had gained far more in tangible benefits than the United States from the period of détente with the Soviet Union in the form of reduced tensions, increased trade opportunities, and improved human contacts. This made Europeans more inclined to see détente as "divisible," that is, to want to protect the gains of détente in Europe even if the Soviet Union misbehaved in the Third World. The United States, carrying the majority of Western global military burdens, had a much greater interest in treating détente as "indivisible," with Soviet actions outside Europe seen as providing cause for Western responses within the European framework. When Russian President Vladimir Putin in 2014 started trying to regain control over former parts of the Soviet Union, starting with the Crimean region of Ukraine, these different European and American perspectives once again came into play (see Chapter 8).

The Cold War experience left several interesting and still-relevant questions open. Does military weakness generate faith in economic and political instruments of national purpose? To what extent did US global military capabilities permit the West European allies to concentrate on non-military approaches? Does military strength generate an inclination to use force to further national objectives? These questions remain just as valid and important for the transatlantic relationship in the twenty-first century as they did at the end of the Cold War, particularly as the United States and its European allies search for the most effective ways to deal with the threats posed by terrorism and the new Russian challenge.

During the 1990s, while most European allies dramatically reduced spending on defense and particularly on investment in new technologies and systems, the US focus on the "Revolution in Military Affairs" created a growing gap between US and European military capabilities. The US Revolution in Military Affairs began revolutionizing the modern battlefield with new intelligence, communications, target identification and acquisition technologies, and "smart weapons" capabilities. After President George W. Bush declared a "war on terrorism" in September 2001, it became clear that the growing transatlantic gaps in military capabilities were reinforcing deeply rooted differences between US and European perspectives about threats and how best to deal with them.

Burden-sharing as a perpetual issue

Elected officials in sovereign, democratic allied states usually seek to get the best security for their populations at the most reasonable price. This means that alliances among sovereign states will always face questions concerning an equitable balance of costs and benefits among the members. This reality caused constant friction between the United States and its allies throughout the Cold War.

The burden-sharing issue was built into the transatlantic bargain, rising up in many ways from the foundation provided by contrasting US and European geographic realities, historical experiences, and military capabilities. The original concept of the alliance was that the United States and Europe would be more or less equal partners and would therefore share equitably the costs of alliance programs. The seeds for a perpetual burden-sharing problem were planted when the original transatlantic bargain was reshaped in 1954 following the failure of the European Defense Community. As described in Chapter 3, the revision of the original bargain meant that the alliance would become heavily dependent both on US nuclear weapons and on the presence of US military forces in Europe to make those weapons credible in deterrence as well as to fortify non-nuclear defense in Europe.

The US burden-sharing complaint took many forms and was translated into a great variety of policy approaches between 1954 and the end of the Cold War. In the early 1950s, the allies made arrangements for common funding of NATO infrastructure costs, such as running NATO civilian and military headquarters and building and maintaining fuel pipelines, communication systems, and so on. Each ally was allocated a share of the infrastructure costs, according to an "ability to pay" formula. As European nations recovered from World War II and experienced economic growth, the US share of infrastructure expenses was progressively reduced. However, such expenses were not the main cost of alliance efforts. The large expenses were the monies spent by nations to build, maintain, and operate their military forces. In this category, the United States always outpaced its European allies.

The administration of President John F. Kennedy in the early 1960s sought a greater European contribution to Western defense. Its policy optimistically advocated an Atlantic partnership with "twin pillars" featuring shared responsibilities between the United States and an eventually united Europe. The Kennedy presidency also witnessed the beginning of the financial arrangements between the United States and West Germany designed to "offset" the costs of stationing US forces in that country. These agreements were renewed and expanded in the administrations of Lyndon B. Johnson and Richard M. Nixon to include German purchases of US Treasury bonds and, in the 1970s, the repair of barracks used by US forces in Germany.

The US experience in Vietnam, French withdrawal from NATO's integrated military structure in 1966, and US economic problems all diminished support in the US Congress for US overseas troop commitments in general, and led the Johnson administration to press the Europeans to increase their defense efforts. This period saw a strong congressional movement, led by Senator Mike Mansfield, to cut US forces in Europe. Senator Mansfield introduced the first of the "Mansfield Resolutions" on August 31, 1966. The resolution judged that "the condition of our European allies, both economically and militarily, has appreciably improved since large contingents of forces were deployed"; the commitment by all members of the North Atlantic Treaty is based on the full cooperation of all treaty partners in contributing materials and men on a fair and equitable basis, but "such contributions have not been forthcoming from all other members. ... Relations between the two parts of Europe are now characterized by an increasing two-way flow of trade, people and their peaceful exchange," and "the present policy of maintaining large contingents of United

States forces and their dependents on the European continent also contributes further to the fiscal and monetary problems of the United States." The Senate was asked to resolve that "a substantial reduction of United States forces permanently stationed in Europe can be made without adversely affecting either our resolve or ability to meet our commitment under the North Atlantic Treaty."[6]

Senator Mansfield reintroduced the resolution in 1967, 1969, and 1970, when the resolution obtained the signatures of 50 co-sponsors. However, US presidents, Republican and Democrat alike, consistently opposed such efforts, and these resolutions and similar efforts through 1974 failed to win final passage. The Nixon administration, after unsuccessfully attempting to get the Europeans to increase "offset" payments, took a new tack. The Europeans objected to the prospect of American troops becoming little more than mercenaries in Europe and argued that the US troop presence was, after all, in America's as well as Europe's interests. Nixon shifted to a focus on getting allies to improve their own military capabilities rather than paying the United States to sustain its. The so-called Nixon Doctrine, applied globally, suggested that the United States would continue its efforts to support allies militarily if they made reasonable efforts to help themselves.

Despite the Nixon Doctrine, which was at least implicitly applied by all US administrations through the end of the Cold War, Congress continued to focus on offset requirements, passing legislation such as the 1974 Jackson-Nunn Amendment requiring that the European allies offset the balance-of-payments deficit incurred by the United States as a result of the 1974 costs of stationing US forces in Europe. However, a combination of events in the mid-1970s decreased congressional pressure for unilateral US troop reductions in Europe. The East–West talks on mutual force reductions that opened in Vienna, Austria, in 1973 were intended to produce negotiated troop cuts, and US administrations argued that US unilateral withdrawals would undercut the NATO negotiating position. Congress turned toward efforts to encourage the Europeans to make better use of their defense spending, and President Jimmy Carter, in 1977, proposed a new "long-term defense program" for NATO in the spirit of the Nixon Doctrine, setting the goal of increasing defense expenditures in real terms 3 percent above inflation for the life of the program.[7]

In 1980, Congress, frustrated by allied failures to meet the 3 percent goal, required preparation of annual "allied commitments reports" to keep track of allied contributions to security requirements. Throughout the 1980s, Congress developed a number of approaches linking the continued US troop presence in Europe to improved allied defense efforts. However, the burden-sharing issue was never "resolved." In fact, the growing US concern with Soviet activities in the Third World put even more focus on the fact that the Europeans did little militarily to help the United States deal with this perceived threat to Western interests.

In sum, throughout the Cold War, the United States felt strongly that the Europeans needed to "do more." US arguments included the following:

1. By all quantitative measures, the United States spent more on defense than its allies (well documented in the annual reports on allied defense spending produced by NATO at the end of each year and published in the NATO Handbook and, in more recent years, as "Financial and Economic Data Relating to NATO Defence" on the NATO website: www.nato.int).
2. American global military commitments contributed to Western security; growing US military commitments in the Persian Gulf region in particular benefited European as well as US security.
3. The economic strength and political maturity of the allies required them to play a larger role on behalf of their own security interests.
4. American military efforts had allowed the Europeans to modernize their industrial plants, producing competitive advantages for European over American firms.
5. American spending on its strategic nuclear capabilities contributed directly to Europe's security.

Although some Europeans agreed that their countries should increase their relative share of the Western defense burden, the prevalent feeling was that many American criticisms of their defense efforts were unwarranted. Their responses to the US critique included a variety of arguments, including the following:

1. The United States overreacted to the threat. Particularly toward the end of the Cold War, the Soviet Union was growing weaker, and Soviet President Mikhail Gorbachev was looking for ways out of the Cold War confrontation.
2. American attitudes toward the Soviet Union swing unpredictably from great pessimism to great optimism. This produces an irregular pattern of US defense spending, with dramatic peaks and valleys, while the Europeans maintain more steady modest growth in defense efforts.
3. Through NATO, the United States protects itself and its global interests more effectively than it could if its defense perimeters were withdrawn to North America and adjacent waters.
4. Some allied contributions to Western security cannot be measured in terms of defense expenditures alone. European countries provide much more development assistance to less developed countries than does the United States, and such efforts help promote stability. Some provide important real estate for NATO bases.
5. British and French strategic nuclear capabilities enhance deterrence.
6. During the Cold War, the allies purchased far more military equipment from the United States than the United States purchased from European arms manufacturers. American industrial profits, employment, and balance of payments all benefited from this one-sided trade.

When the Cold War ended, the foundation for the burden-sharing debate was cut away. The Soviet Union's military capabilities did not disappear overnight, but its capacity to attack Western Europe vanished almost immediately with the democratic revolution in Central and Eastern Europe that demolished the Soviet bloc and the Warsaw Pact. Soviet nuclear forces remained a concern, but more because it was unclear whether they would remain under reliable control at a time when the Soviet Union and its empire were disintegrating.

Perhaps ironically, the biggest burden-sharing issue at the end of the Cold War was how the allies should work together to deal with non-collective defense security threats arising beyond NATO's borders, an issue that had always been a source of division among the allies. That would become one of the biggest challenges for the allies in the 1990s. However, the end of the Cold War in itself was not sufficient to produce dramatic shifts in the burden-sharing equation and did not change the fact that leaders in all NATO nations would continue to try to buy acceptable levels of security at the best price. At least in the first decade after the end of the Cold War, the United States and all its allies would look for a peace "dividend" by reducing defense expenditures, taking the opportunity to shift resources to other priorities.

The end of the Cold War totally changed the context for the tensions and debate among the allies about the best policies to pursue in the face of Soviet power and ideology. However, the underlying sources of differing perspectives that were so prominent during the Cold War did not disappear with the end of that period of history. They simply went underground for a time, waiting to reappear in other ways at other times and perhaps to be changed and modified by future circumstances.

Those circumstances came to the fore after the 9/11 terrorist attacks on the United States, and the variable US and European responses to those attacks. The US attack on Saddam Hussein's Iraq seriously split the alliance across every possible dividing line. But it was the attempt to defeat al-Qaeda and the Taliban in Afghanistan, discussed in Chapter 7, and Russia's new aggressive behavior, discussed in Chapter 8, which provided the new setting for transatlantic and intra-European differences about burden- and risk-sharing in the alliance. The burden-sharing issue would remain a permanent feature of the transatlantic bargain for as long as it should last.[8]

Questions for discussion

1. This chapter highlights some of the factors that separated the United States from the European allies. As a refresher, what were some of the things that the United States and European countries held in common, and how do you think those similarities displayed themselves in the wake of the Cold War?

2. In your opinion, which source of dissimilarity proved the most divisive between the United States and its European allies in the years after the Cold War: geographical, historical, or ideological?

3. How might Stanley Hoffman's "game of historical analogies" apply to conflicting interpretations amongst the NATO allies with regard to more contemporary events?

4. During and immediately after the Cold War, the relative lack of US experience with defeat and vulnerability informed its foreign policy decisions. Since that time, the United States has become more acquainted with failure and negative judgment. How, if at all, have these new experiences changed the country's leadership and decision-making as leader of "the West"?

5. The section on burden-sharing in this chapter lists several arguments from the perspectives of the United States, Canada, and the European allies. Which of these arguments and counter-arguments do you find most compelling? Which remain relevant today?

6. Burden-sharing problems inherently afflict all alliances between sovereign states, but they can be especially frustrating in alliances among countries of substantially differing size and power like NATO. Suggest some possible strategies—ones that have been used and those that might be tried in the future—for keeping burden-sharing issues from becoming divisive and even deal breakers for the transatlantic alliance?

Notes

1 Flora Lewis, "How Europe Thinks of War," *The New York Times*, June 8, 1981, A15.

2 Fritz Stern, "A Shift of Mood in Europe," *The New York Times*, September 2, 1981, A27.

3 Louis J. Halle, *The Cold War as History* (New York: Harper & Row, 1967), 12–13.

4 Stanley Hoffman, "The Crisis in the West," *New York Review of Books*, July 17, 1980, 44.

5 Government of the United Kingdom, *White Paper on Defence* (London: Ministry of Defence, 1980).

6 For analysis of the resolution, see Phil Williams, *The Senate and U.S. Troops in Europe* (London: Macmillan, 1985), 139–67.

7 Fast forward to 2014 when, reacting to renewed Russian aggression in and around Europe, the United States and its allies agreed that all allies that currently did not spend at least 2 percent of gross domestic product on defense would seek to achieve real increases rising to that level in the following decade. See Chapter 8 for further discussion.

8 For an analysis of burden-sharing as an inevitable issue in the alliance, see Wallace J. Thies, *Friendly Rivals: Bargaining and Burden-Shifting in NATO* (Armonk, New York: M. E. Sharpe, Inc., 2003).

Part II

Post-Cold War alliance

6

The 1990s: transitions and challenges

Revolutionary changes

On November 9–10, 1989 East and West Berliners breached the Berlin Wall that was erected in 1961 to prevent East Germans from fleeing to West Germany. This became the first step toward reunification of East and West Germany. On October 3, 1990, the Federal Republic of Germany absorbed the German Democratic Republic, creating a unified Germany. NATO's North Atlantic Council welcomed the unified country as a full member of NATO. Like autumn leaves, communist regimes fell throughout Eastern Europe

The first decade after the end of the Cold War opened with revolutionary changes in Europe that left the transatlantic allies with historic choices about how to organize European security after one "partner" in the Cold War two-bloc system, the Warsaw Pact, and its leading power—the Soviet Union—had been disbanded. Big questions were posed by the fact that new democratic governments in former Warsaw Pact nations wanted to join NATO and the European Union while Russia began a transition away from the Soviet system and into a period of political, financial and economic chaos. The allies were also challenged to deal with the conflicts that broke out in former Yugoslavia which was falling apart largely along ethnic lines.

NATO had been the West's indispensable institution during the Cold War. But as the Cold War era came to an end, many wondered whether the alliance would or should be swept away by the breathtaking winds of change. The NATO members had already been working hard to improve security relations in Europe, largely through negotiating arms control and confidence-building measures with the Soviet Union and its Warsaw Pact allies. As 1990 opened, the authoritarian regimes that had held the Warsaw Pact together were crumbling, and the Warsaw Pact itself was not far behind. The West Germans and the post-communist East German authorities began negotiating reunification under the watchful eyes of the Soviet Union, the United States, France, and the United Kingdom. A new Europe was on the horizon.[1]

In this heady atmosphere, many thoughtful analysts and officials in Western Europe and the United States questioned what NATO's place might be in a world in which the Warsaw Pact had been disbanded and the Soviet Union was withdrawing its forces from Central Europe. On the other hand, new leaders of former Warsaw Pact nations were already focusing on the goal of joining NATO—the alliance seemed particularly relevant to them. In February 1990, Hungarian Foreign Minister Gyula Horn said that he could "imagine that, in a few years, Hungary could become a member of NATO."[2]

Early in 1990, very few Western observers were willing to talk about NATO opening its membership to former Warsaw Pact states. In fact, a variety of quite different concepts for the future organization of European security competed for official and public approval. Some experts speculated that it might be best to keep the Warsaw Pact in business to help organize future security in Europe. Others argued that NATO had outlived its usefulness because there was no longer any threat. Such advocates believed that the Conference on Security and Cooperation in Europe (CSCE), to which all European states, the United States, and Canada belonged, could take over responsibility for maintaining peace and security on the continent. Some Europeans, including French President François Mitterrand and British Prime Minister Margaret Thatcher, tried to find alternatives to German reunification while the United States facilitated accomplishment of West Germany's long-term goal.[3]

With the world changing all around them, the leaders of NATO countries decided that they should address the question of whether NATO was needed. Instinctively, all the governments of all member states, as well as NATO Secretary General Manfred Woerner,[4] believed that NATO should be preserved—even if they were not fully agreed as to why. Some officials argued that NATO was more than a military alliance and was based, in fact, on a community of values that rose above any specific military threat. Others maintained that the Soviet Union remained an alien society that could produce new threats to its neighbors in the future. They saw NATO as an "insurance policy" against a future fire in the European house. Others pointed to new risks and uncertainties that could best be dealt with through NATO's approach, in which like-minded countries work together to handle security problems.

Meeting in London in July 1990, less than nine months after the Berlin Wall had come down, the heads of NATO governments issued the "London Declaration on a Transformed North Atlantic Alliance," announcing a "major transformation" of NATO.[5] They offered to join the Soviet Union and other Warsaw Pact states in declaring that they were no longer enemy states and offered both friendship and cooperation to the former adversaries. Importantly, the leaders also agreed that NATO should revise its military system and its nuclear and non-nuclear strategy. They set in motion a major overhaul of alliance strategy, aimed at producing a "new strategic concept" for the alliance in the course of 1991. With this decision, the NATO members began the process of defining NATO's place in the post-Cold War world.

Figure 6.1 The fall of the Berlin Wall, November 1, 1989, with the Brandenburg Gate in the background.

NATO's evolution throughout the 1990s responded to the changing international environment that the allies encountered at the end of the Cold War. The process of change did not come quickly enough to prevent the conflict in the former Yugoslavia from becoming a bloody civil war. A multinational institution with no supranational powers and an established bureaucracy moves slowly in reaction to change. But the NATO allies worked their way through the inertia of past success and political resistance to new approaches in order to adapt their alliance to the new security environment.[6] And, ultimately, the changes written down in the early 1990s provided the foundation for NATO's critical role enforcing peace in the former Yugoslavia later in the decade.

The process of challenge and change that has faced the Atlantic Community nations since the end of the Cold War is addressed in the next five chapters. During the 1990s, the alliance concentrated on spreading peace, stability and the opportunity for democracy throughout Europe. This mission was performed using military capabilities in the Balkans and, more widely, with political initiatives that included partnership programs and enlargement of NATO's membership. In the 2000s, this mission continued, but the new mission of protecting alliance interests from threats originating beyond Europe, particularly those with roots in Afghanistan, joined the European stability mission.

This chapter, covering roughly the decade of the 1990s, focuses initially on the process of reaching out to other countries by creating the Partnership for Peace program, offering membership to qualified candidates, and cooperating with non-NATO countries in the Mediterranean and Middle Eastern region. It also examines the first steps taken to try to organize NATO's important relationship with Russia. It then discusses NATO's critical role in bringing peace to the Balkans just as it was trying to re-fashion its strategy and forces to a new European security environment. Then it examines the evolution of NATO military—including nuclear—doctrine and forces and takes a look at the initial post-Cold War efforts to produce a more cohesive European contribution to the alliance. In parallel with these developments, the relationship between cooperation in NATO and in the European Union was also evolving, leading toward ambitious goals for the process of European defense cooperation.

The legacy of Harmel

Particularly after NATO adopted the Harmel Report in 1967, NATO governments actively sought to promote dialogue and cooperation with the Soviet Union and its Warsaw Pact allies. The goal was to try to overcome the East–West division in Europe and to prevent the war for which NATO nonetheless continued to prepare. This commitment to détente (discussed in Chapter 4) led the allies to join with the Warsaw Pact and other European countries in 1972 to begin preparations for the CSCE and to open East–West talks on Mutual and Balanced Force Reductions (MBFR) in 1973. It provided the underlying political rationale for negotiations with Moscow on Intermediate-Range Nuclear Forces (INF), which opened in 1985. The CSCE, originally proposed by the Soviet Union primarily to win recognition of the European status quo, was used by the West to promote human rights and other fundamental principles that should govern the behavior of governments—in relations with their own peoples as well as with other states.

The Helsinki Process, as the CSCE forum was called, was widely credited with legitimizing human rights groups in Eastern Europe and weakening the hold of communist regimes on those countries. The CSCE process also included negotiations on confidence-building and stabilizing measures. In 1986, these talks resulted in an agreement signed in Stockholm, Sweden, on Confidence and Security Building Measures and Disarmament. The MBFR talks, after many years of stalemate, were converted into negotiations on Conventional Armed Forces in Europe, which yielded an agreement limiting non-nuclear forces and their armaments deployed in Europe just as the Cold War was ending in 1990. In 1987, the INF negotiations resulted in an agreement to INF from Europe.

NATO's active pursuit of détente through arms control negotiations and security cooperation initiatives in the 1970s and 1980s demonstrated that the allies were prepared to take diplomatic steps to reduce the chance of war even if Warsaw Pact military strength required NATO to maintain a credible defense and deterrence posture. Some political conservatives in the United States doubted the relevance or utility of NATO's détente role, seeing it mainly as a palliative for the left in Europe. Meanwhile, some on the European left regarded NATO's détente role as a political sham, designed for show but not likely to help overcome Europe's division.

Seen at some distance now well after the end of the Cold War, it appears that a combination of allied détente, deterrence, and defense policies contributed to the events that culminated in the end of the Cold War, the dissolution of the Warsaw Pact, and the disintegration of the Soviet Union. Meanwhile, the Harmel formula provided a sufficiently broad rationale for NATO to sustain public support for the alliance in Europe and in the United States, even if the formula was not highly valued by those on the political extremes on either side of the Atlantic.

It therefore was not a desperate or illogical step for the NATO allies in the first years of the post-Cold War period to adopt a new version of the Harmel concept to adapt to the radically new circumstances that had emerged in just a matter of months. In so doing, the NATO allies began the process of engineering another fundamental adjustment to the transatlantic bargain, extending the bargain's reach to include potentially all of democratic Europe.

From the CSCE to the OSCE

One of the first necessities was to adapt the CSCE, shaped as it was by Cold War conditions, to the new circumstances in Europe. The CSCE had played an important role in the Cold War, helping regulate relations among European states and also keeping up a human rights critique of Soviet and Eastern European communist regimes. The Helsinki Final Act, signed by all these states in 1975, was not legally binding on the participants but it provided the "rules of the road" for interstate relations in Europe and constructive guidelines for the development of democracy in all European countries.

At a summit meeting in London in July 1990, NATO leaders had agreed that the CSCE should be strengthened as one of the critical supports for European peace and stability. NATO reasserted this approach at its summit in Rome in November 1991. In an important token of NATO's intentions, a NATO summit meeting in Oslo, Norway, in June 1992 agreed that, on a case-by-case basis, NATO would support peacekeeping operations initiated by the CSCE. Subsequently, NATO called for strengthening of the CSCE's ability to prevent conflicts, manage crises, and settle disputes peacefully.

The key to the CSCE's ability to take on an expanded operational mandate was resources. As a "process," the CSCE had only an ad hoc structure that was not capable of supporting a more ambitious role. In December 1994, a CSCE summit meeting agreed to turn the process into an organization— hence the name change to the Organization for Security and Cooperation in Europe (OSCE) and the decision to provide staff and financial resources so that the OSCE could send missions into European nations to mediate disputes, monitor elections, and conduct other activities designed to prevent conflict.

By the end of the 1990s, NATO and the OSCE were working hand in hand to deal with potential threats to peace. In Bosnia and Herzegovina (hereafter Bosnia), the OSCE played a critical role in helping establish a process of free elections and respect for human rights. NATO provided the military backing required to give such efforts a chance to succeed. OSCE monitors and mediators played important roles in helping to resolve conflicts and build democracy from Abkhazia and Tajikistan to South Ossetia and Ukraine. The relationship between NATO and the OSCE became one of the key ingredients in an evolving cooperative European security system.

Today's OSCE has its headquarters in Vienna, Austria and employs an international staff of some 550 in its various institutions, as well as some 2,330 in its field operations. The OSCE is governed by a council which meets in permanent session as well as at the summit and ministerial level. Its activities are supported by a rotating chairmanship, a secretary-general with an international secretariat, and other institutions including an advisory parliamentary assembly.

Wrapping up Cold War conventional arms negotiations

In 1990, negotiations aimed at cutting non-nuclear forces in Europe, which had begun in 1973 as MBFR talks, concluded with the Treaty on Conventional Armed Forces in Europe (CFE). This landmark agreement produced reductions and controls on non-nuclear military forces from the Atlantic Ocean in the west to the Ural Mountains in the Soviet Union.

The CFE Treaty of November 19, 1990, is the most comprehensive, legally binding agreement on conventional arms control ever produced. Its goal was to reduce imbalances in the numbers of major conventional weapon systems in Europe to eliminate the potential for surprise attack or large-scale offensive operations. Since the treaty entered into force on November 9, 1992, some 60,000 battle tanks, armored combat vehicles, artillery pieces, attack helicopters, and combat aircraft have been removed from the area and destroyed.

Perhaps the CFE Treaty's biggest accomplishment was its contribution to transparency—making all military establishments and forces more visible to all other states. The treaty's required declarations of information and inspection procedures were designed to help reduce concern about intentions and capabilities of neighboring states.

Throughout the 1990s, the countries that signed the CFE Treaty worked to adapt the treaty to the new security conditions in Europe. The adaptation process had to take into account special concerns of states located on the southern and northern flanks of Europe. An adapted version of the treaty was negotiated in 1999, but final ratification has remained a contentious issue between Russia and the alliance.

The treaty was negotiated on a "non-bloc-to-bloc" basis, but nonetheless reflected the reality of two opposing alliances that still existed when the treaty was originally signed in 1990. Over the years, the foundations for the CFE treaty have crumbled with the demise of the Warsaw Pact, disintegration of the Soviet Union, deterioration of Russian military forces, and the membership of former Warsaw Pact and Soviet republics in NATO. Russia ratified the adapted treaty in July 2004, but NATO countries refused to complete their ratification processes "until Russia fulfills commitments it made to Georgia and Moldova. ... Specifically, the Kremlin pledged to finish negotiations by the end of 2000 to close Russian military bases on Georgian soil and to remove all of its troops and weaponry from Moldova by the end of 2002. Neither objective has been met."[7] Russia suspended compliance with the treaty in 2007 claiming that the NATO countries' rationale for not ratifying were illegitimate and that NATO's enlargement steps had increased NATO's equipment totals above treaty limits.

Dialogue and cooperation as a new NATO mission

As democratic governments emerged from the shadow of communism in Eastern and Central Europe at the end of the Cold War, many of the new democracies sought membership in NATO as one of their main national goals. The NATO countries approached these desires carefully, offering the new democracies friendship and cooperation but not initially membership.

Figure 6.2 Secretary General Manfred Woerner played a key role in NATO's transformation to post-Cold War institution.

In July 1991, the Warsaw Pact was dissolved, leaving NATO standing but still in need of greater clarity concerning its future relationship with former members of the Pact. NATO took the first formal step in the November 1991 Rome Declaration, inviting former Warsaw Pact members to join in a more structured relationship of "consultation and cooperation on political and security issues." They created the North Atlantic Cooperation Council (NACC) and invited the foreign ministers of the former Pact countries to the first meeting of the new council in December 1991. When the Soviet Union was dissolved in the same month, the NATO countries immediately invited Russia to join the NACC, and Russia became one of the founding members. The main goal of the NACC was to serve as a forum for dialogue among NATO members and non-member states on a wide range of security topics.[8] Sixteen NATO members and 22 former Warsaw Pact members and former Soviet republics participated in the new body.

The NACC represented a major statement of intent by the allies. They said, in effect, that NATO was not going to remain an exclusive club. Although the allies at that point were reluctant to envision offering NATO membership to former Warsaw Pact members, the creation of the NACC opened the door to that prospect down the road. The Eastern European leaders who wanted their countries to join NATO saw the NACC as totally inadequate for their needs, but they accepted this initial offer and immediately began working for more.[9]

The NACC was essentially the brainchild of US President George H. W. Bush's administration. President Bush and his foreign policy team had played a major role in the process of negotiating German reunification and ensuring that a united Germany would remain a member of NATO. German reunification in effect represented the first expansion of NATO in the post-Cold War era and the first since Spain had been admitted in 1982.

In addition, President Bush made a major contribution to the process of winding down the Cold War by declaring substantial unilateral US reductions in its short-range nuclear forces (discussed below, pp. 152–3). At the same time, Bush developed and maintained a sympathetic working relationship with Soviet President Mikhail Gorbachev, helping support the transition to a post-communist political system in Russia after the Soviet Union was dissolved.

In 1990, neither the Bush administration nor any of the European allies were prepared to signal publicly their acceptance of the possibility that countries that had just left the Warsaw Pact might in the near future become members of NATO. After all, in 1990 the question was whether NATO remained necessary, not whether its membership should be expanded. Moreover, most European governments, as well as President Bush, were focused primarily on how to ensure that the transition in the Soviet Union and then in Russia would confirm the end of the Cold War and not lead to a new one.

Nevertheless, toward the end of the Bush presidency, senior administration officials began acknowledging that the desires of Eastern European governments to join NATO were indeed legitimate. Late in 1992, after Bill Clinton had beaten George Bush in the presidential elections, both Secretary of Defense Richard Cheney and Secretary of State Lawrence Eagleburger suggested that the process of opening up NATO that had begun with the NACC could lead toward NATO membership for some NACC partners.[10]

The advent of the Clinton administration was to bring new and dramatic developments to the process of NATO outreach. The George H. W. Bush administration had put the process on track but had not had time to move beyond the relatively limited and "easy" NACC initiative.

From partnership to membership

When President Bill Clinton came to office in January 1993, the administration took over without a clear line on the issue of NATO enlargement. Its top priority was the economy, following the political rhetoric ("it's the economy stupid") that had helped pave Clinton's electoral path to the presidency. In the administration's first year, Europe was seen mainly as a problem—the source of economic competition for the United States and the locale for a bloody conflict in Bosnia that would not go away. However, one of the important rituals for any new US president is the first NATO summit. Officials in charge of preparations for President Clinton's inaugural NATO summit, scheduled for January 1994, were not of one mind on NATO's future in general and on enlargement in particular. One high-level National Security Council staffer, Jenonne Walker, had written in 1990 that the United States should pull all its troops out of Europe as an incentive for the Soviet Union to withdraw from Eastern Europe.[11] This official was skeptical that the Clinton administration should promote NATO enlargement and had the task of chairing the initial interdepartmental review of the issue. Strobe Talbot, a close personal friend of the president, and leading Russian expert at the Department of State, was concerned that moving too quickly on enlargement would sour prospects for reform in Russia. At the Pentagon, Secretary of Defense Les Aspin and his top officials, including Deputy Assistant Secretary of Defense Joseph Kruzel, were dubious that the United States and NATO should take on the potential burdens of preparing countries for NATO membership that were so far from meeting NATO military standards.

However, as James M. Goldgeier has documented, two key officials leaned in favor of enlargement—National Security Adviser Tony Lake and President Clinton himself.[12] Clinton had not spent much time or energy on foreign policy issues in the campaign, but one of his campaign themes had emphasized that US foreign policy should be focused on "enlarging" the democratic and free-market area in the post-Cold War world. Both he and Lake apparently came to believe that NATO enlargement would directly serve this end. This approach made Clinton ripe for the message from the new democracies in Central Europe, a message that he heard loud and clear when he met with several Central

European leaders, including Poland's Lech Walesa and the Czech Republic's Vaclav Havel, at the opening of the US Holocaust Memorial Museum in Washington, D.C., on April 21, 1993. Clinton subsequently reflected on the meeting, saying, "When they came here a few weeks ago for the Holocaust dedication, every one of those presidents said that their number one priority was to get into NATO. They know it will provide a security umbrella for the people who are members." From the Holocaust meetings on, Clinton had an emotional as well as philosophical predisposition toward enlarging NATO.[13] And even if other administration officials favoring enlargement had geostrategic rationales for the move, such as hedging against future Russian power and ensuring continued US prominence in European security affairs, it was the value-based rationale that would tip the balance in convincing the public and members of the US Congress that NATO enlargement was in the US interest.

Even as official policy largely favored deferring a decision on enlargement at the January 1994 summit, some administration officials and others outside the administration were putting together a case for moving ahead. In an assessment for Congress at the end of 1992, I noted the logic of the case for enlargement, writing:

> How can the existing members of Western institutions, who have throughout the Cold War touted the western system, now deny participation in the system to countries that choose democracy, to convert to free market economic systems, respect human rights, and pursue peaceful relations with their neighbors? This suggests the need for creative and flexible attitudes toward countries making credible efforts to meet the criteria for membership.[14]

And in a statement to a special committee of the North Atlantic Assembly in January 1993, I added that "Poland, Hungary, and the Czech Republic deserve serious consideration for NATO membership in the near future."[15]

In Europe, German Minister of Defense Volker Rühe became the most outspoken official European proponent of enlargement.[16] Early in 1993, he organized a small conference of US and European experts designed to provide ammunition for his position on Europe's future (at the time, Rühe was considered not only a leading official expert on defense but also a potential candidate for the chancellorship). The conference outside Bonn, Germany, provided some of the initial foundations for Rühe's enlargement position.[17] To augment his resources, Rühe contracted the services of a team from the well-respected US think tank Rand. The Rand analysts—Ronald Asmus, F. Stephen Larrabee, and Richard Kugler—had been developing an advocacy of enlargement based on work they were doing under a contract with the US Army and Air Force. In June 1993, Rühe and the Rand analysts were joined by Republican Senator Richard Lugar (R-Ind.), who became the most forceful of US official proponents of enlargement, arguing for early consideration of the membership desires of Poland, Hungary, and the Czech Republic. The Rand team published a major statement of the case for enlargement in the fall of 1993, providing a key reference point for the coming enlargement debate.[18] Senator Lugar remained a strong supporter of NATO and of enlargement, even though his cool relationship with Senate Foreign Relations Committee Chairman Jesse Helms prevented Lugar from playing a formal role in the process.

These proponents of enlargement were in a minority in Europe as well as in the United States, but they were not alone. While most of the US foreign policy bureaucracy was working on finessing the enlargement issue at the January 1994 summit, others, including Lynn Davis, Undersecretary for Arms Control and International Security Affairs, and two key staffers on the Department of State policy planning staff—Stephen Flanagan and Hans Binnendijk—were developing the case for moving enlargement ahead. Both Flanagan and Binnendijk had leaned forward on enlargement in the early 1990s; Davis had close ties to the work of the Rand team.

However, the ship of state changes directions slowly, and the weight of thinking in the bureaucracy and even among the majority of policy-level officials leaned toward deferring the difficult and demanding enlargement issue while continuing to develop ties to the new democracies. As the administration prepared for President Clinton's first NATO summit meeting, the more cautious approach dominated. Secretary of State Warren Christopher observed that NATO enlargement, while possible down the road, was currently "not on the agenda." Deputy Secretary of State Strobe Talbot, with his focus on facilitating Russia's transition to democracy and free markets, reinforced the secretary's cautious inclination.

Meanwhile, US civilian and military officials were searching for a concept to serve as the centerpiece for NATO outreach activities. The concept that developed in collaboration between General John Shalikashvili (the Supreme Allied Commander, Europe), his staff, and senior Pentagon officials, particularly Deputy Secretary of Defense Joseph Kruzel,[19] was premised on the need for aspiring members to meet certain political and military criteria before being considered for membership. The second assumption was that NATO should help such countries become producers, not just consumers, of security. The end result of this thinking was the proposal for the Partnership for Peace (PfP).

The PfP concept was a policymaker's dream. It signaled to those who aspired to NATO membership that they had been heard. Yet it made no commitment concerning the future. Perhaps most crucially, it bought time. It avoided destabilizing relations with Russia at a perilous moment in that country's post-Soviet development. It (temporarily) bridged differences between those in the US administration who favored enlargement and those who were skeptical.

The PfP initiative also served some practical needs. Countries that wanted to join NATO could not expect to do so until they had begun to exchange old Warsaw Pact military systems and habits for those of NATO. Partnership would provide a channel for US and other NATO assistance to aspiring members. And the PfP would serve as a vehicle for aspirants to make contributions to NATO's new role as a regional peacekeeping instrument, potentially spreading burdens among NATO and non-NATO countries.

On the negative side, PfP clearly would not be the end of the story. The Central European democracies recognized that, although active engagement in PfP was essential to their longer-term goal of NATO membership, it could also serve as a long-term excuse for NATO to postpone serious consideration of their membership objective (hence the occasionally heard derogatory references to PfP as a "Policy for Postponement"). In addition, as experience would come to show, under PfP scrutiny of their defense reform and modernization, shortcomings could not easily be hidden from their publics or from NATO members.

The cooperation track

In any case, at the NATO summit meeting in Brussels in January 1994, allied leaders endorsed the PfP program to give countries that wished to develop a detailed cooperative relationship with NATO the opportunity to do so. The program would provide the possibility for non-member military leaders and forces to interact with and learn from NATO militaries. This created a formal framework for the development of NATO military outreach activities and, incidentally, began to shape a new mission for NATO military forces. The PfP was destined to become a successful program in its own right, helping reform regimes in Central and Eastern Europe accelerate the process of democratization as well as to become NATO compatible.

Because these countries were at a variety of stages of political, economic, and military evolution, US and allied officials knew that a program of association with NATO would have to be sufficiently flexible to accommodate such diversity. The NACC already had provided a forum in which such countries could discuss military security issues with NATO allies. The PfP added a way for individual countries to tailor their relationship with NATO to meet their national needs and circumstances. The PfP sought initially to promote greater transparency in national defense planning and budgeting as a way of building confidence in the peaceful intentions of all participants. It also aimed to encourage effective democratic control of defense forces; to help develop each partner as a potential contributor to NATO-led peacekeeping, search-and-rescue, or humanitarian missions; and to enhance the ability of partners' military forces to operate with NATO units. Each partner was invited to identify the extent and intensity of cooperation it wished to develop within the broad agenda of the program.[20]

In mid-1997, the allies decided to add some new and important elements to the PfP agenda to "enhance" the program. When the Clinton administration proposed the PfP, it could not decide what to do with the NACC, even though it could logically have served as a communal consultative forum to complement the more individualized partnership program. (NATO officials observed that the Clinton administration, perhaps in a "not invented here" mode, wanted to ensure that the focus was on the PfP, not on the NACC, which Clinton officials saw as a Bush administration initiative.[21]) The PfP and the NACC existed in parallel but mostly separate worlds until the Clinton administration proposed replacing the NACC with the Euro-Atlantic Partnership Council (EAPC). The EAPC was formally established by the foreign ministers of NATO and partner nations when they met in Sintra, Portugal, in May 1997.

Also at Sintra, the allies gave partners a much stronger role in developing and deciding on PfP programs. They created the concept of partnership "cells," or units made up of partner military and civilian officials working hand in hand with NATO international and member-state officials. A special Partnership Coordination Cell was established in Mons, Belgium, collocated with NATO's top European command, to coordinate activities directly with the Supreme Allied Commander, Europe, and his staff. Through the new Planning and Review Process, partner countries that were making contributions to NATO operations, such as those in Kosovo and Bosnia, could participate more actively in planning and overseeing conduct of such operations. As a result of these changes, the PfP became an important part of the evolving cooperative European security system, even if it was seen as a transitional device by many of its participants.

The EAPC continued as a forum that brought together all NATO allies with all partner countries. The EAPC had 46 members in 2004. The purpose of the EAPC was to serve as the overarching framework for political and security-related consultations and enhanced cooperation under the PfP program. This framework was designed to provide partners with the opportunity to develop a direct political relationship with the alliance. It also gave partner governments the chance to participate in decisions related to activities involving NATO and partner nations.

The EAPC meets twice a year at both foreign and defense minister levels and on a more routine basis at the ambassadorial level monthly in Brussels. The EAPC originally adopted the NACC Work Plan for Dialogue, Partnership and Cooperation, which included regular consultations on political and security-related matters, and then enlarged and adapted that agenda. Consultations have come to include a wide range of topics, such as crisis management issues; regional matters; arms control issues; nuclear, biological, and chemical weapons proliferation; international terrorism; defense planning and budgets; defense policy and strategy; and security implications of economic developments. In addition, the agenda covered consultations and cooperation on emergency and disaster preparedness, armaments cooperation, nuclear safety, defense-related environmental issues, civil–military coordination of air traffic management and control, scientific cooperation, and issues related to peace support operations.

The EAPC has been used as a forum for discussions among the allies and partner countries about the situation in the former Yugoslavia, including developments in Bosnia and the crises in Kosovo and Macedonia, terrorism, and developments in Afghanistan. Under the auspices of the EAPC, a Euro-Atlantic Disaster Response Coordination Center was created in the spring of 1998.

Both allies and partners alike regard the EAPC as an important token of NATO's commitment to openness, cooperation, and extending the benefits of peace and stability to all European nations. However, given the large EAPC membership, formal meetings have consisted largely of set-piece statements by participating governments. This provided an opportunity for participants to put their national positions on the record but hardly a chance for discussion and dialogue. As with many other international organizations, those opportunities come as part of the "corridor" conversations and informal meetings on the margins of the routine EAPC sessions. The EAPC as an institution, therefore, played an important informal role but never became an important factor in NATO's decision-making process.

From cooperation to enlargement

NATO expended considerable time and energy developing or supporting a variety of cooperative security arrangements in its relations with non-members. But the membership track of NATO's outreach program generated the greatest controversy. The January 1994 Brussels summit deferred decisions on enlargement and put the PfP forward as NATO's premier outreach vehicle, but the allies did agree to keep the membership door open.

The drafters of the North Atlantic Treaty in 1949 anticipated that other European states might subsequently wish to join the alliance. The Treaty's Article 10 said that the allies may, "by unanimous agreement, invite any other European state in a position to further the principles of this Treaty and to contribute to the security of the North Atlantic area to accede to this Treaty." The 12 original members were, over the years, joined by Greece and Turkey (1951), Germany (1955), and then Spain (1982). At the NATO summit meeting in Brussels in January 1994, allied leaders said that the commitment in Article 10 would be honored and that NATO's door would be opened to qualified candidates. The allies began a study in December 1994 of the "why and how" of NATO enlargement.

More important, President Clinton left the Brussels Summit apparently ready to move on to the next step, even as those who favored a go-slow approach were reassured that the PfP would buy time and defer tough decisions on enlargement. On a visit to Warsaw in July 1994, interviewed on Polish television, Clinton pushed the issue further down the road, saying:

> I want to make it clear that, in my view, NATO will be expanded, that it should be expanded, and that it should be expanded as a way of strengthening security

and not conditioned on events in any other country or some new threat arising to NATO. ... I think that a timetable should be developed, but I can't do that alone.[22]

Clinton's comments affirmed that NATO should be enlarged because it was the right thing to do. The Warsaw remarks were taken by pro-enlargement officials in Washington as a green light to move ahead.

According to Goldgeier, a number of factors combined to get enlargement on track inside the US administration. These included the appointment as Assistant Secretary of State for European and Canadian affairs of Richard Holbrooke, who had become an enlargement believer during his time as US ambassador to Germany; the shift of Strobe Talbot from enlargement skeptic to enlargement supporter; and the appointment of several enlargement enthusiasts to key positions on the National Security Council staff, including Alexander (Sandy) Vershbow to direct European affairs and Daniel Fried covering Central and Eastern European policy. While the Pentagon remained largely skeptical, administration policy began moving slowly but surely toward an activist enlargement approach.[23]

Meanwhile, the opposition Republicans took control of the US House of Representatives in the fall 1994 mid-term elections. The new leaders of the House brought with them a "Contract with America," listing their policy priorities. Perhaps the only priority on which Clinton and the Republicans could agree was the Contract's advocacy of NATO enlargement. The Contract's enlargement position suggested that despite disparate motivations, NATO enlargement might enjoy a fairly wide bipartisan base of support in Congress.

In Brussels, necessary NATO work on enlargement moved ahead. In September 1995, the allies released the "Study on NATO Enlargement," which explained why enlargement was warranted.[24] It also drew out a road map for countries seeking membership to follow on their way to the open door. The report said that enlargement would support NATO's broader goal of enhancing security and extending stability throughout the Euro-Atlantic area. It would support the process of democratization and the establishment of market economic systems in candidate countries. They said that enlargement would threaten no one because NATO would remain a defensive alliance whose fundamental purpose is to preserve peace and provide security to its members.

With regard to the "how" of enlargement, the allies established a framework of principles to follow, including that new members should assume all the rights and responsibilities of current members and accept the policies and procedures in effect at the time of their entry; no country should enter with the goal of closing the door behind it, using its vote as a member to block other candidates; countries should resolve ethnic disputes or external territorial disputes before joining NATO; candidates should be able to contribute to the missions of the alliance; and no country outside the alliance (e.g., Russia) would have the right to interfere with the process. In this area, the report drew on a set of principles, articulated earlier in 1995 by Secretary of Defense William Perry, which had become known as the "Perry Principles," and on further enlargement analyses by the Asmus, Kugler, and Larrabee Rand team under their contract with the German Ministry of Defense.[25]

The NATO allies made clear that one of the key factors influencing readiness for membership would be the applicant country's ability to work within NATO's military command structure. NATO military leaders were expected to help applicant countries help themselves prepare for becoming effective military contributors to the alliance, adding another important task to NATO's military mission profile.

During 1996–1997, NATO officials conducted intensified dialogues with 12 countries that had expressed an active interest in NATO membership. The candidacies of all countries were thoroughly examined from a wide range of perspectives. It was clear, however, that the United States would play the decisive role in the question of whom to invite for the first round of enlargement.

The enlargement policy debate in the United States

Bringing new members into the alliance constitutes an "amendment" to the North Atlantic Treaty and, as such, has to be ratified by all NATO members. On balance, NATO enlargement had not been a hot issue in Congress, but to the extent that there was interest, there was sustained bipartisan support for NATO and for bringing in new members.[26] This support included passage of the NATO Participation Act of 1994 (Title II of P.L. 103–447), which backed NATO enlargement as a way of encouraging development of democratic institutions and free-market structures in the new democracies. The low-intensity but fairly consistent support was a good foundation for the collaboration between the White House and the Senate that would be critical to eventual ratification of any enlargement decision. Meanwhile, the private, non-profit Committee to Expand NATO was established in 1996 to support the enlargement cause. This group, which involved an impressive collection of corporate leaders, former civilian officials, and retired senior military officers, largely from the ranks of the Republican Party, actively courted congressional support for enlargement and played a major role in the lobbying effort on behalf of the initiative over the next two years.

The United States entered a presidential election year in 1996. Once again, foreign policy was not a big issue in the campaign. On the issue of NATO enlargement, President Clinton and his Republican opponent, Senator Robert Dole, competed mainly to see who could stand closer to the enlargement flagpole. Dole criticized the president for being too attentive to Russia's views—Clinton had worked hard to reassure Russian President Boris Yeltsin that legitimate Russian interests would not be threatened while keeping enlargement moving ahead. But Dole's criticism had virtually no political impact, and most observers saw very little difference between the Republican and Democratic positions on the issue. It was yet another sign of the bipartisan nature of support for bringing new members into NATO, although it certainly did not guarantee that the approach to be taken by the president and the alliance would win the necessary two-thirds majority in the Senate.

The election campaign provided the opportunity for the administration to move ahead decisively. President Yeltsin had survived his re-election campaign in July 1996 and was no longer in imminent danger of being undercut by the US position on enlargement. In September 1996, Clinton called for a NATO summit in 1997 to name the first post-Cold War candidates for NATO membership. In October 1996, Clinton told an audience in Detroit that "by 1999, NATO's 50th anniversary and 10 years after the fall of the Berlin Wall, the first group of countries we invite to join should be full-fledged members of NATO."[27]

The prominent use of the enlargement issue during Clinton's campaign visits to the Midwest—home to many Central European immigrant communities— was subsequently cited by opponents of enlargement in the United States and by skeptics in Europe as evidence that the US position was driven primarily by domestic politics. The history of administration policy, as documented by Goldgeier and observed personally by me, suggests a different conclusion. The president's commitment to enlargement grew much more fundamentally out of his acceptance of and belief in fairly basic Wilsonian principles of international relations, promoting peace and stability through inclusive and cooperative relations among democratic states. Ethnic communities in the United States provided important support for both the president and the issue. But had enlargement not made sense in terms of basic US values and interests, it would have withered on the vine despite the enthusiasm of Polish and other Central European lobby groups.

By the end of 1996 and Clinton's successful re-election effort, collaboration between the White House and Congress was becoming more serious. The White House was fully aware that if the Senate felt it had not participated directly in the enlargement process, the issue could fail to gain the required two-thirds majority even if two-thirds of the Senate leaned toward enlargement, as appeared to be the case. The administration was sensitive to the fact that President Woodrow Wilson had failed to win US involvement in the League of Nations because he had not made the effort to get the Senate on board. It therefore followed President Harry Truman's strategy for Senate consideration of the North Atlantic Treaty in 1948–1949, a strategy that brought key senators into the process early enough to win their commitment but not too early to complicate the policymaking process prematurely.[28]

As the White House began developing working relationships with critical Capitol Hill staff, a related but more immediate question was which countries should be invited when the NATO "enlargement" summit convened in Madrid, Spain, in July 1997. There was virtually unanimous agreement in the administration and among the European allies that the Czech Republic, Hungary, and Poland were a lock. Only Poland would add significantly to the military strength of the alliance. But these three probably could be sold to the Senate as strategically important and politically acceptable. From Germany's point of view, these three satisfied its desire to move off the "front lines" in Central Europe. Being surrounded by NATO members would give Germany a political and military buffer between it and Russia. The United Kingdom preferred to keep the package as small as possible, not being a big fan of the process of enlargement in any case, concerned that too rapid or large an increase in membership would weaken the alliance. However, France, Italy, and some other allies wanted to give enlargement a southern focus as well and favored including Slovenia and Romania in the first tranche. Several members of the Senate, led by Senator Joseph Biden (D-Del.), ranking minority member of the Senate Foreign Relations Committee, and Senator William V. Roth Jr. (R-Del.) favored the inclusion of Slovenia—a small former Yugoslav republic that would add a land bridge between existing NATO territory (Italy) and Hungary.

The Clinton administration decided, despite these senatorial sentiments for Slovenia, that the core package of three candidates would be a sufficient challenge for the process of ratification in the United States as well as for absorption by the alliance. Romania, with an important geostrategic position in southeastern Europe and with substantial military forces, lagged far behind the three core candidates in political and economic development. Slovenia could be kept as a given for the next round. The administration came to an internal consensus on putting just three candidates forward.

Enlargement summit in Madrid

Even though intensive discussions had been held at NATO and among NATO allies in preparation for the Madrid meeting, the US choice of three and only three was publicly revealed in a Pentagon press briefing by Secretary of Defense William Cohen in mid-June. Cohen suggested that, as far as the US government was concerned, the case was closed. His assertion was confirmed by the White House, which claimed that a NATO decision had been made, but in fact NATO consultations had not been completed. The way the United States appeared to close the door to further discussion stunned the allies and was instantly interpreted by the French and others as just one more sign of hegemonic US behavior. The United States had always been "first among equals" in NATO, where decisions are taken by consensus but where US preferences almost always carried the day. Nonetheless, the allies resented what seemed to them a cavalier US approach to the consultation process.

The challenge for the Clinton administration and for US administrations before and after was to be a hegemon without acting like one. The administration had made the mistake of acting like one. The Madrid meeting endorsed the US preference, but not without significant grumbling by French President Jacques Chirac and others. The allies found much to complain about, including the fact that the United States wanted seats in the session for US senators who had been brought along with the US summit delegation to help ensure a favorable ratification process.

At Madrid, to help smooth the many feathers ruffled by US actions, other candidate states were encouraged to continue to work toward eventual membership by following the guidelines laid out in the "Study on NATO Enlargement" and developing bilateral cooperation with NATO through the PfP program. The allies reaffirmed their commitment to the open-door policy in which all European countries meeting the conditions of Article 10 and the guidelines of the study could be considered for eventual membership.

The enlargement process and the US Congress

The next task for NATO was to negotiate the terms of entry with the candidate states. The Clinton administration, however, had its own challenging task: to convince at least two-thirds of the members of the Senate that NATO enlargement was in the US interest. The administration had already begun preparing the ground. A respected former Clinton White House aide and expert on congressional–executive relations, Jeremy Rosner, was brought back to serve as coordinator of the ratification process with both a State Department position and staff and the status of special adviser to the president. The administration had been wise to include senators in the Madrid delegation, but now the serious lobbying work would begin.

In the Senate, the Committee on Foreign Relations, chaired by arch-conservative Jesse Helms, would have primary jurisdiction over the legislation, with the Senate Committee on Armed Services playing an important advisory role. Senate Majority Leader Trent Lott (R-Miss.) had already created the Senate NATO Observer Group, chaired by Senators Biden and Roth, designed to help manage the process in support of the Senate's advice and consent role.

In the summer of 1997, even though it appeared that Rosner and his administration team were starting with a good core of support in the Senate, they would need a strong lobbying effort to ensure final victory. In the course of a luncheon meeting in August hosted by a Scandinavian embassy officer, Rosner and I had a few moments to discuss his challenge. I said that I presumed that President Clinton would be personally involved in the lobbying effort. Rosner assured me that, in the coming months, the president would invite senators to the White House for dinners and private meetings focused on lining up the required votes. However, despite the fact that Clinton had played an important part in getting NATO enlargement on the US and NATO agenda, the fall of 1997 and spring of 1998 found him increasingly captured by impeachment proceedings against him in Congress. He never conducted the lobbying dinners and meetings Rosner had expected. At the numerous official events marking various stages of the ratification process, the president was present and involved, but one had to wonder whether his mind was not on other problems.[29]

Opponents of enlargement in the United States, right up until the Senate vote on April 30, 1998, complained that the issue had not been given the kind of serious attention that was warranted by such an important national commitment. It is true that the issue did not set the public on fire. Public opinion polls showed broad but somewhat shallow support for enlargement. The positive numbers seemed to reflect the public's positive image of NATO and of the idea that the US approach to international cooperation should be inclusive. However, a large percentage of those questioned in polls showed a lack of basic knowledge about what was going on. For example, a large number of respondents in some polls believed that Russia was already a NATO member.[30]

The debate that did rage on editorial and op-ed pages of major American newspapers was largely among the academic and policy elite and was not of great interest to the American public. On the other hand, most foreign policy issues, such as NATO enlargement, are debated and decided largely by the elite public. The public at large is moved to action and involvement only by more headline-making events, particularly those with imminent life-or-death consequences.

In the deliberative body that had to debate and decide the issue, however, there was a thorough and serious process of consideration[31] in keeping with the Senate's role as a "partner" to the transatlantic bargain. Despite the president's "absence" from the process,[32] the work of the NATO Observer Group moved into high gear in close collaboration with the administration. The process relied heavily on teamwork between Rosner and key Senate staffers, particularly Senate Foreign Relations Committee staffer Steve Biegen, Ian Brzezinski, who worked for Senator Roth, and Michael Haltzel from Senator Biden's staff. Other staffers, including Ken Myers of Senator Lugar's staff and David Stevens, who worked for Senator Jon Kyl (R-Ariz.), played key roles in the period leading up to the Senate debate.

The Senate NATO Observer Group, almost completely out of public view, organized a steady stream of classified and unclassified briefings and meetings in the course of 1997–1998. Some of these sessions were intended largely for administration officials to communicate information to Senate staff. Others provided the opportunity for members to meet with senior NATO-nation military officials. One critical session of the NATO Observer Group brought senators together with the foreign ministers of the candidate countries. The meeting appeared to be a turning point for at least one senator who had been skeptical about enlargement. Senator Kay Bailey Hutchison (R-Tex.) had profound concerns about the plan and engaged deeply in the issue, asking her staff, with the help of the Congressional Research Service, to research a number of enlargement issues. At the session with the candidate country foreign ministers, however, it became clear to this observer that Senator Hutchison's feeling of respect and admiration for the accomplishments of the three new democracies would likely bring her into the "yea" column. It did. The Senate Committee on Foreign Relations held a series of public hearings in October and November

1997 in which both supporters and opponents of enlargement were invited to address the committee.[33] Proponents and critics of enlargement in the Senate engaged their staffs in investigation of major issues, calling in a wide range of outside experts to brief senators and staff and engaging hundreds of hours of support from Congressional Research Service analysts.

One of the most sensitive challenges for Jeremy Rosner and other administration officials was to hold together a coalition of Senate supporters and potential supporters who were motivated by substantially different assumptions and objectives. Supporters ranged from conservative Republicans to liberal Democrats. Senator Helms and a few other conservative Republican senators saw NATO enlargement first and foremost as an insurance policy against a resurgent Russia laying claim once again to the sovereignty of Central and Eastern European states. Helms was particularly interested in how the administration saw the future of NATO–Russia relations. In the process of introducing Secretary of State Madeleine Albright at the committee's opening enlargement hearing, Helms cautioned, "NATO's relations with Russia must be restrained by the reality that Russia's future commitment to peace and democracy, as of this date, is far from certain. In fact, I confess a fear that the United States' overture toward Russia may have already gone a bit far."[34]

In addition, many senators had not signed off on the "new NATO" (in which members cooperated to deal with new security challenges, including peace operations in the Balkans), and still believed that the "old NATO" (focused primarily on Article 5, the commitment to assist a fellow member that has come under attack) was what was still needed. On the other hand, some senators found the old NATO to be of decreasing relevance and were more interested in the idea of expanding the number of democratic states that could help deal with new security challenges in and beyond Europe. Others (e.g., Senator Barbara Mikulski, D-Md.) were motivated most strongly by the fact that Poland, the Czech Republic, and Hungary had thrown off communism and committed themselves to a democratic path. How, such proponents asked, could they be denied membership in the Western system, of which NATO was a core part?

The Senate opponents of enlargement were also all over the map politically and philosophically. Senator John Warner (R-Va.) became one of the most severe critics of enlargement. He believed that too many members would make the alliance impossible to manage and would doom it to future irrelevance because it would be unable to make timely consensual decisions with 19-plus members. Senator Warner's attempt to impose a formal pause on the enlargement process was rejected, but a number of senators who voted for enlargement voted with Warner in favor of a pause. Some 41 senators voted for the Warner amendment, enough to block a two-thirds majority of the Senate for the next candidate(s) if they were all to vote against. The most strongly committed enlargement opponent, Senator John Ashcroft (R-Mo.), simply believed that the United States was already overburdened and that NATO enlargement would perpetuate a responsibility that had long ago outlived its utility. Among the opponents, Ashcroft's position came closest to representing a neo-isolationist stance. His perspective related in part to concerns about the potential cost of NATO enlargement. The cost question promised at one point to be the most difficult of issues in the Senate debate. However, conflicting and confusing estimates of the cost blurred the issue and made it a virtual nonfactor in the final debate. Ashcroft's attempt to amend the resolution of ratification to mandate a narrow interpretation of NATO's future mission was defeated through deft parliamentary procedures on the Senate floor. Instead, the Senate passed an amendment offered by Senator Jon Kyl (R-Ariz.) that affirmed the continuing importance of NATO's collective defense role while allowing that NATO now had utility in non-Article 5 missions as well.

The other main school of thought motivating opponents of enlargement was concern about the impact on relations with Russia. George Kennan, the highly respected Russia expert who played a major role in developing the US containment strategy toward the Soviet Union, had opined[35] that NATO enlargement would be a disaster for US–Russian relations, and some members, including Senators Paul Wellstone (D-Minn.) and Patrick Leahy (D-Vt.), cast their votes against enlargement largely on the basis of Kennan's warning.[36] Another opponent, Senator Daniel Patrick Moynihan (D-N.Y.), argued that the European Union, not NATO, should take the lead in including the new democracies in Western institutions. After several abortive attempts to organize a debate and final vote in the Senate, Senator Lott devoted the entire day of April 30 to the enlargement issue. The opponents, led by Senators Warner, Robert Smith (R-N.H.), Moynihan, Ashcroft, and Wellstone, put on a strong show of their concerns. Because Senator Helms was not well, Senator Biden managed the bill for the Senate Foreign Relations Committee with single-minded energy and enthusiasm that left some of his democratic colleagues standing impatiently waiting to be given the floor. Several senators made impressive contributions to the advocates' side, including Mikulski, Joseph Lieberman (D-Conn.), and Gordon Smith (R-Ore.).

The decisive vote was taken late that evening. At the suggestion of Senator Robert Byrd (D-W.Va.) in his role as the unofficial guardian of the procedures and practices of the Senate, all senators took their seats and then rose when called to deliver their "yea" or "nay" vote. Byrd suggested that "the Senate would make a much better impression ... [if senators would] learn to sit in their seats to answer the roll-call ... [rather than] what we have been accustomed to seeing down here in the well, which looks like the floor of a stock market."[37] The Senate, with 99 of its 100 members seated with the decorum requested by Senator Byrd, voted 80 to 19 to give the Senate's advice and consent to ratification of the membership of Poland, the Czech Republic, and Hungary in NATO.

The missing vote was that of Senator Kyl, an enlargement supporter who left Washington on an official overseas trip a few hours before the vote was taken, reassured that his side would win by a clear margin. After observing the daylong drama from the floor of the Senate, I walked out of the Capitol into a pleasant Washington night feeling that I had witnessed a historic event. That impression had been enhanced by the sight of the entire Senate seated in the chamber, thanks to Senator Byrd. Although enlargement supporters managed to beat back all potential "killer" amendments, the number of votes attracted by Senator Warner's proposed "pause" in the enlargement process reflected an important sentiment. Few enlargement advocates were anxious to take on a new round in the near future. Even Jeremy Rosner, who had dedicated so much time and energy to NATO enlargement, judged that the system would not be able to support another round until the first candidates had demonstrated their successful entry into the NATO system.[38]

Some enlargement proponents, however, thought it was important to keep the process moving ahead. The first package had left aside Slovenia, a small but relatively attractive candidate. Senator William V. Roth Jr., one of the leading forces behind the enlargement process, argued that the process should "be carefully paced, not paused." In a special report for the North Atlantic Assembly (now the NATO Parliamentary Assembly) in September 1998, for which the author was rapporteur, Roth proposed that when the allies met in Washington in 1999 to celebrate NATO's fiftieth anniversary, "Slovenia should be invited to begin negotiations aimed at accession to the North Atlantic Treaty. In addition to reflecting Slovenia's preparedness for membership, the invitation would demonstrate that the enlargement door remains open without overloading the enlargement process."[39] Senator Roth's advocacy was considered by, and had some supporters in, the Clinton administration. But the administration ultimately decided that it was too early to move ahead with new candidates. That step was left for the next US administration to manage.

The enlargement process put in motion

Seen two decades later, the US debate on the first round of post-Cold War NATO enlargement was, in effect, a legislative referendum on the future of the alliance. The decision, contested though it was, nonetheless constituted a vote by the United States for NATO's continuing importance. It affirmed and strengthened the transatlantic bargain's important new role of helping emerging European democracies find their way in the world free from control by their large neighbor to the East.

The European allies were relieved that the United States did not want to push ahead immediately with another round of enlargement. The strongest European proponent of enlargement, Germany, accomplished its main objectives with the accession of the first three candidates. It no longer stood on NATO's front lines looking east, and it no longer manifested such great enthusiasm for the enlargement process. Most of the other allies did not look forward to negotiating the next round, in which the potential candidates would likely include one or more of the three Baltic states—former Soviet republics whose NATO membership Moscow strongly opposed.

At the fiftieth-anniversary NATO summit in Washington on April 23–25, 1999, all aspiring candidates for NATO membership were given some cause for hope, even though Slovenia was left standing outside the door. The leaders pledged that "NATO will continue to welcome new members in a position to further the principles of the treaty and contribute to peace and security in the Euro-Atlantic area." The allies created the Membership Action Plan (MAP), which promised cooperation beyond possibilities in the PfP and, perhaps more important, feedback from NATO concerning their progress toward membership. Nine aspirants—Albania, Bulgaria, Estonia, Latvia, Lithuania, Romania, Slovakia, Slovenia, and the Former Yugoslav Republic of Macedonia—initially signed up for the program. These nine were promised that NATO would formally review the enlargement process again no later than 2002.

According to NATO, "The MAP gives substance to NATO's commitment to keep its door open. However, participation in the MAP does not guarantee future membership, nor does the Plan consist simply of a checklist for aspiring countries to fulfill." What MAP did do, however, was to provide "concrete feedback and advice from NATO to aspiring countries on their own preparations directed at achieving future membership." The MAP did not substitute for full participation in NATO's PfP Planning and Review Process, which, in NATO's view, "is essential because it allows aspirant countries to develop interoperability with NATO forces and to prepare their force structures and capabilities for possible future membership."[40]

In 2000, with the United States preparing to elect its next president—the man who would make the next critical decisions on enlargement—the nine candidate states joined together in support of a "big bang" approach to enlargement. Meeting in Vilnius, Lithuania, the nine foreign ministers pledged that their countries would work for entry in NATO as a group rather than compete against each other for a favored position in 2002. Both major presidential candidates in the United States, Vice President Al Gore and Texas Governor George W. Bush, sent letters of support to the session.[41]

Managing the relationship with Russia

As a result of NATO's post-Cold War enlargement and the evolving transformation of the missions and methods of the alliance, NATO's focus with the approach of the twenty-first century could be said to have moved beyond Russia. Russia was no longer the primary security concern for the alliance, even though Russia's evolution remained a critical variable in Europe's future. This process of change began in the early 1990s as the NATO allies reacted to the emerging reality that the Soviet Union and the Warsaw Pact no longer existed as threats to their security. The debate on the first phase of NATO enlargement in the mid-1990s foreshadowed some of the challenges facing the alliance today as controversy continues about how a new NATO strategic concept should shape future alliance goals and activities, particularly in light of the alliance's mission in Afghanistan.

In spite of NATO's efforts to create special partnership status for Russia, Moscow had from the beginning resented the fact that former Warsaw Pact allies and even former Soviet republics were becoming members of what had been the opposing Cold War alliance. After four decades of tension and competition between NATO and the Warsaw Pact, Russian leaders and the public had been well-conditioned to view the United States and its Western allies through an enemy-image prism. In addition, the Russian leadership still viewed what it calls Russia's "near abroad" as legitimately within its sphere of interest, even if Moscow no longer dominates that region. Russians believe they should defend the interests of ethnic Russians in Ukraine and in the Baltic states, even if those populations are now represented by governments in sovereign independent states. The NATO enlargement process directly threatened these perceptions of Russian security interests, even if, from the point of view of its former allies and neighboring republics, it was fully within their right and even in their vital interests to join NATO and the European Union.

The military and ideological threat posed by the Soviet Union, with Russia at its core, along with European concerns about a resurgent Germany, provided the original stimulus for the transatlantic bargain. These two factors also provided motivation for the steps taken in the 1940s and 1950s to initiate the process of European unification. The German "threat" was dissipated by decades of liberal German democracy, loyalty to the Western alliance, and the process of European integration. When the Soviet Union imploded at the end of the Cold War, the United States and its European allies discovered that even though this founding threat was also disappearing, the cooperation that had developed over the years was not only based on solid common values and interests, but also had continuing utility in a post-Soviet world.

Nevertheless, Russia remained a major factor in allied calculations. In spite of Russia's devastated economy, and military forces so weakened as to be incapable of putting down rebellion in the former Soviet Republic of Chechnya, Russia remained a world-class nuclear power with a natural resource base that could serve as the foundation for future economic growth and renewed strategic significance. The development of a liberal democratic system in Russia would constitute a dramatic gain for international peace and stability. An autocratic, deprived and dissatisfied Russia could constitute a major source of instability for the indefinite future. As a consequence, the transatlantic allies moved carefully throughout the 1990s trying to assess how steps that they were taking to adapt their alliance would affect and be affected by Russia. They opened the cooperation path to all former Warsaw Pact members and Soviet republics, including Russia.

Despite the generally positive development of cooperation, the issue of NATO enlargement troubled the relationship. Russia's negative attitude toward NATO enlargement reflected feelings about the alliance that had been reinforced by decades of Soviet propaganda. Even the Russian elite found it difficult to understand the fundamental differences between NATO, a voluntary alliance among independent countries, and the Warsaw Pact, where membership was imposed by the Soviet Union. Expansion of NATO's role and membership meant that US power and influence would stretch ever closer to Russia's borders, displacing what had been Soviet/Russian zones of influence in Central and Eastern Europe. Some Russian officials believed that when Moscow agreed to facilitate German reunification, the Soviet Union had been promised that NATO would not expand up to its borders—a claim rejected by US officials who represented the United States in the negotiations.[42] The Russian perception may help explain Moscow's strong reaction to NATO's enlargement plans. The bottom line, of course, was that even if the negotiations led the Russians to such a conclusion, no such commitment was ever made formal.

In the mid-1990s the NATO allies decided that it was important to respond to the enthusiastic desire of the new democracies to join NATO while at the same time trying to overcome Russian opposition with a cooperative embrace. NATO's attempt to reassure the Russians took several forms. The NATO allies pledged that they had "no intention, no plan, and no reason" to deploy nuclear weapons on the territory of new members. They also said that they planned no permanent, substantial deployments of NATO soldiers in any new member states. Perhaps most important, the allies authorized NATO Secretary General Javier Solana, acting on behalf of the member states, to negotiate a more permanent cooperative relationship with Russia. Those negotiations, guided by Strobe Talbott and other US officials, resulted in the Founding Act on Mutual Relations, Cooperation and Security between NATO and the Russia Federation, signed in Paris in May 1997 just before NATO announced its decision to invite three former Warsaw Pact nations to join NATO.

The Founding Act set a large agenda of topics on which NATO and Russia would attempt to collaborate. It created a Permanent Joint Council (NATO nations plus Russia) as a framework for continuing consultations. Creating this channel for communications was an important step, but there were limits on its effectiveness. From the beginning, there was a tension between the Russian desire to use the forum to "participate in" NATO decision-making while the NATO allies sought to ensure that the Permanent Joint Council remained a place for consultations and not cooperative decision-making. Russia's acceptance of the Permanent Joint Council was always grudging. Russian leaders wanted something more—something that would more directly acknowledge Russia's importance in European security. The NATO countries, on the other hand, did not want to give Russia a direct say in NATO deliberations and certainly not a veto over NATO actions—a concern directly expressed by American conservatives during the 1990s debate on NATO enlargement.

The NATO–Russia relationship was at least superficially enhanced in January 1996 when Russian forces joined NATO troops in the Implementation Force, organized to enforce the military aspects of the Peace

Agreement in Bosnia. Russian forces also joined NATO troops to keep the peace in Kosovo after hostilities had ended in 1999, but were withdrawn from both Bosnia and Kosovo in the summer of 2003. Moscow's participation may have had as much to do with Russia's paternal feeling toward their Serbian cousins, whom they perceived as under attack by the United States and its NATO allies, as it did with wanting to cooperate with NATO.

NATO's evolving military roles

Throughout the Cold War, NATO survived in large part because the allies constantly adapted a fundamentally sound, principled relationship to changing international circumstances. This process of adaptation began with the military build-up and elaboration of a military command structure in the early 1950s after North Korea invaded South Korea—measures not anticipated when the North Atlantic Treaty was signed. The alliance was adjusted again following the failure of the European Defense Community in 1954. In the mid-1960s, NATO was forced to adapt to France's departure from the military command structure. In 1967, the allies revamped NATO's strategy with the doctrine of "flexible response" to a possible Warsaw Pact attack, broadening NATO's military options. In the same year, they approved the Harmel Report, which gave the alliance the mission of promoting détente as well as sustaining deterrence and defense. The process continued in the 1970s and 1980s as NATO allies adapted their alliance to the emerging period of détente in relations with the Soviet Union and sought arms control accords with Moscow to reduce the dangers of an East–West confrontation.

NATO's 1991 Strategic Concept

Since 1949, NATO had always had a strategic concept to guide its policies and force structures. All previous concepts, however, had been classified and were available only in summary form for public consumption. The London Declaration of July 1990 authorized preparation of a new strategic concept. The allies decided that new times required new approaches. In November 1991 in Rome, NATO leaders approved the new concept and released it for all to see.[43]

In Rome, the allies established three areas of particular emphasis for future NATO policies. First, they said that, as part of a "broader" approach to security, they would actively seek cooperation and dialogue among all European states and particularly with the former Warsaw Pact adversaries. Second, they declared that NATO's nuclear and non-nuclear military forces would be reduced and that remaining forces would be restructured to take into account the need for militaries that could handle crisis management tasks (such as the one that soon emerged in Bosnia) as well as collective defense. Third, the allies agreed that the European members of NATO would assume greater responsibility for their own security.

In the 1991 concept, the allies acknowledged the radical changes that had recently occurred in the world and in Europe in particular. When the concept was released, the Soviet Union still existed and still deployed powerful nuclear and non-nuclear military forces. But virtually everything else had changed. Democratic governments were getting organized across Central and Eastern Europe; the terms on which Germany would be reunified had been negotiated; the Treaty on Conventional Armed Forces in Europe had been signed; the Warsaw Pact had been disbanded; an antidemocratic coup against Soviet leader Mikhail Gorbachev had been defeated; and governments in Poland, Hungary, and Czechoslovakia had expressed their wish to be included in NATO activities.

The 1991 concept said that NATO's policies and force posture should be adapted to those remarkable changes. But the allies also reaffirmed some elements of continuity. NATO's core function, they declared, was to defend its members against attack, and NATO's military command structure and coalition approach to defense remained essential to the interests of the members. The transatlantic link between Europe and North America continued to be vital to NATO's future relevance. Defense of democracy, human rights, and the rule of law still constituted the heart and soul of the alliance. Allied leaders noted that, even with all the positive changes, the world remained a dangerous place and that NATO cooperation would be essential to help them deal with the remaining risks and uncertainties. They agreed that the North Atlantic Treaty, in addition to providing for collective defense, included a mandate to work together to deal with threats to the security interests of the members, not just an attack on one of them.

This concept provided a new foundation for NATO initiatives throughout the 1990s and for substantial changes in NATO's military priorities. The allies dramatically reduced and streamlined military forces and NATO's command structure. In 1993, the allies agreed that the peacetime strength of their forces could be reduced approximately 25 percent below 1990 levels. In subsequent years, additional cuts were taken. NATO's command structure was reduced from 65 headquarters down to 20 in the new system.

The force structure implications of the post-Cold War security environment were recognized early in the 1990s, even if most NATO governments were not prepared to act on the implications. The new challenges to allied security arose almost entirely well beyond the borders of NATO countries. Most allies, however, had forces designed largely to defend their own territory or that of a neighbor. They had little capacity to project and sustain forces in operations beyond their borders. The 1991 Strategic Concept assumed that allies would be reducing military spending and forces in view of the reduced threat. The concept also envisioned, however, that allies would restructure remaining military forces to give them greater force projection capabilities.

The Balkan conflicts of the 1990s brought home the importance of these words in the 1991 concept.

The allies addressed directly the reality that the end of the Cold War did not resolve all sources of conflict and tension in the world, even though it certainly improved the prospects for a more peaceful future. Unfortunately, there remained countries and subnational groups, including terrorists, who did not accept the post-Cold War distribution of territory, resources, political influence, or generally accepted norms of international behavior. In some cases, these countries and groups saw the threat or use of force as a way to change the status quo—Saddam Hussein's attack on Kuwait in 1990 was a good example, as were the terrorist acts instigated by the radical Islamic militant Osama bin Laden. Some of these activities rely on conventional weapons and terrorist tactics. But there was reason to be particularly concerned about access of such countries and groups to nuclear, chemical, and biological weapons of mass destruction (WMD) and modern means to deliver such weapons.

At the time, only the United States and a few other allied governments were prepared to move ahead with new military programs designed to respond to the terrorist/WMD problem. Thus, the allies focused initially on the politics of the issue, examining the underlying causes of dissatisfaction with the status quo that gave rise to WMD threats and terrorist activities. They also sought to identify the political, economic, and security tools available to the international community to eliminate the sources of proliferation or to prevent it in some way, including active support for existing arms control regimes. The NATO allies pledged to support political and diplomatic efforts aimed at preventing proliferation without duplicating the work of other organizations. However, the allies never made a serious commitment to coordinate their approaches to terrorist threats or their possible responses to terrorist attacks. This failure was due in part to underlying disagreements about the sources of and appropriate responses to terrorist threats. In addition, the terrorist activities of greatest concern to date had been the responsibility of internal, not external, groups (e.g., bombings of British targets to protest against the United Kingdom's involvement in Northern Ireland and attacks by Basque separatists in Spain) and were regarded by the target states as domestic affairs.

At the same time, WMD and terrorism raised specific security problems for NATO. A terrorist's missile carrying a weapon of mass destruction fired at any NATO country would become a collective defense issue for all the allies. And political efforts to prevent proliferation or deter the use of WMD might not always be successful on their own. The NATO members therefore decided that NATO's military posture must make it clear to any potential aggressor that the alliance cannot be coerced by the threat or use of WMD and that it could respond effectively to threats to its security as they develop.

NATO's 1991 strategy called for maintaining military capabilities that would be sufficient to signal how seriously NATO took the proliferation threat.

Under post-Cold War conditions, the allies decided that they could best communicate their intentions by maintaining a mix of nuclear and non-nuclear response weapons, passive and active defenses, and effective intelligence and surveillance means. NATO forces, they determined, should be capable of anticipating (through high-quality intelligence information and analysis), deterring (through maintenance of credible forces), defending (by protecting against a variety of delivery systems and the effects of biological and chemical agents on troops), and, if necessary, defeating (using whatever force may be required) any threat from WMD that might emerge from any source in the future.

NATO's approach to the new challenges of WMD and terrorism was a contemporary application of the commitment the allies made in the North Atlantic Treaty to cooperate in preserving the peace and dealing with threats to the security of the alliance. Such threats were likely to remain politically complex; they might arise from several different possible directions; and they could be difficult to predict and assess. NATO, however, could help coordinate allied diplomatic efforts to prevent such challenges from arising and, if necessary, develop appropriate responses to more imminent and dangerous military threats that do emerge. Unfortunately, the alliance did little in real terms to respond to the terrorist challenge prior to the September 11, 2001, attacks on the United States.

The allies did, however, make an active commitment to military cooperation with their former adversaries. Even before the 1991 new Strategic Concept was issued, the allies began engaging their military forces in cooperative programs with former Warsaw Pact and other European nations. In support of the dialogues with Russia and Ukraine, NATO military forces tried to reach out to the militaries that had formed the core of the Soviet Union's defense establishment. Thus, while the NATO force structure was being reduced, new roles and missions were being added to the plate of allied military forces. This expansion of functions and responsibilities preceded the burdens that were subsequently imposed by the peace operations in Bosnia and Kosovo.

An important reform of the NATO military command structure began at the January 1994 NATO summit meeting in Brussels when the allies approved the US-proposed idea of establishing Combined Joint Task Force (CJTF) headquarters as part of NATO's military command structure.[44]

The intent of the CJTF initiative was to provide flexible command arrangements within which allied forces could be organized on a task-specific basis to take on a wide variety of missions beyond the borders of alliance countries. Specifically, the concept sought the following:

1. Giving NATO's force and command structure sufficient flexibility to respond to alliance security requirements and new missions other than responses to an attack on a NATO country.
2. Facilitating the dual use of NATO forces and command structures for alliance and/or operations run by the Western European Union, the defense

organization whose membership included only European countries and that had been chosen as the framework for constructing a "European pillar" in NATO; the purpose would be to encourage European nations to undertake missions with forces that are "separable but not separate" from NATO in the context of an emerging European Security and Defense Identity.

3. Permitting non-NATO partners to join NATO countries in operations, exercises, and training as envisioned in the Partnership for Peace program of cooperation open to all non-NATO European states.

All these new directions had direct implications for the NATO command structure and, in April 1994, the Chiefs of the Defense Staffs of NATO countries initiated the "Long-Term Study" intended to form the basis for a new command structure. For starters, it was decided to reduce major NATO commands from three to two—Allied Command Europe and Allied Command Atlantic—with the elimination of the Allied Command Channel. But more difficult issues lay immediately ahead.

NATO's Bosnia experience: from theory to practice

While the NATO nations were trying to calculate how the alliance would relate to and operate in the new international environment of the post-Cold War world, that world was already posing new and difficult challenges. With very little concern for allied preferences and priorities, the real world reminded the United States and its European allies that "life is what's happening while you are busy doing other things."

By 1991, life in the Balkans had already become increasingly conflicted. Yugoslavia was a multi-ethnic communist state that remained relatively independent of the Soviet Union during the Cold War. Following the death of the communist dictator Josip Broz Tito in 1980, the country had been tenuously held together with a power-sharing approach that more or less continued to balance the interests of the country's main ethnic groups (Serbian, Croatian, Muslim, and Albanian). But attempts to modernize Yugoslavia's economic and political system were failing just as the world celebrated the end of the Cold War. The failure became a new Balkan tragedy when the process of disintegration turned violent. The Slovene Republic, a part of the former Yugoslavia that was blessed with a relatively homogeneous population and no substantial minority concentrations, managed to break away with limited fighting. But the Republic of Croatia's breakaway was strongly resisted by the Serbian-controlled military, producing approximately 20,000 dead and more than 350,000 displaced persons.[45]

The conflict quickly spread to Bosnia, where Serbian, Croatian, and Muslim populations were interspersed around the republic and where the conflict became a brutal and bloody internecine battle among the ethnic populations. When the Bosnian War began in March 1992, the NATO countries had just issued their new strategic concept, which, in principle, suggested that they should prepare to deal with such circumstances. But they were nowhere near being ready to do so. In fact, NATO leaders in Rome had made clear their desire to keep NATO at arm's length from the conflict, proclaiming their concern but suggesting that the parties to the Balkan conflicts "cooperate fully with the European Community in its efforts under the mandate given it by the CSCE [Conference on Security and Cooperation in Europe], both in the implementa-tion of cease-fire and monitoring agreements and in the negotiating process within the Conference on Yugoslavia."[46]

A key reason for NATO's reticence was the reluctance of the United States to get involved. President George H. W. Bush was facing a re-election contest in which it was clear that the Democratic opposition would charge him with spending too much time on foreign policy at the expense of domes-tic issues. Bush may have been additionally motivated by Soviet President Gorbachev's warning in the spring of 1991 that the West should not intervene in Yugoslavia, obviously not wanting a precedent for Western intervention to be set that subsequently could be applied to a crumbling Soviet Union.[47]

If the Bush administration needed additional cover for a reticent US approach, a way out had been provided earlier by the European allies. On June 28, 1991, Jacques Poos, the foreign minister of Luxembourg, speaking for the members of the European Community, bravely claimed that the problems in the Balkans presented an opportunity for the Europeans to take charge of their own security affairs, pronouncing that it was "the hour of Europe." According to Poos, "If one problem can be solved by the Europeans, it's the Yugoslav problem. This is a European country and it's not up to the Americans and not up to anybody else."[48] Under these circumstances, the Bush administration was satisfied to leave it at this. NATO's role was restricted to helping enforce the UN embargo against weapons deliveries to any of the warring parties in Yugoslavia. The operation was conducted in parallel with a seaborne monitor-ing operation organized through the Western European Union.[49]

With the United States unwilling to get involved, NATO's role clearly would remain limited. However, the brutality of the conflict and the suffering of non-combatants, broadcast up close and personal for the world to see, could not be ignored.

The international community responded to the immediate consequences of the conflict by mounting a humanitarian relief operation backed up by a UN Protection Force (UNPROFOR), manned largely by lightly armed French, British, and other European troops whose mission was effectively limited to ensuring the safety of the relief efforts. Despite the care that President Bush took not to get involved in the Balkan conflicts, the criticism that he had spent too much time and energy on foreign policy and not enough on the US economy apparently hit home with the American people. In November 1992,

George Bush lost the presidency to Democrat Bill Clinton, who came to office in 1993.

During the US presidential election campaign, Clinton had criticized Bush's hands-off Bosnia policy but, after taking office, he followed much the same approach. In April 1993, the UN Security Council agreed to impose an embargo of all land, sea, and air traffic attempting to enter Serbia and Montenegro. The Clinton administration and the European allies agreed that NATO would help enforce the enhanced embargo, but the new administration remained reluctant to get too deeply involved, fearing that the presidency could in its early months be drawn into what Secretary of State Warren Christopher called "the problem from hell."[50]

Transatlantic relations over Bosnia policy were also troubled by the fact that the United States saw and understood the conflict largely as one involving an aggressor—the Bosnian Serbs, supported by Serbia—against the much weaker Bosnian Muslims. The Europeans, for the most part, believed the conflict should be seen as a civil war in which all parties were to blame. These two different interpretations of the conflict produced divergent policy preferences. The approach to the conflict favored by many members of the US Congress was to lift the embargo against military assistance to Bosnia in order to equip and train Bosnian forces to produce a balance of power in Bosnia that would provide the necessary incentives for peace. This approach was based on the model of Serbia as the aggressor and the assumption that the United States should provide only air power and no ground forces to help resolve the conflict. The European allies strongly objected to any such "lift-and-strike" approach, particularly because the forces they had deployed in UNPROFOR depended on being seen as "neutral" in the conflict and were there only to help mitigate the humanitarian tragedy. The Europeans at that point had put troops in harm's way and the United States had not. This led to the growing perception in the 1990s that the United States would involve itself in overseas conflicts only if risks to American forces could be minimized.

The United States really did not want to touch the Bosnian tar baby. But when it became clear that international relief efforts and UNPROFOR were dealing with some of the consequences but none of the causes of the conflict, the United States, and therefore NATO, were slowly drawn toward deeper involvement. The Clinton administration still hoped to avoid placing US troops on the ground in Bosnia unless they were sent to help enforce a negotiated peace accord. Clinton sent Secretary of State Christopher on a mission to Europe to try to convince the allies to accept the lift-and-strike approach. Christopher made what has been described as a half-hearted pitch to the allies, reportedly conveying the message that he had come in a "listening mode."[51] The Europeans perceived accurately the lack of the administration's commitment to the initiative.

However, by the summer of 1993, Bosnian Serb forces were winning military victory after victory. They had encircled virtually all the "safe areas" that UNPROFOR had established to help protect civilian populations, including the major center of Sarajevo. In response, the NATO members agreed to draw up plans for air strikes by NATO forces against those threatening the viability of UNPROFOR's mission, mainly the Bosnian Serbs. The option was created with a "dual-key" arrangement in which both NATO and the United Nations would have to agree on striking any particular target.

The UN–NATO collaboration was necessitated by the fact that international involvement in the Balkans was largely under the mandate provided by UN Security Council resolutions.[52] Most countries wanted it that way, but the arrangement made for difficult relations between the United States, which provided most of the military capabilities necessary for the NATO air strikes, and the European allies, led by the British and French, whose troops were on the ground and exposed to retaliation by Bosnian Serb forces.

The Bosnian Serbs fully recognized the advantages to their cause of the split between the United States and its allies. They responded to NATO air strikes by backing off when necessary, taking UNPROFOR soldiers hostage when advantageous, and playing for time to complete their military victory.

During 1995, it became increasingly clear that the UNPROFOR approach, even backed up by NATO air strikes, could not be sustained much longer. The European allies suggested that UNPROFOR would have to be withdrawn, and this would require that the United States fulfill its pledge to protect allied forces as they were being pulled out. But such a withdrawal would also mean a victory for those seen by the United States as the aggressors, and such an outcome would have been a serious setback for US foreign policy. Trying to escape from its policy dilemma, the Clinton administration was impelled forward by the Bosnian Serb attack on the UN safe area of Srebrenica early in July 1995. The United Nations rejected the request from Dutch UNPROFOR troops for air strikes to deter the Serb attack. When it came, the Bosnian Serbs conducted a brutal campaign of blatant war crimes in the wake of their military victory. Serbian forces executed some 8,000 Bosnian boys and men, and tortured and sexually abused thousands of women and children. The shocking story emerging in the aftermath of Srebrenica began to galvanize an international view that something more had to be done. The commander of the Bosnian Serb forces bragged that Srebrenica was simply the beginning of the end of the conflict. As one observer has written, "This challenge confronted the United Nations, NATO and especially the leading member states with a fundamental choice. They could act to oppose what was unfolding before them by force of arms or they could declare defeat."[53]

At a meeting in London following the Srebrenica disaster, the United States and its key European allies agreed that Serbian preparations for an attack on the safe area of Gorazde would be met with a strong air campaign, hitting Bosnian Serb targets throughout Bosnia. The United States also produced a plan for negotiations that the allies readily accepted as a way out of the crisis. Operation Deliberate Force began on August 30 after it was determined that a deadly artillery attack on a marketplace in Sarajevo had been conducted by Bosnian Serb forces. The bombing campaign, combined with a successful Croatian offensive against Serbian forces that had begun in early August, brought the Serbs and the other combatants to the bargaining table.

The United States, represented by the bright, ambitious, and controversial Richard Holbrooke and a very capable interagency team of officials, provided much of the energy behind the talks.[54] Following complex and difficult negotiations, a peace accord was completed in Dayton, Ohio, and then signed in Paris on December 14, 1995. The United Nations gave NATO a mandate to help implement the accord, and on December 16, the allies decided to launch what was at the time the largest military operation ever undertaken by NATO. NATO sent to Bosnia an Implementation Force (IFOR) of more than 60,000 troops from NATO, partner, and other nations to maintain the peace, keep the warring factions separated, oversee the transfer of territory between the parties as specified in the peace accord, and supervise the storage of heavy weapons of the parties in approved sites. IFOR had been given one year to accomplish its tasks—a time frame recognized by most observers as inadequate for the purpose of establishing peace but perhaps necessary to appease domestic politics in the United States. At the end of that year, in December 1996, it was decided that peace would not yet be self-sustaining without continued external encouragement. NATO, with a UN mandate, replaced IFOR with a Stabilization Force (SFOR), which remained in Bosnia until replaced by a force under European Union command in December 2004.

Over the years, NATO helped establish relative peace in Bosnia, but questions remained about whether the goal of producing a self-sustaining peace in the multi-ethnic state cobbled together at Dayton would be achieved. According to most observers, international civilian assistance had not achieved a level of effectiveness to stimulate progress toward a more stable society. In addition to a less-than-effective international response to Bosnia's civilian needs, the three ethnic communities—Bosnian, Croatian, and Serbian—had made insufficient efforts to start a serious process of reconciliation that would be needed for a multi-ethnic state to function in the long run.

In 2002, although NATO had reduced the size of SFOR in recognition of the less imminent chance of open conflict, it was still not clear whether the Dayton approach to peace in Bosnia would succeed or fail. In 2004, however, the decision to turn the mission over to the European Union suggested that the challenges had become less military and more political, economic, and social. One of the main tasks of the new European Union command would be to fight crime and corruption, which threatened to undermine Bosnia's democracy. NATO nonetheless decided to keep a small headquarters in Bosnia, partly as a symbol of its continuing support for stability there.

The Bosnia experience demonstrated that the 1991 new Strategic Concept had been on target when it suggested that NATO needed to prepare for non-Article 5 military contingencies. Even though Article 5—the pledge to respond to an attack on another ally—remained the most profound commitment made by each NATO ally, a major attack on a NATO country had become the least likely near-term challenge to the security of the NATO members.

The conflicts in the Balkans did not directly threaten the security of most NATO allies, particularly the United States. This assessment produced the reluctance of the United States and its allies to respond effectively when the Balkan wars broke out. However, the lofty goals of making Europe whole, free, and at peace were challenged directly, as were the moral standards embraced by the United States and its allies. The danger that the conflict would spread to the borders of NATO allies, and perhaps lead to political and even military conflicts between NATO allies, did pose a threat to allied security. And if NATO was not going to be used to deal with this crisis in Europe, would it simply become an insurance policy, ceasing to be an important vehicle for the future management of Euro-Atlantic relations?

NATO's role in helping promote and then enforce peace in Bosnia answered, at least temporarily, some of these questions. NATO's continued value as an instrument for transatlantic consultation and a vehicle for political and military action became more obvious. The original European preference to handle the crisis through the United Nations and the US preference to avoid putting troops on the ground caused a costly delay in bringing an end to the brutal conflict. The fact that NATO's "habits of cooperation" facilitated putting together collaborative responses to contemporary security challenges was demonstrated, as was the utility of NATO's military command structure.

Some questions, however, were not answered. Could the allies in the future respond to an emerging crisis more quickly and therefore minimize the civilian casualties and dislocations that characterized the Balkan conflicts? How could rapid responses be produced by an organization in which one ally, the United States, had a wide range of military options available to it—and therefore might be more inclined to use them—while the rest of the allies had more limited military options and therefore might be more reluctant to resort to the use of force? Would responses to future crises be handicapped because the United States had grown suspicious and mistrustful of the United Nations while the European allies still believed in the necessity of obtaining a UN mandate for military operations? Would the fact that France—one of two European allies with meaningful intervention forces—still did not participate fully in NATO's integrated military structure hamper the construction of future NATO coalition operations? Would the United States be a reluctant participant—and therefore an ineffective leader—in future NATO peace operations, particularly given the attitude of many US conservatives that US military forces should be held in reserve for the "big" contingencies and not wasted on the more menial labor of "doing the windows" in peace operations?

Back to the NATO adaptation process

These and other questions remained very much open in 1996 when, with the Bosnia experience in hand and the difficult process of implementing the Dayton peace accord under way, the allies prepared to take the next steps needed to adapt the alliance to the new security environment. In many respects, the allies found it almost as difficult and time consuming to agree on the principles to guide new arrangements as they did arriving at a common approach to the conflict in Bosnia.[55]

The allies still faced the challenge of implementing agreements that they had made in principle in 1994 designed to give NATO a more flexible structure that would facilitate responses to new security problems. In June 1996, following months of difficult negotiations which on many occasions found the United States and France at loggerheads, the allies neared a breakthrough concerning how to organize responses to future non-Article 5 security challenges. The French had interpreted the Clinton administration's initiatives at the January 1994 Brussels Summit as a sign that the United States was prepared for "Europeanization" of the alliance. The administration, on the other hand, was thinking more in terms of an evolutionary development toward greater European responsibility.[56]

At a critical meeting in Berlin, NATO foreign ministers agreed on significant new steps that, when implemented, would constitute a major transformation of NATO's missions and methods of operation. In Berlin, the allies agreed to move ahead with implementation of the CJTF concept that had been agreed on in principle at Brussels in 1994. In addition, they agreed that a European Security and Defense Identity would be created within the alliance by making NATO "assets and capabilities" available for future military operations commanded by the Western European Union (WEU), the defense organization whose membership included only European countries based on the 1948 Brussels Treaty. Such decisions would be made by consensus on a case-by-case basis. To facilitate such operations, European officers in the NATO structure would, when appropriate, shift from their NATO responsibilities to WEU command positions.[57]

The allies determined that adaptation of the alliance should be guided by three fundamental objectives: to ensure the alliance's military effectiveness and ability to perform its traditional mission of collective defense while undertaking new military roles, to preserve the transatlantic link by strengthening NATO as a forum for political consultation and military cooperation, and to support development of a European Security and Defense Identity by creating the possibility for NATO-supported task forces to perform missions under the direction of the WEU nations.

NATO forces in Europe had always been commanded by an American officer who occupies the position of Supreme Allied Commander, Europe (SACEUR), and the allies unanimously agreed that the United States should retain this top command. But the allies decided that the Deputy SACEUR, a senior European officer, and other European officers in the NATO command structure would in the future wear WEU command hats as well as their NATO command hats.[58] This multiple-hatting procedure would, without duplicating resources and personnel, permit the WEU countries to use the NATO command structure to organize and conduct a military operation largely under European auspices.

The Berlin Accord was designed to help transform NATO's role for the post-Cold War world, respond to calls from Congress for more effective sharing of international security burdens, and accommodate a more cohesive European role in the alliance. The government of France facilitated the outcome by deciding to move toward much closer military cooperation with its NATO allies to help deal with new challenges to security in Europe. The United States and other allies made major contributions to the outcome by agreeing to fundamental changes in the way that NATO had traditionally organized and run its military forces.

The Berlin Accord suggested the importance the allies attached to the need for a flexible and dynamic alliance. It demonstrated the commitment of the United States, Canada, and the European allies to ensure that NATO could respond to contemporary security needs. It revealed transatlantic consensus on the need to accommodate development of greater European defense cohesion and military capabilities.

It was hoped that the agreement, giving the Europeans the potential for a more prominent role in NATO's military affairs, would also lead France to return to NATO's integrated military command. French President Jacques Chirac had implied that such a move might be possible. In the wake of the Berlin Accord, however, a series of events prevented the deal from being consummated. First, in the summer of 1996, Chirac sent a letter to President Clinton suggesting that the reform of NATO should include transfer of the position of Supreme Allied Commander Allied Forces South from the United States to a European country. The French saw such a potential shift in commands as a necessary token of the US willingness to let Europe take more responsibility in the alliance. Given the importance of the Mediterranean region to US interests and the fact that Clinton had just overruled the Joint Chiefs in order to agree to the Berlin Accord, Clinton was not going to "give away" such an important position. Following the small crisis that this request and its rejection caused in US–French relations, the door to a French return apparently was firmly closed early in 1997, when Chirac called early legislative elections (which his party lost, ceding control to the left) and did not want to be accused of abandoning an important Gaullist policy of independence from NATO's integrated command. Only in 2009 did French President Nicolas Sarkozy open the door and walk France back into the military command structure.

Meanwhile, implementation of the Berlin Accord moved ahead slowly, complicated by divergent US and French interpretations of what the agreement actually meant. Even though NATO had already constructed a combined joint task force (IFOR) to conduct the peace enforcement operation in Bosnia and a second one (SFOR) to help keep that peace, the alliance could not declare the CJTF concept operational until the allies had worked through all the details and conducted the requisite tests and exercises. This highly deliberate process gave rise to circulation of a number of anecdotes. Most quoted is the one about a NATO discussion of the CJTF approach in which, after the US representative had described the great virtues of the concept, the French representative supposedly replied, "It looks as though it will work in practice, but will it work in theory?"

The Kosovo campaign

Even as NATO conducted a relatively successful peace enforcement operation in Bosnia, the story of conflict in the Balkans was far from over, and the allies were to get yet another chance to test the CJTF theory in practice. As noted earlier, the disintegration of the former Yugoslavia unleashed several power struggles among ethnic and religious groups whose animosities toward one another had been suppressed for decades. Kosovo, a region in southern Serbia (more formally known as the Federal Republic of Yugoslavia), was populated mainly by ethnic Albanians. In 1989, Serbian leader Slobodan Milosevic removed the region's former autonomy. Kosovo became an explosion waiting to happen.

During 1998, open conflict between Serbian military and police forces and ethnic Albanian forces in Kosovo resulted in more than 1,500 ethnic Albanian deaths and displaced 400,000 from their homes. The NATO allies became gravely concerned about the escalating conflict, its humanitarian consequences, and Milosevic's disregard for diplomatic efforts aimed at peaceful resolution. In October 1998, NATO decided to begin a phased air campaign against Yugoslavia if the Milosevic regime did not withdraw part of its forces from Kosovo, cooperate in bringing an end to the violence there, and facilitate the return of refugees to their homes. A UN resolution had called for these and other measures. At the last moment, Milosevic agreed to comply with the resolution, and the air strikes were called off. In addition, it was agreed that the Organization for Security and Cooperation in Europe (OSCE) would establish a verification mission in Kosovo to observe compliance with UN resolutions.

NATO assumed two special responsibilities in support of the OSCE mission. First, it established an aerial surveillance mission, Operation Eagle Eye, to observe compliance with the agreement. Several partner nations agreed to participate in the operation. Second, NATO established a special military task force, led by France, to be deployed in the Former Yugoslav Republic of Macedonia. Under the overall direction of NATO's SACEUR, this force was designed to rescue members of the OSCE Kosovo verification mission if renewed conflict should put them at risk.

The deteriorating situation in Kosovo in late 1998 led the international Contact Group (the United States, Britain, France, Germany, Italy, and Russia)[59] to produce a draft peace plan on January 29, 1999, that they then proposed to the Serbian authorities and representatives of the Kosovo Serbian population. On January 30, the North Atlantic Council agreed to authorize NATO Secretary General Javier Solana to initiate NATO air attacks against Serbian targets if Milosevic did not accept the terms of the plan. The Kosovo Albanian authorities accepted the plan on March 18, but the Serbians rejected it. NATO initiated air strikes against Serbian targets in both Serbia and Kosovo on March 24. In response, Serbian forces began driving Kosovo ethnic Albanians from their homes, killing some 10,000 ethnic Albanians and torturing and raping many others.

The NATO air campaign, conducted largely by US forces with high-tech capabilities, lasted for 78 days, targeting Yugoslav military forces and important civilian and military infrastructure.[60] The campaign was conducted without a mandate from the UN Security Council, where it could have been vetoed by the Russian and Chinese permanent members. The European allies would have much preferred having such a mandate but accepted the US argument that it was more important in this case to send a forceful message to Milosevic and stop the ethnic cleansing than to stick to international niceties. The allies pledged in the North Atlantic Treaty to "refrain in their international relations from the threat or use of force in any manner inconsistent with the purposes of the United Nations." In this case, the allies judged that the use of force against Serbia was consistent with the purposes of the United Nations, even if they could not get a UN mandate.

Serbian President Milosevic agreed to a peace plan based on NATO conditions on June 3. It required the removal of all Yugoslav forces from Kosovo and provided for the deployment of a NATO-led force to keep the peace while Kosovo was put under international administration until autonomous, elected institutions and officials could be established. Kosovo's final status was left unsettled.

The Kosovo operation ultimately succeeded in driving out Serbian forces and allowing the Albanian population to return, in many cases to homes, neighborhoods, and entire towns that had been destroyed by the Serbs. But the victory was not without a price. Even during the operation, critics complained that NATO's military campaign had provoked the final and most brutal phase of Serbia's ethnic cleansing operation. As the air campaign dragged on with no sign of a Milosevic concession, differences arose among allies and in domestic political debates about an air campaign that was conducted under rules intended to minimize the risks to allied forces and that denied strategically important targets to NATO forces. Some argued strongly that ground forces would have to go in to drive Yugoslav forces out. The debate produced partially accurate images of a United States that thought all wars could be fought without risk to friendly forces versus Europeans who better appreciated the facts on the ground. Perhaps the most dramatic impact, however, was on the perception of a growing gap in deployed technology between the United States and its allies and, from the European side, a realization that Europe could influence the conduct of future military operations only if it could bring more capable forces to the table.

Thus, the end of the war over Kosovo and the beginning of peacekeeping and reconstruction was a victory for NATO albeit a qualified one. The successful outcome of the air campaign meant that the allies avoided the potential casualties, intra-allied divisions, and domestic unrest that a ground force campaign could have produced. However, the interaction between political objectives and military strategy had a lasting effect on US and European attitudes toward NATO management of military operations.

The ultimate success of NATO's strategy surprised the vast majority of military experts and pundits. Most of them had blamed President Clinton, his advisers, and Supreme Allied Commander General Wesley Clark for concocting an air-only campaign designed to avoid NATO casualties but, in their judgment, unlikely to bring Milosevic to heel. In retirement, General Clark answered his critics in a book which argued that a successful end to the campaign had been delayed by constraints imposed on his operations by Washington and interference from other NATO allies, particularly France.[61] Meanwhile, a US General Accounting (now "Accountability") Office report released in July 2001 added to the critique. The report found that the need to maintain alliance cohesion during the conflict led to important departures from standard US military doctrine and resulted in a limited mission with unclear objectives. Many American military officers and civilian officials who participated in this campaign felt that these departures resulted in a longer conflict, more extensive damage to Yugoslavia, and significant risks to alliance forces.[62]

Such critics appear to have been half right and half wrong. They were right that the air campaign allowed Milosevic to continue his ethnic cleansing policies. They were right that Milosevic would have been more convinced of Western resolve if ground forces had been on the table from the beginning. In fact, the build-up of Western forces around Kosovo prior to the end of the conflict did begin to bring ground forces into the military equation, particularly as seen from Belgrade. Moreover, the military revival of the Kosovo Liberation Army, the main Kosovo Albanian fighting force, played a crucial role in forcing Serbian units out of concealment, making them more vulnerable to Western air strikes. NATO did, in the end, have a ground force component to its strategy, even if it developed tacitly and half-heartedly.

Given Milosevic's calculating but stubborn behavior, such critics did not believe that a tacit ground force threat would be sufficient. In addition, the general anti-Clinton perspective of many such experts and, in Europe, the prevailing belief that the United States was no longer willing to take casualties in conflicts not directly linked to "vital" US interests tended to block an objective evaluation of the other important factors at work.[63]

Clinton may have been reluctant to envision US casualties, but he also faced other serious constraints. Only one NATO ally, the United Kingdom, avidly supported the threat of a ground campaign. Some allies were actively opposed, and Clinton supported the air campaign as the only approach that could keep the alliance united and at the same time avoid substantial US casualties. The second important constraint was the absence of good invasion routes, created by a combination of difficult terrain, limited infrastructure in neighboring countries, and the reluctance of some states in the region to be used as launching points for a ground campaign.

At the beginning of the air campaign, and even toward its end, there was no NATO consensus on behalf of even threatening a ground force invasion of Kosovo. The most important missing links were Germany and Greece. If the United States had tried to impose such a strategy on the alliance, divisions among NATO members, never too far beneath the surface, would have burst into the open. The German government might have fallen, and the Greek government, by denying NATO access to its port and road facilities, could have severely hampered ground operations. Even though it was popular in Europe to see NATO as following US policy in lockstep, the fact is that neither the Clinton administration nor its predecessors led the alliance successfully by dictating NATO policy.

The big plus for NATO, in addition to achieving its main declared objectives, was that, not without some difficulty, NATO unity was preserved throughout the conflict. In addition, the fact that the air campaign was conducted with such efficiency left a strong impression concerning the readiness and condition of NATO air forces. The loss of only two aircraft and no NATO military casualties in action was both objectively and statistically convincing of US and NATO military effectiveness.

There may never be another contingency that replicates the Kosovo experience. This likelihood, however, suggested the importance of flexible contingency planning, the training and equipping of NATO forces to deal with a wide range of geographic and climatic conditions, and the availability of excellent tactical and strategic intelligence resources. These directions, however, would require political commitment and resources to implement.

The reality that political factors inhibited NATO's ability to show a stronger hand to Milosevic from the beginning threatened to leave a lasting mark on alliance decision-making. The NATO allies, in the future, might again face a choice between two options: keeping allied unity but compromising its military strategy or abandoning NATO unity, operating with an ad hoc coalition but deploying a more robust military strategy.

NATO theology, followed to a capital "T" by President Clinton, holds that it is almost always better to maintain a unified alliance than to abandon attempts to produce alliance consensus. However, the Kosovo experience suggested that it would not be a surprise if, in some future non-collective defense military contingency, ad hoc approaches were to appear more attractive to NATO's main military players (the United States, the United Kingdom, and France). The United States obviously chose this course when planning its campaign against Taliban and al-Qaeda forces in Afghanistan, partly as a result of the "lessons learned" from the allied management of the Kosovo conflict.

Some European and even American critics of the Kosovo air campaign portrayed it as another example of the United States imposing its hegemonic solutions on a hapless Europe. Such critics echoed themes that came with a vengeance from Chinese and Russian commentaries on the war. The facts of the matter, when fully assessed, suggest the opposite. The role of the United States in this affair was to provide the critical military components for a strategy that was handicapped by political realities in Europe as well as in the United States.

The heavy European reliance on US military capabilities, once again, added urgency to the initiatives of British Prime Minister Tony Blair and other key leaders in the European Union to develop military capabilities more in keeping with Europe's economic and financial resources. There was good cause for Europeans to be concerned about their military capabilities because a healthy US–European security relationship in the future would most likely demand that both burdens and responsibilities be shared equitably. It was no accident that the first peacekeeping forces entering Kosovo were, and remained, mainly European, not American. General Clark and NATO's political leadership were sensitive to the need to balance the perception of the US-dominated air operation with the equally accurate perception of a peacekeeping operation that would rely heavily on European troops.

The question left over from the Kosovo campaign, with its heady mix of positive and negative features, was whether the alliance would in the future use the experience to improve its military preparedness and command arrangements for such conflicts. The fact that the United States and Europe learned different lessons made it difficult to translate the experience into constructive changes for the alliance. The United States learned that it did not like to run military operations largely with US forces but with substantial allied political interference; the Europeans learned that they would prefer to have more influence on the course of a conflict whose outcome directly affected their interests.

The Washington Summit and NATO's evolving mission profile

In April 1999, the NATO allies met at the summit in Washington with the intent of celebrating NATO's fiftieth anniversary and approving guidance to carry the alliance into the twenty-first century. However, before the allies could issue the revised strategic concept on which they had been working for some two years, they were forced by developments in the Balkans to move from debates on principles to decisions in practice. Despite claims by some US officials that the 1999 Strategic Concept would guide NATO for a decade or longer,[64] the summit produced what was largely an incremental step down the road toward twenty-first-century security requirements.

The summit was held under a Kosovo cloud that the summit leaders were unable to dispel. At the time of the summit, it was unclear whether the Kosovo air campaign would ultimately have the desired result. The Clinton administration decided that the main goal of the summit should be to demonstrate allied unity. Most other allied leaders apparently agreed. British Prime Minister Tony Blair clearly had hoped to move allied governments toward a commitment to bring ground forces to bear in Kosovo. But the desire for at least a facade of unity won out. Compromise formulations were fashioned that papered over allied differences about the relationship of NATO to the United Nations and the limits on application of NATO's crisis management operations.

The Washington Summit was the first for NATO's three new members, the Czech Republic, Hungary, and Poland. The allies assured in their final communique that the enlargement process would continue, and the Membership Action Plan (discussed earlier) ensured that the additional nine candidates had a path to eventual membership.[65]

The allies repeated support for the development of a more coherent European role in the alliance. But the goal of giving new impetus to the European Security and Defense Identity largely fell by the wayside, left for the European allies to develop further in subsequent European Union gatherings.

Figure 6.3 Opening of the 1999 Washington 50th Anniversary Summit.

One of the problems addressed by allied defense ministers prior to the summit had been the challenge of preserving the ability of NATO militaries to fight as coalition forces in the future. The greatest concern was the growing technology gap between US armed forces and those of most European nations. European allies had been feasting on the post-Cold War "peace dividend," using reductions in military spending to help meet the requirements for European monetary union. Meanwhile, the United States had continued developing new technologies for its military forces. The consequence—a large capabilities gap between the United States and its allies—was evident in the air campaign against Serbia.

At the summit, the allies agreed on a "Defense Capabilities Initiative (DCI)"[66] designed to try to preserve the ability of allied forces to operate effectively with one another in future decades. The initiative put new political focus on the issue, which surely was needed. But the real problem was money. NATO agreement on what capabilities were needed at a time when threat perceptions were so low throughout Europe would not necessarily open up European treasuries to provide the required funding. In 2001, a NATO Parliamentary Assembly report observed that "the continuing decline in most European defence budgets may jeopardise the success of DCI, and with it the ability of the Alliance to carry out the roles and missions that it set out for itself in the 1999 Strategic Concept."[67]

NATO's 1999 Strategic Concept

One of the most anticipated products of the summit was the preparation of an updated strategic concept. The negotiations leading up to approval of the 1999 concept faced some key differences about NATO's future role and mandate. Perhaps the most important one was the question of how far NATO's mandate should extend beyond collective defense. The United States, with support from the United Kingdom, lobbied for increased alliance focus on new risks posed by the proliferation of nuclear, chemical, and biological weapons of mass destruction and by terrorism.

The North Atlantic Treaty invites the allies to cooperate on "threats" to allied interests, and these emerging risks certainly qualified. The treaty imposes no formal constraints on the ability of the allies to decide to use their cooperative framework to deal with challenges that do not qualify as Article 5 (collective defense) missions. The United States preferred that the 1999 Strategic Concept impose no formal geographic limits on the relevance of NATO cooperation. Most European allies, however, did not want NATO to be seen as a "global alliance" and preferred that decisions on NATO's future operations be made on a case-by-case basis.

In the early months of 1998, as the allies began work on the strategic concept that was to be agreed in April 1999, a major issue developed between the United States and several European allies concerning the relationship between NATO non-Article 5 operations and the United Nations. In preparing the new concept, the United States wanted to keep open the possibility that NATO would from time to time be required to act in the absence of a mandate from the United Nations. France and some other European governments did not disagree with the logic of the US assessment but strongly opposed turning possible exceptions into a new rule. From the French perspective, the rule should be to seek a UN mandate and then decide what to do should such a mandate appear blocked by Russia or China.

This debate, conducted in the corridors at NATO, turned into a real and imminent policy issue over Kosovo. By the autumn of 1998, Russia and China had made it clear that they would not support a UN Security Council resolution authorizing the use of force against Serbia for its activities in Kosovo. Despite this opposition, all NATO allies accepted that Slobodan Milosevic's policies of repression against the ethnic Albanian majority in Kosovo posed a threat, not only to internationally accepted values but also to peace in the Balkans and therefore to stability in Europe.

By late 1998, France and most other allies had accepted that Kosovo could constitute the kind of exception that they still opposed making into a new rule. When in March 1999 the allies saw no choice but to conduct air strikes against Serbia after the breakdown of the Rambouillet negotiations, they went ahead without the blessing of the Security Council.

Nevertheless, French and American differences over how to treat the mandate issue in the new strategic concept persisted, requiring carefully crafted compromises in the document issued by allied leaders in Washington. The strategic concept agreed to in Washington[68] acknowledged that the UN Security Council "has the primary responsibility for the maintenance of international peace and security and, as such, plays a crucial role in contributing to security and stability in the Euro-Atlantic area." The concept also noted that the OSCE "plays an essential role in promoting peace and stability, enhancing cooperative security and advancing democracy and human rights in Europe." The concept pledged that NATO "will seek, in cooperation with other organizations, to prevent conflict, or, should a crisis arise, to contribute to its effective management, consistent with international law, including through the possibility of conducting non-Article 5 crisis response operations." This language essentially met the French requirement for UN Security Council primacy regarding international security but left the door open for the allies, on a case-by-case basis, to act again in the future without a UN mandate if necessary.

The European preference for an international mandate was motivated partly by the need to demonstrate to public opinion that force is being used for the right purposes. Moreover, Europeans have a general preference for basing their foreign and security policies on international law. This is particularly important in Germany for solid historical reasons that have been embedded in both Germany's constitution and its political consciousness. Both the United Kingdom and France prefer to act on the basis of a Security Council mandate, given their positions as permanent (and veto-holding) members of the Council.

France felt this need rather more strongly than the United Kingdom, which believed that it derived influence over US actions through its close ties to Washington. Other European countries, unable to take the law into their own hands, believed that their interests were best served by an international system that runs on a set of predictable rules and regulations to the maximum extent possible. In addition, most Europeans would far prefer to have the Russians on board in support of any military operation in Europe. From their perspective, Russia remained an important European influence even if, at that time, it was weak in virtually all respects (except in its possession of superpower inventories of both strategic and theater nuclear weapons—another good reason for wanting to bring Moscow along).

All the European allies accepted that the new threats identified by the United States were serious and merited their attention. They agreed with the United States when it appeared that NATO might have to use force against Serbia without a specific UN mandate to do so. But most were reluctant to make cooperation more or less automatic in any given peace enforcement or counter-proliferation operation. They saw their willingness to act against Serbia without a UN mandate as an exception.

In the end, such decisions were left to be made on a case-by-case basis, with Kosovo seen neither as a new rule nor as the last time NATO might act without a UN mandate. Nonetheless, the allies agreed to establish a new NATO center to monitor these threats and help plan NATO responses.

The new concept, however, did not settle the question of whether a UN mandate should always be required. By the same token, the concept placed no formal geographic limitations on NATO's activities, nor did it identify a specific area of operations for those activities. This somewhat "fuzzy" outcome in the new concept on such issues accurately reflected the fact that NATO is an alliance of sovereign nation-states that prefer to reserve decisions on future NATO operations that do not involve an attack on a member.

The Washington Summit did not, as some US officials had hoped, lay out the course for NATO's next decade. It made a start down that road but left many crucial questions unanswered. This was not necessarily a failure of allied governments but rather a reflection of the extent to which the Kosovo experience could affect NATO's future development and the more traditional fact that no one meeting in NATO's history has ever resolved all outstanding issues.

Another issue not resolved by the 1999 concept was the question of how to distinguish between Article 5 and non-Article 5 missions, neither of which has ever been differentiated by the scope of the operations. Rather, the distinction is determined by the reason for the operation.

Article 5 is frequently seen as an "automatic" commitment, requiring all allies to come to the defense of one or more under attack. The language in the treaty, however, is more qualified. Allies are committed to regard an attack on one as an attack on all, but then each may "take such action as it deems necessary, including the use of armed force." The virtual automaticity of the guarantee actually was a product not of the language in the treaty but in the way the allies deployed military forces on the front lines in Europe. Multinational layer-cake deployments assured that an attack on frontline ally Germany would at the very outset engage the military forces of the United States and other allies, ensuring that they would have very little choice but to respond with military force sufficient to end hostilities on terms favorable to the allies.

There is no such automaticity either in the treaty or in practice regarding non-Article 5 operations. The response of the alliance in such cases must be determined by individual, independent national judgments, all of which must be at least permissive of the proposed action, if not actively supportive. The strength of the treaty's non-Article 5 provisions is that Article 5 does not provide a mandate to act in the case of threats to interests of the allies, only to deal with circumstances created by an attack on one of them. Article 4, on the other hand, specifically takes into account the possible need to consult concerning threats and to consider joint actions to deal with those threats.

That said, from a military planning perspective, the operations in Bosnia and Kosovo were of impressive size and scope. They were politically complex and militarily demanding. But they differed from traditional Article 5 planning in a number of ways. Most important, NATO planners had a fairly clear idea of what forces would be available in the case of a Warsaw Pact attack on NATO. In both the Bosnia and the Kosovo operations, there was no way to know far in advance what forces member states would send to the operation. This meant that NATO planners were forced to develop a variety of theoretical options to present to their political leaders and then hope that forces would be made available to implement the option selected by NATO national officials. In addition, while a hard core of NATO forces was deployed forward during the Cold War to form the first echelons of a defense against a Warsaw Pact attack, NATO's response to non-Article 5 contingencies must be based on forces that are capable of being moved, establishing themselves in the theater of conflict, and then conducting military operations. The logistics for such deployed operations are much more complicated than those required to support frontline forces engaging in border defense.

Lessons from the Balkans

NATO's initial involvement in the Balkans developed with reluctance and considerable political difficulty during the 1990s, but became seen as the first example of NATO's continued relevance to twenty-first-century security requirements. Only NATO could have organized and conducted the peacekeeping mission in Bosnia and the air war against Serbia over Kosovo. That remained true well into the twenty-first century. NATO's continuing involvement in the Balkans helped sustain a degree of security and stability that provided the opportunity for development of liberal institutions in the states that are emerging from the former Yugoslavia in a more peaceful regional environment.

NATO's experiences in the Balkans made it clear that running a war with multiple centers of political direction can be a demanding, frustrating task. On the other hand, if NATO had not existed, it is unlikely that the many NATO and non-NATO military forces that have played important roles in the Balkan operations could have worked together as effectively as they did. The NATO focus on interoperability and development of habits of cooperation in both political and military relations makes operations among the forces of NATO member states possible. It also created a framework that can accommodate contributions by other countries. It is no coincidence that the European Union is developing the forces for its European Security and Defense Policy under "NATO standards." The bottom line is that the day-to-day collaboration that takes place under the NATO banner has positive practical consequences whose potential benefits stretch well beyond collective defense requirements and well beyond Europe's borders. Even when NATO's military command structure is not used to run military operations, the fact that participants in ad hoc coalitions led by the United States or European Union members start out with a degree of interoperability will make such operations more effective.

In addition, the NATO role in Balkan operations created a framework in which all the NATO allies share responsibility for the security challenges there, even as they divide up tasks required to fulfill the missions. In the early 1990s, some Europeans were tempted to see the Balkan challenge as one that could and should be handled by Europeans, not the Americans. Throughout the 1990s, many Americans felt that the United States should not be required to play such a major military role in the Balkans, given that the Europeans were closer to and had a greater stake in the region. For some, this had meant that the European Union should take over responsibility for Balkan security, allowing the United States to move on to other military tasks. The George W. Bush administration came to office having made such an argument during the 2000 presidential election campaign. Once in office, however, wiser heads in the administration, notably Secretary of State Colin Powell, decided that a unilateral US withdrawal from the Balkans at that point could undermine prospects for continued development of liberal institutions and regional stability. Even though the main responsibilities for Bosnia were turned over to the European Union, NATO continued to provide a security presence in Kosovo pending a more settled situation there.

NATO nuclear weapons in a new strategic environment

From the very beginning, nuclear weapons questions played a central role in the transatlantic bargain. Ensuring that Germany would not become a nuclear weapons power was part and parcel of the transatlantic bargain. In the early 1950s, domestic financial considerations led the Eisenhower administration to make NATO's strategy heavily reliant on the threat of massive retaliation against the Soviet Union should it attack Western Europe. After Soviet advances in long-range missilery and nuclear weapons undermined massive retaliation, the allies shifted to a flexible response strategy based on deploying a spectrum of nuclear and non-nuclear forces to deter a Soviet-led Warsaw Pact attack. Soviet deployment of SS-20 missiles that could target all of NATO European territory provided the rationale for NATO's decision to deploy ground-launched cruise and Pershing II missiles that could hit Russian targets from bases in Western Europe.

When the Cold War ended, the allies faced many decisions concerning whether NATO strategy still required a nuclear component and what should be done about new threats from terrorists and rogue states for which traditional deterrence might not work. Beginning in 1989, the allies focused particularly on countering nuclear proliferation. They reaffirmed that nuclear weapons remained central to NATO's deterrence strategy. In the early glow of the post-Cold War era, the allies called them weapons of last resort, although they subsequently backed away from this description and put more emphasis on the constructive uncertainty that NATO's nuclear capabilities would raise in any potential adversary's mind.

Throughout the 1990s, the allies dramatically reduced NATO nuclear weapons beyond the cuts called for in arms control agreements with the Soviet Union. However, in terms of the transatlantic bargain, nuclear weapons policy was "the dog that didn't bark." The allies chose to move carefully and quietly on nuclear weapons policy, perhaps reflecting the concern that dramatic changes could begin to unravel the transatlantic bargain in which nuclear weapons had played such an important role.[69]

Changes to NATO nuclear strategy and forces

NATO's nuclear strategy and forces were key to the alliance's ability to deter Soviet aggression during the Cold War. In the new political and strategic environment of the 1990s, NATO had to take a long, hard look at the nuclear component of its strategy. Considering that nuclear weapons and strategy had been a prominent and controversial aspect of the transatlantic bargain from the beginning, nuclear issues assumed a relatively low-key role in the 1990s. However, without formal negotiations and with no treaty to bind the two sides, the United States took the initiative to reduce short-range nuclear weapons in its arsenal, many of which were deployed in Europe, and the Soviet Union responded in kind.

On May 3, 1990, President George H. W. Bush told a Washington press conference that the United States would not modernize the obsolescent LANCE tactical nuclear missile system or US nuclear artillery shells deployed in Europe. The president's move came in response to the dramatic changes in Europe and resulting opposition in the US Congress to costly programs that made little sense in terms of the new political and military situation there. He called for a NATO summit conference to agree, among other things, on "broad objectives for future negotiations between the United States and the Soviet Union on the current short-range nuclear missile forces in Europe, which should begin shortly after a CFE [Conventional Forces in Europe] treaty has been signed."

The London Declaration, issued by NATO leaders at their summit meeting in London on July 5–6, 1990, concluded that with eventual withdrawal of Soviet forces from their deployments in Eastern Europe, and implementation of an agreement reducing conventional armed forces in Europe, the alliance would be able "to adopt a new NATO strategy making nuclear forces truly weapons of last resort."[70] This shift in approach would alter NATO's long-standing flexible response doctrine in which the use of nuclear weapons could conceivably have been authorized early in a military conflict. The summit declaration did not, however, forgo the allied option of using nuclear weapons first in a conflict if necessary, and it left open the possibility that nuclear forces will be "kept up to date where necessary." The leaders nonetheless decided that NATO would no longer require all its existing inventory of short-range nuclear weapons consisting largely of nuclear artillery shells, bombs on dual-capable attack aircraft, and the LANCE missile system.

On September 27, 1991, following the failed attempt of hardline communists to seize control in Moscow, President Bush announced a set of wide-ranging changes in US nuclear policy and deployments. He decided to remove and destroy all US land-based nuclear missiles from Europe and withdraw all US sea-based tactical nuclear weapons while inviting the Soviet Union to take reciprocal actions. The president said that the United States should keep a nuclear capability for NATO, but at the same time he discontinued the program to develop the SRAM-II missile, intended for deployment on strategic bombers. A tactical version of this system, the SRAM-T, intended for deployment in Europe, was also discontinued. This left the US nuclear deployment in Europe limited to free-fall nuclear bombs on dual-capable ground attack aircraft.

The president's decisions were positively received throughout Europe and in the Soviet Union. On October 5, 1991, Soviet President Mikhail Gorbachev announced his reciprocal intent to eliminate short-range ground-launched nuclear weapons; he also proposed US–Soviet limitations on air-delivered tactical nuclear weapons. On October 17, 1991, the process of reducing such weapons was taken a step further when NATO ministers of defense, meeting as the Nuclear Planning Group, announced a 50 percent reduction in the inventory of some 1,400 free-fall nuclear bombs deployed primarily by the United States (the United Kingdom also deployed some free-fall nuclear bombs) in Europe.

Nuclear policy in the post-Cold War world

The new NATO strategic concept approved by NATO leaders on November 7, 1991 in Rome declared that "the fundamental purpose of the nuclear forces of the allies is political: to preserve peace and prevent coercion and any kind of war." The allies, at US urging, rejected a no-first-use posture. Some allied governments would have favored a pledge not to be the first to use nuclear weapons. But the United States and some other allies believed that future aggression might be deterred by a potential aggressor's lingering concern that it might face a nuclear counterattack.

The new concept placed principal reliance on the strategic nuclear capabilities of the United States, France, and the United Kingdom. But it also asserted that peacetime basing of nuclear forces on European territory (meaning the residual US freefall bombs) "provides an essential political and military link between the European and the North American members of the Alliance."[71] Even as the leaders met to approve the new concept, however, the Soviet Union itself was breaking apart, raising new issues that allied officials had not been able to take into account in drafting the new approach.

A main focus of NATO and US concern from 1992 forward was to ensure that the tactical and strategic nuclear forces of the former Soviet Union remained under reliable control. The United States and its allies sought to diminish the chances that the dissolution of the Soviet Union would result in nuclear proliferation, either from a number of former republics retaining nuclear weapons or from the transfer of nuclear weapons-making technology and know-how to other nations. By June 1992, all tactical nuclear weapons of the former Soviet Union had been consolidated within Russia, where many of the warheads were scheduled for elimination. By June 1996, Ukraine and Kazakhstan had returned all their strategic warheads to Russia. Belarus did so by the end of 1996.

Early in 1992, with regard to another issue (one much less serious than issues raised by the breakup of the Soviet Union), various French officials suggested that French nuclear forces might one day be placed in the service of a unified European political and defense entity. French President François Mitterrand raised the issue by asking, "Is it possible to develop a European [nuclear] doctrine? That question will rapidly become one of the major considerations in the building of a common European defense."[72] French officials and politicians subsequently answered Mitterrand's rhetorical question in a variety of ways, many of them supporting the idea of eventually dedicating French nuclear capabilities to the European Union. But France's European partners doubted French willingness to make any real sacrifice of national sovereignty on behalf of European integration, and French nuclear strategy remained based on French national deterrence requirements.

In other respects, NATO nuclear issues stayed largely out of sight during 1993 and 1994. In 1995, they began to resurface in the context of the debate on NATO enlargement and as a consequence of French President Jacques Chirac's renewed offer of French nuclear capabilities on behalf of the European Union's defense.[73]

When the NATO defense ministers met in Brussels on June 13, 1996, they reiterated the fundamental purposes of NATO nuclear policy outlined in the new strategic concept. The communiqué also observed that NATO's nuclear forces had been "substantially reduced," and in a direct message to Moscow, the ministers declared that NATO's nuclear forces "are no longer targeted against anyone." The ministers appeared to reinforce the point by noting that the readiness of NATO's dual-capable aircraft "has been recently adapted," presumably to a lower level of readiness for nuclear missions.[74]

The ministers concluded the very brief statement on nuclear policy by expressing satisfaction that NATO's nuclear posture would "for the foreseeable future, continue to meet the requirements of the Alliance." They then reaffirmed the strategic concept's conclusion that "nuclear forces continue to fulfill an indispensable and unique role in Alliance strategy" and emphasized that the remaining US free-fall nuclear bombs for delivery by dual-capable aircraft were still essential to link the interests of the European and North American members of NATO.

In the 1999 Strategic Concept, the allies essentially reiterated their view that "the fundamental purpose of the nuclear forces of the allies is political: to preserve peace and prevent coercion and any kind of war." They maintained that deploying nuclear weapons on the soil of several allied nations was an important demonstration of alliance solidarity. Finally, following another line taken consistently since the 1991 concept, the 1999 concept declared that sub-strategic forces based in Europe "provide an essential link with strategic nuclear forces, reinforcing the transatlantic link."[75]

European Security and Defense Policy (ESDP) in the 1990s

Post-Cold War adaptations in NATO's outreach and membership, relations with Russia, military missions and nuclear deployments responded to the new international realities that emerged in the early 1990s, importantly reshaping the ways and means of the transatlantic alliance. None of these developments, however, altered the basic relationship between the United States and Europe in the alliance. At the same time, however, the process of European integration was shifting some of the terms of the transatlantic bargain.

Transatlantic discomfort with that bargain was on display as the end of the Cold War neared, with members of the US Congress complaining loudly about inadequate defense burden-sharing and European officials grumbling about excessive European reliance on US leadership. As the American political scientist Michael Brenner reflected on transatlantic relations in the 1980s,

"Strategic dependency did not cause European governments to suspend their critical judgment in assessing the wisdom of U.S. policy."[76]

Questions about the sustainability of a relationship that depended so heavily on the United States had been around for a long time. In the mid-1980s this author observed, "The only way to maximize the benefits of alliance will be to encourage a process of gradual evolutionary change in US–European relations toward a new transatlantic bargain." That bargain "must bring greater European responsibility and leadership to the deal; it must ensure continued American involvement in European defense while at the same time constructing a new European 'pillar' inside, not outside, the broad framework of the Western alliance." I then raised questions that are still open two decades into the new millennium: "Will the European allies find the vision and courage to take on added responsibilities? Will the United States be wise enough to accept a more independent European partner?"[77]

In the 1990s, with the main threat to European security gone, that evolutionary process of change accelerated, suggesting that it might be leading toward the new bargain that I wrote about in 1985. That process of change, however, unfolded in fits and starts—not a surprise, given the magnitude of the task. And just as the potential for a new bargain held potential benefits for both US and European interests, it also contained risks that have weighed heavily on US officials. Success in this endeavor nonetheless remains critical to the future of transatlantic relations. Sean Kay, an American international relations expert, has judged that "Balancing the transatlantic relationship is critical to keeping the US–European security partnership vibrant in the future. Indeed, it is a founding task of NATO that remains unfulfilled."[78]

As with the rest of the story of the alliance, the emergence of a more coherent Europe in the area of foreign policy and defense is part of a continuum. In Chapter 4, I discussed the development of European-level foreign and defense policy coordination as one of the significant elements of change in the transatlantic bargain. During the 1990s, this process developed first as an attempt to build a European Security and Defense Identity in NATO and then as a major new initiative to develop an autonomous European Security and Defense Policy within the framework of the European Union (EU). Demonstrating the many challenges posed by the process, it reached a plateau one decade into the twenty-first century, and questions remained concerning whether or not the European allies would have the political will or material resources to take on the levels of responsibility in the alliance to create a "new bargain."

The European Security and Defense Identity (ESDI)

The first response of European governments to the end of the Cold War was to begin cutting defense expenditures to realize a "peace dividend." The United States also hoped for a peace dividend. But the higher priority for President George H. W. Bush and his top officials was ensuring continuity in US international leadership, including leadership of NATO. At a time when some were questioning whether NATO had any future, administration officials were suspicious of the moves within the European Union to give the Union a defense dimension.

American public opinion remained very favorable toward Europe and, in particular, toward EU members, reflecting deep European roots in American society, perceptions of shared values, and alliance relationships, among other factors. But the United States had always been schizophrenic about Europe's role in the world. Throughout the Cold War period, the United States supported the goal of enhanced European economic, political, and defense cooperation. However, the United States had not been forced to confront directly the prospect of European defense cooperation that could actually substitute for what in the past had been done in or through NATO and could supplant traditional US–European roles in the alliance. Even though the United States has always welcomed the potential for a stronger "European pillar" in the transatlantic alliance, it has been wary of approaches that would divide the alliance politically, take resources away from NATO military cooperation, and not yield additional military capabilities to produce more equitable burden-sharing. The US approach could accurately be called a "yes, but" policy, supporting the European effort but warning of the potential negative consequences.[79]

In the early 1990s, traditional support for European integration still dominated the rhetoric of US policy, but the tendency to look somewhat skeptically at US support for European integration became more influential in the absence of the strong geostrategic requirement to support the process during the Cold War. In a "yes, but" policy environment, the "but" therefore received more emphasis.

In 1990, Bush administration National Security Adviser Brent Scowcroft was known to be suspicious of French motivations, and his relationship with officials in Paris was strained. In addition, there may have been a justifiable concern that bringing defense issues within the purview of the European Commission would open the way for anti-American sentiment present in the Commission to influence the evolution of transatlantic defense ties. The administration was also concerned that too much European rhetoric and declarations about taking on responsibility for defense would provide ammunition for traditional US critics of the US commitment to NATO.

As the United States perceived the increased momentum toward European agreement on a defense identity early in 1991, a number of alarm bells were rung by US officials. The US ambassador to NATO, William Taft IV, in speeches delivered in February and March, supported a stronger European pillar in the alliance based on a revival of the WEU but cautioned that the European pillar should not relax the central transatlantic bond, should not duplicate current cooperation in NATO, and should not leave out countries that are not members of the European Community. (These themes foreshadowed the

Clinton administration's 1998 admonition that the European Union should avoid the dreaded "three Ds" of duplication, decoupling, and discrimination.)

The message was put more bluntly in a closely held memorandum sent to European governments by Undersecretary of State for International Security Affairs Reginald Bartholomew in February. According to published reports, the memorandum expressed concern that the United States might be "marginalized" if greater European cohesion in defense led to the creation of an internal caucus within NATO.[80]

Following further warnings issued by Deputy Assistant Secretary of State James Dobbins on visits to European capitals, and expressions of concern by Secretary of Defense Dick Cheney, the US approach to European defense integration appeared to have settled on five main points: the United States supported the development of common European foreign, security, and defense policies; NATO must remain the essential forum for consultations and venue for agreement on all policies bearing on the security and defense commitments of its members under the North Atlantic Treaty; NATO should retain its integrated military structure; the United States supports the European right to take common military action outside Europe to preserve its interests or ensure the respect of international law; and European members of NATO that do not belong to the European Union should not be excluded from European defense policy deliberations.[81]

Toward the end of 1991, the United States backed away from overt protests about a European defense identity, even though substantial ambiguity remained regarding what the United States really wanted from Europe. Tactically, US policymakers concentrated on diplomatic efforts to ensure that the definition of that identity emerging from the NATO summit in Rome and the EU summit in Maastricht, the Netherlands, would be consistent with US interests in NATO as the primary European security institution.

As discussed earlier, NATO's 1991 new Strategic Concept established three areas of particular emphasis for future NATO policies. First, the allies said that, as part of a "broader" approach to security, they would actively seek cooperation and dialogue among all European states and particularly with the former Warsaw Pact adversaries. Second, they declared that NATO's nuclear and non-nuclear military forces would be reduced and that remaining forces would be restructured to take into account the need for militaries that could handle crisis management tasks (such as the one that later developed in Bosnia in the 1990s, and the even more demanding ones in Afghanistan after the 9/11 attacks on the United States) as well as collective defense. Third, the allies agreed that the European members of NATO would assume greater responsibility for their own security. Specifically, the NATO leaders judged that "the development of a European security identity and defense role, reflected in the further strengthening of the European pillar within the alliance, will reinforce the integrity and effectiveness of the Atlantic Alliance." At that time, there was absolutely no concept for how this should come about, particularly when the allies were almost universally focused on how to cut defense expenditures in light of the reduced threats to produce a peace dividend for domestic spending programs.

And in an important footnote to the support for a stronger European pillar, the leaders reiterated that NATO is "the essential forum for consultation among its members and the venue for agreement on policies bearing on the security and defense commitments of Allies under the Washington [North Atlantic] Treaty."[82]

In December 1991, in the wake of NATO's new Strategic Concept, the members of the European Community signed the Maastricht Treaty, transforming the European Community into the European Union and setting the goal of establishing a monetary union and a common currency, the Euro. The treaty importantly included, as part of that Union, a commitment to "define and implement a common foreign and security policy" that would eventually include "framing of a common defence policy, which might in time lead to a common defence." The key articles that followed set the path for enhancement of the role that defense and security would play in the future development of European unification:

Article J.1

The Member States shall support the Union's external and security policy actively and unreservedly in a spirit of loyalty and mutual solidarity. They shall refrain from any action which is contrary to the interests of the Union or likely to impair its effectiveness as a cohesive force in international relations. The Council shall ensure that these principles are complied with.

Article J.2

1. Member States shall inform and consult one another within the Council on any matter of foreign and security policy of general interest in order to ensure that their combined influence is exerted as effectively as possible by means of concerted and convergent action.
2. Whenever it deems it necessary, the Council shall define a common position. Member States shall ensure that their national policies conform to the common positions.
3. Member States shall coordinate their actions in international organizations and at international conferences. They shall uphold the common positions in such fora. In international organizations and at international conferences where not all the Member States participate, those which do take part shall uphold the common positions.[83]

The treaty designated the WEU as the organization responsible for implementing defense aspects of the European Union's decisions on foreign and security policy. The WEU members subsequently agreed (at Petersberg, Germany, in 1992) that they would use WEU military forces for joint operations in humanitarian and rescue missions, peacekeeping, crisis management, and peace enforcement—the so-called Petersberg tasks.

The outcomes in Rome and Maastricht appeared to resolve the conceptual differences between the United States and France about how a European defense identity should relate to the transatlantic alliance, but they really just papered over them. This became patently clear in the first half of 1992, when the United States issued strong warnings to the German and French governments concerning their plans to create a Franco-German military corps of some 35,000 troops. American officials reportedly expressed reservations about the degree to which the corps would displace NATO as the focus of European defense efforts and undermine domestic support in the United States for a continuing US presence in Europe. National Security Adviser Brent Scowcroft was said to have sent a "strongly worded" letter to the German government suggesting that the Germans were not taking a firm enough position against what Scowcroft interpreted as French efforts to undermine cooperation in NATO.[84] The controversy reflected continuing differences between the US and French governments about the requirements for future European security organization.

US policy toward European defense has always been set within a broader US concept of its role in the world and the way in which allies relate to that world. During the George H. W. Bush administration, internal administration studies that suggested the United States should establish and sustain unquestioned superpower status raised questions in Europe as well as in the United States. Concern arose when a draft of the US Department of Defense "defense guidance" memorandum was leaked to the press early in 1992.[85] The document's vision of far-flung US military requirements in the post-Cold War era, apparently designed to ensure that the United States remained the only global superpower, provoked an outcry from a wide variety of observers, who saw the draft plan as seriously out of touch with contemporary political and economic realities.

The reaction among the European allies was that the Pentagon approach seemed to view Europe as a potential adversary rather than an ally. The implication was that the United States should undermine efforts at closer European unity to ensure that no European rival emerged to "balance" the US role in the world. White House and State Department officials characterized the draft as "a 'dumb report' that in no way or shape represents US policy,"[86] suggesting that, even within the Bush administration, there was no consensus on the US role in the world to serve as political guidance for the Department of Defense's strategy.

Following the strong reactions to the leaked draft, a new version was produced that reportedly eliminated most of what the European allies and other observers found objectionable.[87] Nonetheless, the controversial draft, by framing one clear perspective on the future US role in the world, made an important and provocative contribution to the ongoing discussion.

Because the American people clearly wanted the United States to focus its energies on economic and social problems at home, the 1992 election campaign produced very little light on the definition of the future US role in the world. President Bill Clinton's administration came to office against the backdrop of an election in which those voting sent a clear message calling for more attention to domestic issues, including the still-mounting federal deficit.

The Clinton administration hoped to dispel any residual impression that the United States did not want the Europeans to take on more burdens and responsibilities in the alliance. As noted earlier, at least one of Clinton's foreign policy advisers had even argued that withdrawal of US forces from Europe would signal US willingness to envision "Europeanization" of NATO. Less radical approaches prevailed, however, and in January 1994, at Clinton's first opportunity for major initiatives on NATO issues, the NATO Brussels Summit acknowledged the important role that an ESDI could play in the evolving European security system.

The January 1994 NATO summit meeting in Brussels approved the idea, initially proposed by the United States, of creating Combined Joint Task Force (CJTF) headquarters as part of NATO's military command structure. The CJTF initiative, as discussed in Chapter 8, was designed to give NATO's command structure additional flexibility to accomplish a variety of objectives, including facilitating the dual use of NATO forces and command structures for alliance operations and/or those run by the WEU. The purpose was to encourage European nations to undertake missions with forces that are "separable but not separate" from NATO in the context of an emerging ESDI.

The Brussels Summit yielded multiple references in the allied declaration to the importance of European-level cooperation and the constructive role played by the WEU. (The declaration included no fewer than eight references to the WEU, seven references each to the ESDI and European Union, and two each to the Maastricht Treaty on European Union and the Union's Common Foreign and Security Policy goal.)

NATO's work to implement the January 1994 agreements in principle moved ahead slowly but remained hampered by different US and French visions of the future. Many French analysts and officials had interpreted the summit outcome as a US vote for Europeanization of the alliance. In fact, the administration had not intended to go so far and wanted only to open the way toward a stronger European role in the alliance. The perceptual split was suggested by the way each looked at CJTF. The French and some other Europeans saw CJTF primarily as a way for the European allies to engage in more autonomous military actions. The United States saw this as one of the functions of CJTF but regarded the concept's first role as making it possible for NATO itself to operate in more flexible formations and combinations.

In the second half of 1995, the British government began actively searching for ways to create an ESDI within the framework of the alliance and in a fashion that would facilitate France's return to full military integration. Early in 1996, the French and British governments proposed what became known as the "Deputies proposal."[88] The British and French suggested that the Deputy SACEUR, traditionally a senior European officer, and other European officers in the NATO command structure wear WEU command hats as well as their NATO and national command hats. This multiple-hatting procedure would, without duplication of resources and personnel, permit the WEU countries to use the NATO command structure to organize and command a military operation under largely European auspices.

The Deputies proposal reportedly raised serious issues for the US Joint Chiefs of Staff and SACEUR General George Joulwan. Senior US military commanders were concerned that the WEU command arrangements might weaken the European commitment to the NATO structure as well as lessen the American commitment to 57 NATO. However, other US officials, including senior officials at the White House, believed that a continued active US role in the alliance depended on being able to demonstrate to Congress and to the American public that the European allies were willing and able to take on greater responsibility for military missions both inside Europe and beyond.[89] The re-involvement of France in the alliance, with its willingness and ability to participate in military interventions beyond national borders, was seen as the key to the construction of a meaningful and coordinated European contribution to post-Cold War security concerns. The spring 1996 session of NATO ministers, scheduled to be held in Berlin, Germany, emerged as the opportunity to tie the loose ends together. In a discussion prior to that session with a key administration diplomat responsible for NATO policy, I asked whether he would support the Deputies proposal. His answer was, "I'll support it as soon as General Joulwan does," suggesting the depth of resistance from the SACEUR and the Joint Chiefs of Staff more generally. Just days prior to the Berlin meeting, US uniformed military leaders were still resisting the transformation of the Deputy SACEUR position. Senior advisers to the president realized that the time had come for a deal, and the White House overruled the Joint Chiefs—a step not easily taken by a president whose credentials with the military were so suspect.[90] As a consequence, the 1994 summit goals were transformed at Berlin into a plan to build a European defense pillar inside the NATO alliance despite objections from the Joint Chiefs.

In Berlin, NATO foreign ministers agreed to move ahead with implementation of the CJTF concept. In addition, they agreed that an ESDI would be created within the alliance by making NATO "assets and capabilities" available for future military operations commanded by the WEU. Such decisions would be made by consensus on a case-by-case basis. To facilitate such operations, European officers in the NATO structure would, when appropriate, shift from their NATO responsibilities to WEU command positions.

The allies determined that adaptation of the alliance should be guided by three fundamental objectives: to ensure the alliance's military effectiveness and ability to perform its traditional mission of collective defense while undertaking new military roles, to preserve the transatlantic link by strength-ening NATO as a forum for political consultation and military cooperation, and to support development of an ESDI by creating the possibility for NATO supported task forces to perform missions under the direction of the WEU nations.

The Berlin ministerial marked a watershed in the development of US and NATO policy toward creation of a more coherent European role in the alliance. The Clinton administration had clearly gone on the record as supporting a stronger European pillar but, when it came to making significant structural changes in NATO to help bring the concept to fruition, there was profound resistance in the US policy community.

Even after Berlin, the question was what military operations the European allies could actually take on within the framework of the new arrangements. During the intervening years, it was demonstrated that they did not have the combination of military resources and political will to take on operations such as the Implementation Force or Stabilization Force in Bosnia, and the United States provided most of the key resources for the air war against Serbia over Kosovo. In 1997, when impending chaos in Albania threatened to destabilize south-eastern Europe, the Europeans were not even able to agree on organ-izing an intervention under the WEU, but rather sent in an ad hoc coalition force under Italian command. All these experiences led observers to bemoan the fact that Europe did not have the military capacity required to maintain stability on the borders of EU/ WEU member states, to say nothing of the capacity to project significant force beyond the Balkans. As Michael Brenner has written:

> The cumulative record of EU failure and NATO's recovery (in the Balkans) sharpened the issue of whether an ESDI built within NATO on the CJTF principle was satisfactory. For the European allies, the record could be read two ways: as making a compelling case for them to take more drastic measures to augment their military resources and to cement their union, or as providing telling evidence that the quest for an autonomous ESDI was futile. Few drew the first conclusion.[91]

In June 1997, the members of the European Union, in the process of updating and strengthening the Maastricht Treaty, approved the Treaty of Amsterdam. In the area of common defense policy, the Treaty of Amsterdam included a reference to the Petersberg tasks and authorized the adoption of EU common strategies. It also created the position of High Representative for the Common Foreign and Security Policy, one that was not filled until September 1999, when former NATO Secretary General Javier Solana took on the job. Solana had performed well as NATO Secretary General and had won admira-tion in Washington—no small accomplishment for a Spanish socialist who had opposed his country's membership in NATO in the early 1980s. Solana's selection clearly was intended to reassure the United States. In retrospect, the question may be whether Solana's new job was more important than the one he gave up. In fact, it probably was. It would be important for the European Union to move into NATO's exclusive reserve in a way that did not create too much choppy water across the Atlantic, and Solana had a reputation not only for hard work but also for his diplomatic skills—skills that he surely would need in his new job.

An "autonomous" European Security and Defense Policy

In the autumn of 1998, the shape of the discussion on European defense was changed profoundly by British Prime Minister Tony Blair's decision to make a major push for an EU role in defense. Blair first tried out his ideas at an EU summit in Pörtschach, Austria, in October 1998 and then reaffirmed his approach on November 3 in a major address to the North Atlantic Assembly's annual session[92] in Edinburgh, Scotland. Blair bemoaned the fact that Europe's ability for autonomous military action was so limited and called for major institutional and resource innovations to make Europe a more equal partner in the transatlantic alliance. Blair's initiative may also have betrayed some uncertainty concerning NATO's future.[93]

Traditionally, the United Kingdom had been the most reliable, predictable partner of the United States when it came to dealing with defense issues. The British had shared US skepticism regarding initiatives that might create splits between the United States and Europe in the alliance, particularly those with roots in French Neo-Gaullist philosophy. The fact that Blair was moving out in front on this issue produced mixed reactions in the United States.

On the one hand, the United States believed that it still could trust the United Kingdom not to do anything that would hurt the alliance, and Blair claimed that his goal was to strengthen NATO by improving Europe's ability to share security burdens in the twenty-first century. On the other hand, Blair's initiative sounded "too French" to skeptics, and even those who were hopeful were concerned about the political setting for Blair's initiative. It was said that Blair wanted to demonstrate commitment to Europe at a time when the United Kingdom was not going to join in the inauguration of the Euro, the European Union's common currency. Questions about the seriousness of the initiative were also raised by the fact that the proposal seemed to come out of nowhere. In discussions with British foreign office official minutes after the Edinburgh speech was delivered, the author was told that the initiative until then consisted of the two speeches and that on their return to London, they would begin putting meat on the bones of the approach.

At the Edinburgh meeting, Blair and British officials got a foretaste of one of the key aspects of American reactions to the initiative. A report released at the meeting by US Senator William V. Roth Jr. said:

The United States should give every possible help and encouragement to the continuing consolidation of European defense efforts. But the United States must not be held accountable for the inability of European states to develop a more coherent European role in the Alliance. It is the responsibility of the European Allies to develop the European Security and Defense Capabilities to give real meaning to a European Security and Defense Identity.[94]

Any doubts about the serious nature of the Blair initiative were removed when Blair met with President Jacques Chirac at Saint-Malo early in December 1998. The declaration, named for this French resort town, envisioned the creation of a Common European Security and Defense Policy (CESDP) with the means and mechanisms to permit the EU nations to act "autonomously" should NATO decide not to act in some future scenario requiring military action. The French delegation reportedly had lined up support from German Chancellor Gerhard Schroeder prior to the meeting, giving the declaration even more weight. The statement included the following key elements:

1. The European Union needs to be in a position to play its full role on the international stage.
2. On the basis of intergovernmental decisions, the Union must have the capacity for autonomous action, backed up by credible military forces, the means to decide to use them and a readiness to do so, in order to respond to international crises.
3. The NATO and WEU collective defense commitments of the EU members must be maintained, obligations to NATO honored, and the various positions of European states in relation to NATO and otherwise must be respected.
4. The Union must be given appropriate structures and a capacity for analysis of situations, sources of intelligence and a capability for relevant strategic planning, without unnecessary duplication.
5. Europe needs strengthened armed forces that can react rapidly to the new risks, and which are supported by a strong and competitive European defense industry and technology.[95]

US administration officials said the Blair initiative was given the benefit of the doubt.[96] The administration thought that British motivations were solid, even if they remained concerned about those of the French. When the Saint-Malo statement emerged, however, administration officials felt that the British had not been 100 percent transparent about the likely outcome. The administration's formal reaction took the traditional form of the "yes, but" approach characterized earlier. Secretary of State Madeleine Albright, presenting themes originally developed as an opinion piece for publication by National Security Adviser Sandy Berger, formally declared the administration's support but cautioned the Europeans against "the three Ds": duplication, decoupling, and discrimination. Secretary Albright emphasized these concerns at the December 1998 ministerial meetings in Brussels, just days after the Saint-Malo meeting.

According to Albright, the allies should not duplicate what was already being done effectively in NATO. This would be a waste of defense resources at a time when defense spending in most European nations was in decline. More fundamentally, the new European initiative should not in any way "decouple" or "delink" the United States from Europe in the alliance or the European defense efforts from those coordinated through NATO. This could result from a lack of candor and transparency that the United States feared might be an intended or unintended consequence of the new European approach. A process that would encourage European allies to "gang up" on the United States or even its perception on the US side of the Atlantic could surely spell the end of the alliance. Finally, Albright's article insisted there be no discrimination against NATO allies who were not members of the European Union. This point applied in particular to Turkey but also to European allies Norway, Iceland, the Czech Republic, Hungary, and Poland, as well as Canada and the United States on the North American side of the alliance.

The "three Ds" accurately summarized the administration's main concerns and hearkened back to the George H. W. Bush administration's earlier warnings in reaction to the Franco-German development of the Euro-corps. Despite these footnotes to US support for the initiative, it moved ahead in parallel with NATO's conduct of the air campaign over Kosovo intended to wrest the province from Serbian control and allow Kosovo refugees to return to their homes in peace. The campaign, which threatened to cast a dark shadow over NATO's fiftieth-anniversary summit meeting in Washington, also added impetus to the Blair approach. When the numbers were toted up at the end of the air campaign, the United States had conducted nearly 80 percent of the sorties.

From the US perspective, the fact that the allies for the most part were not able to contribute to such a high-tech, low-casualty campaign suggested the wisdom of the Defense Capabilities Initiative (DCI). The DCI, adopted at the Washington Summit, was designed to stimulate European defense efforts to help them catch up with the US Revolution in Military Affairs. From the European perspective, the Kosovo experience clearly demonstrated Europe's (undesirable and growing) military dependence on the United States and the need to get together to do something about it. Even if Washington saw a more assertive European role as a challenge to American leadership, more capable European military establishments could relieve the United States of some of its international security burdens, improving the burden-sharing equation and thereby strengthening, not weakening, transatlantic ties.

The Washington Summit communiqué and the strategic concept for NATO agreed upon at the meeting reflected transatlantic agreement that

European defense capabilities needed a serious shot in the arm, and that it had to be done in ways consistent with the US "three Ds." However, although the Saint-Malo accord was endorsed by all EU members at meetings in Cologne (June 1999) and Helsinki (December 1999), over the course of the year there were growing rumbles and signs of dissatisfaction on the American side. According to one former administration official, as the initiative took shape, British officials came to Washington regularly prior to each major stage of negotiations with France and the other EU members to reassure US officials that they agreed completely with American perspectives. However, the Saint-Malo outcome and its subsequent implementation at Cologne and Helsinki gave much more emphasis to "autonomy" than the administration would have liked. This official noted that British reassurances throughout this period were often followed by outcomes that reflected compromises with French positions that were not entirely to the liking of administration officials, raising concerns about the eventual impact of a "European caucus" on transatlantic cooperation.

On the European side, NATO and government officials chafed under the impression left by the "three Ds" that the US superpower was putting too much emphasis on the negative. European experts and officials openly cautioned US State and Defense officials at transatlantic discussions of defense issues not to allow this negative approach to capture US policy. Former British Minister of Defense George Robertson, after succeeding Javier Solana as NATO Secretary General, offered a more positive approach. Addressing the forty-fifth annual session of the NATO Parliamentary Assembly, Robertson said, "For my part, I will ensure that ESDI is based on three key principles, the three I's: *improvement* in European defense capabilities; *inclusiveness* and transparency for all Allies, and the *indivisibility* of transatlantic security, based on shared values" (emphasis added). Moving from "Ds" to "Is," Robertson tried to put a positive spin on the American concerns that would make the same points but in a fashion less offensive to the Europeans.

By the end of 1999, the European Union had tied a major package together based on the guidelines of the Saint-Malo statement. The EU members agreed that Javier Solana, in addition to serving as the Union's High Representative for the Common Foreign and Security Policy, would become WEU Secretary General to help pave the way for implementation of the decision confirmed at Cologne to merge the WEU within the European Union. In Helsinki, the EU members declared their determination "to develop an autonomous capacity to take decisions and, where NATO as a whole is not engaged, to launch and conduct EU-led military operations in response to international crises." They noted that the process "will avoid unnecessary duplication and does not imply the creation of a European army." The EU members continued to reiterate that collective defense remained a NATO responsibility and would not be challenged by the new EU arrangements. They agreed on a series of substantial steps, called the "Helsinki Headline

Goals," required to implement their political commitment, including the following:

1. To establish by 2003 a corps-size intervention force of up to 60,000 persons from EU member-state armed forces capable of deploying within sixty days and being sustained for at least one year;
2. to create new political and military bodies to allow the European Council to provide political guidance and strategic direction to joint military operations;
3. to develop modalities for full consultation, cooperation, and transparency between the European Union and NATO, taking into account the "needs" of all EU member states (particularly the fact that four EU members— Austria, Ireland, Finland, and Sweden—are not NATO members);
4. to make "appropriate" arrangements to allow non-EU European NATO members and others to contribute to EU military crisis management;
5. to establish a non-military crisis management mechanism to improve coordination of EU and member-state political, economic, and other non-military instruments in ways that might mitigate the need to resort to the use of force or make military actions more effective when they become necessary.

The EU members moved quickly to implement the goals. By March 2000, the Political and Security Committee (PSC, also known by the French acronym COPS), the European Union Military Committee, and the EU Military Staff started functioning as interim organizations. The PSC was to be the political decision-making body for CESDP, preparing decisions for EU Council consideration on foreign policy and crisis situations and implementing decisions of the EU members. The European Union Military Committee, like the NATO Military Committee, was designed to provide military advice and recommendations to the PSC and to implement the military aspects of EU decisions. The EU Military Staff was to support the work of the Military Committee.

The most immediate task was to prepare a catalog of forces that would be made available to actions authorized under the CESDP. This work resulted in the European Union Capabilities Commitment Conference, which convened November 20–21, 2000. The conference produced an impressive inventory of resources, including about 100,000 soldiers, 400 combat aircraft, and 100 ships, including two aircraft carriers. In addition, non-EU NATO members and EU associate partners pledged capabilities that could join in future EU operations. One well-informed commentator has emphasized that there were "certain realities" about the pledging operations that were missed by some observers. According to former high-level British defense official Michael Quinlan:

> First, there was no suggestion that the forces to be contributed by countries towards the Goals would be entirely new and additional ones created for that purpose; they would be existing ones though ... much improvement or redesign might be required. Second, there was no suggestion that they would be separate

from forces declared to NATO. European countries in the integrated military structure already customarily declared all that they could to NATO; there was no separate reservoir of similar forces available beyond those. Nothing in the CESDP concept rested on hypotheses of extensive autonomous EU action at a time when NATO itself needed to employ forces, and alternative earmarking did not therefore entail illegitimate or confusing double-count (any more than did the long-familiar fact that almost all Alliance members had sometimes used their NATO-declared forces for national or U.N. purposes). Third, the capability was not intended as a European Army—a description specifically rejected in EU utterances—or even a European Rapid Reaction force in the customary usage of that term in NATO.[97]

The main issue during 2000, however, was how these new EU institutions would relate to their NATO counterparts. The problem grew out of the strong desire of some in the European Union, particularly in French diplomatic and political circles, for an "autonomous" EU approach, less vulnerable to US influence. This conflicted with the hope in NATO that the European Union's role in defense would be integrated as fully as possible within the overall transatlantic alliance.

An evolving NATO–EU relationship

Until the beginning of the new millennium, the relationship between NATO and the European Union had been informal and lacking much substance. Even though these two organizations constituted the core of intra-European and Euro-Atlantic relations, they existed largely as separate, disconnected organizations with bureaucracies and political cultures, particularly on the EU side, which were interested primarily in keeping a safe distance from one another. Because the United States had in so many ways been the dominant influence in NATO, EU national and international officials historically feared that too close a relationship with the alliance would bring too much US influence into European councils. In the 1990s, former US Ambassador to NATO Robert Hunter frequently lamented the lack of any working communication and coordination channels between NATO and the European Union. During Hunter's years at NATO in the mid-1990s, NATO Secretary General Javier Solana met informally with the president of the European Commission, the European Union's top official. And the NATO Berlin decisions of 1996, intended to give life to NATO's support for development of an ESDI, led to closer coordination between NATO officials and those from the WEU. But a huge gap remained between NATO and the European Union.

With the proclaimed EU goal of establishing an "autonomous" CESDP, a more formal NATO–EU relationship clearly was required. The process was slow in developing, partly because of the residual concern among a few EU governments, particularly the one in Paris, that the construction of CESDP not be overly influenced by the United States. For the first half of 2000, this view led the French government to argue that CESDP institutions should be developed prior to serious discussions of how the European Union's decision-making process would relate to NATO. However, according to NATO Secretary General Lord Robertson, by September 2000 the process of linking NATO and EU institutions was well under way and moving in positive directions. Speaking to the SACLANT Symposium in Reykjavik, Iceland, on September 6, 2000, Robertson noted that:

> already, NATO and the EU are working together closely—meeting together to decide on how to share classified information and drawing on NATO's experi-ence to help the EU flesh out the requirements of its headline goal. ... Put simply, NATO-friendly European defence is finally taking shape—and it is taking the right shape.[98]

In September 2000, NATO's North Atlantic Council (NAC) and the European Union's "Interim" Political and Security Committee (PSC) began meeting to work out details of the arrangement and to establish a pattern and format for cooperation. The first joint NAC/PSC meeting took place on September 19, 2000, followed by a second meeting on November 9, 2000. Meanwhile, four EU–NATO working groups began to work on their assigned issues: security of sensitive information; Berlin-plus (ESDI initiatives designed to facilitate more coherent European contributions within the NATO frame-work); military capabilities; and permanent EU–NATO institutional arrange-ments. In addition, Robertson and his predecessor, Javier Solana, actively collaborated to ensure that the NATO–EU liaison worked effectively.

In the Clinton administration's last major initiative regarding EU–NATO relations, Secretary of Defense William Cohen on October 10, 2000, delivered informal but important remarks to a meeting of NATO defense ministers in Birmingham, United Kingdom.[99] Cohen strongly endorsed the development of CESDP, saying that "we agree with this goal—not grudgingly, not with resig-nation, but with wholehearted conviction." At the same time, Cohen dismissed the logic sometimes used to provide a rationale for CESDP, saying, "The notion that Europe must begin to prepare for an eventual American withdrawal from Europe has no foundation in fact or in policy."

In addition, Secretary Cohen suggested that it was hard to imagine a future case in which the United States and the European Union would diverge dra-matically on whether a crisis situation warranted a joint response. According to Secretary Cohen:

> It is overwhelmingly likely that in any situation where any ally's involvement on a significant scale is justified, and where there is a consensus in Europe to undertake a military operation, the United States would be part of the operation. In addition, it is difficult to imagine a situation in which the United States was prepared to participate, but our European Allies would prefer to act alone.

With regard to the question of whether the European Union should establish its own military planning capacity, Cohen argued for a NATO–EU approach that would be "unitary, coherent, and collaborative." He suggested that NATO and the European Union should create a "European Security and Defense Planning System" that would involve all NATO and EU countries. In Cohen's judgment, "It would be highly ineffective, seriously wasteful of resources, and contradictory to the basic principles of close NATO–EU cooperation that we hope to establish if NATO and the EU were to proceed along the path of relying on autonomous force planning structures." Cohen concluded:

> The NATO–EU relationship, Ministerial Guidance, and implementation of DCI [an initiative agreed to at the NATO Washington summit in 1999 designed to improve allied defense capabilities] are not separate, parallel processes that we can allow to proceed in isolation from one another. Rather, they are all vital strands in the powerful and enduring fabric of Euro-Atlantic security.

Secretary Cohen's remarks made it clear how important it would be to ensure that NATO and EU military planning move forward hand in hand in whatever institutional construct proved acceptable to all parties. In the best case, NATO and EU military planners would in fact be largely the same people working toward the same ends, whether they wore NATO or EU hats. It was also hoped that the dynamics created by the European Union's defense objectives might help reinvigorate and give new sense of direction to the NATO planning process.

The fact that the Cohen proposal for resolution of the planning issue was not received enthusiastically by the European Union (particularly by the French) led the secretary of defense, at his last NATO meeting in December 2000, to put more emphasis on the "but" side of the "yes, but" equation. Cohen warned that CESDP could, if handled incorrectly, turn NATO into a "relic of the past."[100]

At the end of the year, the NATO–EU negotiations came close to agreement on how to work together in the future. During the December 14–15 meeting of the NAC, the NATO allies were able to note that progress had been made in the four working groups. They welcomed the European Union's agreement at its summit in Nice, France, earlier in December that there should be a "regular pattern" of meetings at all levels between the European Union and NATO. According to the NAC communiqué, "Meetings between the North Atlantic Council and the Political and Security Committee outside times of crisis should be held not less than three times, Ministerial meetings once, per EU Presidency (in other words, every six months); either organization may request additional meetings as necessary."[101]

The communiqué also noted favorably the European Union's agreement that consultation would be intensified in times of crisis. In addition, the allies welcomed the Nice provisions for inviting the NATO Secretary General, the chairman of the Military Committee, and the Deputy SACEUR to EU meetings. NATO reciprocated by agreeing to invite the EU presidency and Secretary

General/high representative to NATO meetings and providing that the chairman of the European Union Military Committee or his representative would be invited to meetings of the NATO military committee.

The allies also stated their intention to make arrangements for:

> assured EU access to NATO planning capabilities able to contribute to military planning for EU-led operations; the presumption of availability to the EU of pre-identified NATO capabilities and common assets for use in EU-led operations; the identification of a range of European command options for EU-led operations, further developing the role of Deputy SACEUR in order for him to assume fully and effectively his European responsibilities; and the further adaptation of the Alliance's defence planning system, taking account of relevant activities in and proposals from the European Union. Allies will be consulted on the EU's proposed use of assets and capabilities, prior to the decision to release these assets and capabilities, and kept informed during the operation.[102]

However, at the end of the day, the government of Turkey blocked consensus to permit the European Union "assured access" to NATO planning and therefore prevented final agreement on the whole NATO–EU package. Ankara had wanted the European Union to grant the Turkish government veto power over the Union's deployment of a military force under circumstances that could affect Turkey's security. That, of course, was a nonstarter with the European Union.

When the George W. Bush administration came to office in 2001, most details of the NATO–EU arrangement had been agreed to, but it was left to the new administration in Washington to help find a way around the EU–Turkish impasse and perhaps also to review aspects of the NATO–EU agreement that it found of concern.

The 1990s as prelude

As the transatlantic alliance moved into the new millennium, the members of NATO and the European Union had faced major changes in the international and European systems and had adjusted their political/military relationships to the new realities. Several processes were put in motion:

- former Warsaw Pact states and Soviet republics began solidifying their independence establishing democratic political systems and western-style market economies while building their case for inclusion in NATO and the European Union;
- NATO specified terms under which new members would be accepted, and created new partnership structures;
- the allies agreed on new Strategic Concepts in 1991 and 1999 that reflected their opinion that the alliance still served their interests, even in the absence of a Soviet threat;

Box 6.1	**Some key developments (November 1989–April 1999)**

Nov 1989   Berlin Wall fell
July 1990   NATO leaders approved London Declaration on a Transformed North Atlantic Alliance
Oct 1990   East and West Germany reunified
July 1991   Warsaw Pact dissolved
Nov 1991   NATO Rome summit approved 1991 Strategic Concept
Dec 1991   Soviet Union dissolved
Feb 1992   Maastricht Treaty signed, creating European Union
March 1992   Bosnian war began
Jan 1993   Bill Clinton entered office as President of the United States
Jan 1994   Partnership for Peace program launched and Combined Joint Task Force approved at NATO Brussels summit
Dec 1994   Conference on Security and Cooperation in Europe became Organization for Security and Cooperation in Europe
Aug 1995   NATO bombing campaign, Operation Deliberate Force, commenced in Bosnia
Sep 1995   NATO allies released "Study on NATO Enlargement" supporting enlargement
Dec 1995   Peace accord signed in Paris ended the Bosnian war
May 1997   Euro-Atlantic Partnership Council established NATO/Russia Founding Act on Mutual Relations, Cooperation and Security signed
July 1997   NATO Madrid summit invited Czech Republic, Hungary, and Poland to begin accession talks
Dec 1998   France and UK signed Saint-Malo accord, envisioning Common European Security and Defense Policy
March 1999   NATO initiated air campaign against Serbian targets in Serbia and Kosovo after breakdown of proposed peace plan
April 1999   NATO Washington Summit issued 1999 Strategic Concept, welcomed Czech Republic, Hungary, and Poland to alliance

- major reductions in nuclear and non-nuclear forces began;
- the United States and its allies started to take their "peace dividend" in reduced military spending;
- NATO took on the challenge of enforcing peace in the Balkans and protecting Kosovo from Serbia;

- Russia swerved toward political and economic chaos and then back toward a directed economy and more authoritarian political control; and.
- European Union members began laying the foundation for construction of an ambitious foreign and defense component of the process of European integration.

These and other developments in the 1990s could not have prepared the allies for the challenges to their security as well as to the political cohesion of the alliance that would burst on the scene early in the next decade.

Questions for discussion

1. Were the NATO allies wise in not only preserving NATO after the Soviet threat had disappeared but in also placing it at the center of the European security system?
2. What do events in the 1990s say about the importance of US leadership to NATO's success—at war, and in diplomacy?
3. What did the conflicts in Bosnia and Kosovo suggest about the respective roles and capabilities of NATO and the European Union in the post-Cold War period?
4. Could NATO and the European Union have done more to accommodate Russian interests in the 1990s? If so, what, and how might it have changed Russian behavior in subsequent years?

Notes

1 Elizabeth Pond, *The Rebirth of Europe* (Washington, D.C.: Brookings Institution Press, 1999), 56, 57.
2 Speech by Gyula Horn, Hungarian foreign minister, at the meeting of the Hungarian Society of Political Sciences, Budapest, February 20, 1990.
3 For a variety of perspectives on the process by which Germany's was reunified, particularly the role of the United States, see Stephen F. Szabo, *The Diplomacy of German Unification* (New York: St. Martin's Press, 1992); Philip Zelikow and Condoleezza Rice, *Germany Unified and Europe Transformed: A Study in Statecraft* (Cambridge, Mass.: Harvard University Press, 1995); James A. Baker, *The Politics of Diplomacy: Revolution, War and Peace, 1989–1992* (New York: G. P. Putnam's Sons, 1995); George Bush and Brent Scowcroft, *A World Transformed* (New York: Knopf, 1998); Hans-Dietrich Genscher, *Rebuilding a House Divided* (New York: Broadway Books, 1998); and Alexander Moens, "American Diplomacy and German Unification," *Survival* 33 (November–December 1991): 531–45.
4 Woerner, a German Christian Democrat and former West German defense minister, played an important creative role in the process of adapting NATO to the new international circumstances.

5 North Atlantic Council, *London Declaration on a Transformed North Atlantic Alliance*, July 6, 1990.

6 For an excellent, thoroughly documented account of NATO's transformation in the 1990s, see David S. Yost, *NATO Transformed: The Alliance's New Roles in International Security* (Washington, D.C.: United States Institute of Peace Press, 1998).

7 Wade Boese, "Dispute over Russian Withdrawals from Georgia, Moldova Stall CFE Treaty," *Arms Control Today*, September 2004.

8 David Yost has documented the fact that France was the only NATO ally to have serious reservations about the NACC. According to Yost, "The French had two preoccupations in this regard: resisting the tendency to give more substantial content to NACC activities, which might increasingly compete with those of the CSCE and maintaining coherence with the Alliance participation policy they had pursued since 1966." It is also evident that France's Socialist President François Mitterrand did not want to strengthen NATO's position in post-Cold War Europe at a time when other options might better suit French preferences. See Yost, *NATO Transformed*, 95–6.

9 In the fall of 1990, on one of my lectures at the NATO College in Rome, I served on a panel with a West European security expert and a Polish professor to discuss the future of NATO. The Polish panelist urged that the NATO countries take Polish pleas seriously, while the West European judged that the question of membership in NATO was many years away from serious consideration. Sympathetic to the Polish case, the best I could do was to suggest that Poland be patient and that the logic of their case would bring them through.

10 James M. Goldgeier, *Not Whether but When: The U.S. Decision to Enlarge NATO* (Washington, D.C.: Brookings Institution Press, 1999). Goldgeier's account of the enlargement decision-making process in the Clinton administration is an insightful look at the US decision-making process that led to the entry of the Czech Republic, Hungary, and Poland into the alliance.

11 Jenonne Walker, "U.S., Soviet Troops: Pull Them All Out," *The New York Times*, March 18, 1990, E19.

12 Goldgeier, *Not Whether but When*, 23–4. Goldgeier reports that at the first meeting of the interagency working group formed to prepare for Clinton's first NATO summit in January 1994, "Walker announced that there were two people in the White House who thought NATO expansion was a good idea—Bill Clinton and Tony Lake."

13 Goldgeier, *Not Whether but When*, 20.

14 Late in 1992, within constraints imposed by the Congressional Research Service mandate to produce "objective and non-partisan" analyses, I anticipated the issue facing the new administration:

The goals of supporting democracy, the development of free market economies, and the observance of human rights probably will be served best by an inclusive rather than an exclusive approach to participation in components of a new European security system. In spite of the complications involved, inclusion may have to be the rule; exclusion the exception. How can the existing members of Western institutions, who have throughout the Cold War touted the Western system, now deny participation in the system to countries that choose democracy, attempt to convert to free market economic systems, respect human rights, and pursue peaceful relations with their neighbors? This suggests the need for creative and flexible attitudes toward countries making credible efforts to meet the criteria for membership. (Stanley R. Sloan, "The Future of U.S.–European Security Cooperation," Congressional Research Service Report for Congress 92–907, Washington, D.C., December 4, 1992, 2–3.)

15 In a statement to the North Atlantic Assembly Presidential Task Force on America and Europe, on January 21, 1993, I carried the point to its logical conclusion, arguing at that early date for an approach that eventually became US policy:

Full membership in specific institutions, such as NATO, should be based on the desire and demonstrated ability of countries to adopt the norms and obligations of membership. Not all former members of the Warsaw Pact may be able to meet such standards in the near future. But can the allies in good conscience deny participation in their security system to countries that have overthrown communist dictatorships and committed themselves to a democratic future?

This suggests, in practical terms, that Poland, Hungary, and the Czech Republic deserve serious consideration for NATO membership in the near future. Clearly, taking such a step would require that the NATO countries reassure Russia and other non-NATO European states that growing membership in the alliance will help create conditions of stability and peace that will support their own attempts to become constructive participants in the international community. (Stanley R. Sloan, "Trends and Transitions in U.S.–European Security Cooperation," statement before the North Atlantic Assembly Presidential Task Force on America and Europe, Washington, D.C., January 21, 1993.)

16 Gebhard Schweigler, "A Wider Atlantic?," *Foreign Policy*, September–October 2001, 88.
17 The invitation to me and others suggested that the session was designed as an off-the-record opportunity to think and talk prospectively about transatlantic security issues.
18 Ronald D. Asmus, Richard L. Kugler, and F. Stephen Larrabee, "Building a New NATO," *Foreign Affairs*, September/October 1993, 28–40.
19 Kruzel, a central and creative participant in NATO policy formulation in the early Clinton years, Col. Nelson Drew, the main architect of the Combined Joint Task Force concept, and respected career diplomat Robert Frasure, who played a key role in the process leading to the peace accord in Bosnia, all lost their lives when the vehicle in which they were riding plunged off a dirt road outside Sarajevo. Just days before the tragic accident, my wife and I were guests along with Kruzel and his wife at an informal dinner in Washington hosted by then-Danish Minister of Defense Hans Haekerrup. In the course of our conversation over dinner, I asked Joe if he did not sometimes regret the price he had to pay in lost time with his

family given his demanding job. He acknowledged that this cost was the most difficult part of the job. In the end, he and his family paid a much larger price than either of us could have contemplated that enjoyable evening.

20 By the end of 1996, after Switzerland had joined, the Partnership for Peace had 28 members. Since that time, an additional six countries have become PfP partners, while three of the original members graduated to the status of NATO membership in 1999, seven more in 2004, and two in 2009. Most partners have seen their participation as a road to NATO membership. The Czech Republic, Hungary, and Poland used their PfP involvement constructively as a way to strengthen their bid for membership. Albania, Bulgaria, Croatia, Estonia, Latvia, Lithuania, Romania, Slovakia and Slovenia, have followed their example.

21 Off-the-record interviews with the author.

22 Goldgeier, *Not Whether but When*, 68.

23 Goldgeier, *Not Whether but When*, 69–70.

24 NATO, "Study on NATO Enlargement," (Brussels: NATO, September 1995).

25 Goldgeier, *Not Whether but When*, 94–5.

26 At the time, I was the lead Congressional Research Service NATO expert and a source for Congress of objective and nonpartisan analysis on NATO issues. When the NATO Observer Group was established in the Senate to manage the process of NATO enlargement, I was asked to serve as adviser to the group and as the Congressional Research Service liaison with both the Senate Observer Group and the Senate Foreign Relations Committee on NATO enlargement issues.

27 White House, "Remarks by the President to the People of Detroit," October 22, 1996.

28 For a thorough, well-documented history of this process, see Lawrence S. Kaplan, *NATO 1948: The Birth of the Transatlantic Alliance* (Lanham, Md.: Rowman & Littlefield, 2007).

29 As a participant in several such ceremonies, I was impressed by the distant look in the president's eyes, suggesting, even as he artfully presented prepared remarks, his thoughts and priorities were elsewhere.

30 See, for example, results of polls conducted by the Pew Research Center for the People and the Press, Washington, D.C., in *America's Place in the World, Part II*. The data, released on October 7, 1997, found that support for enlargement ran more than three to one in favor (63 percent for, 18 percent opposed); however, only 10 percent of the public could identify even one of the potential new members.

31 A partial record of Senate activities related to NATO enlargement, along with the Foreign Relations Committee's Resolution of Ratification and separate views of the Senate Committee on Armed Services and the Senate Select Committee on Intelligence can be found in US Senate Committee on Foreign Relations, *Protocols to the North Atlantic Treaty of 1949 on Accession of Poland, Hungary and the Czech Republic*, 105th Cong., 2d sess., Exec. Rept. 105–14, March 6, 1998.

32 This aspect of the ratification process went completely unnoted in Goldgeier's otherwise excellent account of NATO enlargement decision-making.

33 US Senate Committee on Foreign Relations, *The Debate on NATO Enlargement*, 105th Cong., 1st sess., October 7, 9, 22, 28, and 30 and November 5, 1997, S. Hrg. 105–285.

34 US Senate Committee on Foreign Relations, *The Debate on NATO Enlargement*, 2.

35 US Senate Committee on Foreign Relations, *The Debate on NATO Enlargement*, 2.

36 Following one Senate NATO Observer Group session in the weeks before the Senate vote, Wellstone engaged me in a discussion of the Russia issue. I attempted to provide a balanced perspective but suggested that Kennan's prediction was probably exaggerated. It was clear from that discussion, however, that Wellstone's vote probably would be with the enlargement opponents. Following Russian aggressions against Ukraine in 2014, critics of NATO enlargement pointed to Kennan's arguments as having warned of likely problems with Moscow.

37 Even though the Standing Order of the Senate says that "votes shall be cast from assigned desk," roll-call votes are routinely taken with senators walking into the chamber and milling about the clerk's desk until their names are called. Byrd's comments can be found in *Congressional Record*, 105th Cong., 2d sess., April 30, 1998: S3906.

38 Discussion with author in 1998.

39 William V. Roth Jr., *NATO in the 21st Century* (Brussels: North Atlantic Assembly, September 1998), 53.

40 NATO, "NATO's Membership Action Plan," *NATO On-line-Library Fact Sheet* (Brussels: NATO, April 20, 2000).

41 William Drozdiak, "9 NATO Candidates Pledge to Join in a 'Big Bang' Bid," *International Herald Tribune*, May 20–21, 2000, 1.

42 Yost, *NATO Transformed*, 133–4.

43 North Atlantic Council, *Strategic Concept*, November 8, 1991.

44 North Atlantic Council declaration, January 11, 1994.

45 Susan Woodward, *Balkan Tragedy, Chaos and Dissolution after the Cold War* (Washington, D.C.: Brookings Institution Press, 1995).

46 "The Situation in Yugoslavia" (statement issued by the heads of state and government participating in the meeting of the North Atlantic Council in Rome, November 7–8, 1991), paras. 1, 4.

47 Stanley R. Sloan, "NATO Beyond Bosnia" (CRS Report for Congress 94–977 S, December 7, 1994), 3.

48 As cited by James Gow, *Triumph of the Lack of Will: International Diplomacy and the Yugoslav War* (New York: Columbia University Press, 1997), 48, 50.

49 For an insider's perspective on the role of the Western European Union, see the account by the Union's secretary-general of the time, Willem van Eeckelen, *Debating European Security, 1948–1998* (The Hague: Sdu Publishers, 1998), 140–83.

50 For an excellent, concise account of Clinton administration decision-making concerning "the problem from hell," see Ivo H. Daalder, *Getting to Dayton: The Making of America's Bosnia Policy* (Washington, D.C.: Brookings Institution Press, 2000).

51 Daalder, *Getting to Dayton*, 16.

52 For a discussion of the UN–NATO relationship during the early stages of the Balkan conflicts, see Dick A. Leurdijk, *The United Nations and NATO in Former Yugoslavia, Partners in International Cooperation* (The Hague: Netherlands Atlantic Commission, 1994).

53 Daalder, *Getting to Dayton*, 68.

54 For Holbrooke's perspective on the Bosnia peace process and his role in it, see Richard Holbrooke, *To End a War* (New York: Random House, 1998).

55 For an excellent insider's perspective on the political and bureaucratic struggles within NATO during the adaptation process through 1996, see Rob de Wijk, *NATO on the Brink of the New Millennium: The Battle for Consensus* (London: Brassey's, 1997).

56 Subsequent discussions with US and French officials.

57 North Atlantic Council, Berlin Accord, June 3, 1996.

58 For background on the development of NATO's missions in addition to Article 5 contingencies, see Stanley R. Sloan, *NATO's Future: Beyond Collective Defense* (Washington, D.C.: National Defense University Press McNair Papers, 1996). This study was originally issued as a Congressional Research Service Report for Congress in 1995, advancing the idea of strengthening the Deputy SACEUR's role, a concept that became one of the key reforms in the June 1996 Berlin Accord.

59 The Contact Group had been formed in April 1994 among the United States, Russia, Great Britain, France, and Germany as a way of coordinating Bosnia policy in a small group of major powers. Italy was very unhappy about its original exclusion from the group, engineered by its European partners, not the United States. Italy joined the group in 1996 during its six-month term as president of the European Union's Council of Ministers and remained in the group thereafter. The tradition of smaller groups of allies forming a special committee is well established in the alliance, even if not always appreciated by allies excluded from the group. For example, during the Cold War, the Berlin Group, consisting of the United States, France, the United Kingdom, and Germany, used to meet prior to NATO ministerial meetings to discuss issues related to Berlin and Germany.

60 For a dispassionate assessment of NATO's operations in the Kosovo conflict, see John E. Peters, Stuart Johnson, Nora Bensahel, Timothy Liston, and Traci Williams, *European Contributions to Operation Allied Force: Implications for Transatlantic Cooperation* (Washington, D.C.: Rand, 2001).

61 Wesley K. Clark, *Waging Modern War: Bosnia, Kosovo, and the Future of Combat* (New York: Public Affairs, 2001).

62 US General Accounting Office, "Kosovo Air Operations: Need to Maintain Alliance Cohesion Led to Doctrinal Departures" (GAO-01-784), Washington, D.C., July 27, 2001, 2.

63 For a US perspective on the Kosovo campaign, see Ivo H. Daalder and Michael E. O'Hanlon, *Winning Ugly: NATO's War to Save Kosovo* (Washington, D.C.: Brookings Institution Press, 2000).

64 This claim was made in off-the-record administration briefings to the Senate NATO Observer Group, in which the author participated. In fact, the 1999 concept was not replaced for more than a decade, but mainly because the allies were reluctant to set a new path for the alliance in partnership with the Bush administration in Washington whose judgment they mistrusted. The decision of the allies that NATO would take command of the International Security Assistance Force in Afghanistan constituted a dramatic change from the caution of the 1999 concept concerning NATO and military operations beyond Europe. With that decision, NATO's strategy changed much more radically in practice than it had in theory.

65 North Atlantic Council, Washington Summit Communiqué, April 24, 1999, para. 7.

66 North Atlantic Council, *Defense Capabilities Initiative*, April 25, 1999.

67 NATO Parliamentary Assembly, Defense and Security Subcommittee on Future Security and Defense Capabilities, "Interim Report on NATO's Role in Defence Reform" (Brussels: NATO Parliamentary Assembly, October 2001), para. 90.

68 "North Atlantic Council, The Alliance's Strategic Concept, April 24, 1999."

69 This discussion is based on my chapter in *Controlling Non-Strategic Nuclear Weapons: Obstacles and Opportunities*, eds. Jeffrey A. Larsen and Kurt J. Klingenberger (Colorado Springs, Col.: USAF Institute for National Security Studies, 2001).

70 North Atlantic Treaty Organization, "London Declaration on a Transformed North Atlantic Alliance, Issued by the Heads of State and Government Participating in the meeting of the North Atlantic Council in London on 5–6 July 1990" (printed in *NATO Review* 38, no. 4 [August 1990]: 32–3).

71 North Atlantic Treaty Organization, "The Alliance's New Strategic Concept, Agreed by the Heads of State and Government Participating in the Meeting of the North Atlantic Council in Rome on 7–8 November 1991" (printed in *NATO Review* 39, no. 6 [December 1991]: 25–32).

72 Mitterrand was speaking at a meeting in Paris on January 10, 1992, as reported by *Atlantic News*, no. 2387, January 14, 1992, 4.

73 Many Europeans looked skeptically on the French offer as an effort to deflect criticism of France's nuclear testing program.

74 M-DPC/NPG 1(96)88, Meeting of the Defense Planning Committee in Ministerial Session, Brussels, June 13, 1996.

75 "The Alliance's Strategic Concept, Approved by the Heads of State and Government Participating in the Meeting of the North Atlantic Council in Washington D.C. on 23rd and 24th April 1999" (NATO press release NAC-S [99]65).

76 Michael Brenner, *Terms of Engagement: The United States and the European Security Identity*, The Washington Papers no. 176, Center for Strategic and International Studies (Westport, Conn.: Praeger, 1998), 23.

77 Stanley R. Sloan, *NATO's Future: Toward a New Transatlantic Bargain* (Washington, D.C.: National Defense University Press, 1985), 191.

78 Sean Kay, *NATO and the Future of European Security* (Lanham, Md.: Rowman & Littlefield, 1998), 149.

79 This discussion draws on the author's examination of US attitudes toward European defense where he first described the "yes, but" nature of US policy. See: Stanley R. Sloan, "The United States and European Defence," Chaillot Paper no. 36 (Paris: Western European Union Institute for Security Studies, April 2000).

80 Catherine Guicherd, "A European Defense Identity: Challenge and Opportunity for NATO," Congressional Research Service Report 91478 (Washington, D.C.: Congressional Research Service, June 12, 1991). For the text of the "Bartholomew Telegram" of February 20, 1991, see Willem van Eekelen, *Debating European Security, 1948–1998* (The Hague: Sdu Publishers, 1998), 340–4.

81 Guicherd, "A European Defense Identity," 60–1.

82 Rome Declaration on Peace and Cooperation, Issued by the Heads of State and Government Participating in the Meeting of the North Atlantic Council in Rome on November 7–8, 1991.

83 Single European Act, Title V: Provisions on a Common Foreign and Security Policy, Articles J 1, 2.

84 Frederick Kempe, "US, Bonn Clash over Pact with France," *Wall Street Journal*, May 27, 1992, A9.

85 Patrick E. Tyler, "Senior US Officials Assail Lone-Superpower Policy," *The New York Times*, March 11, 1992, A6.

86 Tyler, "Senior US Officials Assail Lone-Superpower Policy," 6.

87 Barton Gellman, "Pentagon Abandons Goal of Thwarting US Rivals," *Washington Post*, May 24, 1992, A1.

88 This concept was developed in a Congressional Research Service report originally prepared for Senator William V. Roth Jr. (R-Del.). See Stanley R. Sloan, "NATO's Future: Beyond Collective Defense," Congressional Research Service Report 95–979 S (Washington, D.C.: Congressional Research Service, September 15, 1995), 21–4, 30–2. French officials subsequently acknowledged that the report contributed to what eventually became a British–French initiative. British officials have suggested that London was beginning to think along similar lines when the report appeared.

89 Discussions with administration officials in 1996.

90 This point is based on interviews with US officials involved in the decision.

91 Brenner, *Terms of Engagement*, 35.

92 In the course of that session, the Assembly renamed itself the NATO Parliamentary Assembly to emphasize its role as the parliamentary component of the transatlantic alliance.

93 Jolyon Howorth, *European Integration and Defence: The Ultimate Challenge?* (Paris: Western European Union Institute for Security Studies, 2001), 108.

94 William V. Roth Jr., *NATO in the 21st Century* (Brussels: North Atlantic Assembly, September 1998), 57.

95 "Statement on European Defence" (text of a joint statement by the British and French governments, Franco-British Summit, Saint-Malo, France, December 4, 1998).

96 Interviews conducted with Clinton administration officials.

97 Michael Quinlan, *European Defense Cooperation: Asset or Threat to NATO?* (Washington, D.C.: Woodrow Wilson Center Press, 2001), 38.

98 Lord Robertson, "NATO's New Agenda: More Progress than Meets the Eye" (remarks at the SACLANT Symposium, Reykjavik, Iceland, September 6, 2000).

99 William Cohen, "Meeting the Challenges to Transatlantic Security in the 21st Century: A Way Ahead for NATO and the EU" (remarks at the Informal Defense Ministerial Meeting, Birmingham, United Kingdom, October 10, 2000).

100 Reuters News Service, "Cohen Warns Europe That NATO Could Become 'Relic,'" *International Herald Tribune*, December 6, 2000, 7.

101 Final Communiqué, Ministerial Meeting of the North Atlantic Council held at NATO Headquarters, Brussels, December 14–15, 2000, para. 31.

102 Final Communiqué, para. 33.

7

The 2000s: turbulent transatlantic ties

Shocks to the transatlantic system

George W. Bush's election as President of the United States in November 2000 raised many questions about how the transatlantic alliance might fare under his leadership. He brought with him a team that conveyed the impression of confident leadership on defense issues. His Secretary of State, retired general Colin Powell, had already served as national security advisor (to President Reagan) and Chairman of the Joint Chiefs of Staff (under presidents George H. W. Bush and Bill Clinton). Powell came to office well-respected on both sides of the political aisle in the United States and by America's NATO allies. Bush chose as Secretary of Defense Donald Rumsfeld, an out-spoken and experienced official who, in the 1970s, had served as the US Permanent Representative to NATO (under President Nixon), White House Chief of Staff and Secretary of Defense (under President Ford).

From the outset, the Bush administration faced a mix of European fears and expectations as it confronted relations with the NATO allies. Candidate Bush had made some statements suggesting the United States should begin to pull back from some of its overseas commitments, but the overall thrust of administration policy was in unilateralist, not isolationist, directions, at least as seen by most Europeans.

The first foreign policy actions of the Bush administration raised warning flags for European governments. Unilateral US decisions not to join in the International Criminal Court, to remain outside the Kyoto Protocol on greenhouse gas emissions, and to terminate the Anti-Ballistic Missile Treaty with Russia were all seen as signs that the United States was heading in new directions based almost exclusively on short-term US policy choices and with no regard for their impact on the views or interests of its closest allies.

The new Bush administration was alert to any signs that the EU's Common European Security and Defense Policy (CESDP) might be undermining NATO. British Prime Minister Blair hurried to Washington to reassure President Bush.

In his meetings with Blair in February 2001, President Bush accepted on good faith that CESDP would not hurt NATO. Following Camp David discussions with Blair, the president said:

> He [Blair] assured me that NATO is going to be the primary way to keep the peace in Europe. And I assured him that the United States will be actively engaged in NATO, remain engaged in Europe with our allies. But he also assured me that the European defense would no way undermine NATO. He also assured me that there would be a joint command, that the planning would take place within NATO, and that should all NATO not wish to go on a mission that would then serve as a catalyst for the defense forces moving on their own. And finally, I was very hopeful, when we discussed the prime minister's vision, that such a vision would encourage our NATO allies and friends to bolster their defense budgets, perhaps. And so, I support what the prime minister has laid out. I think it makes a lot of sense for our country.[1]

Some observers speculated that Bush endorsed CESDP in return for Blair's support for the new administration's goal of strengthening missile defenses, but it seems more likely that the two issues were considered on their own merits by both sides. The reaffirmation of US support for the initiative was necessary because the incoming administration was known to have concerns similar to those expressed earlier by the Clinton administration and by private experts outside the administration—some of whom were appointed to positions of influence inside the new administration.[2]

Even among Euro-enthusiasts, there was lingering concern that CESDP would produce rhetoric, promises, and institutions but no additional capabilities. The EU pledge to create a 60,000-troop intervention force with 400 aircraft and 100 ships was impressive. But there was little evidence that European governments were increasing defense spending to buy the strategic lift and other assets required to make the force credible. On balance, the Europeans still lagged well behind the United States in deployed military capabilities for force projection, intervention, and high-tech warfare.

Following President Bush's meeting with Prime Minister Blair, the new administration appeared to settle into a relatively passive approach toward CESDP, perhaps in the belief that nothing dramatic affecting US interests was likely to happen in the near term. The more urgent priority in the first half of 2001 was to develop US policy toward ballistic missile defense and sell it to the allies, Russia, and China, as well as to reform and repair the US defense establishment.

Another priority—the war against terrorism—displaced all others on September 11, 2001, when terrorists killed almost 3,000 Americans and citizens of more than 80 other countries. Bands of terrorists coordinated by al-Qaeda hijacked four civilian airliners, crashing two of them into both towers of the World Trade Center in New York, and one into the Pentagon in

Washington, D.C. The fourth hijacked aircraft, perhaps headed for the White House or the US Capitol, crashed in a field in Pennsylvania after passengers learned of the other three hijackings and decided to try to wrest control of the aircraft from the terrorists. As the United States, Europe, and the world turned their eyes toward the threat posed by international terrorism, important questions remained unanswered about the relationship between the United States and Europe in the alliance.

September 11 and transatlantic relations

On the morning of September 12, the Paris daily *Le Monde* headlined their story on the 9/11 attacks with the proclamation that "We are All Americans." The headline suggested the extent to which terrorism would affect the terms of the transatlantic bargain. The event was traumatic for Americans and Europeans alike. The *Le Monde* headline was indicative of European empathy and support for the United States.

But Americans, led by the George W. Bush administration, adopted a war mentality, whose perpetuation Bush officials actively encouraged through the November 2004 elections and beyond. US President George W. Bush declared a "Global War on Terrorism" in response to the attacks. The United States prepared to mount a campaign against the Taliban leadership and forces in Afghanistan that had hosted and supported the al-Qaeda organization and its leader, Osama bin Laden, and had refused to turn bin Laden and his associates over to the United States for prosecution. Europeans, acting more like Europeans, were inclined to see September 11 as a major event in the struggle against terror, but not the beginning of a war whose outcome would be determined anytime soon.

In any case, on September 11, 2001, the challenges to transatlantic relations became much more complex and demanding. Within 24 hours the attack on the United States was addressed by the North Atlantic Council (NAC) in Brussels, which decided to invoke Article 5 of the North Atlantic Treaty if it was determined that the attack was the responsibility of a foreign source, and not domestic terrorism, from which many allies had suffered but which does not fall under the collective defense provisions of the treaty. On September 12, the NAC declared:

> The Council agreed that if it is determined that this attack was directed from abroad against the United States, it shall be regarded as an action covered by Article 5 of the Washington Treaty, which states that an armed attack against one or more of the allies in Europe or North America shall be considered an attack against them all.
>
> The commitment to collective self-defence embodied in the Washington Treaty was first entered into in circumstances very different from those that exist

now, but it remains no less valid and no less essential today, in a world subject to the scourge of international terrorism. When the Heads of State and Government of NATO met in Washington in 1999, they paid tribute to the success of the alliance in ensuring the freedom of its members during the Cold War and in making possible a Europe that was whole and free. But they also recognized the existence of a wide variety of risks to security, some of them quite unlike those that had called NATO into existence. More specifically, they condemned terrorism as a serious threat to peace and stability and reaffirmed their determination to combat it in accordance with their commitments to one another, their international commitments, and national legislation.

Article 5 of the Washington Treaty stipulates that in the event of attacks falling within its purview, each ally will assist the Party that has been attacked by taking such action as it deems necessary. Accordingly, the United States' NATO allies stand ready to provide the assistance that may be required as a consequence of these acts of barbarism.[3]

On October 2, 2001, NATO Secretary General Lord Robertson announced the allies had concluded the attacks had been directed from abroad and they therefore would be regarded as covered by Article 5. The United States had made it clear that, even though it appreciated the alliance's declaration of an Article 5 response, it would conduct military operations itself, with ad hoc coalitions of willing countries. Initially this included only the United Kingdom among NATO allies. The United States decided not to ask that military operations be conducted through the NATO military command structure. Such a request would have created serious political dilemmas for many allies. The discussion of NATO's area of operation had basically been put aside since the debates leading up to the 1999 Strategic Concept, and there was no enthusiasm for reopening these debates in the middle of this crisis. Furthermore, the United States obviously preferred to keep tight control of any military operations.

Nonetheless, NATO was asked to provide a number of services on behalf of the war against terrorism. On October 4, NATO allies agreed to: enhance intelligence sharing and cooperation; provide assistance to allies and other states which are or may be subject to increased terrorist threats as a result of their support for the campaign against terrorism; provide increased security for facilities of the United States and other Allies on their territory; backfill selected allied assets in NATO's area of responsibility that are required to support operations against terrorism; provide blanket overflight clearances for the US and allied aircraft for military flights related to operations against terrorism; provide access for the United States and other Allies to ports and airfields on the territory of NATO nations for operations against terrorism, including for refueling.[4]

The NAC also agreed that the alliance was prepared to deploy elements of its Standing Naval Forces to the eastern Mediterranean in order to provide a NATO presence and demonstrate resolve, and that NATO was ready to deploy elements of its Airborne Early Warning force to support operations against terrorism. In fact, on October 8 it was announced that NATO Airborne Warning and Control aircraft would be deployed to the United States to help patrol US airspace. The move freed up US assets for use in the air war against Taliban forces in Afghanistan. Just as NATO had invoked Article 5 for the first time ever, the dispatch of NATO forces to protect US territory, according to NATO's Supreme Allied Commander General Joseph Ralston, the Supreme Allied Commander Europe, was "the first time NATO assets will have been used in direct support of the continental United States."[5]

NATO's reaction to the terrorist attacks was quick and unequivocal. The reaction was initially applauded by the Bush administration. Two months after the attacks, the US ambassador to NATO, R. Nicholas Burns, argued that NATO had responded strongly to the terrorist challenge, and that the response demonstrated NATO's continuing relevance: "With the battle against terrorism now engaged, it is difficult to imagine a future without the alliance at the core of efforts to defend our civilization."[6]

Initially, preparing for and conducting operations in Afghanistan, the US administration sought help from the allies mainly through bilateral channels, not through NATO. In the weeks following the attacks, some Pentagon officials privately dismissed NATO's formal invocation of the alliance's mutual defense provision and complained that the alliance was not relevant to the new challenges posed by the counter-terror campaign. Meanwhile, some NATO allies were led to believe that the United States did not value or want contributions that they might make in the battle against terrorism. The Italians, for example, were embarrassed by their exclusion from British–French–German talks about counterterrorist operations held on the fringes of a European Union summit in Ghent, Belgium, combined with rumors, apparently from French sources, that the United States had rejected Italian offers of military assistance.[7]

By November, many allies, including Germany, had pledged forces to the counterterrorist campaign, and their offers had been explicitly welcomed by the administration. As the campaign stretched into 2002, more NATO country forces were brought to bear on the conflict. Many allies pledged forces for post-conflict peacekeeping duties. Several Danish and German soldiers were killed trying to destroy Taliban munitions. Canadian forces saw combat against al-Qaeda and Taliban elements in the eastern Afghan mountains, and the British deployed a force of some 1,700 Royal Marines to join in the fight against residual al-Qaeda and Taliban forces.

In the aftermath of the terrorist attacks and the US reactions, one British expert judged that the US choice not to use NATO to run the military operations against terrorist targets in Afghanistan means "It's unlikely the Americans will ever again wish to use NATO to manage a major shooting war."[8] The Bush administration did not initially ask that NATO run the military actions in Afghanistan because it did not want to repeat the Kosovo experience, where the conduct of military operations was complicated by allied criticism of US targeting strategy. Specifically, the French government on several occasions vetoed targets that had been identified by US planners. Complaints by Bush administration Pentagon officials about NATO's limited utility apparently were registered without the administration even asking the allies to give the alliance a more substantial role.

With regard to the other US partner to the transatlantic bargain, the US Congress, the traditional burden-sharing debate took on a new and pointed direction. Leading members of the US Senate argued strongly that Europe's failure to take the war on terrorism seriously could undermine the US commitment to NATO and destroy the alliance altogether. At the Thirty-eighth Annual Munich Conference on Security Policy, defense expert Senator John McCain (R-Ariz.) joined leading Bush administration officials stressing "the need for the European allies to acquire better capabilities for their armed forces so that they can cope with sudden terrorist threats and possibly join US troops in a campaign to overthrow Saddam Hussein in Iraq."[9] This argument came in the wake of President Bush's State of the Union address in which he argued that Iraq, Iran, and North Korea constituted an "axis of evil" that could be the target of US preemptive strikes.[10]

Senator Richard G. Lugar (R-Ind), long-time NATO supporter and leading commentator on the alliance, hit hard in a speech to the US–NATO Missions Annual Conference in Brussels on January 19, 2002, arguing that a division of labor in which the United States did the war fighting and Europe did the peacekeeping was unacceptable. Senator Lugar summed up his view saying:

> America is at war and feels more vulnerable than at any time since the end of the Cold War and perhaps since World War II. The threat we face is global and existential. We need allies and alliances to confront it effectively. Those alliances can no longer be circumscribed by artificial geographic boundaries. All of America's alliances are going to be reviewed and recast in light of this new challenge, including NATO. If NATO is not up to the challenge of becoming effective in the new war against terrorism, then our political leaders may be inclined to search for something else that will answer this need.[11]

On the European side, allied officials complained that, after showing their support and willingness to contribute, the United States largely proceeded with a strategy focusing on dividing, not sharing, responsibilities. According to press reports, the situation "irritated European leaders. Behind their unflagging public political support for Washington are private complaints about the constant risk of being caught flatfooted by the US refusal to limit its own options by revealing its plans. Accustomed to being consulted about or at least alerted to US moves, these leaders are now embarrassed."[12] One French official reportedly observed that the message from the United States was "We'll do the cooking and prepare what people are going to eat, then you will wash the dirty dishes."[13] It subsequently became popular to observe that the new formula for international security management was "the US fights, the UN feeds, and the EU finances and does peacekeeping."

To some extent, the situation can be attributed to factors for which the Europeans themselves were to blame. First, they did not, for the most part, have significant military assets to contribute to the first phase of the Afghan campaign, which relied heavily on air-delivered precision-guided munitions. Second, officials in the Bush administration were fully aware of past NATO-nation resistance to involving the alliance in military operations beyond their borders, to say nothing of beyond Europe.

On the other hand, it appeared that the United States missed an opportunity to move the NATO consensus well beyond the 1999 Strategic Concept following the September 11 events. Given the invocation of Article 5 and the explicit willingness of many NATO allies to contribute military capabilities to the war against terrorism, a political consensus existed that perhaps could have been used to expand NATO's horizons and establish a mechanism for NATO contributions in the future. For example, the allies could have taken NATO's involvement at least one step further by creating a NATO Counterterrorism Combined Joint Task Force.[14] Creation of a special task force would have provided the organizational focus required for a serious NATO contribution to the counterterrorist campaign. It would have provided a reliable framework for allied involvement in the campaign, built on the foundation of NATO's military command structure, for as long as such support was required. As it happened, while the 9/11 events produced strong supportive reactions among the allies, they did not yield much in terms of creative or even substantial improvements in allied capabilities. Part of this failure could be attributed to the reticence of the Bush administration about making NATO a key part of the response.

Implications for NATO

The terrorist attacks on the United States and the nature of the US response had a major impact on US–European relations. The attacks left fundamentally different impressions on Americans and Europeans. The "war mentality" adopted by the Bush administration seemed to warrant all necessary steps to defend the country, irrespective of the views of other countries or the accepted norms of international law. Europeans, although shocked and sympathetic, did not see the attacks as changing global realities in any profound way. They remained convinced that international cooperation and law were vitally important foundations for international stability and, indeed, for a struggle against international terrorism.

The actions required to respond militarily to the terrorist attacks nonetheless demonstrated in many ways the wisdom of the allied approach to adaptation of the alliance that began in the early 1990s. NATO never abandoned the critical Article 5 commitment, but it began preparing for the new kind of security challenges alliance members thought likely in the twenty-first century.

The implications for force structure were clear: NATO needed more forces capable of being moved quickly to conflicts beyond national borders and prepared to fight as allies in a variety of topographic and climatic conditions in coalitions using a synergistic mix of conventional and "high-tech" weaponry. Even though the September 11 attacks constituted a clear case for invocation of Article 5, the response required the kinds of forces and philosophies that the allies had been seeking to develop for so-called "non-Article 5 contingencies."

Unfortunately, the directions suggested by NATO strategy documents and incorporated in the 1999 Defense Capabilities Initiative had not been taken seriously by most European governments. This was a major factor encouraging the cynicism of Bush administration and Pentagon officials concerning the utility of NATO and European military forces. NATO acknowledged allied shortcomings in December 2001 when allied defense ministers in a special statement observed that:

> Efforts to improve NATO's ability to respond to terrorism must be an integral, albeit urgent, part of the more general ongoing work to improve Alliance military capabilities. There has been some progress in this wider regard since our last meeting, but a great deal more needs to be done. We are especially concerned about persistent longstanding deficiencies in areas such as survivability, deployability, combat identification, and intelligence, surveillance, and target acquisition. The full implementation of DCI is essential if the Alliance is to be able to carry out its missions, taking into account the threat posed by terrorism.[15]

In 1999, the allies had finessed the issue of whether or not NATO could be used for military operations beyond Europe. The United States had argued strongly that most applications of allied cooperation in the future would likely be well beyond allied borders. If given the mandate, NATO could have begun assessing allied forces that could be used in different conditions of weather and terrain and the means available for delivering them to zones of operation. But most European allies had opposed any open-ended commitment to employ NATO on a more global basis. As the war on terrorism unfolded in Afghanistan, far from Europe, the alliance had no agreement in principle concerning where NATO could be used. Legally, they needed no such agreement once they had declared the attacks on the United States to fall under NATO's collective defense provisions. But the lack of a commitment to and planning for operations far from NATO's borders meant alliance activities, mindsets, and force structures were not oriented toward being helpful in such contingencies.

In spite of such handicaps and the Bush administration's initial reluctance to involve NATO in the war on terrorism, many allies ultimately contributed forces to post-conflict peacekeeping duties in Afghanistan. In 2003, discussed below (pp. 205–7), NATO itself took command of the peacekeeping part of military operations there. NATO command of the International Security Assistance

Force, a UN-mandated force initially responsible for providing security in and around Kabul, became NATO's first mission beyond the Euro-Atlantic area.

The Iraq crisis in transatlantic relations

Immediately following the 9/11 attacks, if not before, some key officials in the Bush administration began to act on the assumption that Saddam Hussein was part of the terrorist problem that should, and could, be eliminated. By early 2002, it seemed clear that the United States was intent on bringing about regime change in Iraq.

While the United States was laying the groundwork for an attack against Saddam Hussein's Iraq, the European allies were not prepared to come to the same conclusions reached already by Bush administration officials. Europeans generally agreed that Hussein was a problem and that his regime was in clear violation of international law. Further, they shared some of the US frustration that international sanctions had done much to hurt the Iraqi people but little to undermine Saddam's rule.

However, most Europeans and many European governments reacted strongly to the Bush administration's determination to go to war against Iraq no matter what other countries thought, irrespective of how unilateral action might affect the future of international cooperation, and with little regard for the impact on international law.

The largely unilateral US approach to Iraq was the instigating event for the crisis in US–European relations, but French President Jacques Chirac and German Chancellor Gerhard Schroeder helped ensure that the crisis would produce deep divisions among Europeans as well as between many Europeans and the United States. Given German public opinion in the summer of 2002, Chancellor Schroeder undoubtedly needed to take a stand against attacking Iraq in order to be returned as chancellor in the fall elections. But Schroeder disappointed many Americans, and surely President Bush, by failing to soften his opposition after the election. France's criticism of the US stance was seen in Washington, and across the country, as typical Gaullist grandstanding designed to show France's flag and to rein in the US hegemon. As in the case of Germany, however, US expectations concerning French behavior ultimately led to disappointment and even anger.

Many Americans expected France to be with the United States when the time came to use force, to ensure that France would have a say in the important post-conflict period in Iraq. Damage to the transatlantic alliance and to European solidarity, already serious, was aggravated when France not only remained opposed but happily took on the role of leader of the opposition. France's attitude, supported by French and broader European public opinion, nonetheless was highly divisive in the European framework, particularly when President Chirac "derided those Central and Eastern European countries

Figure 7.1 'NATO Team' by Kevin Kallaugher.

that have signed letters expressing their support for the United States as 'childish,' 'dangerous,' and missing 'an opportunity to shut up.'"[16]

For its part, the Bush administration further fanned the flames of European concern when, in September 2002, the White House released a policy statement on the "National Security Strategy of the United States." The paper focused on "those terrorist organizations of global reach and any terrorist or state sponsor of terrorism which attempt to gain or use weapons of mass destruction (WMD) or their precursors." With regard to such threats, the document laid out an unambiguous strategy of preemption, saying "as a matter of common sense and self-defense, America will act against such emerging threats before they are fully formed." It then added that "while the United States will constantly strive to enlist the support of the international community we will not hesitate to act alone, if necessary, to exercise our right of self-defense by acting preemptively against such terrorists."[17] Even though much of what the document said reflected realities of the contemporary security environment, it was widely interpreted as a unilateral assertion of rights beyond the accepted norms of international law, which could be misused by the United States or copied by other countries with destabilizing results.

The irony of success in Prague and continued enlargement

Just as Kosovo had been the uninvited guest at the 1999 Washington Summit, Iraq was the new dark cloud shadowing alliance leaders when they met in Prague, the Czech Republic, in November 2002. The Prague meeting fortuitously fell at a time when the United States, the UK, France, and Germany were still trying to develop a common approach to Iraq through the United Nations. This brief lull in the Iraq controversy helped produce a better environment for the Prague meeting. Somewhat ironically, the Prague Summit yielded significant steps forward for the alliance at a time when political relations in the alliance were headed for new lows. One suspects that the Bush administration and the European allies wanted to show that their differences over how to deal with Iraq would not prevent them from making the Prague Summit a success. Not only did the allies invite seven new members (Bulgaria, Estonia, Latvia, Lithuania, Romania, Slovakia, and Slovenia) to join the alliance—another major step toward a Europe "whole and free"—but they also took giant strides toward making NATO an important player in security well beyond Europe.

In anticipation of the summit, Czech Republic President Vaclav Havel wrote that for "the Alliance to define clearly the role it wants to play in the global campaign against terrorism, the Prague Summit will have to involve a fundamental re-examination of the way in which NATO operates. Moreover, it will have to set in motion a still more radical transformation of the Alliance in order for NATO to reaffirm its position as a key pillar of international security."[18]

Havel's goals for the summit were largely met. The leaders confirmed the decision to create a NATO Response Force intended to be capable of taking on virtually any military mission anywhere in the world. They approved reform of NATO's command structure to move away from its old geographic focus into a new functional approach organized around a command for "operations" and another for "transformation."

As a result of decisions taken at Prague and after, NATO was given a mandate and some of the instruments required to play a meaningful role in dealing with twenty-first-century security challenges (the Prague Summit decisions on NATO transformation and its consequences are discussed below, pp. 224–6). It began using these new tools with the International Security Assistance Force in Afghanistan in 2003 and in Iraq, where it supported NATO ally Poland's role there, and in 2004 began helping train Iraqi security forces.

In addition, the agreements between NATO and the European Union, known as "Berlin Plus," designed to facilitate cooperation between the two organizations finally were agreed upon and implemented. The accords did not guarantee smooth sailing in the NATO–EU relationship, particularly given the suspicions about the purposes of European defense integration still harbored by key Bush administration officials. But their implementation did provide a new and constructive foundation on which NATO–EU relations could develop.

NATO enlargement door opens again

With regard to the enlargement process, the Bush administration and the NATO allies faced a number of issues as they confronted the next enlargement decision. They included several questions that played into the first enlargement debate and some others that were created by specific circumstances surrounding the next batch of candidates. The issues included the following:

1. Had the first round of enlargement (with the Czech Republic, Hungary, and Poland) proceeded successfully enough to warrant a second round? Did shortcomings in military reform and defense improvements of the three new members suggest that leverage on candidate states disappears when they become members?
2. Did the increase to 19 members have any discernible effect on NATO's decision-making ability? Was there a magic number beyond which NATO's consensus-based deliberative process would become unworkable?
3. If countries that did not fully meet the military guidelines for membership laid out in the NATO enlargement study are nonetheless invited to join, would this imply that NATO was becoming "more political," making military capabilities of potential members less relevant?
4. What were the likely consequences for relations with Russia of various possible enlargement scenarios?
5. How would further enlargement interact with other policy initiatives, for example, the Bush administration's attempt to develop a collaborative approach with Moscow on nuclear missile reductions and ballistic missile defenses?
6. Could the financial costs of the next enlargement be kept reasonable and shared effectively?
7. Would senators be more wary of extending defense commitments to additional, less familiar countries than they were for the first three candidates?[19]
8. How should further NATO enlargement be linked to the process of EU enlargement, given that several leading candidates for NATO enlargement were headed for EU membership?
9. Should enlargement be linked in any way to the process of further reforming NATO to make it more relevant to the war on terrorism?[20]
10. Would membership of the Baltic states in NATO and a closer NATO–Russia relationship lead Finland and Sweden to seek membership? If they did would Austria and Ireland, the other two of four formerly neutral EU members, follow?

In a speech in Warsaw on June 15, 2001, President George W. Bush outlined his vision of a Europe "whole, free, and at peace," and said that all new European democracies, "from the Baltic to the Black Sea and all that lie between," should be able to join European institutions, especially NATO. Bush's declaration opened the way for a second enlargement round—one that might have been expected to be controversial but which turned out to be far less contentious than the first one.

Before the September 11, 2001, terrorist attacks, political interest in and support for NATO's second enlargement round could not be compared to that for the first round. President Bush said that his administration was a strong supporter of NATO enlargement. But the administration had no eager European partner on this issue. Germany, the key European architect of the first round, had less of a strategic stake in the next stages and, until late in 2001, had been reluctant to upset Moscow.

In the wake of the terrorist attacks on the United States, some observers questioned the wisdom of moving ahead with NATO enlargement. However, within a few months of the attacks it appeared that a consensus was growing in favor of a major enlargement initiative when allied leaders met in Prague, the Czech Republic, in November 2002.

According to a study by the Brookings Institution released late in 2001:

> the case for enlargement ... is stronger than before. Enlargement will contribute to the process of integration that has helped stabilize Europe over the past fifty years and promote the development of strong new allies in the war on terrorism. ... Far from backing away from NATO enlargement, the Bush administration should welcome all those European democracies whose political stability, military contributions, and commitment to NATO solidarity would be assets to the Alliance. Now more than ever, Alliance leaders can and should pursue a wider, integrated NATO and a strong and cooperative relationship with Russia at the same time.[21]

As it turned out, the track record of the three countries in the first round, while not perfect, did not hurt prospects for the second. Predictions of opponents that enlargement would be expensive for the United States, other NATO states, and the candidates never materialized. The military performance of the new members was mixed: Poland was seen as having done quite well in modernizing its forces, and Hungary and the Czech Republic less so. But all three were generally judged to have made contributions to stability in Europe and to the war on terror and other security challenges.[22]

The credentials of the nine candidates (countries participating in the Membership Action Plan: Albania, Bulgaria, Estonia, Former Yugoslav Republic of Macedonia, Latvia, Lithuania, Romania, Slovakia, and Slovenia) were uneven, measured against the standards set in the 1995 NATO Enlargement Study.[23] In the end, neither Albania nor Macedonia was deemed ready for membership. Slovenia, a small country that almost made it into the first round, was judged to be the strongest candidate, at least in terms of how far its democracy and reform of its military establishment had progressed. Slovakia had removed a potential question mark about the development of its democracy when elections in September 2002 supported continued democratic reform in the country. Romania and Bulgaria had large military establishments that had a long way to go to meet NATO standards, but southern NATO allies (Italy, Greece, and Turkey) supported their accession. NATO's northern European members advocated membership for the three Baltic states: Estonia, Latvia, and Lithuania. Russia's potential reaction remained the main concern about membership for these candidates.

Because the Bush administration had offered US support for a "big bang" enlargement, the path became relatively clear for the seven leading candidates. The Republican-controlled Congress fell in behind the president. In October 2002, the House of Representatives passed by an overwhelming margin of 358–9 H. Res. 468 strongly supporting NATO membership for the group of seven.[24] When the NATO leaders met at Prague in November 2002, membership invitations were issued to these leading candidates. The enlargement process had originally been expected to be the main focus of the meeting. For the seven countries it undoubtedly was. For the alliance overall, however, the process of adapting the alliance to the new challenges posed by terrorism and NATO's emerging role beyond Europe (see discussion in Chapter 8) became the big news out of Prague. The ratification process went smoothly, with virtually no controversy or debate in the US Senate or in other NATO countries. By March 29, 2004, all 19 current and the seven prospective members of the alliance had deposited their instruments of ratification with the United States government, and the alliance had grown to 26 members.

This process left five potential candidates in the alliance waiting room. Albania, Croatia, and the Former Yugoslav Republic of Macedonia appeared likely to qualify for membership in the not-too-distant future. Albania and Croatia joined in 2009, and Macedonia was on track to join except for the fact that it had not been able to resolve the issue of its formal name. Greece, which would have to approve Macedonia's membership along with all other allies, objected to the use of "Macedonia" because it believed its neighbor's use of the name implied claims on the adjoining Greek province by the same name. Two former Soviet republics of Ukraine and Georgia stood out as issues, inside their countries, in relations with Moscow, and among the NATO allies.

Crisis over ensuring Turkey's security

Even with the successful Prague meeting, the Iraq issue continued to plague the alliance. Early in 2003, the question of whether to begin planning defensive assistance to Turkey should it be attacked by Iraq during a presumptive US-led coalition attack on Saddam Hussein's regime exploded, threatening the very underpinnings of the alliance. On January 15, US Deputy Secretary of Defense Paul Wolfowitz formally asked NATO allies to consider what supporting roles they might play in case of a US-led war on Iraq. Six areas of assistance were discussed, including: sending Patriot missiles and Airborne Warning and Control surveillance planes to defend Turkey, the only NATO country that borders Iraq; sending naval forces to help protect ships in the eastern Mediterranean; providing personnel to help protect US military bases in Europe; access to airspace, ports, bases, and refueling facilities in Europe; backfilling US forces that are sent to the Gulf; and deploying NATO troops to Iraq after a possible war to help rebuild and govern the country.

After considerable discussion within the NAC, Belgium, France, and Germany publicly announced their opposition to allowing NATO to begin planning to provide military assistance to Turkey. The three recalcitrant allies said they were not opposed to aiding Istanbul but believed that planning for such action was premature while UN arms inspectors were still seeking to disarm Iraq peacefully. The initiative was seen as an attempt by the United States to get preemptive NATO support for a military action that was not sanctioned by the UN Security Council. Once before, in the case of Kosovo, NATO had acted without a Security Council mandate. In that case, however, all the allies agreed that Russia and China should not be allowed to block a military action in Europe deemed necessary by the NATO allies. In this case, the three allies wanted to make it clear that a NATO mandate would not be sufficient to justify military action against Iraq. The choices of the United States to put the issue before the alliance, and of the three allies to block the requested planning, brought existing political differences over Iraq into NATO in a way that put NATO's mutual defense commitment on the line.

To break the stalemate, NATO Secretary General Robertson and some member states suggested bringing the issue before the Defense Planning Committee, in which France, at that time, still chose not to participate. Agreement was finally reached in the French-less Defense Planning Committee when Belgium and Germany dropped their opposition to beginning planning possible military aid to Turkey.

Iraq war opens with divided alliance

The scenario illustrated to what extent the Iraq issue had frayed political bonds among the allies. It also demonstrated that NATO remained an alliance of sovereign states, and that it works only when serious efforts have been made to build a political consensus behind a course of action, particularly when that action requires the use of military force.

The Bush administration worked hard to get as many European governments as possible on board in support of the war. In addition to the Blair government, the most responsive European governments were those that had been liberated from Soviet control by the successful end of the Cold War. For many of these countries, the goal of eliminating one of the world's most despotic dictators undoubtedly seemed more compelling than for those countries which for decades had experienced peace, democracy, and financial well-being.[25] The list of European countries that supported the war effort in principle was substantial.[26] The UK contributed combat troops and played a significant role in the attack on Iraq and in the post-war occupation. Poland took charge of a post-war military region in Iraq, and Spain and Italy contributed paramilitary and intelligence units. However, even in countries whose governments supported the war, public opinion remained strongly critical.

The initial war against Hussein's regime in Iraq was militarily successful, resulting in the overthrow of Hussein and the eventual capture of the former leader and elimination or capture of most of his top lieutenants. But Europeans remained unconvinced. In the summer of 2003, when asked "was the war in Iraq worth the loss of life and other costs," 70 percent of all Europeans polled answered "no," while only 25 percent said "yes." Even in states whose government supported the war effort, majorities answered in the negative, including the UK (55 percent); the Netherlands (59 percent); Poland (67 percent); Italy (73 percent); and Portugal (75 percent). In the two leading European opponents of the war, the results were more emphatic: France (87 percent) and Germany (85 percent).[27] (In subsequent years, American public opinion tended to produce similar margins against the decision, restoring transatlantic unity, at least on that point!)

An in-depth analysis of European public opinion following the Iraq war came to the conclusion that opposition to the war was at least partly rooted in the perception that the United States was acting unilaterally, and without reference to international opinion. According to this analysis, "it makes a significant difference whether a potential military action involved a unilateral US move or one supported by NATO or the U.N. In Europe support increases from 36% for the U.S. acting alone to 48% for an action under a U.N. mandate."[28]

After the initial hostilities in Iraq, one influential European commentator who had earlier defended the US role as a benign hegemon cautioned the Bush administration and other Americans not to sacrifice the good will and cooperation that had for decades constituted part of the foundation for American power. Pro-American commentator Josef Joffe responded to the growing US unilateralist tendencies by observing that the United States would remain the dominant force in international affairs for some time to come, and that no traditional power balance would be provided by another power or combination of powers. However, in Joffe's view, US self-interest would not be well served by a strategy based on a "with us or against us" philosophy like that deployed by President Bush following the 9/11 attacks. Rather, according to Joffe, the United States should assume the inevitable costs that are associated with international leadership:

> Primacy does not come cheap, and the price is measured not just in dollars and cents, but above all in the currency of obligation. Conductors manage to mold 80 solo players into a symphony orchestra because they have fine sense for everybody else's quirks and qualities—because they act in the interest of all; their labour is the source of their authority. ... Power exacts responsibility, and responsibility requires the transcendence of narrow self-interest. As long as the United States continues to provide such public goods, envy and resentment will not escalate into fear and loathing that spawn hostile coalitions.[29]

Late in 2003, when it appeared the Bush administration was attempting to broaden the base of international support for Iraqi stabilization and reconstruction, and just before George W. Bush was scheduled to call the leaders of Germany, France, and Russia to ask them to forgive old Iraqi debt, the administration took another unilateral step that surprised and angered the European governments that had opposed the war. A directive from Deputy Secretary of Defense Paul Wolfowitz—cleared by the White House—was posted on the Pentagon website making it clear that only Iraq coalition members would be eligible to serve as prime contractors for US-financed reconstruction projects in Iraq. This eliminated three key countries Bush was about to ask for Iraqi debt relief and others, including Canada. The predictable reaction was immediate. German foreign minister Joschka Fischer said that the move would "not be acceptable" to Germany. "And it wouldn't be in line with the spirit of looking to the future together and not into the past."[30] The move undermined the diplomatic efforts of Secretary of State Colin Powell to build international support for Iraqi debt relief. Russian defense minister Sergei Ivanov spoke out in opposition to forgiveness of Iraq's $120 billion debt, $8 billion of which is owed to Russia. Ivanov remarked, "Iraq is not a poor country."[31]

Just prior to release of the contracting decision, former Secretary of State James Baker had been asked to travel to Europe to convince key allied states to forgive Iraqi debt as a contribution to Iraqi recovery from the war. Baker found a cool reception in Paris, Berlin, and Moscow, but the three key governments all agreed to negotiate some package of debt reductions. Irritated by the US contracting decision, French President Chirac, German Chancellor Schroeder, and Russian President Putin all decided to handle the debt reduction issue via normal diplomatic channels, which in this case would be through the "Paris Club, a group of 19 industrialized nations that have collaborated since 1956 on easing financial burdens of heavily indebted nations."[32]

In the first half of 2004, the international character and political depth of the US-led coalition in Iraq took a serious hit. On March 14, national elections in Spain removed the party of Prime Minister Jose Maria Aznar from power. Voters apparently blamed Aznar's support of the US-led war in Iraq for the terrorist bombings that killed just under two hundred people in Madrid on March 11, and rebuffed the government's attempt to blame the bombings on Basque nationalists. Voters overwhelmingly endorsed candidates from the opposition Socialist Party, whose leader, Jose Luis Rodriguez Zapatero, had promised to withdraw Spain's 1,300 troops from Iraq, move Spain's foreign policy away from such close links to the United States, and restore good relations with European allies France and Germany that had opposed the Iraq war. Zapatero moved quickly and, as promised, all Spanish troops were out of Iraq by the end of May.

As the United States struggled to move Iraq from a war in progress toward self-rule and democratic elections, the allies softened their reaction to the requests for assistance from the United States but stopped far short of providing the kind of help the United States wanted. At the NATO Istanbul Summit in

June 2004 the allies agreed that NATO's mission in Iraq could be expanded beyond backing up the Polish command there to include training for Iraqi forces. The allies were careful, however, to avoid giving President Bush any "victory" that he could use to good effect in his re-election campaign. This reluctance was reinforced by the fact that Bush administration claims about Iraqi weapons of mass destruction and ties to terrorist groups, used to justify the war, were not supported by the evidence, validating European reticence about participating in the conflict.

Following the November 2 elections that returned George W. Bush for another four-year term, the Europeans almost immediately moved to begin the process of rebuilding bridges to Washington. British Prime Minister Tony Blair, who had stood behind the Bush administration on Iraq, in spite of strong opposition to the war at home as well as around Europe, flew to Washington to try to get US–European relations back on track. Blair seized on the death of Palestinian leader Yasir Arafat as a possible opening for US and European diplomacy to cooperate in making another push for an Israeli–Palestinian peace accord. During Blair's White House talks, President Bush responded to Blair's efforts by acknowledging that "the world is better off, America is better off, Europe is better off when we work together."[33]

The European countries responded to the Bush victory by compromising on Iraqi debt, agreeing to forgive much of that debt, in spite of Iraq's potential future oil income.[34] But French President Chirac continued to call for a multi-polar world,[35] and President Bush said he would use the "capital" he earned in the elections in support of his policy preferences. These positions left questions about how quickly US–European relations would recover from the Iraq and 9/11 traumas.

In addition, the allies agreed at the December 2004 ministerial meetings in Brussels to expand NATO's Baghdad training presence from 60 to some 300 officers. Six countries—France, Germany, Belgium, Greece, Spain, and Luxembourg—while not blocking the initiative, refused to assign officers to the training program. US Secretary of State Powell and NATO Secretary General Jaap de Hoop Scheffer both expressed their concern that officers from these countries, serving on NATO's International Military Staff, would not be allowed to participate in the program.[36]

The bottom line early in 2005 was that US prestige in Europe had dropped to an all-time low, by almost any measure. The image of US intelligence capabilities, brought low by US claims that Saddam Hussein had an active weapons of mass destruction program, had suffered as well. Would the United States be able to convince European governments to follow its lead on some future issue that relied on US intelligence capabilities and judgments? The Euro-Atlantic debates over Iraq had left obvious scars on transatlantic relations as well as on intra-European ties.

Many European governments remained supportive of US policy even though all European governments faced public opinion that opposed the war and thought little of US leadership in general. Additional members of the Iraq war coalition were preparing to pull their troops back from Iraq, making very little difference in the capabilities of the "coalition" but further exposing the fact that the United States, with the exception of Tony Blair's loyal support, was carrying most of the burden of maintaining security there. George Bush's "fence mending" trip to Europe in February 2005 helped establish a better atmosphere for the US–European dialogue, and even made some progress toward coordination of US and European approaches to Iran and other issues. Good will was evident on both sides. But many underlying suspicions and unresolved issues remained.

How and why did NATO survive the crisis?

The case could have been made in the mid-2000s that NATO would, in fact, not survive for long and that the issues that came to a head in the crisis instigated by the policies of George W. Bush's administration would return to undermine the alliance down the road. If, however, "survival" is defined by the will of the member states to sustain the alliance relationship, the alliance survived this most recent in a long line of crises in the relationship.

The fact that NATO moved past this confluence of events cannot be explained in terms of the need for a response to an existential threat. Such a threat from the Soviet Union had been history for a decade before George W. Bush came to office, and had not been reconstituted. It also cannot be explained by the Bush administration's post-9/11 argument—an argument not accepted by most Europeans—that the United States and its allies were at war with radical Islamic extremism.

Even though the Bush administration carried unilateralism to new levels, the European allies had already experienced a taste of it in the alliance-friendly Clinton administration. The Bush administration's actions, however, on top of the Clinton experiences, convinced many Europeans that US unilateralism and hegemonic behavior were becoming the norm in transatlantic relations. The suggestion by some that Bush administration behavior was an American anomaly was undermined by the fact that in 2004 the American people re-elected George Bush for a second term.

These European perceptions increased support for building up the European Union as a counterbalance to US power. They fed support for the European Constitution agreed by EU governments in 2003. Such attitudes toward US behavior also led to the "rump" meeting of France, Germany, Belgium and Luxembourg in April 2003, which produced agreement on establishing a separate EU military planning cell independent of NATO, which US Ambassador to NATO Nicholas Burns subsequently called "the most significant threat to NATO's future."

What could have been seen as a reason for European states to get used to America's hegemonic behavior, started to turn into a dynamic that could have led to the end of alliance. Why did it not? The paragraphs that follow discuss some of the possible explanations.

The Bush administration in its second term recognized the need for allies and the importance of NATO in mustering allied contributions to security and made serious efforts to show that the United States remained committed to the alliance.
The Bush administration in its second term mounted a campaign to win back the trust and cooperation of European governments. Both Secretary of State Condoleezza Rice and President Bush visited European capitals early in 2005 explicitly seeking to repair some of the damage done by the administration in its first term, and most particularly by the decision to go to war against Iraq. US policy became more solicitous of allied views, more cooperative and less confrontational.

The shift perhaps reflected the Bush administration's acceptance that more traditional approaches to dealing with its allies would be to the US advantage. In the late 1990s, German commentator Joe Joffe had argued that the United States was different from previous dominant powers: "It irks and domineers, but it does not conquer. It tries to call the shots and bend the rules, but it does not go to war for land and glory." Further, he argued, the dominating US position is based on "soft" as well as "hard" power: "This type of power—a culture that radiates outward and a market that draws inward—rests on pull, not on push; on acceptance, not on conquest."[37] In its second term, the Bush administration tried to rely more on these natural strengths of the United States, and to push more gently.

Failure of the EU Constitution to win popular acceptance implied that arguments being made for the EU to become a "balancer" of US power internationally could not be sustained by reality, at least not in the near term.
The failure of the EU Constitution to win approval in 2005 referenda in France and the Netherlands did not signify popular rejection of the "balancer" argument. Decisions in France and the Netherlands were based far more on the desire to preserve national identities and cultures and on concerns about economic consequences than on any grand strategic arguments.

But this failure did squelch talk about the EU as a "balancer," and led to serious introspection among EU governments. How could one imagine the EU counterbalancing the United States if even the most "Gaullist" of European countries, whose government had promoted the concept of making the EU an international pole of power, could not win popular approval for a document that would establish the platform for such a role?

New European democracies in Eastern and Central Europe were strongly committed to NATO's continuation, particularly because their historical and geographic proximity to Russian power and influence convinced them that NATO provided an essential link to US power that was not provided by EU membership.

Former Soviet satellites in Central and Eastern Europe and three former Soviet Republics (Estonia, Latvia, and Lithuania) had worked hard to adopt "Western" political and economic systems. They wanted to align with the United States and to protect themselves against Russian influence. They wanted to be EU and NATO members to ensure that they were fully part of Europe with strong links to the United States.

Those who wanted the EU to become a "balancer" of American power were disappointed and even angered by the fact that the new democracies wanted a form of European unity that remained compatible with transatlantic alliance. The net impact, however, was to reaffirm the importance of the transatlantic link and NATO.

European governments simply had no alternative to remaining in alliance with the United States, and NATO was still the most important symbol and operational component of the relationship.

Even before the EU Constitution went down in defeat, there were serious questions about the EU balancer concept. In a new balance of power system, the EU would have been required to align itself with Russia and China from time to time in response to disagreements with the United States. One presumes this could also mean that the United States would be free to align with other countries, let's say India and Japan, or even Russia or China, against the European Union. It doesn't take much imagination to envision how unstable international relations could become in such an environment.

Moreover, how comfortable would Europeans feel about aligning themselves with autocratic or even authoritarian states against the American democracy? Somehow this model of international relations never made much sense.

One answer, of course, is that the EU could be a "soft" balancer, simply opposing US policies as necessary and acting as a friendly critic of the United States and not formally aligning itself with any other power. This, however, was not much different from the contemporary state of transatlantic relations. A healthy dialogue over differing points of view remained in the interests of democracies on both sides of the Atlantic.

West European governments remained split concerning the future construction of Europe, and the default position (of European integration within the broader context of transatlantic cooperation) was sufficiently compelling to discourage other options.

The debate in Europe over the US invasion of Iraq reflected the fact that there were very different attitudes and assumptions concerning the relationship with the United States. While some European states opposed the US action based on their judgment that the case for war had not been made, others lined up in support. Among some traditional NATO allies, the United States was supported by several governments led by conservative parties. In the United

Kingdom, the powerful influence of the "special relationship" in the hands of Prime Minister Tony Blair aligned the United Kingdom with its American ally.

The divisions among allies and even within allied governments were based not just on the merits of the case for war but also on differing images of Europe's future. When the model of the EU as a balancer fell apart, the idea of a uniting Europe with the framework of continued transatlantic cooperation reasserted itself.

In addition, the change of leaders in two key countries—France and Germany—substantially improved the dynamics of their bilateral and alliance relations with the United States. When Christian Democrat Angela Merkel assumed the chancellorship in Germany in 2005 she consciously sought to repair some of the damage to Germany's relations with the United States, and to make NATO "a high priority for German foreign policy."[38]

Similarly, when Nicolas Sarkozy won the French presidency in 2007 he brought with him a fundamentally changed attitude toward NATO and relations with the United States. Sarkozy's intent to return France to NATO's integrated military command and to develop the European Union's Security and Defense Policy in NATO-friendly directions was welcomed by the Bush administration.[39]

The fact was that, in spite of differences over Iraq and international relations generally, the United States and its European allies still shared an impressive collection of values and interests.
For those who argued in the 1990s and into the 2000s that Europe and the United States were inevitably drifting apart, the standard assertion of common Euro-Atlantic values appeared undermined by the many issues on which there seemed to be serious differences: the death penalty, global warming, abortion, gun control, and when to use military force, among others. However, in spite of these differences, what made the transatlantic alliance special was the fact that it still stood in defense of core values such as individual liberty, democracy, and the rule of law. The validity of this value foundation was strongly reaffirmed by the former members of the Warsaw Pact and former Soviet Republics that put these values at the heart of their new democratic systems.

The financial and economic fortunes of the United States and Europe had become so mutually interdependent that a political/security break with the United States could put vital European and American interests at risk.
In addition to shared political values, the United States and EU member states had market-based economic systems in which competition drives the market but is governed by democratically approved rules and regulations. European and American market economies remained the essential core of the global economic system.[40] The European Union was the largest US partner in the trade of goods and services. The members of the EU had over $860 billion of direct investment in the United States. The United States had some $700 billion invested in EU states.

The EU and the United States together accounted for more than 40 percent of world trade and represented almost 60 percent of the industrialized world's gross domestic product. Joseph P. Quinlin concluded in his excellent 2003 study of US–European mutual economic interdependence that: "In sum, the years since the fall of the Berlin Wall have witnessed one of the greatest periods of transatlantic economic integration in history. Our mutual stake in each other's prosperity has grown dramatically since the end of the Cold War. We ignore these realities at our peril."[41]

Finally, in 2008, developments in Russian policy (see below, pp. 232–3) starkly highlighted what could return as another reason why NATO survived the Bush administration crisis in transatlantic relations.
Since the end of the Cold War, NATO's members had attempted to develop cooperative political, economic and security relations with Russia. This had not stopped the allies from taking steps that they saw as warranted by their own values and interests, such as admitting former Warsaw Pact allies and Soviet republics to alliance membership. However, other dynamics were working on Russian policies.

After the collapse of the Soviet Union, there was a chance that Russia itself would fall apart, as the Chechen separatist movement seemed to suggest. It was therefore not a surprise that Russia moved into a new, perhaps prolonged, period of authoritarian tendencies designed to keep the country from disintegrating.

Afghanistan: NATO goes "out of area"

All the efforts made to ensure continued NATO cohesion were made necessary not just by the US attack on Iraq but also by the initial US approach to the potential role of NATO and the allies in Afghanistan. NATO's invocation of Article 5 and allied offers of assistance immediately following the al-Qaeda attacks on the United States met a lukewarm response in Washington, where skepticism about NATO and allies in general was rampant in the new administration's Pentagon. When Secretary of Defense Donald Rumsfeld proclaimed in September 2001, "The mission determines the coalition. And the coalition must not be permitted to determine the mission," the message to the NATO allies was loud and clear: thanks, but no thanks.

NATO did provide some early assistance to the United States, such as sending NATO Airborne Warning and Control aircraft to patrol US airspace while similar American systems were supporting operations against the Taliban and al-Qaeda in Afghanistan. Despite inviting a select group of individual allies to contribute forces to operations in Afghanistan, NATO as an organization was largely left aside, owing to the Bush administration's belief that alliance involvement would only complicate decision-making and slow the pace of operations.

It was not long before the United States, recognizing the scope of the task of pacifying Afghanistan, sought additional help from the international community. The Bush administration did not initially call on NATO but asked the United Nations to authorize NATO allies to help man and manage the operation.

Within two months of initiating military operations, the United States and its allies, including Afghan anti-Taliban elements known as the "United Front" or Northern Alliance, had broken the Taliban's control over most of the country. On December 5, the "Bonn Agreement Pending the Re-establishment of Permanent Government Institutions," brokered by the United Nations, established the central role of the United Nations and the US-led coalition in the reconstruction of the country (alongside Hamid Karzai's interim Afghan government). The Bonn meeting of various Afghan factions had designated Karzai, from the ethnic Pashtun majority, to take on the interim role. This agreement was confirmed by United Nations Security Council Resolution (UNSCR) 1386 on December 20, which also called for the establishment of an International Security Assistance Force (ISAF) to "assist the Afghan Interim Authority in the maintenance of security in Kabul and its surrounding areas, so that the Afghan Interim Authority as well as the personnel of the United Nations can operate in a secure environment." The UK accepted initial responsibility for command of the operation, which was originally intended to rotate among troop-contributing nations.

When the ISAF was established, US and allied military operations against residual Taliban and al-Qaeda elements continued as a coalition of the willing under the auspices of Operation Enduring Freedom (OEF), which had been created by the United States in October 2001 following the 9/11 attacks as the umbrella under which Afghanistan operations and other aspects of the Global War on Terror were conducted. Thus, the OEF coalition in Afghanistan and ISAF forces initially operated under parallel but separate command structures.

After a six-month period, the United Kingdom handed over command of the ISAF to Turkey and, at the end of 2002, it was commanded jointly by Germany and the Netherlands with support from NATO. During 2002, the Karzai government advocated an expanded role for the ISAF, which it hoped would help extend the authority of the fledgling central government to the provinces. This proposal was opposed by some domestic Afghan elements and the United States. The United Front feared the erosion of Afghanistan's sovereignty and the marginalization of its own forces, while the US was concerned that the move might constrain its own combat operations.[42] Furthermore, European allies were reluctant to engage more fully in the struggle.

In 2003, however, as the United States began military operations intended to remove Saddam Hussein from power in Iraq, the Bush administration began to see a larger NATO role in Afghanistan as potentially relieving some pressure on US forces, which were increasingly occupied with the new and demanding operation in Iraq. Moreover, Germany and Canada saw a more prominent NATO role as politically facilitating their participation in Afghan operations, and alliance officials in Brussels leaned toward NATO taking on more responsibility.

NATO assumes command of the ISAF

Despite determined French and German opposition to US Iraq policy and related divisions cutting across the entire alliance, consensus was reached at NATO to take command of the ISAF; the decision to do so was confirmed in Brussels on April 16, 2003. In historical perspective, this was a stunning event. Not only were the allies divided over Iraq, but, just four years earlier, the Europeans had resisted any suggestion in NATO's 1999 Strategic Concept that the alliance could be used to mount military operations beyond Europe. With very little debate or dissent, the allies agreed to take on a demanding military mission on soil far from Europe, for which the military forces of many allied countries were ill-prepared. The mission would become seen by many as a litmus test for the ability of the alliance to be an effective contributor to contemporary security challenges.

NATO formally assumed command of the ISAF in August 2003. UNSCR 1510 (October 13, 2003) subsequently confirmed the ISAF mandate to operate outside of Kabul, using joint military-civilian Provincial Reconstruction Teams (PRTs) to bring both security and reconstruction projects to other parts of the country. As Afghanistan moved toward presidential elections scheduled for October 2004, the need to broaden NATO's operations to help ensure security for the vote became more evident. NATO allies pledged in June 2004 to increase the NATO presence from 6,500 to around 10,000 by the time of the election. When the allies met at the summit in Istanbul in June 2004, it seemed an open question whether the forces would be provided. In the end, allies made up the shortfall and helped ensure a relatively peaceful election process. In December 2004, NATO ministers meeting in Brussels agreed to continue the process of expanding NATO's role in Afghanistan by deploying PRTs to the country's western provinces, yet no allies pledged additional troops for the effort.

Based on the UN mandate, the allies developed a plan to work through progressive stages in Afghanistan with the goal of ultimately providing security and reconstruction programs across the entire country. The first stage, carried out in 2003–2004 by French and German troops, was to secure the more stable northern regions. Stage 2 began in May 2005, when Spanish and Italian forces moved into western Afghanistan. Establishment of ISAF command in the more volatile southern and eastern regions began on July 31, 2006 with the initiation of stage 3 and continued with the final stage 4 on October 5 of the same year. Some forces from the separate, US-led OEF remained for counter-terror operations but, by the end of 2006, the ISAF was responsible for providing security for all of Afghanistan. As of June 2009, there were 61,130 ISAF troops in the country from 42 contributing nations and 89,500 soldiers in the Afghan National Army. The operation was organized around five conceptual phases: (I) assessment and preparation (in Kabul); (II) geographic expansion through Afghanistan; (III) stabilization; (IV) transition to domestically provided security; and (V) redeployment of ISAF troops.

Provincial Reconstruction Teams (PRTs)

PRTs were the main organizational instrument for the ISAF's contributions to the stabilization and development of Afghanistan. The alliance's comprehensive approach to the ISAF mission has brought together "civilian-military units of varying sizes, designed to extend the authority of the central government into the countryside, provide security, and undertake projects to boost the Afghan economy."[43] As of July 2009, there were 26 PRTs under ISAF jurisdiction with various lead countries, some taking over from teams formerly controlled by the United States, including those in Kandahar (Canada), Lashkar Gah (Britain), and Tarin Kowt (the Netherlands).

Despite some successes, the PRT program came under criticism for a variety of reasons, many stemming from the disconnected and non-standardized nature of the operations. One expert observed that PRTs seemed to be largely a localized form of support, leaving large swathes of territory unprotected and unaided.[44] Germany was criticized for its operation of PRTs due to the politically imposed caveats that prevented both civilians and military PRT elements from operating beyond the borders of their PRTs. Some non-governmental organizations (NGOs) complained that PRTs were treading on their feet, bringing heavy firepower and inexperienced operatives to bear on situations in which they (the NGOs) had specific experience and skills.[45] Their claims suggested that the civilian-military nature of PRTs had blurred the lines between combatants and aid workers, and thus endangered independent NGO staff, whose supposed neutrality was thus compromised, consequently exposing them to increased risk of kidnap and death.[46]

The PRT concept, even with its shortcomings, responded to the accurate perception that the war in Afghanistan could not be won without the kind of reconstruction and development that the PRTs were intended to produce. The provision of stability in Afghanistan required a "comprehensive approach,"[47] one that sought to provide a degree of security for the development of Afghan infrastructure, economy, educational opportunities, public health programs, and a modern legal system. The main shortcomings seem to have been the low number of teams and lack of security, both of which prevented the program from achieving its goals on a national scale. In addition, the fact that the PRTs were designed and operated on a nation-by-nation basis stood in the way of any consistent NATO or ISAF design for the country-wide operation.

Operation Enduring Freedom and the ISAF

From its inception with UNSCR 1386, the ISAF existed in parallel with, but separate from, the US-led OEF that had successfully ousted the Taliban from power and continued to pursue al-Qaeda and Taliban elements. In 2009, the OEF continued as a counter-insurgency combat operation with approximately 38,500 troops under US command, while the ISAF was expressly mandated by the United Nations to provide security and development for Afghanistan. With completion of stage four of ISAF, in which NATO assumed responsibility for providing security for the entire country, the line separating the objectives of the two operations became increasingly blurred, as the necessity of combating a growing Taliban/al-Qaeda insurgency forced ISAF troops into more combat roles.

Some way of consolidating the commands seemed logical from early on. However, the idea met with mixed emotions on both sides of the Atlantic. Some experts claimed that initial US rejection of proposals to integrate the operations was based on its desire to retain autonomous control over its forces in the region.[48] One of these experts, Amin Saikal, claimed it was an extension of American aversion to UN supervision that kept the ISAF and OEF separate. European resistance, Saikal said, resulted from some NATO contributors not wanting to see their troops redirected into harm's way in the unstable south of the country.[49] In addition, Markus Kaim reported that the public perception in Germany was "that Enduring Freedom is the 'bad' American part of the Afghanistan mission, bombing villages and killing innocent civilians, whereas the ISAF is the 'good' one, focusing on state building and reconstruction."[50]

Nevertheless, ISAF stage four requirements and the intensification of the Afghan insurgency finally forced a partial consolidation of the OEF and ISAF commands. The separate commands led to differences in both strategy and tactics, compromising attempts to produce an Afghanistan-wide approach to dealing with the insurgents and the accompanying need for development of governmental and civilian systems and infrastructure.

While the ISAF was making the transition to a more active combat capacity, the OEF continued to conduct its own, separate operations against high value targets and other militant concentrations. NATO and US planning began to reflect the realization that withdrawing from areas after completion of combat operations was resulting in the re-establishment of Taliban influence. As a result, the operational strategy for NATO forces was changed to "clear, hold and build."[51] Instead of clearing territory of Taliban and promptly leaving, ISAF troops began to hold newly won territory and develop indigenous security forces and services in the hopes of fostering a more persistent stability. However, there were still insufficient forces and inadequate (corrupt, compromised, or incompetent) government infrastructure to implement the concept successfully on a large-scale basis.

The Pakistan complication

Beginning in 2007, violence caused by the Taliban and al-Qaeda insurgencies escalated, with significant increases in ISAF and US casualties. The expansion of Taliban capabilities was in no small measure due to the fact that the insurgents had established their base of operations and support facilities across the border in Pakistan. The insurgent leadership, having been dislodged from Afghanistan by persistent NATO and coalition action, began operating from safe havens nearby, in Pakistan's Federally Administered Tribal Areas (FATA) and Baluchi region. The traditional Taliban under Mullah Muhammad Omar, along with two other Taliban groups with links to al-Qaeda, operated from these territories. In addition, Pakistani Jihadist elements under the separate leaderships of Gulbuddin Hekmatyar and Jalaluddin Haqqani operated from the FATA. The latter established the so-called "Islamic Emirate of Waziristan" with several thousand fighters and claimed responsibility for several suicide bombings in Afghanistan.[52]

Dealing with this challenge was complicated by the fact that the government of Pakistan, for a wide variety of reasons, until the second half of 2009, was unwilling or unable to take on the Taliban and other extremist elements that had solidified their base along Pakistan's border with Afghanistan. In addition, reports suggested that elements of the Pakistani government (especially the Inter-Services Intelligence organization) were complicit in the operation of cross-border insurgent groups.

Despite their reluctance until 2009 to pursue the Taliban presence in their border frontiers, the Pakistani military did engage in combat in the FATA against foreign fighters and took part in dialogues both with the ISAF and the Afghan National Army through the Tripartite Joint Intelligence Operations Center, which aimed to coordinate military action on the border between the three forces.

By this stage of the war, there was widespread agreement that stability could never be secured in Afghanistan until Pakistan controlled its border and resolved its own problems with the Taliban/al-Qaeda insurgency. The resignation of President Pervez Musharraf in 2008, and the restoration of civilian rule to the country, were followed by rapid deterioration of the economy, and despite the new government's pledge to combat growing insurgency and terrorism in the country, pro-Taliban militancy grew bolder, notably in the northwestern city of Peshawar. But the departure of Musharraf led to improved relations between Afghanistan and Pakistan, and the program of "peace jirga" meetings between prominent tribal elders from both countries began anew.

After coming to office in January 2009, the Obama administration made it clear that it would deal with Afghanistan and Pakistan as key parts of the same problem. Subsequently in 2009, the government of Pakistan took a more active and effective approach to dealing with Taliban and extremist elements in the regions adjacent to Afghanistan. The Pakistan military mounted a major operation in the fall of 2009 seeking to take control of Taliban and al Qaeda strongholds in Waziristan from which the insurgent leaders mounted operations and sought refuge from US and ISAF forces on the other side of the border. The operation, for which Pakistan authorities claimed major successes, led almost immediately to an upsurge in attacks against Pakistani civilian and governmental targets. It remained clear that close cooperation among all players—the United States, NATO ISAF, Afghan authorities, and Pakistani officials—would be required to reduce the threat of radical extremists in both countries, and that sustaining domestic support in Pakistan for its role in the conflict would be a challenge to the government in Karachi.

The mission: a self-governing, secure Afghanistan

The NATO allies agreed that "NATO's main role in Afghanistan is to assist the Afghan government in exercising and extending its authority and influence across the country, paving the way for reconstruction and effective governance."[53] When the NATO leaders celebrated the alliance's 60th anniversary at Strasbourg (France) and Kehl (Germany) in April 2009, they issued a Summit Declaration on Afghanistan elaborating on the mission and its rationale, declaring:

> In Afghanistan we are helping build security for the Afghan people, protecting our citizens and defending the values of freedom, democracy and human rights. Our common security is closely tied to the stability and security of Afghanistan and the region: an area of the world from where extremists planned attacks against civilian populations and democratic governments and continue to plot today. Through our UN-mandated mission, supported by our International Security Assistance Force (ISAF) partners, and working closely with the Afghan government, we remain committed for the long-run to supporting a democratic Afghanistan that does not become, once more, a base for terror attacks or a haven for violent extremism that destabilizes the region and threatens the entire International Community.[54]

The task of establishing a legitimate, competent, centralized government presented a unique challenge to the international community, because Afghanistan had a long history of decentralized rule and had frequently looked much like a failed state, in which no one power possessed a monopoly on the legitimate use of force. Rule of law and provision of security was administered informally on an ad-hoc basis across the country, with little or no standardization, training, or even literate officials. The Bonn Agreement of 2001 set the goal of establishing governmental legitimacy and consolidating central control following the defeat of the Taliban, but widespread corruption and the perception of weakness in the face of the Taliban's continued insurgency cast doubts about the ability of the government to sustain itself. In fact, the Bonn Agreement itself, while seeking to strengthen the government in Kabul, led to an international approach that may have worked against the stated objective. Pursuant to the accord, NATO nations and international organizations focused many of their efforts locally and regionally without a clear national strategy and without necessarily strengthening the influence of the central government over distant and historically autonomous regions and population centers.

A new Afghan constitution was ratified in January of 2004, establishing a strong presidency counterbalanced by a legislature, confirming equal rights for men and women, and laying a framework of Sunni Islamic law for the judiciary.[55] The head of the interim administration, Hamid Karzai, was subsequently elected with 55 percent of the popular vote and was then free to appoint a 27-member cabinet. The international community recognized that the fledgling government would require significant financial and organizational support. At the national level, the United Nations Development Program focused its efforts on increasing the government's ruling capacity through developing structures such as an independent election commission, support mechanisms for the newly elected Afghan Parliament, training for civil servants, financial and logistical support for police forces, and other measures.

At the provincial level, NATO-ISAF supported various efforts to extend governance by providing security, PRT operations, and support of various initiatives such as the Afghan Social Outreach Program, which increased dialogue between provincial authority figures and their populations.

The August 2009 elections were conducted without major terrorist attacks, although it appeared that the relatively light turnout had been induced by Taliban threats and attacks prior to the elections, particularly in the southern and eastern parts of the country. President Karzai won a decisive victory over his one major opponent, former Foreign Minister Dr Abdullah Abdullah, but evidence of widespread voter fraud led to demands and plans for a runoff election. However, Abdullah withdrew from the election, arguing that the runoff election would not be conducted fairly. President Karzai was returned to power, but with a large black cloud over his head.

Despite some areas of success, the establishment of a self-sufficient, legitimate government proved in many ways to be fraught with difficulty. It was widely acknowledged that President Karzai had tolerated corruption and appeased faction leaders with appointments to facilitate stability,[56] but endemic corruption consistently stood out as a crippling factor in the extension of effective governance, and reports indicated that the government consistently failed to provide basic services to the population. Various international efforts to provide local delivery of aid through PRTs, NGOs, Special Forces, and other programs often conflicted both with one another and with domestic government processes that remained unregulated and disconnected from one another. Inefficient, highly centralized ministries in Kabul were often responsible for delivery of services across the country, and while efforts were made to delegate authority to lower levels, results were limited.

Provision of essential services was critical for establishing the legitimacy of a central Afghan government, but as of 2009 the government lacked even the means to collect taxes. Indeed, bookkeeping, even at the national level, was so underdeveloped that the government could not keep track of aid flows. Instead it left the task of accountancy up to individual donors, who had varying recordkeeping methods that further complicated information sharing.[57]

According to the former Interior Minister of Afghanistan Ali A. Jalali, writing in 2007, "The structural legitimacy of the current Afghan government suffers from a lack of capacity, particularly at the subnational level, where the vacuum is filled by insurgents, militia commanders, [and] local gangs, all of whom undermine human security, local governance, democratic values and the delivery of basic services."[58] The weakness of the government, he claimed, has caused a crisis of confidence and the erosion of its legitimacy. Apparently, the fundamentals had not changed by 2009 when the Congressional Research Service observed that "The Karzai government's own problems are apparent: discontented warlords, endemic corruption, a vigorous drug trade, the Taliban, and a rudimentary economy and infrastructure. In the view of former NATO General, speaking as the US Ambassador to Afghanistan, Karl Eikenberry said 'The enemy we face is not particularly strong, but the institutions of the Afghan state remain relatively weak.'"[59]

Rule of law and an operational justice system, often considered keystones to the establishment of a legitimate regime, were still woefully underdeveloped and, according to a World Bank assessment, the Afghan system was still one of the worst in the world.[60] Reports indicated that warlord control over regions had dramatically disrupted attempts by the central government to appoint judges and establish authority, and allegations of serious corruption were lodged against both the attorney general's office and the Supreme Court in Kabul.

Corruption and incompetence in the newly reconstituted police force proved disastrous for its credibility. A report by the International Institute for Strategic Studies asserted in 2007 that "The Afghan National Police has been a source of insecurity for communities across the country, rather than a solution to it."[61] The report charged that informal bribe earnings for police in the country ranged between $200 and $30,000 per month, and that besides failing to prosecute in instances of murder and torture, the police themselves engaged in crimes, such as bank robberies and kidnappings for ransom.[62] Reforms were slow-moving and, despite efforts by the European Union Police and the United States to raise standards, it was concluded in July 2007 that only 40 percent of the Afghan National Police was adequately equipped.[63]

These problems continued virtually unabated into 2009. NATO's annual assessment reported that "The capacity of the Afghan government at the national, provincial and district levels remains limited and suffers from corruption. Continuing insecurity, criminality and, in places, the influence of the narcotics trade further impede efforts to improve good governance."[64]

In the United States, the new Obama administration immediately placed a high priority on improving training of the Afghan police and sent an additional 4,000 troops to Afghanistan to strengthen the program. The United States hoped that the injection of additional trainers would make a difference in combating corruption. The unscrupulous nature of the force was pervasive: ranking positions on police forces and judiciary frequently went to the highest bidder and, as one provincial police official observed, "This is the reason no one accepts the rule of law ... because the government is not going by the rule of law."[65]

The irony in all this was that the Taliban reportedly were reaping large financial benefits from the illicit narcotics trade—a line of business they suppressed when in power. For many Afghans, growing poppy for that trade had become their main way of life as well as the main source of revenue for the Taliban.

Since the Taliban was removed from power, opium poppy cultivation in Afghanistan had increased to supply 93 percent of the world's opium. Part of the answer to the drug problem was destroying poppy fields and disrupting production and transportation of opium to the international market. US, ISAF, and Afghan forces cooperated in such destruction and interdiction activities. However, these approaches did not present a long-term solution to the problem, in part because so much of the Afghan economy depended on the revenue from the trade.

The Afghanistan National Security Forces: toward self-defense capabilities?

A critical key to the security component of Afghanistan's future was the development of domestic security forces capable of defending the political system from its enemies. This also proved to be a daunting task. However, according to NATO, in 2008 "The [Afghanistan National Security Forces] grew in strength and capability and Afghan forces assumed responsibility for security in the Kabul area for the first time."[66]

Responsibility for training the Afghan National Army (ANA) had been primarily taken on by the United States, but included the cooperation of French, British, Turkish, and other nations' trainers in establishing an officer corp. In the Summit Declaration on Afghanistan in April 2009 NATO leaders announced the establishment of a NATO Training Mission-Afghanistan to provide higher-level training for the ANA and additionally confirmed the target for army expansion to be 134,000 troops.[67] Newly trained units experienced early successes in combat operations alongside foreign forces and, in 2008, 62 percent were led by the ANA.[68] ISAF and coalition troops were deployed with ANA units through the Embedded Training Team and the Operational Mentoring and Liaison Team programs, monitoring and supporting the development of the force. By mid-March 2009, the ISAF was operating 52 Operational Mentoring and Liaison Teams with at least 30 additional teams planned to enter service by the end of 2010.[69]

NATO also provided support for the ANA through its Equipment Support Program and the ANA Trust Fund, which the NAC set up in 2008. Various NATO nations donated equipment with the intention of modernizing the Soviet-era armaments of the ANA, but internal complaints persisted regarding the dismal state of the army's weaponry and, as of early 2009, contributions to the trust fund were still limited, totaling approximately 18.5 million euros.[70]

Despite some successes, the ANA was criticized for its crippling dependence on foreign military assistance, in the form of embedded NATO/Coalition troops, air-support, and funding,[71] and for its high attrition rate.[72] That said, developments, such as the creation of the Afghan National Army Air Corps, spearheaded by the United States, gave the ANA greater independence.

At the end of the decade, the development of self-sufficient Afghan military forces remained a long-term project, but one that perhaps had made more progress than the development of the judicial and legal system. This was not surprising, given the fact that the US and ISAF military forces in Afghanistan had been able to provide the resources to help mold an Afghan military with its own standards and internal relationships that perhaps would rise above those seen in Afghan civilian society.

Implications for NATO

The ISAF mission became NATO's most ambitious and demanding task in its history. The Cold War required large armies and defense budgets, but never brought alliance forces into a combat environment. Afghanistan became a groundbreaking experience for the alliance, both because it required active combat and counter-insurgency operations and because it was so far from the alliance's base in Europe.

At least initially, assumption of the ISAF mission appeared to be a vote of confidence in unity and cooperation on both sides of the Atlantic. The Bush administration had been forced to acknowledge that it needed help from allies and the alliance to deal with the demands of two conflicts: one in Iraq, which was given highest priority, and the other in Afghanistan, which had begun as the immediate reaction to the 9/11 attacks. The fact that the allies fell in behind the ISAF mission at a time when the alliance was so profoundly divided over Iraq suggested that the alliance could survive its most heated disagreements.

By 2008, it was clear that the combination of ISAF and OEF operations had not been enough to turn the tide against the Taliban or to capture Osama bin Laden. Subsequent paragraphs examine the shortcomings of ISAF that are deeply rooted in Europe. However, it seems appropriate to start with a brief acknowledgment that the US decision to invade Iraq and remove Saddam Hussein from power led to such a demanding commitment there that the goals in Afghanistan became a secondary priority. In 2007, Chairman of the US Joint Chiefs of Staff, Admiral Mike Mullen, said pointedly: "In Afghanistan, we do what we can. In Iraq, we do what we must." In May 2009, Mullen reversed field, and declared that Afghanistan was the US military's "main effort"— a priority that would guide troop assignments, equipment purchases and deployments, and allocation of other resources.[73]

The United States did not dedicate the military manpower needed to establish and maintain control against the Taliban. It did not devote enough civilian capabilities and financial resources to help the government in Kabul establish itself throughout the country. However, the specific problems and history associated with Afghanistan suggest that even with a devoted and persistent effort, the United States still might not have been able to achieve its objectives there.

None of the European allies portrayed the deficient US commitment as a rationale for the shortcomings of their own contributions. And, it could be further argued that the more the United States does, the less the Europeans will feel their efforts to be essential. Nevertheless, if leadership by example has any value, the fact is that the United States constructed a very poor model for the Europeans to emulate.

Weak allied public support

European involvement in ISAF combat operations never enjoyed wide-spread support among the domestic populations of the contributing nations. According to the German Marshall Fund's 2008 Transatlantic Trends public opinion survey, support for deploying their troops in combat operations gained majority support only in the United Kingdom (64 percent favor) and France (52 percent favor). In Germany, 62 percent opposed using their troops to conduct operations against the Taliban. The overall results in the 12 European countries polled found an average of only 43 percent in support of troops being used for combat operations. When asked if they favored deploying troops for non-combat roles such as providing security for reconstruction, training Afghan soldiers and police, or combating narcotics production, all European countries polled produced strong majorities in support. Respondents in the United States showed strong majority support for the use of American troops in combat and non-combat operations.[74] In Canada, a country that had been on the front lines in combat operations, support for its role in ISAF eroded in 2008–2009, with its mission set to expire in 2011.[75]

The aversion to combat in Afghanistan did not necessarily reflect public loss of confidence in NATO. Despite strong European disapproval of the Bush administration and its policies, public opinion of NATO's importance to their country's security remarkably remained relatively strong. An average of around 60 percent of European respondents in the 2008 Transatlantic Trends polling agreed that NATO was "still essential" to their country's security, a number almost identical to the percentage of Americans who thought the alliance still essential to US security.

The reluctance of NATO members to provide forces to the ISAF underlined the limited enthusiasm for its mission. While the alliance touted the fact that all members and several partners had provided forces to the ISAF, many made only token contributions. The difficulty that European members of NATO had in 2006 finding 2,200 troops to replace departing soldiers demonstrated the failure of the allies to shoulder the burden that NATO accepted in taking command of the ISAF. Despite the UN's authorization "to take all necessary measures to fulfill its mandate," many NATO European allies were either unable or unwilling to commit forces to the Afghanistan conflict.

Secretary of Defense Robert Gates, preparing to leave for meetings with his counterparts in June 2009, nonetheless took an upbeat approach, telling a US Senate committee that the United States was not alone in Afghanistan and that more than 40 allies deployed a total of 32,000 troops there. Gates avoided criticizing those that avoided combat missions, but specifically commended Canada, Denmark, the UK, and Australia, all of which had put their troops in harm's way and taken heavy casualties.[76] In the past, Gates had taken the allies to task for the limits on their contributions, but apparently the United States decided that public praise for allied efforts would be more effective than public criticism of their shortcomings.

National caveats, casualty differentials, and burden-sharing

Ambiguity in the UN mandate for the ISAF and the level of decision-making discretion given to NATO allies led to a wide variety of approaches to how individual nations deployed and used PRTs and other programs and what limits governed the troops they committed to the ISAF. National caveats, or restrictions, placed by many nations on their forces in Afghanistan, exacerbated tensions within the alliance. They also reduced the flexibility of commanders to allocate forces in the country, while nationwide reconstruction programs, undertaken by various allies, met with mixed effectiveness and occasional charges of inefficiency and redundancy. One NATO general was quoted as saying "Opponents and national caveats have polluted ISAF's command-and-control system ... If politicians don't trust their military commanders, they should kick them out, but they should not try to run local battles from faraway capitals. It is wrong and it can kill people."[77]

In mid-2009, nearly half of all troops under ISAF command had some sort of restrictions on their operational capacities, relating to geographic deployment, mission profiles, and the use of force. According to the Congressional Research Service:

> While caveats in themselves do not generally prohibit the kinds of operations NATO forces can engage in, caveats do pose difficult problems for commanders

who seek maximum flexibility in utilizing troops under their command. Some governments' troops lack the appropriate equipment to function with other NATO forces. Some nations will not permit their troops to deploy to other parts of Afghanistan. Still others prohibit their troops from participating in combat operations unless in self-defense. NATO commanders have willingly accepted troops from some 42 governments but have had to shape the conduct of the mission to fit the capabilities of and caveats on those troops.[78]

These limitations, while often a reflection of the domestic political realities of the allies, were widely criticized outside the countries with the most constraining caveats. At the 2008 Munich Security Conference, Secretary of Defense Gates issued an unequivocal condemnation of national caveats, saying "in NATO, some allies ought not to have the luxury of opting only for stability and civilian operations, thus forcing other allies to bear a disproportionate share of the fighting and the dying."[79]

The nationally imposed limitations on Germany's ISAF contribution were the focus of greatest controversy. Germany's troops, largely confined to the relatively stable northern regional command, were required to go to great lengths to avoid confrontations with militants and were prohibited from initiating combat operations, authorized by the German government to fire only in self-defense. Demilitarization and the legacy of World War II in the German collective conscious, according to German foreign policy expert Markus Kaim, led to what military sociologists call "post-heroic society" which is "casualty-shy and risk averse," needing to rationalize military involvement as a noble, humanitarian mission of state-building.[80] Politically, taking an anti-Afghanistan war stance became tremendously profitable in Germany, and left-wing parties gained serious traction by advocating immediate withdrawal and painting entanglement in Afghanistan as an outgrowth of following the Bush doctrine.[81] Chancellor Merkel's coalition government was forced to walk a fine line between placating an increasingly impatient public and destabilizing the entire NATO operation by heeding their demands. The disaffection of the German populace was not unique, and similar trends were seen in other contributing nations as well, including France and the Netherlands, and even staunch US ally the United Kingdom.

The German situation in some ways illustrated the success of Western policy after World War II. Every possible political, legal, social, and educational attempt was made to ensure that Germany would never again be a threat to European or international peace. The campaign was embraced by West Germany's leaders and its educational system. Furthermore, German reunification at the end of the Cold War brought in a population that had been trained to be suspicious of the West, the United States, and NATO. For some German politicians, the limits on Germany's role in Afghanistan may be largely a way of avoiding difficult decisions and commitments. But, for others, it is a matter of strong political beliefs concerning Germany's role in the world.

Despite public pressures on European governments, and increased intensity of the conflict in Afghanistan, some took steps to reduce the number and severity of restrictions on their ISAF forces. In 2009, the French contingent was authorized to offer emergency assistance to other NATO forces and the Italian and Spanish commanders were granted discretionary authority concerning the use of the troops under them in urgent situations.[82]

Perhaps the greatest danger to success in Afghanistan and to the future utility of NATO was the development of a multi-tiered alliance, in which some countries assumed much greater risks than others on behalf of a shared mission. In the relationship between the United States and the European allies, this concern took the form of the traditional burden-sharing issue, in which the United States appeared to carry most of the weight and became resentful of the less-robust European contributions. With the Obama administration's shift in US priorities and resources from Iraq to Afghanistan, the gap between the North American and European military contributions and risks taken—as well as similar gaps among the Europeans themselves—grew, generating grounds for a new-burden-sharing debate on both the transatlantic and intra-European levels.

Moreover, there were serious differentials in the casualties suffered by alliance members as a result of their contributions. Grim reality dictated that the countries deploying their forces on the front lines of combat with the Taliban and al-Qaeda would suffer the greatest casualties. The forces of the United States, the United Kingdom, Canada, Denmark, and the Netherlands consequently faced the greatest risks and took the heaviest casualties. Countries like Germany, deployed in the more stable north, took fewer risks and sustained lighter casualties. This is an aspect of the burden-sharing debate that cut across the alliance at a very personal level. It was not a matter of money, but rather concerned the lives of soldiers. Should the life of a soldier from one allied country be more valuable than that of another? Of course not. But the consequences of political decisions taken by various allies produced the appearance of such a difference, and this casualty differential threatened to leave long-term scars on the alliance.

A continuing story ...

As the process of progressively turning combat responsibilities over to the central Afghan government began, the process of evaluating the performance of the United States, its allies, and the alliance had just begun. Mistakes were made. The United States made the first one by invading Afghanistan without devoting the time, attention, and resources to the task of stabilizing the defeated and failed state. Yet the European allies also contributed to the problem by severely limiting the manpower and resources they were willing to commit to the conflict. The constraints many allies placed on the forces they did deploy made if difficult if not impossible for NATO to construct a coherent effort on the ground. The European Union, which has access to many of the non-military assets not commanded by NATO, was slow and tentative in contributing, some say because EU officials were reluctant to play second fiddle to NATO and the United States in Afghanistan.[83]

In the second half of 2009, a challenge to such a successful outcome emerged in the United States itself. The Obama administration's attempt to refocus American military priorities on Afghanistan, based on a calculated assessment of US interests, was challenged by shifting American public opinion. As the increased number of US troops in Afghanistan and much higher tempo of operations against Taliban targets produced growing numbers of American casualties, public opinion in the United States began to turn against continuing the war.[84] The polling results raised questions about whether the Obama administration could sustain the American presence in Afghanistan without resorting to the kind of fear-mongering that so successfully produced initial public support for the Bush administration's war against Iraq. It was obvious that, if the United States could not sustain its role in Afghanistan, that of NATO would fail as well.

The administration was put in a particularly difficult bind by the fact that as public opinion was running away from support for the war, Obama's military advisors were recommending a large increase in US forces devoted to the effort. The recommendation by the commander of US and ISAF forces in Afghanistan, General Stanley A. McChrystal—that as many as 40,000 additional American troops would be required to avoid mission failure—presented the administration with a difficult set of choices: go against the president's political base or the advice of his top military commanders.

In November 2009, Obama announced he had decided to order substantial increases in the US military forces in Afghanistan. In so doing, he largely followed the advice of his military commanders. In response to concerns, expressed strongly in his own party, about escalation of the conflict, Obama declared that his strategy placed a high priority on training up the ANA to be able progressively to take over responsibilities for security, allowing the United States to begin withdrawing forces by the middle of 2011. He also called for NATO allies to increase their own commitments during the same time period. He still faced criticism from the right for setting a deadline by which time to begin withdrawing forces and from the left for sending more troops in the near term and not receiving sufficient support from the international community.

While NATO, the European allies, and the European Union could all be faulted for either ineffective or insufficient contributions to the effort in Afghanistan, the United States carried part of the blame for not making Afghanistan a higher priority. For its part, the United States did not want the Afghan problem to be "Americanized," and the formal involvement of NATO and NATO allies in shaping the outcome helped ensure that the conflict remained internationalized. NATO's involvement, even as flawed as it was, provided a critical link to international legitimacy for US policy objectives. That link ran through NATO directly to the United Nations, hopefully (from the US point of view) ensuring that the broader international community would share responsibility for guaranteeing that Afghanistan did not return to a failed state offering a welcoming habitat for future terrorist operations. However, when the Obama administration on December 28, 2014 announced the formal end of the US (and NATO) combat role in Afghanistan (see Chapter 8), Afghanistan's future remained up for grabs.

NATO's defense planning response to post-9/11 requirements

Even though NATO was not immediately given a role to play following the September 11, 2001 terrorist attacks, it was clear to most observers that NATO would have to contribute to the struggle against international terrorism to remain relevant to the security needs of its member states. But NATO did not yet have the mandate from the member states to operate beyond Europe where many of the military operations against terrorist organizations were being conducted. The alliance was neither organized nor equipped to play a meaningful role.

As noted above (pp. 191–2), it was ironic that, at a time when the allies were becoming seriously divided over what to do about Iraq, they nonetheless were able to move forward on a number of NATO initiatives designed to overcome barriers to a more central NATO role in the fight against terrorism. The work produced a package of measures approved at the summit meeting in Prague, the Czech Republic, in November 2002.

Perhaps the most important development came without particular notice. Discussions at NATO during the year had, with little controversy, moved beyond the problems encountered in Washington in 1999 concerning NATO's area of operation. NATO foreign ministers, meeting as the NAC in May 2002 in Reykjavik, Iceland, declared that the allies must be capable of carrying out "the full range of ... missions ... to field forces wherever they are needed."[85] By the time of the Prague Summit, the allies were agreed that NATO had to be ready to intervene militarily anywhere the interests of NATO countries were threatened. The old "out of area" debate had ended, with no major fanfare.

Given the nature of the challenges NATO had faced since the end of the Cold War, it was not surprising that the topic of how to "transform" the alliance came front and center in the 2000s. After all, Russia was no longer perceived as a military threat, while challenges well beyond NATO's borders were becoming more demanding. The concept was developed originally with the thought that NATO militaries needed to transform the contingency plans, capabilities, equipment, and training to move away from border defense and toward force projection. The NATO nations even dedicated a major command to the transformation task when, in 2002, they converted the Allied Command Atlantic in Norfolk, Virginia to the Allied Command Transformation. The new command was given no operational responsibilities, but instead was intended to promote transformation of alliance military capabilities. Allied Command Transformation's goal was to ensure that NATO military forces, concepts, doctrines, and training were focused on the new security challenges faced by alliance forces. At the same time, Allied Command Europe, NATO's other strategic command, was renamed "Allied Command Operations."

In an attempt to plant the transformation goal more firmly in the decision-making processes of the member states, the leaders formulated a "Prague Capabilities Commitment," saying they did so as part of the continuing alliance effort to improve and develop new military capabilities for modern warfare in a high threat environment. The Prague communiqué declared that "Individual allies have made firm and specific political commitments to improve their capabilities in the areas of chemical, biological, radiological, and nuclear defence; intelligence, surveillance, and target acquisition; air-to-ground surveillance; command, control, and communications; combat effectiveness, including precision guided munitions and suppression of enemy air defences; strategic air and sea lift; air-to-air refueling; and deployable combat support and combat service support units."[86]

The Defense Capabilities Initiative (DCI) approved at the 1999 Washington Summit had ambitiously covered about every imaginable shortcoming of NATO forces. The allies tried to give the Prague Capabilities Commitment a more narrow focus on capabilities that would be required by the NATO Response Force in the hope that it also would be more successful than the DCI. The underlying problem in most European countries remained a shortage of funds devoted to defense, but the new capabilities commitment at least identified areas where available funds should be concentrated. One area of particular concern was the challenge of dealing with potential chemical, biological, and nuclear attacks. At Prague, the allies agreed to create a Multinational Chemical, Biological, Radiological and Nuclear Defense Battalion, which was brought to operational status by December 2003. The battalion, led by the Czech Republic, helped provide security for the summer 2004 Athens Olympics.

The Allied Command Transformation describes itself as "NATO's leading agent for change; enabling, facilitating and advocating continuous improvement of military capabilities to enhance the military interoperability, relevance and effectiveness of the Alliance." In a vacuum, this might have been a spectacular undertaking to occupy NATO and member state militaries for many years. In the real world, NATO military interventions in the Balkans and then in Afghanistan demonstrated the need for transformation and, at the same time, made it more difficult.

In fact, NATO must use its real world experiences as the main drivers for transformation, rather than looking at them as getting in the way. The fact is that the experience in Iraq, as troubled as it was, has been a transformational experience for the United States military. US forces encountered serious asymmetric responses from Iraqi and al-Qaeda fighters, particularly the use of Improvised Explosive Devices against allied troops and armored vehicles. The threat forced changes not only in tactics but also in equipment, leading to a new generation of armored vehicles more resistant to attacks by Improvised Explosive Devices.

Much of the discussion of the failures and successes of transformation revolve around the story of the NATO Response Force (NRF). The concept of such a force was developed in think tank studies, and originally was supposed to bring together highly capable American forces with forces from European allied militaries. The goal was to produce a force that was highly capable and able to respond quickly to contingencies before other forces could be mustered. In addition, it was thought that such an integrated NATO force would help spread American know-how and technological sophistication to allied militaries.

The NRF concept called for development of a combined (multiple nations participating), joint (army, air, and naval units) force some 21,000 strong. The force was designed to have modern, highly capable fighter aircraft, ships, army vehicles, combat service support, logistics, communications, intelligence, and all other attributes required to make it an agile, effective force.

When the allies approved the NRF concept in 2002, it more or less followed the plan that had been developed by experts, but did not include extensive contributions to the force, in part because Afghanistan and Iraq were already American preoccupations. From the perspective of the George W. Bush administration, the NRF became a challenge to the European allies to transform their forces to make them more relevant to contemporary security threats and responses.[87]

It could be argued that the NRF became more of a distraction than a help to the alliance's ability to perform its missions by holding back for NRF purposes forces that were desperately needed in Afghanistan. But the forces assigned are not "locked up in a drawer," and can be used as necessary by the states from which they originated. There is no doubt that NATO's military forces still required substantial transformation at all levels. The main obstacle was the lack of political will in national capitals to devote the priority and resources to the necessary upgrading and reorientation of military forces.

Between the end of the Cold War and 2009, a number of factors produced this lack of will, including the desire to realize the post-Cold War peace dividend, the constraints imposed on discretionary spending, notably including defense, by the deficit spending limits imposed by EU monetary union, and differences with the United States over the best mix of hard and soft power to deal with international security challenges. At the end of the 2000s, even though the allies no longer had the "Bush alibi" for limiting their defense efforts, one can add the global economic downturn to the list of factors that made political leaders unwilling and, in some cases, unable to support even current levels of defense spending. Only a handful of NATO's European members were achieving the informal alliance goal of spending at least two percent of gross domestic product on defense. The estimated average for NATO Europe in 2008 was 1.7 percent of gross domestic product, while the United States came in at 4.0 percent.[88]

Throughout the 2000s, NATO planning focused strongly on the need to refocus the alliance's planning and capabilities on force projection missions, like the one in Afghanistan and potential future efforts in the Middle East. Never completely out of mind for some allies, however, was the potential of a future threat from Russia and the need to deter potential attempts to restore Moscow's control over its "near-abroad."

A decade of deteriorating Russia–NATO relations

Relations between NATO and Russia started out the 2000s with some signs of hope for the future, but deteriorated seriously toward the end of the decade. Vladimir Putin, in the early stages of his initial presidential term (which ran from December 31, 1999 until May 7, 2008), appeared to be leading Russia toward a pragmatic and even constructive relationship with NATO, while trying to restore a degree of internal order following the tumultuous presidency of Boris Yeltsin. The most important stimulus was provided by the September 11 terrorist attacks, which prompted Putin to offer assistance in the US-declared war against terrorism. Putin's position clearly helped strengthen his relationship with President George W. Bush, and facilitated work toward agreements on dramatic cuts in strategic nuclear weapons arsenals and possible agreements on missile defenses. Putin also hinted at new Russian perspectives regarding its relationship to NATO and Russia's attitude toward NATO enlargement.

In November 2001, Bush's political ally, British Prime Minister Tony Blair, initiated discussion of a new Russia–NATO relationship by proposing the creation of an updated forum for Russia–NATO cooperation. Blair, in a letter to NATO Secretary General George Robertson, suggested the creation of a "Russia/North Atlantic Council", which would take decisions by consensus on certain issues affecting both NATO and Russia including, for example, terrorism, arms proliferation, and peacekeeping. According to press reports, British officials suggested privately that post-9/11 events could lead to a new world order, ending old enmities and building new bridges. "The prime minister believes the fact that the world is such a different place since September 11 does give us opportunities as well as threats," one official said.[89]

Apparently with the blessing of the Bush administration, Secretary General Robertson put the idea forward during an official visit to Moscow. Headlines shouted "Russia Could Get Veto Power in New NATO."[90] Russian conservatives worried that Putin was about to give away the farm, while other Russian analysts speculated that the move would give Russia associate membership in the alliance. American conservatives remained concerned that the move might end NATO's useful existence. Polish observers fretted that this might

Figure 7.2 Secretary General George Robertson and Russian President Vladimir Putin meeting in Brussels after Putin's reaction to the 9/11 attacks had led to one of the few high points in Russia–NATO relations.

be the first step toward Russian membership in NATO. French observers wondered if events were moving too fast for rational consideration of their consequences.

Two former officials responsible for the Clinton administration's NATO enlargement policy, Jeremy D. Rosner and Ronald D. Asmus, argued for simply revitalizing current NATO–Russia relations: "Mr. Putin has complained that the existing NATO–Russia relationship is moribund. He is right. But the reason why it is moribund is that Russia walked away from the table in protest over NATO's air campaign in Kosovo and has since pursued an obstructionist policy. That fact alone should give us pause. There is nothing wrong with the NATO-Russia Permanent Joint Council that a dose of good will and hard work could not fix."[91]

On December 6, 2001, in spite of such arguments, the allies agreed to establish a new Russia-NATO council to identify and pursue opportunities for joint action between Russia and the NATO allies. The ministers made it clear that the new council would not give Russia a veto over NATO decisions.

Agreement on the new arrangements was confirmed at a NATO-Russia summit outside Rome, Italy on May 28, 2002. The Permanent Joint Council was replaced by a new Russia-NATO Council. The new council was intended to meet more regularly, and to make decisions on some subjects. However, the regular agenda of the NAC would not be shifted to the new framework. The

NAC would decide when issues should be submitted to decision by the NATO-Russia Council and when they should be kept within usual NATO decision-making channels. Unlike the Permanent Joint Council, however, the allies would not bring "pre-cooked" NATO positions to the table with Russia. If the new council became deadlocked on an issue because of Russian disagreement, this would not block the NATO members from acting in the NAC without Russian agreement or participation. Lord Robertson argued that the real differences between the former arrangement and the new forum were a matter of "chemistry rather than arithmetic, as even the best format and seating arrangements can be no substitute for genuine political will and open minds on both sides."[92] In other words, the change was largely cosmetic, intended as a political statement rather than a structural change.

In spite of the new consultative arrangements, resentment of NATO's enlargement to include the three former Soviet republics of Estonia, Latvia, and Lithuania persisted in some Russian quarters. In March 2004, Russia's lower house of parliament adopted a resolution denouncing NATO enlargement and the deployment of four Belgian F-16 fighter jets to a Lithuanian air base to patrol the air space of the new Baltic members of NATO. This, however, did not stop President Putin just one week later from signing agreements with NATO Secretary General Jaap de Hoop Scheffer establishing Russian military liaison offices at NATO's top military headquarters.

One of the most difficult policy issues confronting the process of enlarging NATO, particularly to the Baltic states of Latvia, Lithuania, and Estonia, was the question of how to reassure Russia that a growing NATO would not diminish Russian security. The allies faced the challenging task of keeping their commitment to enlarge while avoiding a new confrontational relationship with Moscow. The issue was a very broad one that included important political, psychological, security, and economic dimensions.

Russian officials expressed particular concern that NATO enlargement could lead to the deployment of nuclear weapons on Russia's borders. This complaint could be dismissed as, at best, a bargaining strategy to the extent that Russian defense officials and experts knew that NATO had no nuclear-armed missiles or other nuclear weapons systems that it would want to deploy forward on European territory.

As it happened, the nuclear issue did not create a serious crisis with Russia in the first enlargement (when the Czech Republic, Hungary, and Poland were admitted to NATO) or even in the potentially more sensitive second enlargement (when Estonia, Latvia, and Lithuania as well as the Slovak Republic, Slovenia, Bulgaria, and Romania were admitted). Russian President Vladimir Putin decided not to make a major issue out of the nuclear aspects of enlargement, and the NATO countries were not required to make any apparent concessions to win Putin's relatively grudging acceptance of the new reality. Some Russian politicians and defense officials still grumbled about the fact that NATO membership for the three Baltic States had brought NATO forces close to the Russian heartland. But, for the most part, nuclear weapons in the context of NATO enlargement had never become as difficult an issue as had been feared when the enlargement process began in the 1990s.

Missile defense issues

The question of missile defenses sparked the big differences, however, between Russia and NATO. One of the first actions of the Bush administration after taking office in 2001 was to withdraw from the 1972 Anti-Ballistic Missile (ABM) Treaty with the Soviet Union, freeing the United States from any treaty obligation not to deploy such systems. The administration argued that looming missile threats from nuclear weapons state North Korea and nuclear weapons aspirant Iran warranted US movement toward deployment of systems that could protect the United States and its allies from such future threats. The ABM Treaty stood in the way, and the United States did not plan to deploy a system that would neutralize Russian nuclear missile capabilities in any case.

In 2001, the Bush administration argued, with some logic, that continuing to base relations with a post-Cold War Russia on premises and agreements that governed relations with a Cold War Soviet Union would not lead to new, constructive ties. The administration saw the ABM Treaty as a relic of the Cold War. Moreover, the treaty blocked the testing the United States deemed necessary to develop critical missile defense capabilities. European allies accepted that relations with Russia needed to be set on new ground but generally believed that treaties such as the ABM accord still helped shape a framework of stability that should not be thrown away lightly. These differing approaches began the process of splitting the transatlantic allies in the first month of the Bush administration.

The September 11, 2001 attacks on the United States added new elements to the missile defense debate. On the one hand, those who had been skeptical about Bush missile defense plans could interpret the September 11 attacks as demonstrating that building defenses against strategic missiles was pointless. Terrorists and rogue states clearly could find ways around US defenses to attack and destroy select US targets, create fear, and disrupt the US economy and way of life. On the other hand, those who supported a robust missile defense program could see the September 11 events as fully justifying their position. The demonstrated willingness of the al-Qaeda network to attack US targets using hijacked aircraft made it even more likely that such groups or rogue states in the future might acquire ballistic missiles to deliver weapons of mass destruction on US or allied targets.

While the United States was tied down fighting in Iraq, new concerns arose about the potential for neighboring Iran, led by a radical Islamic regime that no longer was pre-occupied with Saddam Hussein's Iraq, to develop both nuclear weapons and the missile systems to deliver them on European and American targets. In 2007, this concern led the administration to decide to negotiate deployment of missile interceptors in Poland and a radar facility in the Czech Republic as key components of a defense against long-range Iranian missiles. The administration decided to move ahead with preparatory steps even though the missile intercept system had not proven itself ready for deployment.[93]

The strong Russian reaction against this decision had many components. Russian officials knew that the number (10) and location of the planned deployments posed no threat to their intercontinental ballistic missile capabilities. They also knew that the proposed systems had not yet proven their viability. They nonetheless chose to characterize the decision as a threat to their security. Even though their arguments were in part disingenuous, designed largely for domestic consumption, they did reveal continued Russian sensitivity to the fact that NATO and US power were moving even closer to their borders. And Russian officials argued that the missile deployments could, in the future, be used as the basis for expansion to pose a threat to Russian missiles.[94] In November 2008, Russian President Medvedev, presumably attempting to raise the stakes on the issue, suggested that the deployment of the US anti-missile systems could lead Russia to deploy the conventionally armed tactical ballistic Iskander-M missile system in the Russian enclave of Kaliningrad.[95]

The US decision created political divisions among the allies and within the deployment countries. One particularly serious issue was the fact that the interceptors might be able to protect some NATO allies from attack, but would not be capable of stopping attacks against others, particularly to the south of the locations of the interceptors. The Polish and Czech governments in 2008 nonetheless confirmed their participation in the program.

In 2009, one of the early decisions of the new Obama administration in Washington was to slow the pace of progress toward deploying missile defense systems in Europe, largely due to questions about whether the system would work or not, but also consistent with its attempt to "reset" US relations with Russia.[96] Following President Obama's discussions with Russian President Medvedev in July 2009, the Pentagon announced that the European missile plans were "not set in concrete," and that, in consultation with the Polish and Czech governments, the deployments could be adjusted depending on future developments.[97] In September 2009, following the advice of his senior military advisors, including Secretary of Defense Robert Gates, Obama announced that the scheduled deployments in Europe would be canceled. The United States would instead deploy a new missile defense land- and sea-based system focused on the Iranian short- and medium-range missile threat.[98]

The Russian reaction to Obama's Moscow visit suggested that a renewed dialogue and nuclear arms control negotiations with the United States might be more important to the Russian leadership than persistent opposition to NATO plans and policies. Russia had always valued the bilateral US–Russian relationship because it was seen in Moscow as implying Russia's continued status as a major power. However, internal political developments in Russia continued to give rise to concern, and could in the longer term create demands on Russian policy that would make progress in arms control and missile defense relations with the United States and NATO more difficult.

Growing autocracy in Moscow

Even as Putin took some practical steps in relations with NATO, he increasingly adopted an autocratic approach to governance in Moscow, which carried over into the term of his hand-picked successor, Dmitry Medvedev. Initially using the struggle against Chechen separatists as his rationale, Putin began re-centralizing power. In 2004, he involved himself actively in the presidential election campaign in Ukraine, supporting the pro-Moscow candidate Viktor Yanukovych against the more Western-oriented opposition.

In July 2006, as Putin continued consolidating power, Russia hosted the Group of Eight Nations (G8) economic summit—the annual gathering of the leaders of the world's industrial powers. Russia had become a full participant in the G8 in 1998, having been invited partly to encourage and facilitate Russia's democratization and modernization process as well as to acknowledge Russia's natural resource base and nuclear weapons capabilities (at the time, Russia was just the seventeenth leading industrial power). Meeting in Moscow, the G8 leaders successfully sought a non-controversial meeting, generally regarded as a success for the host government.[99] Many observers hoped that Russia might be on its way to becoming a respected and influential member of the international community. But those hopes were dashed when Putin, after returning to the presidency in 2012, reacted to pro-Western developments in Kiev by seizing The Crimea region and supporting separatists in South-Eastern Ukraine (see Chapter 8).

Ukraine as an issue between NATO and Moscow

In the early years of the twenty-first century, Russia's economic fortunes brightened considerably with its international sales of oil and gas, apparently encouraging Russian leaders to begin flexing their foreign policy muscles again. Russia first began deploying its new-found sense of confidence and bravado in relations with former Soviet republics Ukraine and Georgia. The accession of the Baltic States to NATO had been viewed in the 1990s as a step that could lead back to a new "Cold War" environment. But there was little that Russia could do when NATO's "big bang" expansion took place in 2004. The crunch did not come until both Ukraine and Georgia began moving closer to membership at a time when Russia was feeling more confident about throwing its weight around once again. Moscow used various forms of hard and soft power to pressure the Ukrainians against joining NATO, including restricting access to gas supplies that flowed to and through Ukraine. In the unstable Caucasus, the Kremlin vocally supported the separatism of two Georgian regions and then invaded Georgia to enforce the regions' independence.

NATO's relationship with the next most significant independent country formed by a former Soviet republic, Ukraine, had been of an entirely different character than that with Russia. As part of the unwinding of the Cold War, Ukraine gave up the Soviet-era nuclear weapons that had been deployed on its territory in return for Western financial assistance and the tacit promise of acceptance into the Western community of nations. In the Budapest Memorandum of December 5, 1994, the leaders of The Russian Federation, Britain, and the United States, in return for Ukraine's nuclear weapons abstinence, reaffirmed "their obligation to refrain from the threat or use of force against the territorial integrity or political independence of Ukraine, and that none of their weapons will ever be used against Ukraine except in self-defence or otherwise in accordance with the Charter of the United Nations." (Vladimir Putin obviously ignored this pledge in 2014 when Russia seized control and then annexed the Crimea region of Ukraine.) By the mid-1990s, many in the Ukraine elite quietly aspired to eventual membership in both NATO and the European Union. However, domestic political divisions called for a cautious approach. Ukraine did not ask to be considered for NATO membership but strongly supported the process of NATO enlargement. The NATO allies responded to Ukraine's aspirations at their summit meeting in Madrid in July 1997, agreeing to establish a Ukraine–NATO Charter on Distinctive Partnership, creating an intensified consultative and cooperative relationship between NATO and Ukraine.[100]

In May 2002, President Leonid Kuchma announced Ukraine's goal of eventually joining NATO. Following this pronouncement, and building on the cooperative relationship established with Ukraine in the 1990s, NATO–Ukraine cooperation was deepened and broadened with the adoption of the NATO–Ukraine Action Plan in November 2002. In subsequent years, Russia worked hard to ensure its future political and economic influence in Ukraine, leaving Ukraine's future orientation and role in Europe open to question.

Ukraine sent forces to join in NATO's military operations in Bosnia and Kosovo and contributed over 1,600 troops to the Polish-led multinational division in Iraq. NATO-member Poland, in fact, committed itself to helping Ukraine sustain its independence and become a full member of the Euro-Atlantic security system. Illustrating Poland's concern about Ukraine's future, Janusz Onyszkiewicz, a Polish member of the European Parliament and former Polish defense minister, noted that "Poland is extremely worried about the future of Ukraine and Russia's policies in that country. If Russia establishes a dominance over Ukraine, it could give rise to new, imperialistic tendencies. If Russia can manage to do that with Ukraine, why not Belarus, Moldova, and other countries in the Caucasus?"[101]

Entering the twenty-first century, Ukraine remained torn between its past and its future. The eastern cities of Ukraine were traditionally more russified—both linguistically and politically, while the more rural western regions of the country preserved their ethnically Ukrainian character and were a hotbed for nationalistic sentiments. The United States, NATO, and the European Union sought to encourage Ukraine to work toward becoming part of the Euro-Atlantic community of democracies. This goal is supported by significant elements in the political elite and among the public. But another powerful contingent in Ukraine—largely living in Ukraine's eastern half—favored close links to Moscow, if not reintegration with Russia. This constituency was actively lobbied and encouraged by Russia, which viewed Ukraine as its missing half. Russia is an important country on its own, but it would be much more powerful if reunited with Ukraine. As Zbigniew Brzezinski wrote in the mid-1990s, "Without Ukraine, Russia ceases to be a Eurasian empire. ... if Moscow regains control over Ukraine, with its 52 million people and major resources, as well as access to the Black Sea, Russia automatically again regains the wherewithal to become a powerful imperial state, spanning Europe and Asia."[102]

The electoral crisis in Ukraine at the end of 2004 illustrated how divided Ukraine was between the pro-Western and pro-Russian tendencies. The conflicting interests translated into international discord at the December 2004 ministerial meeting of the Organization for Security and Cooperation in Europe (OSCE). Russia, led by President Putin's overt support for the pro-Moscow presidential candidate, had actively intervened in the election campaign, and the results of the first round were marred by serious charges of voting fraud. OSCE foreign ministers were unable to reach agreement on a statement, including language, on the Ukrainian Supreme Court's ruling that the "victory" of the pro-Moscow candidate in the November 2004 presidential polling should be invalidated and new elections held. Agreement was reportedly blocked by Moscow's refusal to include the references.[103]

The "Orange Revolution" in Ukraine following the disputed presidential elections not only brought a pro-Western leader, President Viktor Yushchenko, to power in internationally monitored run-off elections, but also resulted in Ukraine's changing from a NATO partner to a country actively seeking membership in the alliance. Yushchenko's ambitions for his country were received enthusiastically in Washington, where the Bush administration supported the membership aspirations of both Ukraine and Georgia, while Russia kept up its active opposition.

In addition to overt political pressure and, presumably, clandestine assistance to Yushchenko's pro-Moscow opponents, Moscow turned to its most powerful non-military weapons to influence Ukrainian behavior. Already in 2006, Russia threatened to cut supplies of natural gas that flows via pipelines to Ukraine and onward to Western Europe. A more serious disruption came early in 2009, when the Russian gas supply monopoly Gazprom suspended gas shipments to Ukraine, accusing Ukraine of stealing gas that should be going through the system and not paying an adequate price for the gas it consumed. Regardless of whether the Russian claims reflected reality or not, the move by Gazprom was widely seen as a blatant attempt to demonstrate Ukraine's, and the rest of Europe's, dependence on Russian gas supplies.

Another sensitive issue was the Ukrainian port of Sevastopol, which had been home to Russia's Black Sea Fleet for 225 years and remained an important symbol of Russian power and influence in south-eastern Europe. Russia paid rent to Ukraine for use of its territory, a lease arrangement that was scheduled to expire in 2017, at which time Ukraine had said that the fleet could no longer be based on Ukrainian territory. Russia's potential loss of this facility and its embodiment of Russian power was a source of consternation for Russian leaders. Russia was building a new naval base on Russian territory at Novorossiysk, but the head of Moscow's general staff had expressed the hope that the new base would be in addition to, and not instead of, continued Russian use of the Sevastopol base.[104]

The Bush administration had wanted the alliance to grant both Ukraine and Georgia entry to NATO's Membership Action Plan (MAP) at the NATO summit scheduled for April 2008 in Bucharest, Romania. President Bush, visiting Kiev on April 1, 2008, on his way to Bucharest, unconditionally advocated offering both Georgia and Ukraine MAPs to put them on the path to NATO membership. Bush told reporters "I strongly believe that Ukraine and Georgia should be given MAP, and there are no tradeoffs—period."[105] Both countries had contributed troops to the war in Iraq, and Bush's support for their NATO membership goal was widely seen as a reward for their contributions. President Bush's advocacy of giving the two aspirants MAP status was not convincing for many European governments, led by France and Germany, who thought such a decision would be premature. The summit, instead, issued a statement that surprisingly promised that Georgia and Ukraine would one day become NATO members.[106] Russia had won a tactical victory, but was surprised and disturbed by the long-term NATO commitment to the membership of Ukraine and Georgia—a victory for the lame-duck American president.

In 2009, the new US administration led by President Barack Obama supported the "open door" for NATO enlargement but did not put a high priority on pushing the matter ahead with any urgency. This suggested that the alliance would work with Ukraine and Georgia to help them move toward meeting the requirements for NATO membership without specifically putting them on the track toward membership. This also meant that Russia would continue to lobby against the eventuality and would likely use sources of influence available to it to support the outcomes it prefers. As we will see in Chapter 8, this came to the use of force against Ukraine, as it had against Georgia (discussed in the coming paragraphs).

Georgia as an issue between NATO and Russia

When the Cold War ended and the Soviet Union began to break apart, the Georgian province of South Ossetia sought to break away, leading to serious fighting between the separatists and Georgian forces. (South Ossetia had pursued independence in the 1920s until forcibly incorporated in the Soviet Union as an autonomous region in Georgia.) A peace agreement was brokered by Russia, and "peacekeepers" from Russia, South Ossetia, and Georgia were authorized for the region. Tensions continued, however, over the next two decades, while Russia worked to support South Ossetia's goal of secession from Georgia, including issuing Russian passports to South Ossetians who wanted them. Georgia never accepted the South Ossetian claims to independence and resented Moscow's active efforts to support that goal.[107]

Following the 2003 pro-democracy "Rose Revolution" in Georgia, the new Western-leaning Georgian government led by Mikheil Saakashvili pledged to re-establish Georgian authority over South Ossetia and Georgia's other separatist region of Abkhazia. Both the pro-Western nature of Saakashvili's government and its goal of regaining central government control of the separatist regions ran counter to Moscow's perceived interests.

After a number of failed attempts to negotiate a settlement between Georgia and the two regions, tensions began to build in July 2008, leading to skirmishes between Georgian and South Ossetian units in the province, followed by Russian intervention and attacks on Georgian forces and targets in the two regions and in Georgia itself. Russia took the opportunity not only to "punish" Georgian forces involved but also to push into Georgia, destroy Georgian military and civilian infrastructure, and seal off Georgia from its two break-away republics. Russian officials claimed they would never again be part of Georgia.

The process of controlling conventional armed forces in Europe suffered serious collateral damage from Russia's aggression toward Georgia and Ukraine. Russia suspended compliance with the Treaty on Conventional Armed Forces in Europe's terms, and refused requests from NATO states for inspections provided for under the treaty.[108] Final approval of the treaty remained potentially important from a confidence-building perspective, but had become largely irrelevant to contemporary security relations in Europe.

The last thing the NATO nations wanted was a new cold war with Russia, but Russian actions in Georgia chilled the atmosphere across Europe, as well as between Russia and the United States. As one expert observed, NATO and the European Union needed to work together on this difficult relationship and "Russia must be reminded that cooperation with NATO, as an alliance of democratic states, requires compliance with democratic rules."[109]

The longer-term consequences of this affair remained to be seen, but, at the very least, many European states, particularly those in Russia's neighborhood, saw Russia's actions as a sign that they would be safer in the future with a

NATO security blanket than without. The impression of a more threatening Russia was enhanced by Russian behavior in other areas. In 2007, a number of Estonian government web sites suffered "denial of service" attacks at a time of tension between Estonia and Russia over Tallinn's decision to move a Soviet-era war memorial to a less prominent spot in the capitol. The source of the attacks was not publically confirmed, but the likelihood that the attacks originated in Russia raised questions about how such attacks in the future could pose serious security threats to NATO allies.[110]

The Russian alternative for European security

From the early stages of the post-Cold War period, Russian leaders struggled to create or propose alternatives to a European security system dominated by NATO and the United States. The Russian-led Commonwealth of Independent States, founded in December 1991, was Moscow's first attempt to reassert a degree of Russian leadership of former Soviet republics. However, Russian weakness in the early 1990s gave their leaders no real possibility of having decisive influence over the unfolding developments that were leading former Warsaw Pact allies and key Soviet Republics into alliance, or at least partnership, with NATO. This weakness inevitably led to resentment of the fact that the United States and its NATO allies were largely dictating the terms of the new European security system, even if the Western powers made serious attempts to develop a special partnership with Russia.

With the advent of the new century, Russia was beginning to realize some of the financial and political benefits from demand for its natural resources, particularly natural gas, on international markets. Even though the Russian military was still in disastrous condition, the improved financial situation gave rise to a belief in Moscow that it could take certain initiatives to counter what appeared to be increasing Western dominance all around Russia's borders. In 2002, Russia led a group of former Soviet republics to establish the Collective Security Treaty Organization (CSTO). Armenia, Belarus, Kazakhstan, Kyrgyzstan, and Tajikistan joined Russia as members. Uzbekistan joined the organization in 2006. The members pledged to come to the defense of a member that had been attacked, and agreed to create a peacekeeping force that could be deployed at the request of the United Nations. Most objective observers saw the CSTO mainly as a way for Moscow to attempt to maintain its influence in former Soviet republics that were not yet seeking close relations with NATO. The extent to which Russia was successful in pursuing its interests through the CSTO was called into question by the fact that no CSTO member immediately followed Russia's lead in recognizing the governments of the breakaway Georgian regions of South Ossetia and Abkhazia.

In June 2008, Russian President Medvedev proposed creating a new all-European security organization, suggesting that the OSCE as well as NATO were increasingly irrelevant to the new circumstances in Europe. Perhaps more importantly, Russia was willing to use its veto to limit the OSCE's role in issues important to Russian interests, particularly in the aftermath of Russia's August 2008 invasion of Georgia. In the spring of 2009, Russia blocked extension of the mandate for both United Nations and OSCE monitors in Abkhazia and South Ossetia.[111] As one expert has noted, "Russia's relations with the Euro-Atlantic community in its institutional formats are characterized by a sense of strategic dissonance."[112]

The initial Medvedev proposal seemed to suggest that the new framework should be constructed by Europeans, implying no role for the United States or NATO. However, when the European response raised many questions about Russian intentions and motivations, Medvedev softened the approach to suggest that all existing security organizations, as well as all key players in European security, should be involved in shaping the new system.[113] By early 2010, the European security initiative had not been formally presented in full detail, but it remained part of a larger Russian package of initiatives apparently designed to begin restructuring European and international security, energy, and political relations along lines more favorable to Russian influence and interests.[114]

None of the Russian initiatives initially achieved much traction in Europe, and were viewed with great skepticism in particular by the former Soviet republics and Warsaw Pact countries that had achieved or aspired to NATO membership. With international condemnation of Russian behavior in Georgia, and with Russian economic fortunes hard hit by the global recession in 2009, Moscow adopted what appeared to be a more modest approach. The focus of Russian policy turned tentatively toward developing a new and more constructive policy with the American government led by Barack Obama. But that movement in the late 2000s was dashed in the next few years.

NATO and the EU

The 2000s saw a surge in the development of the European Union's attempt to develop a more capable approach to foreign and defense policy. The political stimulus for the surge came strongly from concern about the foreign policy and strategic directions taken by the Bush administration, in particular the decision to invade Iraq. But by the end of the decade the EU had failed to put its money where its mouth was or the sovereignty of the member states up for submission to an overall European defense system.

NATO–EU relations during the George W. Bush administration

The Bush administration, despite the early-1991 reassurances from Tony Blair discussed at the opening of this chapter, seemed wary of the potential for a Common European Security and Defense Policy (CESDP) to create artificial distinctions among NATO allies, undermining NATO's political cohesion. The CESDP process and the demands of its institutional creations could encourage "we/they" distinctions between Europeans and the United States and even among European members of NATO. The Clinton administration was quite restrained in its response to French diplomatic initiatives in Eastern and Central Europe that appeared designed to convince states that were candidates for EU membership that they should line up with EU positions in the ongoing negotiations with NATO concerning the EU–NATO relationship.[115]

During 2002, while the allies were enmeshed in the divisive debate over Iraq, the EU/Turkey problem was resolved, and cooperative arrangements between NATO and the European Union were quietly put in place. On December 16, NATO Secretary General Lord George Robertson and EU foreign policy chief Javier Solana issued the "EU–NATO Declaration on ESDP,"[116] elaborating the principles on which the NATO–EU strategic partnership in crisis management would be based.

Tensions in the US relationship with those allies who opposed the Iraq war escalated in April 2003 when the leaders of Belgium, France, Germany, and Luxembourg held a meeting in Brussels to discuss developing a European defense union that would be independent of NATO. The four European leaders said they were not trying to weaken NATO but to strengthen the European pillar of the alliance and to give the EU the ability to become a strong partner of the United States. Many of the proposals they issued built on existing plans for an EU defense force and proposals for strengthening European defense cooperation being developed by the European constitutional convention. Their brief declaration also included plans for their own rapid-reaction force centered on the Franco-German brigade and two new European military institutions: "a multinational deployable force headquarters" for operations that do not involve NATO, and a "nucleus of collective capability for planning and conducting operations for the European Union."[117]

This "rump" European meeting was ill-timed and disruptive, both in transatlantic relations and inside Europe, irritating many EU governments that were not invited to participate in the session. Dutch Foreign Minister Jaap de Hoop Scheffer explained his country's decision not to participate, saying "Belgium and France will not guarantee our security. ... Germany will not guarantee the security of the Netherlands. I cannot imagine world order built against the United States."[118] In the meantime, getting the NATO–EU relationship right was becoming even more important, as the EU constitutional convention moved ahead. The shape of the NATO–EU relationship at the end of 2003 would likely provide a critical part of the foundation on which the EU Constitution's provisions on defense would be constructed.

Late in 2003, Tony Blair, seeking to find some common ground on which the UK, France, and Germany could restore a degree of unity following their split on Iraq, worked out a compromise giving the green light for the EU to develop a small defense planning capability. Reacting to the development at a meeting of the NAC on October 16, the US Permanent Representative Nicholas Burns, presumably under instructions from Washington, told fellow ambassadors that the European Union's pursuit of greater military autonomy posed "one of the greatest dangers to the transatlantic relationship."[119] In the end, however, the United States backed away from Burns' warning and accepted the approach. It hasn't been proven, but US acquiescence may well have been at least a partial payoff to Blair for his support on Iraq.

On December 12, 2003, EU leaders, meeting in Brussels, agreed to create a small EU military planning cell. British Prime Minister Tony Blair said the final accord fully met London's requirements not to do harm to NATO, telling reporters, "This gives us the opportunity to keep the transatlantic American alliance very strong, but make sure that in circumstances where America is not engaged in an operation, and where the vital European interests are involved, that Europe can act, and that is exactly what we wanted, and doing it in a way that is completely consistent with NATO as the cornerstone of our alliance."[120] The unit is co-located with the EU's military staff in Brussels. A separate EU unit attached to SHAPE, NATO's military headquarters in Mons, Belgium, was also made permanent.

Once again, Blair's leadership on the question of how European defense cooperation should relate to the transatlantic defense relationship was crucial. The Iraq war debate had badly split the NATO allies, but was equally devastating to the image of foreign policy unity among current and future EU members. Blair's success in finding a solution to the EU planning cell issue not only helped find a transatlantic compromise but also promoted the process of healing the wounds to EU unity.

What did the Bush administration's acquiescence in the EU planning cell demonstrate? President Bush undoubtedly saw it as a reward for Blair's cooperation on Iraq. Pentagon Euro-skeptics perhaps decided it really didn't make much difference, given their low expectations about the EU, NATO, and the "old" Europeans. Some at the Department of State may have seen it as a signal of US moderation and reason, opening the way for European countries and the EU to take over more responsibility for the defense and security of Europe.

During 2004 it appeared that the relationship between NATO and the European Union was developing constructively. The Atlanticist and Europeanist requirements had more or less been compromised in the new NATO/EU cooperative arrangements. Those arrangements carried forward the practical elements of the 1996 Berlin Accords while acknowledging the need for a degree of autonomy in development of an EU military capability.

Perhaps most importantly, the Europeans demonstrated their willingness to take on more responsibility in the transatlantic security relationship. In August 2004, the Euro-corps took command of the NATO-led International Security Assistance Force (ISAF) in Afghanistan for a six-month rotation. Then, in December 2004, the European Union took over from NATO in Bosnia. On December 2, a ceremony in Sarajevo, Bosnia, marked the end of NATO's

Stabilization Force (SFOR) mission and the beginning of the European Union's follow-on EUFOR. The EUFOR mission was organized under the "Berlin Plus" arrangements for NATO to support European Union missions and represented the first major operational test of those arrangements.

Beyond the transatlantic battles

Transatlantic relationships during the Bush administration's first term suggested that if the United States and its allies did not manage the NATO–EU relationship effectively, it could intrude dramatically on a wide range of issues in which their common interests are likely served by pragmatic cooperation rather than conflict inspired by current international power realities.

This reality was modestly reflected in the second term of President George W. Bush, during which Bush and other officials attempted to repair relations with American allies, particularly European states. Early in 2005, both Secretary of State Condoleezza Rice and President Bush visited European capitals, explicitly seeking to repair some of the damage done by the administration in its first term, and most particularly by the decision to go to war against Iraq. The administration made few formal changes in its policies toward the alliance, and many of the same officials whose statements had seriously damaged relations with the allies remained in place. But there was a change toward more conciliatory and less confrontational approaches to the allies. The new US attitude notably included support for NATO taking over command of the ISAF in Afghanistan.

Following a NATO summit meeting in February 2005, President Bush praised the alliance saying "NATO is the most successful alliance in the history of the world. ... Because of NATO, Europe is whole and united and at peace. ... NATO is an important organization, and the United States of America strongly supports it."[121]

During the question and answer period, one reporter suggested that Europeans remained skeptical about administration intentions, particularly as Secretary of Defense Donald Rumsfeld was still suggesting "the mission should determine the coalition." The reporter asked what the United States would do to improve transatlantic relations. The President's answer was relatively straight-forward: we had a major difference with some allies over Iraq and now we need to put that issue behind us.

For the most part, European governments did appear to put the issue behind them, by agreeing to disagree about the wisdom of invading Iraq, but accepting the new more NATO-friendly US attitude as reaffirmation of US support for the alliance. Few Europeans were convinced that the administration's words and actions could be undone simply by a "charm offensive" by the President and his Secretary of State, but the more productive Euro-Atlantic relationship suggested that attitudes do matter. The new US approach also seemed to take some of the drive out of the European temptation to try to develop the European Union as a "pole" with which they could balance American power.

As for the EU's role as an international security actor, early in 2009, Javier Solana, the EU High Representative for the Common Foreign and Security Policy, told the European Parliament that the EU had in recent years been very active in contributing to international security challenges: "more than 20 civilian and military operations are or have been deployed on almost every continent, from Europe to Asia, from the Middle East to Africa. Thousands of European men and women are engaged in these operations, ranging from military to police, from border guards to monitors, from judges to prosecutors, a wide range of people doing good for the stability of the world."[122] Solana also pointed to the fact that EU actions under the ESDP have been guided by the European Security Strategy of 2003, as updated by a new report in December 2008.

As impressive and helpful as the EU's operations had been, they were limited in many ways. The failures of the EU Constitution temporarily blocked some of the consolidating and streamlining measures that were intended to give stronger leadership to the Common Foreign and Security Policy and the ESDP. Those failures reflected the fact that divisions among and within EU members remained substantial, and that national sovereignty on foreign and defense policy issues remained closely guarded by EU member states. It also reflected the fact that the EU had neither the command structures and military capabilities nor the political will to conduct military operations that are particularly demanding. Moreover, the agreement on a European Security Strategy, defining threats and desirable responses from a purely European perspective, failed to generate additional European military capabilities.[123]

From Bush to Obama

With the inauguration of President Barack H. Obama in 2009, the United States was presented with an opportunity for a new beginning with American allies. Obama, having achieved something close to rock star status in Europe during the 2008 presidential campaign, came to office explicitly acknowledging the importance to US interests of allies, alliances, and international cooperation and organizations more generally.

In addition, the decision by French President Nicolas Sarkozy that brought France back into full participation in NATO's military command structure in 2009 mitigated suspicions in Washington about French intentions and the potential for a competing European pole in international relations. Part of the deal for France's return called for appointment of a senior French officer as the new commander of Allied Command Transformation. The move rewarded France for its return to the military command structure and also symbolized France's commitment to intensified cooperation in the transatlantic framework.

Figure 7.3 EU High Representative for the Common Foreign and Security Policy (and former NATO Secretary General 1995–1999), Javier Solana and NATO Secretary General, Jaap de Hoop Scheffer, meet in October 2008 in the context of a joint session of NATO's North Atlantic Council and the EU's Political and Security Committee.

These political developments enhanced the prospects for a more effective alliance, but did not guarantee transatlantic tranquility. For example, a continuing challenge was in the area of defense industrial relations. There remained a danger that US unilateralism combined with the EU desire for "autonomy" could increase transatlantic trade and industrial tensions by supporting development of a "fortress Europe" mentality in defense procurement. This was an area where the United States could take much of the blame for the lack historically of a "two-way street" in transatlantic armaments trade, and failure to devise ways of sharing new technologies with the European allies to help them participate in the "Revolution in Military Affairs." ESDP did not necessarily require that Europe increase protectionism or favoritism for its own defense industries. Lagging far behind American defense firms in adjusting to post-Cold War market conditions, the necessary mergers and consolidations were finally beginning to rationalize the European defense industrial base. The next logical step would have been for rationalization of the *transatlantic* industrial base through a variety of means. This next step would have to be facilitated by governments, and both the United States and the EU members would have to make alliance solidarity and cooperation a high priority to overcome existing barriers to transatlantic armaments cooperation. An EU that puts a higher priority on developing ESDP could easily put new obstacles in the way of alliance cooperation in armaments, and particularly in the way of purchasing US systems.[124]

One strong but critical supporter of the European Union, Charles Grant, assessed the progress of the development of EU foreign and security policy capabilities and found them wanting. Grant observed that:

> In 2004 the EU launched the idea of "battlegroups." In theory the EU should be able to send up to two battlegroups to a crisis zone at any time. Each of these is a rapid reaction force of some 1,500 troops provided by a single member-state or a group of them. But no battle group has yet been deployed. In 2008 the UN asked the EU to send battlegroups to eastern Congo, Britain and Germany were "on call" to provide their battlegroups, but refused to send them. Some of the battlegroups that exist on paper are probably not useable: unfortunately, each government—rather than an independent body—is allowed to verify whether its battlegroup is operational.[125]

According to Grant, the EU's shortcomings in the areas of foreign policy and defense have multiple causes, not the least of which is the strong desire of member states to retain ultimate control over these core aspects of their sovereignty. In addition, the member states come from very different histories and experiences, meaning that today they have no common strategic culture. EU states simply look at foreign and defense issues through very different prisms, and come up with national assessments and conclusions that make common positions impossible on many issues.

On balance, the European Union of 2009 was far advanced from the European Community of 1973, when the author drafted the first US intelligence estimate of the European integration process.[126] But the even-more solidified core of the process remained seriously hedged by its member states. The European Union was much more of an international actor than it was in 1973, although it was still misleading to speak of "Europe" as if it consisted of like-minded, similarly-thinking and acting, states and citizens. It perhaps was never that "united," but the EU's post-Cold War enlargement made creation of a unitary European actor across the entire range of international relations even more problematic. And, Europe's "identity" remained clouded by questions about future expansion, particularly whether or not Turkey should be brought into the European fold or left with tenuous European moorings.

The unilateralist character of US foreign and defense policy under George W. Bush led some Europeans to favor using integration in the European Union to "balance" US power in the international system. This multi-polar temptation, like the US unilateral temptation, threatened trans-Atlantic cooperation and therefore international stability. François Heisbourg, director of the French

Fondation pour la Recherche Stratégique, argued persuasively that his nation's government should avoid the divisive rhetoric of multipolarity and pursue a multilateral agenda of cooperation with the United States and others.[127]

The failure of the EU Constitution to win approval in France and the Netherlands undermined the argument that Europe could effectively balance US power, and strengthened the case for building Europe in parallel with maintenance of a cooperative transatlantic relationship—a position favored by several EU members led by the UK and many of Europe's new democracies.

The Treaty of Lisbon,[128] otherwise known as the "Reform Treaty," a more modest version of the EU Constitution, took effect in December 2009 confirming the continuity of the process of integration. But it also confirmed the judgment that the emergence of anything like a United States of Europe remained for future generations to manage. As the respected German commentator Theo Sommer observed, "the United States of Europe is a long way off. But the United Europe of States is a realistic short-term goal."[129]

With regard to foreign and defense policy, the treaty created a High Representative of the Union for Foreign Affairs and Security Policy, merging the post of High Representative for the Common Foreign and Security Policy and the European Commissioner for External Relations and European Neighbourhood Policy. The High Representative was given the right to propose defense or security missions, with the decisions on such missions remaining in the hands of the member states. The High Representative was put in charge of an External Action Service also created by the Treaty of Lisbon, giving the EU its own diplomatic corps.

The EU governments agreed in the treaty that members should assist each other in the case of terrorist attacks or natural or man-made disasters. Joint military operations, however, remained subject to member state approval. The treaty projected the ESDP eventually leading to a common defense for the EU, with the provision that such a transition would require a unanimous decision of the European Council, approved through the normal constitutional procedures of the member states—something that was nowhere on the near political horizon.

Perhaps at this point it became more appropriate to talk about a "multi-player" international system, in which the European Union is an important player in many policy areas. Advocating a "multi-polar" system implies competition, shifting alliances and balance of power politics—a system that would serve neither American nor European interests. The European Union was already an important participant in a multi-player world. A continuing trend back toward a position of a "pillar" in the transatlantic relationship and away from "polar" pretensions would augur well for both the United States and Europe.

A key question about ESDP and NATO remained that of what additional military responsibilities the European allies would be capable of taking on in the near future. According to Michael Quinlan, one should be encouraged by the fact that "most European countries now accept that their forces should in the future be configured, equipped, trained, and available much more than before for expeditionary or similar use, in support of international order, rather

---

Box 7.1	Some key developments (January 2001–April 2009)
Jan 2001	George W. Bush entered office as President of the United States
Sep 2001	Al-Qaeda-coordinated terrorist attacks struck the World Trade Center towers in New York and the Pentagon in Washington. Within twenty-four hours, the North Atlantic Council announced the intention to invoke Article 5
Oct 2001	The US, supported by the UK, initiated Operation Enduring Freedom with attacks on al-Qaeda and Taliban forces and facilities, opening war in Afghanistan
May 2002	NATO Russian summit established the new Russia-NATO Council
Nov 2002	NATO allies met in Prague where they invited seven new members to the alliance, confirmed the creation of a NATO Response Force and agreed on the Multinational Chemical, Biological, Radiological and Nuclear Defense Battalion
Dec 2002	NATO and the EU reached the Berlin Plus agreements designed to facilitate cooperation between European and NATO defense efforts
April 2003	France, Germany, Belgium, and Luxembourg held "rump" meeting to establish a separate EU military planning cell
Aug 2003	NATO assumed command of the International Security Assistance Force in Afghanistan
April 2004	Bulgaria, Estonia, Latvia, Lithuania, Romania, Slovakia, and Slovenia became members of NATO
Nov 2004	George W. Bush re-elected President of the United States The "Orange Revolution" began in Ukraine, leading Kiev to shift from NATO partner to active seeker of NATO membership
April 2008	At Bucharest summit, NATO invited Albania and Croatia to join the alliance, but US desire to invite Georgia and Ukraine was not supported by allies
Jan 2009	Barak Obama entered office as President of the United States
April 2009	NATO leaders celebrated alliance's 60th anniversary in Strasbourg and Kehl

than for direct homeland defense against massive aggression."[130] In 2009, it seemed unlikely that the European allies would find substantially more resources to devote to defense. The question, therefore, was whether they would find ways to make current levels of spending more effective.

The 2000s in retrospect

This decade began with large questions about the future, in spite of the spirit of relative optimism with which transatlantic relations had emerged from the 1990s. After 9/11, the approach taken by the Bush administration during the early stages of the war against terrorism, beginning with the campaign in Afghanistan, produced mixed reactions. On the one hand, the administration's strategy was based on building a broad international coalition against terrorism. The rhetoric and formal approach of US policy remained true to this goal. On the other hand, the United States initially conducted the campaign with little reference to offers from the allies to help out and without making much institutional use of the NATO framework.

US management of alliance relations during George W. Bush's first term suggested that when the United States appears to be overbearing in its relations with other countries, it might find it difficult to build international consensus on behalf of its policies. Early Bush administration policy toward allies and NATO in its first term demonstrated that there are costs associated with policies that build coalitions by trying to use overpowering political force rather than by consultation, persuasion, and compromise.[131]

One consequence of the US response to the 9/11 attacks was the simultaneous creation of transatlantic unity over a response to the attacks in Afghanistan and transatlantic dissensus over the decision to attack Iraq. The allies responded to the attacks directed by al-Qaeda from their bases in Afghanistan by declaring them as an Article 5, collective defense situation, calling on all allies to react as if the attack had been on all of them. They rallied around US efforts to remove al-Qaeda from Afghanistan as well as the Taliban government that had hosted the terrorist bases. The alliance then took on the mission of coordinating the military response in Afghanistan under a mandate from the United Nations.

The US decision to attack Iraq and remove Saddam Hussein from power created divisions not only across the Atlantic but also among European allies and even within their foreign and defense policy establishments. While the United Kingdom and some other European states—particularly those who had just joined NATO or wished to do so—supported the US mission, France, Germany, and several other European states remained skeptical of the merits of US policy and opposed to the intervention. This opposition translated into political support for intensified collaboration on an EU-based autonomous alternative to leadership of the United States in NATO and in transatlantic relations more generally. As tensions eased over the Iraq issue, and it became clear that most European states would not produce the resources necessary to support an alternative to NATO, support for European defense cooperation took a softer line, both politically and in terms of actual activities.

In the meantime, tensions with Russia were growing, particularly as Vladimir Putin took control in Moscow and began planning to re-establish the former greatness of the Soviet Union in the somewhat more constrained framework of post-Cold War Russia. In spite of frequently repeated Western desires for cooperation, Putin increasingly saw the process of NATO enlargement as threatening Russian interests, particularly as shaped by the emerging authoritarian regime in Moscow.

Over the course of the next decade, the conflict between NATO and the EU on one hand and Russia on the other would intensify, while the conflict would also produce divisions among the allies. During the 2000s, Russia had become an important source of energy for almost all of Europe, as well as an important market and commercial partner for its western neighbors. The intersection between the aspects of conflict and cooperation with Russia would once again prove challenging for the West, as would the increasing turbulence in north Africa and the Middle East.

Questions for discussion

1. Which of the following conflicts, events, and countries caused the most strain on US–European relations in the 2000s, and which were the most uniting: 9/11, Iraq, Afghanistan, Russia, NATO enlargement, and NATO–EU relations?
2. Which European countries supported, and which opposed, the US-led invasion of Iraq, and why?
3. What are the potential advantages and disadvantages for their interests of the EU members trying to balance US power and influence in the international system?
4. What made Afghanistan such a novel and "groundbreaking experience" for NATO?
5. What role did the values articulated in the North Atlantic Treaty play in overcoming the Iraq crisis in transatlantic relations?

Notes

1 Transcript of President Bush and British Prime Minister Tony Blair's news conference following their first meeting at Camp David, February 23, 2001.
2 For example, Peter Rodman, who had written and commented widely on CESDP from his position at the Nixon Center, moved into a senior policy position at the Department of Defense; Robert Zoellick, a supporter of European defense coop-

eration, became the US trade representative; and John Bolton, a strong skeptic, moved to a position at the National Security Council.

3 Statement by the North Atlantic Council, NATO Press Release (2001) 124, September 12, 2001.

4 George Robertson, NATO Secretary General, statement to the press on the North Atlantic Council Decision on Implementation of Article 5 of the Washington Treaty following the September 11 attacks against the United States, October 4, 2001.

5 "NATO Airborne Early Warning Aircraft Begin Deploying to the United States," SHAPE News Release, October 9, 2001.

6 R. Nicholas Burns, "NATO is Vital for the Challenges of the New Century," *International Herald Tribune*, November 10–11, 2001, 8.

7 Not-for-attribution discussion with Italian government officials in October 2001.

8 Charles Grant, "Does This War Show That NATO No Longer Has a Serious Military Role?," *The Independent*, October 16, 2001.

9 Joseph Fitchett, "Pentagon in a League of Its Own," *International Herald Tribune*, February 4, 2002, 3.

10 George W. Bush, State of the Union Address, The White House, January 29, 2002.

11 Richard G. Lugar, "NATO Must Join War on Terrorism," speech to the US–NATO Missions Annual Conference, January 19, 2002.

12 Joseph Fitchett, "US Allies Chafe at 'Cleanup' Role," *International Herald Tribune*, November 26, 2001, 1.

13 Joseph Fitchett, "US Allies Chafe at 'Cleanup' Role," 1.

14 As discussed in Chapter 6, NATO in 1994 accepted the US idea of creating Combined Joint Task Force (CJTF) headquarters as a means of making the alliance's command structure more flexible to deal with new threats to security. A NATO Counterterrorism Task Force would not have been designed to run military operations against terrorist targets. However, such a task force could have been developed as a support mechanism for Afghanistan and future operations. In addition to military officers, the task force could have involved participation by representatives from the foreign and finance ministries of task force countries to bring to bear the wide range of resources needed to wage the campaign. One of the beneficial attributes of the CJTF structure is that non-NATO allies can be invited to participate. In addition, a Counterterrorism Task Force would have provided a framework for enhanced NATO–Russia cooperation. Russia could have been represented in the task force command and support counterterrorist operations even if it did not join openly in attacks on terrorist targets.

The author recommended such an initiative following the September 11, 2001 terrorist attacks: first in an October 7, 2001 presentation to the Political Committee of the NATO Parliamentary Assembly, during the Assembly's annual meeting in Ottawa, Canada, entitled "A Perspective on the Future of the Transatlantic Bargain;" in a lecture at the NATO Defense College on October 22, 2001; and then in the *International Herald Tribune*: Stanley R. Sloan, "Give NATO a Combined Task Force against Terrorism," November 13, 2001, 8.

15 NATO North Atlantic Council in Defence Ministers Session, "Statement on Combating Terrorism: Adapting the Alliance's Defence Capabilities," NATO Press Release (2001) 173, December 18, 2001.

16 Craig S. Smith, "Chirac Upsets East Europe by Telling It to 'Shut Up' on Iraq," *The New York Times*, February 19, 2003.

17 US Government, the White House, "The National Security Strategy of the United States," September 2002.

18 Vaclav Havel, "Prague Predictions," *NATO Review*, Spring 2002. Text available at: www.nato.int/docu/review/2002/issue1/english/art1.html [accessed May 11, 2015].

19 For a discussion of this issue by Professor Lawrence S. Kaplan, a distinguished NATO historian and enlargement skeptic, see Lawrence S. Kaplan, "NATO Enlargement: The Article 5 Angle," *Bulletin of the Atlantic Council of the United States* 12(2) (February 2001), entire issue.

20 Sean Kay, "Use NATO to Fight Terror," *Wall Street Journal Europe*, November 16, 2001.

21 Philip H. Gordon and James B. Steinberg, "NATO Enlargement: Moving Forward," Policy Brief (Washington, D.C.: The Brookings Institution, December 2001), 1.

22 Paul E. Gallis, "NATO Enlargement," Congressional Research Service Report for Congress RS21055 (Washington, D.C.: Congressional Research Service), May 5, 2003, 2.

23 A particularly thorough study by the Rand Corporation released in 2001 judged Slovenia to be the strongest candidate for membership, with Slovakia next in line. Estonia, Latvia, and Lithuania were judged to be "mid-term (or longer) candidates" because of the "strategic ramifications" of their accession—meaning the potential costs of contemporary and future Russian reactions. Bulgaria and Romania were rated next, their "relative strategic attractiveness ... offset by their inability to meet NATO's criteria." Macedonia and Albania were judged to be least advanced in this group. The report also examined the standing of European Union members that had not applied for NATO membership, concluding that Austria and Sweden were reasonably well-prepared for membership. Finland was rated below these two because of the "strategic costs it would impose on NATO," with reference to Finland's long border with Russia and Russia's potential reaction to Finland's joining NATO. Thomas S. Szayna, "NATO Enlargement, 2000–2015: Determinants and Implications for Defense Planning and Shaping (MR-1243-AF)," The Rand Corporation, 2001, 100–3. See also Jeffrey Simon, *Roadmap to NATO Accession: Preparing for Membership* (Washington, D.C.: Institute for National Strategic Studies, National Defense University, October 2001).

24 Gallis, "NATO Enlargement," 6.

25 The White House even noted in a press release on March 20, 2003, "it is no accident that many member nations of the Coalition recently escaped from the boot of a tyrant or have felt the scourge of terrorism. All Coalition member nations understand the threat Saddam Hussein's weapons pose to the world and the devastation his regime has wreaked on the Iraqi people."

26 On April 3, 2003, almost two weeks after the opening of hostilities in Iraq, the White House listed some 49 Iraq Coalition members, including the following

23 European (including former Soviet republics) states: Albania, Azerbaijan, Bulgaria, Czech Republic, Denmark, Estonia, Georgia, Hungary, Iceland, Italy, Latvia, Lithuania, Macedonia, the Netherlands, Poland, Portugal, Romania, Slovakia, Spain, Turkey, Ukraine, United Kingdom, and Uzbekistan.

27 Data quoted are from Ronald Asmus, Philip P. Everts, and Pierangelo Isernia, "Power, War and Public Opinion: Thoughts on the Nature and Structure of the Trans-Atlantic Divide," *Transatlantic Trends 2003*, a project of the German Marshal Fund of the United States and the Compagnia di San Paolo.

28 Asmus, Everts, and Isernia, "Power, War and Public Opinion," 12.

29 Josef Joffe, "Gulliver Unbound: Can America Rule the World?," the Twentieth Annual John Bonython Lecture, The Centre for Independent Studies, Sydney, Australia, August 5, 2003.

30 Erin E. Arvedlund, "Allies Angered at Exclusion from Bidding," nytimes.com, December 11, 2003. 12.

31 Arvedlund, "Allied Angered at Exclusion from Bidding."

32 Craig S. Smith, "France Gives Baker Lukewarm Commitment on Iraqi Debt," nytimes.com, December 16, 2003.

33 Richard W. Stevenson and Steven R. Weisman, "Bush Says U.S. Will Push Hard on Peace Plan," nytimes.com, November 13, 2004.

34 Craig S. Smith, "Major Creditors in Accord to Waive 8% of Iraq Debt," nytimes.com, November 22, 2004.

35 In a speech sponsored by the International Institute for Strategic Studies in London on November 18, 2004, Chirac observed "It is by recognizing the new reality of a multi-polar and interdependent world that we will succeed in building a sounder and fairer international order." Patrick E. Tyler, "Chirac Hints France Will Help Rebuild Iraq," nytimes.com, November 19, 2004. The day before Chirac left for London, he told interviewers that "To a certain extent Saddam Hussein's departure was a positive thing. But it also provoked reactions, such as the mobilization in a number of countries of men and women of Islam, which has made the world more dangerous." Craig S. Smith, "Chirac Says War in Iraq Spreads Terrorism," nytimes.com, November 18, 2004.

36 Joel Brinkley, "NATO Agrees to Expansion of Forces Training Soldiers in Iraq," *The New York Times*, December 10, 2004.

37 Josef Joffe, "How America Does It," *Foreign Affairs*, September/October 1997. 16.

38 Christian Hacke, "The Merkel Miracle? The Promising Beginnings of a Readjusted German Foreign Policy," American Institute for Contemporary German Studies Analyses, Washington, D.C., March 17, 2006, www.aicgs.org/analysis/c/hacke031706one.aspx.

39 See, for example, Leo Michel, "Getting to Oui," *Internationale Politik*, German Council on Foreign Relations, Berlin (Summer 2008), www.ip-global.org/archiv/2008/summer2008/getting-to-oui.html.

40 See Joseph P. Quinlin, "Drifting Apart or Growing Together? The Primacy of the Transatlantic Economy," Center for Transatlantic Relations [Washington] March 2003.

41 See Quinlin, "Drifting Apart or Growing Together?," xi.

42 Amin Saikal, "Afghanistan's Transition: ISAF's Stabilization Role?" *Third World Quarterly* 27(3) (June 2006), 528.

43 Vincent Morelli and Paul Belkin, "NATO in Afghanistan: A Test of the Transatlantic Alliance," Congressional Research Service Report RL33627, July 2009, 7–8.

44 North Atlantic Treaty Organization, *Afghanistan Report 2009* (Brussels: NATO Public Diplomacy Division, 2009), 18, 35, 36.

45 Anthony Cordesman, "Sanctum FATA," *The National Interest* 101 (May–June 2009), 31.

46 Saikal, "Afghanistan's Transition," 532.

47 The lessons of NATO operations in the Balkans and then in Afghanistan led the alliance to recognize formally that military interventions on their own are insufficient to "win the peace." NATO has also acknowledged that, as an organization, it does not have the mandate or the in-house resources to provide everything that is required to deal with a defeated or failed state. At the April 4, 2009 Strasbourg/Kehl Summit, allied leaders in their "Declaration on Alliance Security" noted: "We aim to strengthen our cooperation with other international actors, including the United Nations, European Union, Organization for Security and Cooperation in Europe and African Union, in order to improve our ability to deliver a comprehensive approach to meeting these new challenges, combining civilian and military capabilities more effectively. In our operations today in Afghanistan and the Western Balkans, our armed forces are working alongside many other nations and organisations." PRTs and cooperation with other international organizations formed the core of NATO's comprehensive approach to the ISAF mission in Afghanistan.

48 See, for example, James Sperling and Mark Webber, "NATO: From Kosovo to Kabul," *International Affairs* 85(3) (May 2009), 509, and Saikal, "Afghanistan's Transition," 532.

49 Saikal, "Afghanistan's Transition," 532.

50 Markus Kaim, "Germany, Afghanistan, and the Future of NATO," *International Journal* 63(3) (Summer 2008), 613.

51 Michael O'Hanlon, "Toward Reconciliation in Afghanistan," *The Washington Quarterly* (April 2008), 142.

52 Cordesman, "Sanctum FATA," 31.

53 The goal is found in numerous locations on the NATO website. See, for example, www.nato.int/cps/en/natolive/topics_8189.htm [accessed July 28, 2019].

54 North Atlantic Treaty Organization, "Summit Declaration on Afghanistan, Issued by the Heads of State and Government participating in the meeting of the North Atlantic Council in Strasbourg / Kehl on 4 April 2009."

55 Kenneth Katzman, "Afghanistan: Government Formation and Performance," CRS Report for Congress, RL30508, June 2009 (updated regularly), 15.

56 Katzman, "Afghanistan: Government," 16.

57 Daniel Korski, *Afghanistan: Europe's Forgotten War* (European Council on Foreign Relations, 2008), 24.

58 Ali A. Jalali, "Afghanistan: Regaining Momentum," *Parameters* 37(4) (Winter 2007), 8.

59 Morelli and Belkin, "NATO in Afghanistan," 31.

60 Seth G. Jones, *Counterinsurgency in Afghanistan: RAND Counterinsurgency Study–Volume 4* (Arlington: RAND Corporation, 2008), 84.

61 Cyrus Hodes and Mark Sedra, *The Search for Security in Post-Taliban Afghanistan* (Abingdon: Routledge for the International Institute for Strategic Studies, 2007), 2.
62 Hodes and Sedra, *The Search for Security*, 62.
63 Hodes and Sedra, *The Search for Security*, 64.
64 North Atlantic Treaty Organization, *Afghanistan Report 2009*, 5.
65 Richard A. Oppel, Jr., "Corruption Undercuts Hopes for Afghan Police," *The New York Times*, April 8, 2009.
66 North Atlantic Treaty Organization, *Afghanistan Report 2009*, 5.
67 North Atlantic Treaty Organization, "Summit Declaration on Afghanistan."
68 North Atlantic Treaty Organization, *Afghanistan Report 2009*, 13.
69 North Atlantic Treaty Organization, *Afghanistan Report 2009*, 13.
70 North Atlantic Treaty Organization, *Afghanistan Report 2009*, 14.
71 Jones, *Counterinsurgency in Afghanistan*, 75.
72 Hodes and Sedra, *The Search for Security*, 57.
73 Ann Scott Tyson, "Afghan Effort is Mullen's Top Focus," *The Washington Post*, May 5, 2009, 1.
74 German Marshal Fund of the United States et al., "Transatlantic Trends 2008 Topline Data," October 2008.
75 Morelli and Belkin, "NATO in Afghanistan," 23.
76 Al Pessin, "Gates to Meet with Allies on Afghanistan, Wants Progress Within a Year," VOANews.com, June 9, 2009.
77 Joris Janssen Lok, "Defining Objectives: Taliban and European Politics Challenge NATO Mission in Afghanistan," *Defense Technology International* 1(6) (August 2007), 16.
78 Morelli and Belkin, "NATO in Afghanistan," 10.
79 Thomas Omestad, "NATO Struggles Over Who Will Send Additional Troops to Fight in Afghanistan," USNews.com, February 13, 2008.
80 Kaim, "Germany, Afghanistan," 614.
81 Kaim, "Germany, Afghanistan," 613.
82 Eric Chauvistré, "Don't Shoot, We're German! Obstacles to a Debate on the Bundeswehr's International Missions," *Internationale Politik*, Summer 2009, 69, 77.
83 While not officially documented, the author heard this rationale widely rumored among European officials.
84 Jennifer Agiesta and Jon Cohen, "Public Opinion in U.S. Turns against Afghan War," *The Washington Post*, August 20, 2009.
85 Final Communiqué, Ministerial Meeting of the North Atlantic Council held in Reykjavik on May 14, 2002, para. 5.
86 Prague Summit Declaration, Issued by the Heads of State and Government participating in the meeting of the North Atlantic Council in Prague on November 21, 2002.
87 The Rumsfeld initiative owes much to the research completed at the National Defense University by Hans Binnendijk and Richard Kugler. The two experts developed the basic concept for the Response Force. See Hans Binnendijk and Richard Kugler, "Transforming European Forces," *Survival* (Autumn 2002), 117–32.

88 North Atlantic Treaty Organization, Public Diplomacy Division, "Financial and Economic Data Relating to NATO Defence," 19 February 2009. See: www.nato.int/docu/pr/2009/p09–009e.html [accessed May 17, 2015].

89 Mike Peacock, "Blair Pushes for a New NATO/Russia Relationship," *Reuters*, November 16, 2001.

90 Michael Wines, "Russia Could Get Veto Power in New NATO," *International Herald Tribune*, November 23, 2001, 1.

91 Ronald D. Asmus and Jeremy D. Rosner, "Don't Give Russia a Veto," *The Washington Times*, December 5, 2001, A19.

92 Lord Robertson, "NATO in the 21st Century," Speech at Charles University, Prague, March 21, 2002 (full text on NATO web site at www.nato.int/).

93 Sean Kay, "Missile Defenses and the European Security Dilemma," Paper Prepared for Presentation at the Annual Meeting of the International Studies Association, New York, February 2009, 5–6.

94 An excellent analysis of Russia's attitudes can be found in John P. Caves, Jr. and M. Elaine Bunn, "Russia's Cold War Perspective on Missile Defense in Europe," *Foundation pour la Recherche Stratégique*, May 3, 2007: www.isn.ethz.ch/Digital-Library/Publications/Detail/?lng=en&id=141194 [accessed May 14, 2015].

95 GlobalSecurity.org, "9K720 Iskander-M (SS-26 Stone)", www.globalsecurity.org/wmd/world/russia/ss-26.htm [accessed May 14, 2015].

96 Tomas Valasek, "Obama, Russia and Europe," Centre for European Reform Policy Brief, London, June 2009, 1–2.

97 Gordon Lubold, "European Missile Shield Not Set in Stone, Pentagon says," *Christian Science Monitor*, July 14, 2009.

98 Barack Obama, "President Obama Delivers Remarks on Missile Defense," Transcript, washingtonpost.com, September 17, 2009: [accessed September 17, 2009]. www.washingtonpost.com/wp-dyn/content/article/2009/09/17/AR2009091701818.html [accessed May 14, 2015].

99 Claire Bigg, "Russia: Putin 'Satisfied' as G-8 Summit Winds to a Close," RFE/RL Report, July 17, 2006.

100 For an excellent collection of analyses of Ukraine's early post-Cold War role in European security, see David E. Albright and Semyen J. Appatov, *Ukraine and European Security* (New York: St. Martin's Press, 1999).

101 Judy Dempsey, "Neighbors See Need for Kiev Incentives," *International Herald Tribune*, November 23, 2004.

102 Zbigniew Brzezinski, *The Grand Chessboard: American Primacy and its Geostrategic Imperatives* (New York: Basic Books, 1997), 46.

103 Joel Brinkley, "Powell Trades Tough Talk with Russian Leaders over Ukraine," *The New York Times*, December 8, 2004.

104 Denis Dyomkin, "Russia Hopes to Keep Naval Base in Ukraine," *Reuters India*, July 14, 2009.

105 Luke Harding, "Bush backs Ukraine and Georgia for NATO membership," *The Guardian*, April 1, 2008.

106 North Atlantic Treaty Organization, "Bucharest Summit Declaration," para. 23, April 3, 2008.

107 For an excellent unbiased account of the Russia/Georgia conflict see: Jim Nichol, "Russia–Georgia Conflict in August 2008: Context and Implications for U.S.

Interests," Congressional Research Service Report for Congress RL34618, March 3, 2009.

108 Wade Boese, "Russia Unflinching on CFE Treaty Suspension," *Arms Control Today,* June 2008.

109 Karl-Heinz Kamp, "Frozen Conflict," *Internationale Politik,* German Council on Foreign Relations, Berlin (Summer 2008): https://ip-journal.dgap.org/en/ip-journal/topics/frozen-conflict [accessed May 14, 2015].

110 In 2009 a Russian State Duma Deputy claimed that his assistant had initiated the attacks. This claim was not accepted by Estonian authorities who judge that such an attack was too intense and complex to have been mounted by one individual. See Robert Coalson, "Behind the Estonian Cyberattacks," Radio Free Europe, Radio Liberty Transmission, March 6, 2009: www.rferl.org/content/Behind_The_Estonia_Cyberattacks/1505613.html [accessed May 14, 2015].

111 At the time, Greek Foreign Minister and OSCE chair Dora Bakoyanni regretted the Russian move, observing that "As a result, one of the largest on-the-ground missions of the OSCE in the region was led to an end—despite the clear need, recognized by many states taking part in it, for the organization to be present in order to contribute toward security and stability in the region." Matt Robinson, "U.N. monitors leave Georgia, OSCE mission shut," www.boston.com, June 30, 2009.

112 Andrew Monaghan, "At the Table or on the Menu? Moscow's Proposals for Strategic Reform," NATO Defense College Research Division Research Report, June 2009, 1.

113 Bobo Lo, "Medvedev and the New European Security Architecture," Centre for European Reform Policy Brief, July 2009, 3–5.

114 Monaghan, "At the Table or on the Menu?," 2–3.

115 The perception among many Eastern and Central European officials was that this was the intent of French diplomacy for a period early in 2000, even though it has been denied by French officials.

116 During 2001 the EU members dropped the word "Common" and began referring to the policy as the "European Security and Defense Policy (ESDP)."

117 Joint Statement of the Heads of State and Government of Germany, France, Luxembourg, and Belgium on European Defence, 29 April 2003.

118 John Vinocur, "4 Nations Agree to Set up Autonomous Europe Defense Body," *International Herald Tribune,* April 30, 2003. Jaap de Hoop Scheffer's clear statement may have served as a leading credential for his appointment as NATO Secretary General in 2004.

119 Judy Dempsey, "NATO Urged to Challenge European Defence Plan," *The Financial Times,* October 17, 2003.

120 Ian Black, "Iraq Splits EU Summit as Blair backs US," *The Guardian,* December 12, 2003: www.theguardian.com/world/2003/dec/13/usa.eu [accessed May 16, 2015].

121 President and Secretary General Hoop de Scheffer Discuss NATO meeting, White House Press Release, February 22, 2005.

122 Javier Solana, "EU High Representative for the CFSP, Addresses the European Parliament on the EU Common Security and Defence Policy," Council of the European Union, Brussels, February 18, 2009.

123 For an excellent, albeit arguably an excessively optimistic, assessment of the process of developing security and defense policy competence in the EU, see: Jolyon Howorth, *Security and Defence Policy in the European Union*, The European Union Series (New York: Palgrave Macmillan, 2007).

124 For an excellent survey of transatlantic defense industrial issues see Burkard Schmitt editor, with Gordon Adams, Christophe Cornu, and Andrew D. James, "Between Cooperation and Competition: The Transatlantic Defence Market," Chaillot Paper no. 44, Western European Union Institute for Security Studies, January 2001. For additional background see Gordon Adams, Alex Ashbourne, et al., *Europe's Defence Industry: A Transatlantic Future* (London: Centre for European Reform, 1999) and Robert P. Grant, "Transatlantic Armament Relations under Strain," *Survival*, 39(1), Spring 1997, 111–37.

125 Charles Grant, *Is Europe Doomed to Fail as a Power?*, Centre for European Reform essays, July 2009.

126 In April 1973, National Security Advisor Henry Kissinger gave a speech entitled "The Year of Europe," which led to European concern and speculation about Kissinger's "agenda." The questions Kissinger raised about how transatlantic relations would be affected by the process of European integration undoubtedly gave rise to the US intelligence community's decision to prepare an estimate on the development of a "common" European approach.

      Many of the issues raised in 1973 are still open today, and the overall conclusion in the estimate remains reasonably accurate. The draft approved in the interagency review process noted that the United States should think in terms of a "uniting Europe," observing that European integration was a long historical process, with no clear outcome foreordained. The estimate concluded that as integration advanced, and as more common policies were decided, a "uniting Europe" would nonetheless present a mixed picture to the outside world, a blend between areas in which the central institutions had been given authority over key decisions and implementation of community policies and areas in which national identities, interests and prerogatives still prevailed.

127 François Heisbourg, "Chirac Should be More Cynical," *The Financial Times*, June 4, 2003.

128 For the text of the treaty, see: http://eur-lex.europa.eu/legal-ontent/EN/TXT/PDF/?uri=OJ:C:2007:306:FULL&from=EN [accessed June 14, 2015]

129 Theo Sommer, "Not a Cinch, but a Success," *The Atlantic Times*, 4(7), July 2007, 1.

130 Quinlan, *European Defense Cooperation*, 54.

131 For a more extended treatment of this issue see Stanley R. Sloan, Robert G. Sutter, and Casimir A. Yost, *The Use of U.S. Power, Implications for U.S. Interests* (Washington, D.C.: Institute for the Study of Diplomacy, Georgetown University, 2004). See also Fareed Zakaria, "The Future of American Power, How the United States Can Survive the Rise of the Rest," *Foreign Affairs*, 87(3), May/June 2008, 41, and Richard Haass, "The Age of Nonpolarity, What Will Follow U.S. Dominance," *Foreign Affairs*, 87(3), May/June 2008, 56.

8

The 2010s: new tasks, new traumas

Two key developments in the late 2000s played a major role in shaping the opening of the next decade in transatlantic relations. One of those developments was the 2008 election of Barak Obama to replace George W. Bush as president of the United States. The second development was the descent of the Western economic system into the worst decline since the great depression of the 1930s.

Barack Obama entered the White House in January 2009 pledging to end the combat roles of the United States in both Iraq and Afghanistan and to pursue a less interventionist American international role. His election produced a honeymoon period in transatlantic relations, as European governments hoped that a more liberal American administration would find itself more frequently in agreement with their perspectives on international issues. The "honeymoon" lasted perhaps six months, by which time transatlantic relations returned to a more normal set of agreements and disagreements. Nevertheless, Obama's commitment to end the wars in Iraq and Afghanistan provided a better context for the relationship than had the contentious Bush years.

The second development—what became known as the "great recession"—reinforced the already strong tendencies of the European allies to cut spending on defense while controlling government spending and protecting important social programs. President Obama came to office just as the "great recession" (from January 2007 to June 2009) had brought the Western economic system to its knees. The recession was a global one, based on the fact that annual real world gross domestic product per-capita actually declined in the single calendar year of 2009.[1] At the same time, war fatigue and domestic pressures in the United States increased support for the case that America's allies, particularly the European ones, should pick up more international security burdens to relieve American ones. Clearly, this was a formula for transatlantic friction.

By the middle of this decade, as Western economies still struggled to recover from the great recession, two new threats to Western security intruded on the hope for peace in a post-Iraq and Afghanistan War world. One was posed by the emergence of a new radical Islamist group variously called the "Islamic State of Iraq and the Levant (ISIL)," "Islamic State of Iraq and Syria (ISIS)," or, from the Arabic language, the acronyms "Da'ish," "Da'eesh," or "Daesh" (this text will, for convenience, use the first of these acronyms, ISIL). The others came from new Russian aggression against Ukraine and implicit or explicit threats to other neighboring European states from Russian President Vladimir Putin's increasingly autocratic regime in Moscow.

This chapter examines these transitions and traumas to bring this volume's analysis to the point where we can move toward consideration of the future defense of the West and the role that NATO and the European Union may play in that defense.

Obama is not Bush

When Barack Obama emerged in 2008 as the Democratic nominee for the presidency, he was greeted with acclaim and a degree of wonder in Europe. Even though President Bush had, in his second term, regained some of the ground that he had lost with the European allies, most European governments and electorates were looking for a change. On a swing through Europe during the electoral campaign, Obama was greeted by huge, admiring crowds, hopeful for new leadership from their senior ally and amazed that the United States might actually elect a black man to the presidency—something many Europeans remarked could not yet happen in their countries. In a speech to a cheering throng of over 200,000 in Berlin, Obama responded to European hopes by promising a new appreciation of the value of US allies, but also called for more substantial European contributions to the alliance.[2]

Obama's election seemed to signal a new era in transatlantic relations. But after six years of his administration, despite high hopes for Obama, there was less enthusiasm for US leadership. There was however, a greater realization that a leading American role in the alliance remained essential to their security.

As a gift of sorts for the new American president, French President Nicolas Sarkozy announced in March 2009 that his government would return France to participation in NATO's military command structure. In fact, for several years French officers had been actively engaged in NATO's military command structure, and Sarkozy's move seemed to reflect a judgment that French national interests had more to gain from full formal involvement than from remaining partly outside the Western tent.

The first NATO summit following Obama's ascent to the presidency (and France's return to the military command structure) took place in Strasbourg, France and Kehl, Germany on the occasion of NATO's 60th

Figure 8.1 NATO leaders at 2009 Strasbourg/Kehl 60th Anniversary Summit (British Prime Minister Brown, US President Obama, NATO Secretary General Jaap de Hoop Scheffer, German Chancellor Merkel, French President Sarkozy).

anniversary. Allied leaders celebrated NATO's birthday in a positive mood, calling for the preparation of a new strategic concept to reflect more than a decade of change since the previous concept, with the hopes of establishing a foundation for NATOs future. The alliance had been in need of a new concept for many years, particularly given the fact that since 1999 the allies had taken the alliance "out of area" for the first time, in spite of the earlier European reluctance to consider such operations. The 9/11 attacks profoundly affected allied views on this question, but many allied governments preferred to defer preparation of a new concept until the post-Bush period had dawned.

The process of transition continued for the rest of 2009, as a new leadership team came into NATO. Allied leaders at Strasbourg/Kehl confirmed one of their own—Danish Prime Minister Anders Fogh Rasmussen—as NATO's next Secretary General, replacing Jaap de Hoop Scheffer. Rasmussen would play a major role in shaping the alliance's 2010 Strategic Concept. On NATO's military side, US Navy Admiral James G. Stavridis replaced Army General Bantz J. Craddock as the new head of the US European Command and as NATO's Supreme Allied Commander, Europe (SACEUR). Stavridis, the first naval officer to become SACEUR and seen as "perhaps the ultimate warrior scholar of his generation,"[3] took charge of NATO forces at a time when the alliance was facing a growing number of emerging challenges.

By the end of the year, President Obama had been convinced that, in order to leave Afghanistan responsibly, one final military "surge" would be required, as had been done in preparation for leaving Iraq. The idea was to surge US and coalition force numbers and operations to improve the security situation before Afghanistan national forces took on primary responsibility for dealing with the persistent threat from Taliban forces. In a major speech at the US West Point Military Academy in December 2009, Obama announced that the United States would send an additional 30,000 troops to Afghanistan with the goal of beginning the process of withdrawing US forces by July 2011. He described the deployment as part of an international effort, reporting:

> I've asked that our commitment be joined by contributions from our allies. Some have already provided additional troops, and we're confident that there will be further contributions in the days and weeks ahead. Our friends have fought and bled and died alongside us in Afghanistan. And now, we must come together to end this war successfully. For what's at stake is not simply a test of NATO's credibility—what's at stake is the security of our allies, and the common security of the world.[4]

While there was not great enthusiasm in Europe about sending more troops to Afghanistan, the promise of a surge leading to the eventual departure garnered a degree of allied support. Three days after the President's speech, NATO announced that 25 countries had pledged a total of around 7,000 additional troops to support the US-led surge in Afghanistan.[5]

Meanwhile, the dislocations caused by the recession forced leaders on both sides of the Atlantic to focus on the resultant financial and economic challenges as a leading threat to their national security. It guaranteed that, set against the perception that there were no imminent threats to European security, European governments would focus on trying to restore economic growth, support the Euro currency, reduce unemployment and save domestic social programs. In this environment, the downward path for defense spending and investment that had followed the end of the Cold War would not be reversed.

In fact, it took the dual threat posed in 2014 by ISIL in the Middle East, and Russian aggression in Europe, to help stimulate support for renewed growth in defense expenditures and investment in defense systems. (See discussion below of the NATO Wales Summit in September 2014, pp. 286–91.)

Toward a new strategic concept

As work continued on a new strategic concept for the alliance, the threat environment in Europe actually seemed to be improving. In December, 2009 NATO and Russia agreed at a meeting of the NATO-Russia Council to revitalize their relations.[6] This led to a formal resumption of NATO-Russia military ties on January 26, 2010.[7] The next day it was announced that Russia had agreed to enhance cooperation with the alliance in Afghanistan, including opening more transit routes for supplies to international troops and helping service Soviet-built helicopters used by the International Security Assistance Force (ISAF).[8]

As a vehicle for developing the new concept, NATO Secretary General Rasmussen had established a special "Group of Experts" under the leadership of former US Secretary of State Madeleine Albright to lay the groundwork. On May 20, 2010, the Albright group delivered its report, examining all aspects of the alliance, its purpose and its future directions.[9] The report provided a wealth of information and perspectives, but it was not in any way a "pre-draft" of the new concept.

In the past, strategic concepts had been developed through interactive drafting exercises managed by national permanent representatives at NATO headquarters with contributions by visiting experts from capitols. On this occasion, with the mandate provided by the North Atlantic Council (NAC), Secretary General Rasmussen took over: "Having followed the Albright group's work closely, the Secretary General himself drafted the first version of the Strategic Concept that was to serve as the basis for the final negotiations in the NAC."[10]

Even though the draft concept dealt with a number of issues on which there was not a full allied consensus, consultations in the NAC apparently were not particularly difficult. According to one account, there were some "dramas" in discussion of the draft, particularly on the issues of the priorities to be assigned to nuclear deterrence versus nuclear disarmament, new threats to allied security, and the relationship with and role of partners.[11] The new concept, entitled "Active Engagement, Modern Defence,"[12] was issued by alliance leaders at their summit in Lisbon, Portugal on November 19–20, 2010.

The new concept (subsequently referred to also as "SC2010") laid out three "core" missions for the alliance:

1. *Collective defence.* "NATO members will always assist each other against attack, in accordance with Article 5 of the Washington Treaty. That commitment remains firm and binding. NATO will deter and defend against any threat of aggression, and against emerging security challenges where they threaten the fundamental security of individual Allies or the Alliance as a whole."

2. *Crisis management.* "NATO has a unique and robust set of political and
   military capabilities to address the full spectrum of crises—before, during
   and after conflicts. NATO will actively employ an appropriate mix of those
   political and military tools to help manage developing crises that have
   the potential to affect Alliance security, before they escalate into conflicts;
   to stop ongoing conflicts where they affect Alliance security; and to help
   consolidate stability in post-conflict situations where that contributes to
   Euro-Atlantic security."
3. *Cooperative security.* "The Alliance is affected by, and can affect, political
   and security developments beyond its borders. The Alliance will engage
   actively to enhance international security, through partnership with relevant countries and other international organisations; by contributing
   actively to arms control, non-proliferation and disarmament; and by
   keeping the door to membership in the Alliance open to all European
   democracies that meet NATO's standards."

In addition to laying out NATO's three core missions, the new concept
confirmed NATO's role as a pre-eminent forum for transatlantic security
relations. It asserted that NATO remained a "nuclear alliance;" supported
allied cooperation on missile defense, cyber security, non-proliferation,
counter-terrorism, and energy security; acknowledged the importance of
UN responsibilities for international security and the European Union's contributions to security; and re-affirmed the importance of cooperation with
Russia.

Documents such as the SC2010 very seldom create new realities. Rather,
they confirm and acknowledge the level of consensus among the allies that
existed in the year or two prior to agreement on the document. However, in
this case, two important aspects of the SC2010 weighed directly on the question of NATO's role in the transatlantic bargain, having recognized a new
consensus that goes well beyond what was possible in NATO's last Strategic
Concept agreed in Washington in 1999.

First, SC2010 provided a substantially new definition of collective defense,
the key underlying commitment made by each ally to the others. In the
past, collective defense was defined almost exclusively by the North Atlantic
Treaty's Article 5, in which the allies agreed that an attack on one ally would
be treated as an attack on all, and that each ally would determine on the basis
of its sovereign decisions what it would do in response.

The end of the Cold War, and the dissolution of the Warsaw Pact and
the Soviet Union, made a direct attack on a NATO country appear much
less likely, but "threats" to security and territorial integrity subsequently
emerged from a number of new sources, including non-state actors. In
these circumstances, Article 4, which called for cooperation to deal with
threats, not predicated on an attack having taken place, became more
relevant.[13]

Box 8.1   North Atlantic Treaty, Articles 4 and 5

Article 4

The Parties will consult together whenever, in the opinion of any of them, the territorial integrity, political independence or security of any of the Parties is threatened.

Article 5

The Parties agree that an armed attack against one or more of them in Europe or North America shall be considered an attack against them all and consequently they agree that, if such an armed attack occurs, each of them, in exercise of the right of individual or collective self-defence recognised by Article 51 of the Charter of the United Nations, will assist the Party or Parties so attacked by taking forthwith, individually and in concert with the other Parties, such action as it deems necessary, including the use of armed force, to restore and maintain the security of the North Atlantic area.

Any such armed attack and all measures taken as a result thereof shall immediately be reported to the Security Council. Such measures shall be terminated when the Security Council has taken the measures necessary to restore and maintain international peace and security.

In SC2010, the allies conflated Articles 4 and 5 to produce an amended definition of collective defense. In this updated interpretation of the treaty, SC2010 stated that "NATO members will always assist each other against attack, in accordance with Article 5 of the Washington Treaty. That commitment remains firm and binding. *NATO will deter and defend against any threat of aggression, and against emerging security challenges where they threaten the fundamental security of individual Allies or the Alliance as a whole*" (emphasis added).[14]

This new presentation of collective defense arguably provided NATO with a much broader mandate than understood by the original treaty. It opened the door to more extensive cooperation to deal with potential as well as imminent threats. Those threats were not geographically limited, nor were they necessarily limited to "armed" threats. Threats can be, and have been, interpreted as including a wide variety of challenges to the security of individual member states as well as to the collective including, for example, cyber threats and energy supply manipulation. The Strategic Concepts of 1991 (Rome) and 1999 (Washington) identified such threats but did not commit to the use of NATO to deal with them. Afghanistan changed all that, and SC2010 appeared to open the NATO door even wider to potential cooperation on security challenges regardless of the type or location from which a threat originates.

The second important contribution of the concept to NATO's future role was the expanded interpretation of comprehensive security. For over a decade, some analysts had argued that future security would require more effective integration of military and non-military instruments of security.[15] Now that this argument had been more-or-less accepted as conventional wisdom, the challenge became one of producing the institutional and intergovernmental cooperation to make the concept work in the real world. So far, this had been frustratingly difficult. For many years, some European governments, France in particular, resisted the idea of expanding NATO's mandate to coordinate cooperation on non-military instruments of power and influence. When it was suggested that perhaps a new framework of cooperation be developed, this approach met resistance from those who opposed creating new consultative frameworks as well as those skeptical about the future of transatlantic security cooperation altogether.[16]

The frustrations over developing comprehensive approaches to security were deepened by the experience in Afghanistan. The fact that NATO was in charge of the ISAF there made the European Union reluctant to get deeply involved with its non-military strengths and resources which could have been very helpful to stabilizing the country. NATO and the EU had not been able to have serious formal consultations about anything other than Bosnia due to the deadlock between Turkey, Greece, and Cyprus, and therefore between Turkey and the EU, over future European security arrangements.

SC2010 nonetheless suggested that NATO should develop further its capabilities in coordinating non-military components of future security cooperation, under the broadened definition of NATO's collective defense mandate. The concept declared that crisis management is one of NATO's "core tasks," and that "NATO has a unique and robust set of political and military capabilities to address the full spectrum of crises—before, during and after conflicts. NATO will actively employ an appropriate mix of those political and military tools to help manage developing crises that have the potential to affect Alliance security before they escalate into conflicts; to stop ongoing conflicts where they affect Alliance security; and to help consolidate stability in post-conflict situations where that contributes to Euro-Atlantic security."[17]

The logic of the strategic concept suggested that the evolving transatlantic bargain was one in which allied nations, still belonging to a "unique community of values," aspired to plan and work together to deal with threats to their interests, and do so with a wide spectrum of capabilities, including diplomacy, political and economic incentives and sanctions, and, if necessary, the use of force. This evolving bargain was based on a deepened concept of what constitutes collective defense and a broadened scope of cooperative measures to be used in response. It was also based on the concept of all alliance members contributing to alliance missions, and to equitable sharing of alliance burdens.

A bargain based on these objectives required more intensive, comprehensive, and informed planning among NATO allies than had been the case to date. SC2010 made it clear that NATO alone did not aspire to assume responsibility for all crisis management functions, even if it hopes to plan for effective management of pre-conflict, conflict, and post-conflict stages of crises. The concept specified that NATO will look to other organizations to carry part of the comprehensive approach load: "The Alliance will engage actively with other international actors before, during and after crises to encourage collaborative analysis, planning and conduct of activities on the ground, in order to maximise coherence and effectiveness of the overall international effort."[18]

The concept therefore recognized that future US–European security cooperation would require a good working relationship between NATO and the EU, and between the United States and EU members bilaterally and in NATO. However, attempts to meld the resources of the two most important Euro-Atlantic institutions, NATO and the European Union, and the work of United Nations agencies and non-governmental organizations, into comprehensive approaches, whether in Afghanistan or more generally, have run into serious political obstacles. The main concern of other organizations is that they will either become too associated with or subordinate to NATO's combat mission, while they are engaged in humanitarian or development work.

Prospects for multilateral cooperation can be further complicated when UN and non-governmental organizations are reluctant to get too close to NATO military operations, fearing that their humanitarian purposes will be perceived as part of a war effort.

SC2010 therefore begged the question: what must happen for NATO to be able to develop more comprehensive approaches to security issues? This is a key element of the "crisis management" component of SC2010's approach. If the allies seek to prevent crises from developing into armed conflicts, dealing with such conflicts if they do, and helping manage the transition from armed conflicts into more peaceful settings, it will need either very good collaboration with the European Union, the United Nations and other international organizations and non-governmental humanitarian and assistance groups; or, it will need an expanded mandate of its own to organize and coordinate the diplomatic, financial, military and other resources required for effective crisis management.

When the concept was released, NATO had neither a high level of effective coordination with partner organizations, in spite of institutional efforts to improve such cooperation, nor did the members give NATO the mandates that would have been required for NATO to take on responsibility itself for the full range of crisis management tasks.

First test of the new concept: Libya

The ink was barely dry on the new concept when developments on the southern rim of the Mediterranean challenged the allies to deploy their crisis management commitment so highly touted in the new Strategic Concept. Libya's dictator Moammar Gaddafi had ruled his country with an iron fist for over four decades when, in February 2011, he ordered his military forces to quash a peaceful protest against his regime in the eastern regions of his country. When Gaddafi's forces killed dozens of protestors in the eastern city of Benghazi, the United Nations Security Council (UNSC) ordered an arms embargo against Libya and authorized additional sanctions (UNSC Resolution 1970[19]).

When Gaddafi's forces appeared on the verge of defeating resistance in Benghazi, the UNSC on March 17 approved Resolution 1973[20] authorizing "all necessary measures" to establish a no-fly zone, protect civilian areas, and impose a ceasefire on Gaddafi's military. Five countries abstained: China, Russia, India, Brazil, and Germany. This outcome followed urging by France and the UK in particular and then by the Arab League. The United States was able to support the initiative without being out front—perhaps exactly the right stance for a country already engaged in conflicts in two Muslim countries. But the vote produced a deep schism between EU members Germany, on the one hand, and France and the UK, who were the prime advocates of the measures against Gaddafi, on the other.

A week after Resolution 1973 was approved, several UN members in an ad hoc coalition of North American, European, and Arab countries led by the United States initiated military action against Gaddafi's forces under what the United States called "Operation Odyssey Dawn."[21] The ad hoc coalition cobbled together to run military operations against Gaddafi's forces was not initially run by NATO, but it could not have functioned if NATO did not exist. The infrastructure and interoperability for the operation relied on the cooperative arrangements stimulated and rationalized by NATO commitments. Access to Italian bases from which many operations were run was facilitated by their NATO roles.

The critical importance of the NATO framework was recognized when the alliance was given a key coordinating role in the operation. NATO entered the action in the third week of March. The North Atlantic Council decided that "Operation Unified Protector" would take up the UN arms embargo mandate and began interdicting the flow of weapons and fighters to Libya, establishing a no-fly zone around the country. On March 31, NATO took control of all military actions against Gaddafi's military.

Operation Unified Protector, with heavy air strikes on Libyan forces and other assistance,[22] enabled the anti-Gaddafi forces to push back Gaddafi into small pockets around the capitol of Tripoli. The insurgent National Transitional Council forces captured and executed Gaddafi on October 20, 2011. The mission was declared ended on October 31, 2011.

Lessons learned

Operation Unified Protector illustrated, in particular, the limitations on the potential for the European Union to perform as a unitary military actor on the international scene—as well as the handicaps that such limitations impose on NATO. Just prior to Libya, it had been common for many Europeans to project the image of a Europe growing into a new "pole" in a multi-polar international system. It was equally popular for American academics and officials, perhaps too impressed by rhetoric from Europe, to hope for an EU that would be able to take over security responsibilities, providing effective burden relief for the United States.

The image of European solidarity was smashed when Chancellor Angela Merkel's German government joined Russia, China, Brazil, and India abstaining on the UN resolution that sanctioned use of force against Libya. The German attitude was consistent with its desire not to be seen as taking aggressive actions against any state, in Europe or beyond. This well-engrained attitude, born of the lessons learned from World War II, had led Germany to stake out a largely non-combat role in Afghanistan as well.

However, German reluctance to authorize a mission strongly advocated by its leading European allies and supported by its American partner, combined with willingness to join Russia and China in abstention, raised serious questions about the potential for Europe to act together on any future decisions that require or support use of force.

Discussing these difficult times, a senior Belgian diplomat wisely told audiences at the NATO College that fault lines over the invasion of Iraq ran not just across the Atlantic, but across Europe and even through all European governments and ministries. German refusal to participate in or support the UN-authorized action against Gaddafi provided a fresh illustration of this diplomat's observation about the limits on European cohesion.

Perhaps more telling, however, was that EU governments, when it came to serious military and security questions, still acted as nation states. This was simply a reflection of reality, and suggested that at least some of the rhetoric about a European pole in the international system simply did not wash when it comes to vital security interests.

At the other end of the spectrum from Germany, France and the UK, just prior to the Libya crisis, advanced their bilateral military cooperation,[23] intending to enhance their role within the alliance. They did leverage their expanded cooperation into effective international activism in support of removing Gaddafi from power. However, even this success revealed limitations on their ability to perform such missions: much like the United States, they had voiced frustration that other European countries were not willing or able to do more to support their efforts. After the mission turned out to be much more demanding than expected, they also complained that US reticence was to blame for NATO's shortcomings. In the process, both Paris and London discovered some of the questionable benefits of leadership that the United States knows all too well. The United States has often been damned if it did and damned if it didn't provide strong leadership for the alliance. In the case of Libya, the French and British experienced both the highs and lows of taking a strong leadership position.

On the Western shores of the Atlantic, some Members of Congress—both on the left wing of the Democratic Party and among Tea Party Republicans—looked at US commitments to NATO as a prime target for spending cuts. For some, the difficulties of the Libyan mission only underscored their arguments. One American commentator, Lawrence F. Kaplan, criticized the Obama administration's leaving Libya to the Europeans, saying that "someone on the Obama team ought to have inquired about European capabilities—that is, whether the Europeans *can* do this or, more to the point, [can do] anything at all?" (Emphasis in original)[24] Particularly disconcerting was the fact that some European forces ran out of some munitions and had to get more from the United States. Kaplan quoted French expert Bruno Tertrais as saying: "The Libyan crisis has strikingly exposed the lack of a European defense policy: no ability to achieve a common political vision and no capacity to take on an operation of this kind."[25] Adding to the distressing picture, only eight of the 28 NATO allies took on combat missions in the conflict and "most ran out of ammunition, having to buy, at cost, ammunition stockpiled by the United States."[26]

It may be true that NATO's problems in managing the anti-Gaddafi mission are in large part due to the fact that the United States took a back seat in the operation, "leading from behind." However, President Obama could also have been seen as simply applying the lessons the United States had learned from the previous decade of US-led military operations: get an international mandate; do not put the United States in the position of attacking another Muslim country; try to get allies to do as much of the grunt work as possible; and keep US boots off the ground. President Obama also was responding to the message he heard from the American people: tend to our own problems; let the world take care of itself. Unfortunately, when the administration said it was turning leadership of the mission over to NATO, it helped perpetuate a long-standing flawed view of the alliance: many Americans regard NATO as simply meaning "those damned Europeans," while at the same time, many Europeans look at the alliance as "those damned Americans."

The top two American officials in NATO at the time, the United States Permanent Representative Ivo H. Daalder and the SACEUR, James G. Stavridis, praised the alliance for being capable of conducting the Libya mission in spite of the difficult circumstances surrounding the operation. However, they also noted that "The heavy reliance of alliance members on the United States during the conflict highlighted the cost of a decade of European underinvestment in defense."[27]

It was not long after the end of NATO involvement in Libya that the country descended into political chaos with the so-called Islamic State (ISIL) taking advantage of the turmoil to establish presence in or near several Libyan cities. From this perspective, the NATO operation can be seen as another case of well-intentioned removal of a dictator resulting in anarchy and civil war (as in Iraq).

From a transatlantic perspective, however, the Libya experience should have convinced most that NATO remains critically important when allies need/want to coordinate the use of military force. Political divisions among key EU members made it impossible for the EU to enforce UN Security Council Resolution 1973, while NATO was able to function in spite of such differences.

The Libya experience induced no progress toward overcoming the continuing barriers to effective cooperation between NATO and the European Union. But it did suggest that such cooperation would be essential in any efforts to shape a new transatlantic bargain in which NATO would play a key role in implementing comprehensive approaches to security with burdens shared on a basis that is politically acceptable to electorates and deliberative bodies on both sides of the Atlantic. The global economic recession, from which recovery had just begun, inclined the United States, Canada and the European allies to seek burden-shifting rather than burden-sharing outcomes. This was not an environment conducive to the production of bold new initiatives with uncertain outcomes.

Back to the future: burden-sharing and shifting priorities

In the midst of the Libya crisis, the perpetual burden-sharing issue once again reared its head. The United States had avoided putting "boots on the ground" in Libya but nonetheless was called on to provide essential components of the military operations and to bail out the Europeans when they ran out of munitions to use against Gaddafi's forces. The fact that only some of the European allies joined in combat operations made it clear that burden-sharing is not just a transatlantic issue but also a trans-European one.

For NATO, the ability of the alliance to conduct the operation in spite of the lack of universal allied enthusiasm, had a bright side: NATO can be operationally successful even when all allies do not participate, just as long as no ally uses its dissent to prevent an operation from happening. However, the dark side was that the variable contributions to an alliance mission was indicative of growing divisions among the members.

US Secretary of Defense Robert M. Gates, speaking at a Brussels symposium on June 11, 2011, delivered his final message to the alliance prior to leaving government service.[28] While critically examining allied contributions to NATO's roles in Afghanistan and Libya, Gates focused on the fact that some allies chose to take on the "softer" missions and tasks, leaving the heavy lifting for other allies, suggesting that this tendency was creating divisive levels of contributions to the alliance.

In the past, I've worried openly about NATO turning into a two-tiered alliance: Between members who specialize in "soft' humanitarian, development, peace-keeping, and talking tasks, and those conducting the "hard" combat missions. Between those willing and able to pay the price and bear the burdens of alliance commitments, and those who enjoy the benefits of NATO membership—be they security guarantees or headquarters billets—but don't want to share the risks and the costs. This is no longer a hypothetical worry. We are there today. And it is unacceptable.[29]

Gates concluded with a warning to allied governments:

The blunt reality is that there will be dwindling appetite and patience in the U.S. Congress—and in the American body politic writ large—to expend increasingly precious funds on behalf of nations that are apparently unwilling to devote the necessary resources or make the necessary changes to be serious and capable partners in their own defense. Nations apparently willing and eager for American taxpayers to assume the growing security burden left by reductions in European defense budgets.

Indeed, if current trends in the decline of European defense capabilities are not halted and reversed, Future U.S. political leaders—those for whom the Cold War was *not* the formative experience that it was for me—may not consider the return on America's investment in NATO worth the cost.[30]

Gates's warning echoed similar messages that had come from Washington for many years, if not decades. It was perhaps more bluntly delivered to try to break through the resistance to increased defense expenditures and investment prevalent in most allied nations. But it accurately reflected the increasing deterioration in shared commitments and burdens in the alliance as well as the dangers that a future US administration might reduce Europe and NATO's position in US foreign and defense policy priorities.

The message was sent at a time when the United States was in the final stages of withdrawal from Iraq, and in a dramatic reduction of US and NATO presence and activities in Afghanistan. In July 2011, the government of Afghanistan began the process of taking over combat missions from NATO forces with the goal of Afghani forces assuming responsibility for all combat missions by 2014. In December, NATO informed Iraq that it would withdraw its small training mission by the end of the year after Baghdad refused to grant it, or US forces, legal immunity. The end of the mission would therefore parallel the final withdrawal of US forces from Iraq.

The Asia pivot seen through a burden-sharing lens

While planned withdrawals from Iraq and Afghanistan were progressing rapidly, the Obama administration announced another major policy initiative that would have a large impact on its European allies—on their perceptions at least, if not on their planning. In the fall of 2011, the administration, in a series of announcements, said that the United States would be focusing increased political, military, and economic attention on the Asia/Pacific region. This policy, described initially as a "pivot" to Asia and subsequently re-defined as a "rebalancing" toward Asia, was presented as a major policy shift. But, as a Congressional Research Service Report noted, "Many aspects of the "Pacific Pivot" represent an expansion rather than a transformation of U.S. policy."[31]

To some, it seemed unnecessary to describe the policy focus as a "pivot," as the United States had been actively engaged in Asia since World War II, and had even fought two wars there over the previous 70 years (Korea and Vietnam). Therefore, it was not unreasonable for some observers to suggest that the not-so-subtle message to our NATO allies, and to European and Middle Eastern nations more generally, was that they could not in the future count on continuation of an active US role in guaranteeing security and controlling conflicts.

If the "pivot" was intended in part as a burden-sharing message to the European allies, it came at a very bad time. The focus in Europe was in bringing European troops home from NATO's ISAF in Afghanistan and trying to get their domestic economic house in order. In January 2012, France announced it would withdraw its troops from Afghanistan a year earlier than the 2014 date previously agreed by NATO. Other NATO governments were looking forward to being relieved of their Afghani commitments.

Under some circumstances, one might expect that the end of combat operations in Afghanistan would allow NATO countries to reallocate expenditures to other military needs. To some extent, this happened. France still had responsibilities in former African colonies, and intervened in Mali early in 2013 to help the government defeat jihadist forces that were threatening Mali's capital of Bamako. Central European governments, led by Poland, and the Baltic states were anxious to focus their energies on defense of their region against increasingly ominous indications that Vladimir Putin's Russia was pursuing a revisionist agenda in Europe.

Had Europe's recovery from the recession been moving ahead more smoothly, there might have been some margins available to support at least minimal defense improvements. Had the European Union not been beset by a multitude of issues emerging from the recession and the very slow recovery, there might have been more optimism available to drive real European acceptance of greater security burdens and responsibilities in and around Europe, as the United States would have liked. However, this was not to be.

The European Defense Agency (EDA), an intergovernmental agency of the European Union's Council, reports that, even though membership in the EDA increased from 26 to 27 Member States (Croatia having become a member) in 2013, total defense expenditure from 2012–2013 decreased by EUR 1.7 billion, or 0.9 percent. EDA reported that "total defence expenditure has been declining since 2006, dropping by over EUR 32 billion or about 15% from 2006 to 2013."[32] The report notes that as a share of gross domestic product and of total government spending, 2013 defense expenditure decreased to its lowest level since 2006.

Two main factors drive European defense spending: available resources and threat perception. In 2011–2013, Europe did not have excess resources to devote to defense and, given the low level of threat perception, no reason to re-allocate domestic spending to defense. The attempt by the US administration in the Gates warnings and the Asia pivot message to add a third factor—the threat of US abandonment—was concerning to European governments but insufficient to overcome the dynamic created by limited discretionary resources and modest threat perceptions. As one European expert observed in 2012, in spite of the Gates warning, "as European countries respond to the financial crisis, they have continued to cling to national prerogatives. Instead of coordinating their military spending cuts within NATO and the EU, governments have sidelined both organizations and scaled back their armed forces with scant regard for their allies. By proving Gates right, however, Europeans are undermining their ability to contribute to international security and creating significant political strains for the transatlantic alliance."[33]

As for threat perception, while concerns had been growing in Poland and the Baltic States, stimulating support for defense improvements there, most of Europe did not at that point feel directly threatened by the emerging Russian challenge. There was growing concern about the spillover from turmoil in the Middle East. But the Libya operation left most European allies unenthusiastic about taking on or even preparing for ambitious military operations in the region.

NATO comes to Obama's home: the Chicago Summit

The next decision point for the allies was to be a summit meeting held in President Obama's home town of Chicago in May 2012. When first planned, NATO governments anticipated that the main goal of the Chicago meeting would be to produce "deliverables" in response to the programs initiated at or suggested by the new Strategic Concept agreed in Lisbon in 2010. Such outcomes were to include: a clear plan for ending NATO's combat role in Afghanistan; a re-evaluation of NATO's approach to nuclear deterrence; progress on development of a missile defense plan; and a vision for the future of the alliance beyond Afghanistan. In addition, the pressure was on for a positive outcome: President Obama, facing a tough re-election battle, needed good news and support from America's key allies at this session to be held in the president's home town.

As the summit date came near, it appeared that it would produce some sort of NATO agreement with Afghan President Hamid Karzai's government, modeled on the US–Afghan pact signed in April 2012. The US–Afghanistan accord promised continuing US assistance to Afghanistan for many years after the scheduled transfer of security responsibilities to Afghan forces at the end of 2014, while laying out terms for a continued American presence in the country.

As for NATO's deterrence review ("Deterrence and Defense Posture Review"), there was no indication that the process of consultations, begun under the Lisbon Summit mandate, had managed to unravel the nest of complicated issues and profound differences among allies over the role of nuclear weapons in NATO's future strategy. The process had been complicated by continuing uncertainty about Russia's future, which particularly concerned those allies who only two decades ago escaped from Russian domination.

Newly inaugurated Russian President Vladimir Putin decided not to attend the Chicago meeting, where a session of the NATO-Russia Council was planned. It probably was just as well, because there seemed to be little prospect of significant progress being made in the NATO–Russia relationship in Chicago. NATO had continued to keep its arms open to cooperation with Russia, but the Russian response had largely kept the relationship in an icy limbo. As long as Russia's rulers intended to maintain autocratic, Moscow-centered rule—which seemed likely to be the inclination during Putin's third presidential term—the Kremlin will likely want to keep NATO available as an imagined external threat to reinforce public support for its domestic political control.

The difficult relationship with Russia had also complicated NATO's work on a missile defense system aimed at countering missile threats to Europe originating in the Middle Eastern region—Iran in particular. Russia's terms for cooperating in any such system included the unacceptable (for NATO) demand for a "two-key" system in which the Kremlin would have veto power over whether or not to launch interceptors against a ballistic missile attack.

The summit work plan also included NATO's "internal agenda": how to keep the alliance relevant and serving the interests of its members in the wake of the long war in Afghanistan and the short war over Libya. Neither of these conflicts were seen as models for NATO operations in the future, even though both of them had already produced lessons for the alliance. Some of the lessons had to do with American political judgment—the George Bush administration's decision to attack Iraq, leaving the Afghanistan mission as a poor stepchild, for example. Some had to do with European shortcomings, such as the inability of key European powers to conduct the Libyan campaign without vital US assistance, combined with the unwillingness of several European allies to participate in the campaign.

Moreover, the Obama administration's intention to pivot US defense priorities toward Asia, on top of former Secretary of Defense Robert Gates' parting shot across NATO's bow the previous summer, raised fundamental questions about the US commitment to the alliance. How might the Chicago Summit affect perceptions around this key existential issue for NATO?

The fact that the Obama administration planned to remove two army combat brigades from Europe, as part of broader cuts in defense spending, had fueled speculation that NATO was, or should be, coming to the end of its useful life. Some analysts argued that it was long overdue for Europeans to take care of their own defense, and that the United States should turn NATO's leadership over to its European allies.[34]

In Chicago, the allies issued the Chicago Summit Declaration.[35] The declaration covered the usual wide range of issues that concern the allies, but focused in particular on the process of making the transition from a combat to an advisory role in Afghanistan. The allies said, in part:

> Today we have taken further important steps on the road to a stable and secure Afghanistan and to our goal of preventing Afghanistan from ever again becoming a safe haven for terrorists that threaten Afghanistan, the region, and the world. The irreversible transition of full security responsibility from the International Security Assistance Force (ISAF) to the Afghan National Security Forces (ANSF) is on track for completion by the end of 2014, as agreed at our Lisbon Summit.[36]

The allies also approved a statement on the Deterrence and Defense Posture Review,[37] a study they had mandated at the Lisbon Summit. The study, however, did not resolve the issue of what nuclear capabilities were required to be stationed on European territory in support of NATO deterrence strategy. The allies did offer to consider further reductions in non-strategic nuclear weapons assigned "in the context of reciprocal steps by Russia, taking into account the greater Russian stockpiles of non-strategic nuclear weapons stationed in the Euro-Atlantic area."[38]

With regard to missile defenses, the allies supported moving ahead with the new approach proposed by the Obama administration in 2009.[39] At a time when relations with Russia seemed to be deteriorating rapidly, the allies called on Moscow to understand that the deployments were not intended to degrade Russian strategic missile deployments, saying:

> NATO missile defence is not oriented against Russia nor does it have the capability to undermine Russia's strategic deterrent. The Alliance, in a spirit of reciprocity, maximum transparency and mutual confidence, will actively seek cooperation on missile defence with Russia.[40]

At this point, the allies seemed well-aware that relations with Russia were rapidly moving toward confrontation, even if they wanted to keep the door open for cooperation. Russia's aggression against Georgia was noted in the summit declaration, and the allies called "on Russia to reverse its recognition of the South Ossetia and Abkhazia regions of Georgia as independent states."[41] Not only did Putin not attend the summit (as a NATO partner), but he even canceled out of the US-hosted Group of Eight Nations (G8)[42] economic summit that preceded the Chicago meeting,[43] sending Prime Minister Dmitry Medvedev in his place. The allies repeated the perhaps-incautious 2008 pledge that Georgia "one day" would join NATO—a sore point with Moscow. They were more cautious and less explicit regarding the same pledge that was made to Ukraine. While declaring that "An independent, sovereign and stable Ukraine, firmly committed to democracy and the rule of law, is key to Euro-Atlantic security," the allied leaders noted that "Recalling our decisions in relation to Ukraine and our Open Door policy stated at the Bucharest and Lisbon Summits, NATO is ready to continue to develop its cooperation with Ukraine."[44]

Against the backdrop of severe financial difficulties in member states, the leaders issued a Summit Declaration on Defence Capabilities: Toward NATO Forces 2020,[45] declaring that:

> NATO allows us to achieve greater security than any one Ally could attain acting alone. We confirm the continued importance of a strong transatlantic link and Alliance solidarity as well as the significance of sharing responsibilities, roles, and risks to meet the challenges North-American and European Allies face together. We recognise the importance of a stronger and more capable European defence and welcome the efforts of the European Union to strengthen its capacities to address common security challenges. These efforts are themselves an important contribution to the transatlantic link.[46]

This declaration included brave words and perhaps empty promises, given the fact that European defense spending and investment continued to decline, that the European Union was struggling to keep the Eurozone[47] together while recovering from the "Great Recession," and that the Obama administration was in the process of trying to "pivot" or "rebalance" toward Asia.

On the positive side, the summit celebrated the many successes of NATO's partnership program. (See table 8.1 below for participation in European security organizations.) Based on the fact that the Lisbon Strategic Concept had made "cooperative security" one of NATO's core missions, the leaders pledged to enhance the effectiveness of NATO's partnerships, including the Euro-Atlantic Partnership Council, Partnership for Peace, Mediterranean Dialogue,[48] Istanbul Cooperation Initiative,[49] and the "partners across the globe."[50] The latter category is perhaps the most interesting, because it opens the possibility for cooperation with like-minded states well beyond the Euro-Atlantic area. The value of such cooperation had been clearly demonstrated by global partner Australia's major contributions to the ISAF in Afghanistan. To provide an even stronger foundation for that relationship, shortly after the summit, NATO and Australia signed the "Australia-NATO Joint Political Declaration,"[51] noting the values shared by NATO member states and Australia and the commitment to consult and work together on areas of mutual interest. While there were no prospects of NATO opening up its ranks to include Asian members, the declaration opened the door even wider to further NATO cooperation with Australia.

Table 8.1 *Participation in Euro-Atlantic Security Institutions (2020)*

NATO: North Atlantic Treaty Organization
EAPC: [NATO] Euro-Atlantic Partnership Council
PFP: [NATO] Partnership for Peace
EU: European Union
OSCE: Organization for Security and Cooperation in Europe

Country	NATO	EAPC	PFP	EU	OSCE
Albania	*	*			*
Belgium	*	*		*	*
Bulgaria	*	*		*	*
Canada	*	*			*
Croatia	*	*		*	*
Czech Republic	*	*		*	*
Denmark	*	*		*	*
Estonia	*	*		*	*
France	*	*		*	*
Germany	*	*		*	*
Greece	*	*		*	*
Hungary	*	*		*	*
Iceland	*	*			*
Italy	*	*		*	*
Latvia	*	*		*	*
Lithuania	*	*		*	*
Luxembourg	*	*		*	*
Montenegro	*	*			*
Netherlands	*	*		*	*
North Macedonia	*	*			*
Norway	*	*			*
Portugal	*	*		*	*
Romania	*	*		*	*
Slovakia	*	*		*	*
Slovenia	*	*		*	*
Spain	*	*		*	
Turkey	*	*			*
United Kingdom	*	*		**	*
United States	*	*			*
Austria		*	*	*	*
Cyprus				*	*
Finland		*	*	*	*
Ireland		*	*	*	*
Malta		*	*	*	*
Sweden		*	*	*	*
Switzerland		*	*		*
Armenia		*	*		*
Azerbaijan		*	*		*
Belarus		*	*		*
Bosnia-Herzegovina		*	*		*
Georgia		*	*		*
Kazakhstan		*	*		*
Kyrgyzstan		*	*		*
Moldova		*	*		*
Mongolia			*		*
Russian Federation		*	*		*
Serbia		*	*		*
Tajikistan		*	*		*
Turkmenistan		*	*		*
Ukraine		*	*		*
Uzbekistan		*	*		*
Others***					*

* = Member
** = Former member, after Brexit
*** = Andorra, the Holy See, Liechtenstein, Monaco, and San Marino.

The Chicago Summit provided a good touchstone for President Obama to carry into the fall presidential elections, in which he defeated the Republican nominee, Mitt Romney. But it left open many questions about NATO's future. It was clear that the alliance would be leaving its combat commitment in Afghanistan behind by the end of 2014, but it seemed likely that being left with only a "war on terrorism" to fight, new questions would be raised about the future purpose and tasks of this alliance.

Toward a new Cold War? Russia/Ukraine crisis

Some NATO allies, particularly Poland and the Baltic states, already had a clear idea of where they thought NATO's focus should be in the post-Afghanistan period. All of them had contributed to the war effort in Afghanistan, but their security concerns were much closer to home. In their view, a resurgent Russia, financed in part by growing energy sales to the West, combined with Vladimir Putin's increasingly combative approach, warranted a laser-like focus on NATO's core mission of collective defense. And, in response, the alliance had made a mild nod[52] in the direction of their concerns by endorsing the decision to continue NATO's Air Policing Mission in the Baltic States.[53]

While the United States and its partners in the ISAF worked toward the transfer of security responsibilities to the government of Afghanistan at the end of 2014, developments in the relationship between Russia and Ukraine captured the attention and concern, not just of the already-nervous Poles and Baltic States, but also of other NATO countries on both sides of the Atlantic. (See Chapter 7's discussion of "Ukraine as an Issue between NATO and Moscow" for background, pp. 231–6.)

The crisis was precipitated by developments in Kiev, Ukraine, around the negotiations on a Ukraine–European Union Association Agreement. The negotiations, underway for over two years, had produced the text of an accord, but the European Union said that it would not ratify the accord unless the government of Ukraine, led by President Viktor Yanukovych, established democratic conditions, improved the rule of law in Ukraine, and released former Prime Minister Yulia Tymoshenko to leave the country for medical treatment. On November 21, 2013, Yanukovych announced that Ukraine would not sign the accord. Moscow had lobbied against the accord for many months, using both political pressure and economic measures as levers. It was widely reported that Russian President Putin had advised Yanukovych not to sign the agreement, but instead to move Ukraine's economy into closer economic integration with Russia's.[54]

The Yanukovych decision to abort the deal with the EU sparked protests among opposition, pro-Western, political parties and groups. They coalesced in what became known as the "Euromaidan," a series of protests and demonstrations centered on the "Maidan Nezalezhosti," or Independence Square, where the protest continued into 2014. On February 18, 2014, the confrontation between protestors and police in Independence Square turned violent, with dozens killed in the conflict, eventually leading to the ouster of Yanukovych. When many members of Yanukovych's party joined him in leaving Kiev or simply switched allegiances, the opposition, having become the majority, passed laws impeaching Yanukovych and establishing a new pro-Western government. Elections were scheduled for May.

The United States and the EU welcomed events in Kiev, as they appeared to put Ukraine back on the path toward democracy and away from Yanukovych's lean toward Moscow.[55] However, the outcome was seen in Moscow as a direct challenge to Russia's influence in Ukraine and security interests more broadly. In a matter of days, the Russian response became clear: Russian troops, not wearing any national or unit identification, began pouring into the Crimea. Moscow's actions came in reaction to recent developments in Kiev, but planning for the operation apparently had been underway for some time, some sources claiming since 2003.[56]

For Russia, Crimea was the most sensitive of Ukraine's regions from both historic and strategic perspectives. In 1954, the Supreme Soviet Presidium approved the transfer of the region from the Russian Republic to the Ukrainian Republic in the former Soviet Union. At the time, it made very little difference whether the region was in the Russian or Ukrainian republic, and Soviet leader Nikita Khrushchev apparently viewed it as a friendly gesture to Ukraine.[57] When the Soviet Union disintegrated at the end of the Cold War, a referendum in Ukraine supported independence from Russia. The vote in Crimea was in favor, but by the smallest margin of all Ukrainian regions. After six years of difficult negotiations, Ukraine and Russia concluded the Treaty of Friendship, Cooperation and Partnership between the Russian Federation and Ukraine.[58] The treaty settled a wide variety of bilateral issues between the two countries, including the status of Russian military forces and facilities in Ukraine, most importantly the headquarters and port of the Russian Black Sea Fleet in Sevastopol, Crimea.

With Yanukovych in charge in Kiev, Russia had seen a Ukrainian move toward NATO membership as a less imminent prospect. However, with the new regime in Kiev, the prospect of losing access to the Sevastopol Black Sea fleet headquarters loomed on the near horizon, from the Russian perspective.

Ukrainian forces in Crimea did not resist the Russian military moves, and by early March Crimea was clearly dominated by Russian military units. On March 16, a referendum organized by pro-Russian Crimean authorities allegedly approved Russian annexation of the region by 96.77 percent of those voting, with a turnout of 83.1 percent. "Ukraine, the United States, the European Union and other countries denounced the referendum as illegal and not held in a free or fair manner."[59] On March 18, Russian President Vladimir Putin signed an agreement with pro-Russian Crimean leaders that incorporated Crimea into Russia. Subsequently, Putin acknowledged that Russian Federation military forces had invaded Crimea.

Russian annexation of the Crimea was a gross violation of the Budapest Memorandum, a 1994 agreement in which Russia, the United States, and the United Kingdom agreed that, in exchange for recognition of its borders by all parties, Ukraine would give up the residual nuclear forces left over from their deployment there during the Soviet period. The memorandum also recognized Ukraine's signature of the Treaty on the Non-Proliferation of Nuclear Weapons as a non-nuclear-weapon State.[60]

At the same time, anti-Maidan forces were rallying against Kiev in the Russian-leaning Ukrainian regions of Donetsk and Luhansk, apparently with covert support from Moscow. These two regions had consistently stood against Ukrainian membership in NATO and preferred closer ties to neighboring Russia than to the European Union. While Ukraine had not resisted the swift Russian takeover in Crimea, it was not going to give up Donetsk and Luhansk without a fight.

As the crisis escalated, NATO foreign ministers challenged Russia's actions. Meeting in Brussels on April 1, the ministers declared:

> We, the Foreign Ministers of NATO, are united in our condemnation of Russia's illegal military intervention in Ukraine and Russia's violation of Ukraine's sovereignty and territorial integrity. We do not recognize Russia's illegal and illegitimate attempt to annex Crimea.[61]

The ministers suspended all "practical civilian and military cooperation" between NATO and Russia, even though a political dialogue, particularly about the current crisis, could continue. The statement reflected what would eventually become the framework for the Western response to Russia's actions. The approach would be to try to deter Russia from further meddling in Ukraine, while reassuring NATO allies in the region that the alliance had their backs. In the early stages, the steps taken appeared to have little deterring effect on Moscow, and NATO members Bulgaria, Estonia, Latvia, Lithuania, Poland, and Romania did not seem particularly reassured.

The strongest actions against Russia were managed not in NATO but in bilateral financial and economic venues. Already early in March 2014 the United States had begun applying financial sanctions against Russian "individuals and entities responsible for violating the sovereignty and territorial integrity of Ukraine, or for stealing the assets of the Ukrainian people."[62] At the same time, the European Union was condemning Russia's action and beginning to apply a variety of sanctions and travel limitations.[63] Subsequently, as Russia's unresponsive behavior was judged to warrant stronger sanctions, they were developed though informal cooperation between the European Union, the United States and other Western countries, and imposed on a bilateral but coordinated basis.

By mid-2014, two important aspects affecting the Western response became clear. First, not everyone in the West was willing to put full blame on

Russia for the crisis. Second, the Western response would be handicapped by the many areas in which Europe, in particular, but also the United States had become dependent on economic, energy, and other aspects of relations with Russia.

Who's to blame, and what to do?

On the first count, some leading experts in the West began to argue that the United States and its NATO allies had created the problem by enlarging NATO in the 1990s and then promising NATO membership to both Georgia and Ukraine in 2008. John J. Mearsheimer, a leading member of the "realist" school of international politics, made the case:

> the United States and its European allies share most of the responsibility for the crisis. The taproot of the trouble is NATO enlargement, the central element of a larger strategy to move Ukraine out of Russia's orbit and integrate it into the West. At the same time, the EU's expansion eastward and the West's backing of the pro-democracy movement in Ukraine—beginning with the Orange Revolution in 2004—were critical elements, too. Since the mid-1990s, Russian leaders have adamantly opposed NATO enlargement, and in recent years, they have made it clear that they would not stand by while their strategically important neighbor turned into a Western bastion. For Putin, the illegal overthrow of Ukraine's democratically elected and pro-Russian president—which he rightly labeled a "coup"—was the final straw. He responded by taking Crimea, a peninsula he feared would host a NATO naval base, and working to destabilize Ukraine until it abandoned its efforts to join the West.[64]

According to Mearsheimer, the combination of liberal values and an interventionist bent led US and European leaders since the end of the Cold War to favor the expansion of the Western political and economic system with little regard for the consequences. In his view, "They tend to believe that the logic of realism holds little relevance in the twenty-first century and that Europe can be kept whole and free on the basis of such liberal principles as the rule of law, economic interdependence, and democracy."[65] The policy implication, Mearsheimer argued, was that the United States, NATO and the EU should learn from their mistakes and stop pulling Ukraine toward the West, as it inevitably would be seen in Moscow as threatening to Russian security and a cause for responses that could deepen the crisis and even risk war.

Such "realist" arguments were reflected in the work of other respected authors. Stephen F. Cohen, a well-known Russia scholar, warned early on in the crisis of the potential consequences, even if a war with Russia was avoided:

Even if the outcome is the non-military "isolation of Russia," today's Western mantra, the consequences will be dire. Moscow will not bow but will turn, politically and economically, to the East, as it has done before, above all to fuller alliance with China. The United States will risk losing an essential partner in vital areas of its own national security, from Iran, Syria and Afghanistan to threats of a new arms race, nuclear proliferation and more terrorism. And—no small matter—prospects for a resumption of Russia's democratization will be terminated for at least a generation.[66]

Another realist scholar, Sean Kay, wrote that there was a way out of the crisis:

Realism suggests that stability is the priority in Ukraine—and that the vital interest at stake for America and its allies is de-escalation. The obvious deal that can end this crisis is also one from the Cold War playbook—[President John F.] Kennedy's bargain to end the Cuban Missile Crisis—in which we withdrew missiles from Turkey and promised not to invade Cuba. Today, with a promise that Ukraine will not be a NATO member, while Russia withdraws from its posture on Crimea and demonstrates it will be a constructive actor in Ukraine's future by recommitting to its sovereignty (verified by the OSCE), this crisis can be resolved.[67]

While such arguments found substantial favor in some European quarters, the opposing arguments were just as strongly made and tended to have the dominant influence on Western governmental decisions.[68]

As for the causes of the crisis, NATO enlargement proponents argued that while it may have been incautious in 2008 to promise that Georgia and Ukraine would eventually become NATO members, the overall process was warranted by the circumstances. NATO did not go out seeking new members in the 1990s; rather former Warsaw Pact states and Soviet republics came begging to be let in to protect them from future Russian influence or even reassertion of dominance. Many NATO members in the early 1990s were reluctant to open NATO's doors, and there were concerns about the effect on relations with Russia (all discussed in Chapter 6). Moreover, when NATO did open its door, it did so with a set of guidelines and requirements that pushed prospective members to enact democratic reforms, settle issues with neighboring states, develop market economies, and prepare to be a contributor, not just a consumer, of security.

As well-respected NATO expert and official Michael Rühle wrote:

The dissolution of the Warsaw Pact and the end of the Soviet Union in 1991 later created a completely new situation, as the countries of Central and Eastern Europe were finally able to assert their sovereignty and define their own foreign and security policy goals. As these goals centered on integration with the West, any categorical refusal of NATO to respond would have meant the de facto continuation of Europe's division along former Cold War lines. The right to choose one's alliance, enshrined in the 1975 Helsinki Charter, would have been denied—an approach that the West could never have sustained, neither politically nor morally.[69]

Rühle suggested that as long as Russia ignored the reasons why former Warsaw Pact countries and republics want to join the West, Putin and his successors will see both NATO and EU enlargement as a threat.

Anne Applebaum was an outspoken critic of Russia, and advocate of NATO enlargement from the beginning of the enlargement process. In 2014 she took on the arguments of Mearsheimer and others with a strong defense of the West's desire to support "Westernization" by states formerly part of or dominated by the Soviet Union. From her perspective:

> Instead of celebrating this achievement on the 25th anniversary of the fall of the Berlin Wall, it is now fashionable to opine that this expansion, and of NATO in particular, was mistaken. This project is incorrectly "remembered" as the result of American "triumphalism" that somehow humiliated Russia by bringing Western institutions into its rickety neighborhood. This thesis is usually based on revisionist history promoted by the current Russian regime—and it is wrong.[70]

Applebaum concluded that the problem was never American "triumphalism,"; that Russia had been given many opportunities to develop constructive relations, and was never "humiliated" by the West. Indeed, the United States and the EU members supported Russia's desire to keep the Soviet Union's seat on the UN Security Council and invited Moscow to join the G8 even though neither Russia's political conditions nor economic standing warranted it. NATO consistently responded to Russian complaints by creating fora in which Russia could engage with the NATO allies on a wide range of security issues. Western corporations, encouraged by their governments, engaged with Russia in trade, investment and energy supply enterprises. The bottom line, Applebaum argued, is that "Our mistake was not to humiliate Russia but to underrate Russia's revanchist, revisionist, disruptive potential."[71]

Michael McFaul, who served as the US Ambassador to Russia during 2012–2014, argued, after returning to his academic life, that Russian domestic political developments played a major role in the crisis: Putin's perceived requirements for sustaining his regime were at the root of Russia's foreign policies and its aggression in Ukraine. McFaul noted that the Clinton, Bush, and Obama administrations had all attempted to develop a strong relationship with Russia, in spite of differences on specific policy issues. The first Obama administration even produced the concept of a "reset button" for US–Russian relations. Rather than "humiliating" Russia, as Putin claimed, US administrations had treated Russia with great respect.

The problem, according to McFaul, was that "To sustain his legitimacy at home, Putin continued to need the United States [and NATO] as an adversary."[72] Authoritarian regimes need external enemies to warrant extreme measure of internal control. As for policy implications, McFaul offers this conclusion:

> This crisis is not about Russia, NATO, and realism but about Putin and his unconstrained, erratic adventurism. Whether you label its approach realist or liberal, the challenge for the West is how to deal with such behavior forcefully enough to block it but prudently enough to keep matters from escalating dramatically.[73]

As NATO and EU governments struggled to fine tune a reaction to Putin's annexation of Crimea and support for separatists in Donetsk and Luhansk, the differing interpretations of the roots of the crisis produced different advice on how to respond. For those who blamed the West (NATO and the EU) for creating conditions for the crisis by taking advantage of a weak Russia, the advice was to go slow, try to repair relations with Moscow, do not provide arms to Ukraine, and pledge that Ukraine would not be invited to join NATO. For those who saw Russia as the main problem, the policy recommendations included imposing financial costs on Russia for its aggression through a variety of sanctions, removing some of the "benefits" Moscow had received from Western institutions (suspending Russia's membership in the G8, for example), providing arms to Ukraine, and strengthening NATO's deterrence posture in central and northern Europe. Despite these differences, both schools of thought recognized that Ukraine itself needed substantial political and economic reform, supported by extensive financial assistance.

The influence of economics, trade, and investment

Putin's Ukraine offensive created many dilemmas for the United States and its European allies. Since the early 1990s both the United States and the Europeans had come to assume that Russia had more-or-less bought into the post-Cold War status quo, even if there were gray areas around its borders, and complaints about NATO enlargement. The United States decided it could depend on Russia to transport US astronauts to and from the international space station. Europeans became even more dependent on Russian energy sources, as well as markets for European products. And, many Europeans became intellectually and emotionally dependent on the wishful thinking that they no longer had to worry about Russia, even if the Russian Federation fell far short of European democratic standards. This false assumption led European countries in 1996 to invite Russia to join the Council of Europe—the pan-European organization dedicated to democracy and human rights.

For several years, Moscow had used the energy supply weapon to try to keep Ukraine in line. In the early stages of the Maidan protests, Putin had offered then-President Yanukovych a very favorable price on Russian gas sales as to encourage Ukraine to reject the association deal with the European Union. After Yanukovych had been removed, Russia then began using the price of gas less as a carrot and more as a stick.[74]

Ukraine's dependence on Russian energy supplies was just the tip of the iceberg. The fact was that the rest of Europe had become significantly dependent on Russian oil and gas—sufficiently impressive to give many European leaders pause about the potential costs of sanctions.[75] In the medium term, according to *The Economist*, "Europe remains highly vulnerable to Russian control over gas supplies. This vulnerability is one of the reasons why Mr. Putin thinks Europe will not act decisively against him over the annexation of Crimea, or any further territorial depredations he may have in mind."[76]

To some extent, Europe's energy vulnerability came from the fact that some of the Russian gas came through pipelines that run through Ukraine. In 2009, Russia turned off the natural gas supply tap to Ukraine, resulting in immediate shortages for some European countries, which depended on gas that passed through pumping stations in Ukraine. Bulgaria, for example, was cut off from virtually all its supply of natural gas.

Europe's vulnerabilities included more than just energy. London's banking industry included significant participation by Russian banks, raising questions about British willingness to sanction Moscow's banking sector. France was under contract to provide two Mistral-class helicopter carrier ships to Russia, one virtually ready for delivery and the next not far behind. The $1.3 billion sale was put on hold by French President Hollande until a ceasefire was in place in Ukraine and there had been progress toward a settlement. By mid-2015, France was still looking for an alternative buyer, including China, for the two ships, but the market was complicated by the fact that the ships were designed to Russian specifications and would require expensive alterations to meet the requirements of another navy.[77] German diplomacy depended heavily on balancing Western defense efforts with a cooperative attitude toward Moscow—an approach dating back to Prime Minister Willy Brandt's "Ostpolitik" that was carried forward enthusiastically into the post-Cold War era. And Germany's economic and financial interests were deeply into doing business in Russia. This perhaps was best personified by the fact that former Chancellor Gerhard Schroeder in 2006 had become an official of the Russian gas pipeline operator Nord Stream after being defeated by Angela Merkel, and now was speaking out in opposition to German sanctions against Russia.[78]

The sanctions approved by the United States and the European Union in the early stages of the crisis focused primarily on limiting Russian access to Western weapons technology and restricting the finances and travel of individuals close to Putin. As the crisis escalated, more seemed warranted. A major turning point came when Malaysian Air Airlines flight MH17 from Amsterdam was shot down near the village of Grabove, Ukraine in rebel-held territory, with the loss of 298 lives, including many Dutch citizens. The rebels denied responsibility for the attack and Moscow produced a variety of alternative explanations. But most Western governments believed that sepa-ratist forces, using a ground-to-air missile system produced and provided by Russia, had brought down the flight. At the same time, fighting was escalating and Western sources detected an increasing number of Russian forces and weapons systems coming into Ukraine to join the fight.

The situation had become sufficiently grave, and Russian actions so appar-ently uninhibited by earlier sanctions, that the members of the European Union overcame their dependence-based concerns and joined the United States by imposing a new set of much tougher sanctions. While explicitly resisting pres-sure from some Republicans, President Obama rejected sending lethal arms to Ukraine, arguing that "They are better armed than the separatists."[79]

The separate but coordinated US and EU sanctions cut off additional Russian banks from medium- and long-term capital markets, and also: prohibited Americans from dealing with a large Russian shipbuilding firm; suspended US export credit and development finance for Russia; embargoed European arms sales to Russia; and sanctioned additional Russian individuals. As one account noted, the EU sanctions posed some risk to already vulnerable European econo-mies, but were hedged against significant costs:

> European governments moved ahead despite concerns that Europe would pay an economic price for confronting the Kremlin more aggressively. While their actions went far beyond any previously taken against Russia over the Ukraine crisis, they were tailored to minimize their own costs. The arms embargo, for instance, applies only to future sales, not to the much debated delivery [to Russia] by France of Mistral class helicopter carriers that resemble bigger aircraft carri-ers. And the energy technology restrictions do not apply to Russian natural gas, on which Europe relies heavily.[80]

Toward the Wales Summit

With the United States and the European Union ratcheting up sanctions, the NATO allies were preparing for what had become a potentially historic summit meeting, scheduled to be hosted by British Prime Minister David Cameron in Wales early in September. NATO Secretary General Anders Fogh Rasmussen and NATO's Supreme Allied Commander General Philip M. Breedlove (who had succeeded Admiral Stavridis in May 2013) promised that the summit would "make NATO fitter, faster and more flexible to address future chal-lenges, from wherever they come."[81]

In spite of the brave projection by NATO's top two leaders, it was very possible that the outcome in Wales might not meet maximum expectations. NATO is an alliance that honors the sovereignty of each member, while at the same time promising defense of that sovereignty. For that reason alone, NATO decisions inevitably represent compromises between the most ambitious positions and the most cautious ones. At this summit, every decision would be seen in the context of relations with Russia, as well as transatlantic and intra-European burden-sharing issues. If the compromises made left the alliance lacking credible conviction, Washington and its allies would have failed both in terms of deterring further Russian aggression and in terms of reassuring NATO's most threatened allies—Poland, Estonia, Latvia and Lithuania.

NATO governments had a wealth of recommendations to consider, some produced by intergovernmental discussions and others coming from private experts and observers. The suggestions floated fell into three broad categories: how to adapt NATO to its new and much reduced role in Afghanistan; how to react to Russia's destabilizing aggression against Ukraine, and how to reaffirm NATO unity, at a time when there had been a lot of disunity on display both among European allies and across the Atlantic. And these three areas came together around the question of whether or not the alliance would remain the main geo-strategic expression of "the West."

The traditional burden-sharing issue framed one of the more difficult challenges for the allies. The NATO guideline for allied defense spending had, for some time, been in the range of 2 percent of gross domestic product. To be sure, it is a rough measure and does not tell the whole story of the contributions that countries are making to the security of the alliance. But with the Ukraine crisis, which had unmasked Putin's European objectives, the question of relative defense efforts became more urgent. At the same time, it was important to look at what that 2 percent was actually purchasing. American NATO expert John Deni noted that the government of Greece spends more than 2 percent but produced little in deployable capabilities, while Denmark spent less than the goal but had a "highly capable, deployable military." He concluded, "The two percent goal appears increasingly arbitrary and hence meaningless."[82] If so, perhaps the primary focus should be on usable capabilities rather than spending levels.

The biggest challenge for the summit was in establishing a firm and balanced alliance approach to relations with Russia. It was well known that the allies bordering Russia were strongly motivated to reinforce NATO's collective defense capabilities, particularly at their borders. Poland wanted a permanent NATO base hosting significant numbers of allied forces on its territory, and General Breedlove had proposed expanding a current NATO command in Szczecin, Poland, into a "permanent and enhanced NATO base." This command was staffed by Danish, German, and Polish troops, but it would send a much stronger signal if the United States took the lead and deployed forces there, either on a permanent or rotating basis.

Some allies opposed steps that could be perceived by Moscow as particularly provocative. Some press reports suggested that, prior to the MH17 shoot-down, German Chancellor Angela Merkel and Russian President Vladimir Putin had discussed a deal to settle the crisis.[83] It reportedly would have included acceptance of Crimea's incorporation into Russia plus a pledge from Ukraine not to join NATO in return for an end to Moscow's support for Ukrainian separatists and a long term deal for Russian supplies of natural gas to Ukraine. A "soft" German line—one which explicitly accepted Moscow's control of Crimea and denied Ukraine any chance of joining NATO—would surely push the summit outcome in many areas toward a "lowest common denominator" that would seriously disappoint Poland and the Baltic states, and therefore betray rifts in the alliance that Russia could continue to exploit.

The bottom line was that the NATO summit would be a "success" if Moscow believed that the allies had left Wales having achieved a sense of unity and demonstrated common purpose. The outcome would inevitably reflect compromises between those allies who wanted dramatic steps in response to Russia's aggression and those who favored a more cautious approach. A sign of weakness or division at the summit would only have encouraged Putin on his aggressive path.

Wales Summit outcome

To what extent did the Wales Summit succeed, and in what ways did it fail to meet expectations? As with any such question, the answer depends heavily on the expectations of the respondent as well as the political perspective in which the answer is set. If the most important goal of the summit was to maintain solidarity among NATO members, the meeting was a great success. But the long-term judgment would be determined by the outcomes sought or hoped for in the final decisions of the allied leaders.

The United States, for its part, while not abandoning the "Asia pivot," found itself called on to put together a strong allied front on both European and Middle Eastern security challenges.

Perhaps the most important strategic observation about the summit was that the alliance explicitly linked *threats* to the security and territorial integrity of individual allies—not just *attacks*—as causes for possible collective action. NATO's 2010 Strategic Concept set the ground for this shift when it conflated the pledge that an attack on one ally would be regarded as an attack on all—as described in Article 5—with the less well-known terms of Article 4. To remind, Article 4 commits the allies to consult with each other "whenever, in the opinion of any of them, the territorial integrity, political independence or security of any of the Parties is *threatened*" (emphasis added).

The allies thus made clear that a threat would henceforth be sufficient to agree on a collective response, including the possible use of military force. The "Wales Declaration on the Transatlantic Bond"[84] detailed the affirmation by 28 NATO leaders that "should the security of any Ally be threatened we will act together and decisively, as set out in Article 5 of the Washington Treaty." This language brought the "threat" coverage of Article 4 into the collective defense coverage of Article 5.

In keeping with this declaration, the allies produced responses to the challenges posed by Russian aggression against Europe, as a "major challenge to Euro-Atlantic security," and by the emergence of ISIL whose "barbaric attacks" pose a "grave threat to the Iraqi people, to the Syrian people, to the wider region, *and to our nations*" (emphasis added).

As expected, the allies elevated the role of cyber defense in NATO's strategy. According to the summit communiqué,[85] "Cyber attacks can reach a threshold that threatens national and Euro-Atlantic prosperity, security, and stability. ... We affirm therefore that cyber defence is part of NATO's core task of collective defence." NATO members would have to agree to invoke Article 5, and primary responsibility for cyber defense would rest initially with each nation, but NATO cooperation would be intensified.

At a time when NATO was ending its combat role in Afghanistan, the members took on new roles in promising to provide a variety of assistance to its "distinctive partner" Ukraine and to cooperate in attempting to defeat ISIL. Neither of the two areas represented official NATO missions, and the most significant actions in both areas would likely come from individual allies.

Members did not repeat the 2008 pledge that Ukraine would eventually become a NATO member, even though they did so for Georgia; however, they did pledge that, in general, NATO's door to qualified applicants remained open. Still, the allies offered strong rhetorical support for Ukraine and once again condemned Russia's "illegal and illegitimate" annexation of Crimea and its aggression in Ukraine's eastern and southern regions.

Allied leaders left Wales with approved plans for increased defense cooperation with Ukraine, as well as with the potential that individual allies could begin providing lethal arms to Ukraine. No NATO country had acknowledged the intent to provide lethal arms, but Ukraine's President Petro Poroshenko had said that he expected such help.[86] Assistance like this, which might not be provided through normal arms sales channels, would be designed to help Ukraine defend against Russian-supported separatists as well as regular Russian forces, which by that time, according to NATO, were attacking Ukrainian government forces from locations inside Ukraine and from firing positions just across the border in Russia.

To reassure those allies most immediately threatened by Russia's aggressive posture, the allies laid plans for a continuing (not permanent) NATO presence in Poland and the Baltic states. In addition to allied forces rotating through this region bordering Russia for collective defense exercises and monitoring, members said they would establish a Very High Readiness Joint Task Force (VJTF), which would be able to deploy a few days after a request from a member state.

Whether or not the VJTF could reassure allies in the region would depend on the commitment of sufficient, capable, and ready forces. Perhaps more important would be the question of whether and what the United States would contribute to the force. NATO's still-existing Response Force, established in 2002, had been seen by the Bush administration largely as a way to get the Europeans to take on more responsibility for their own defense—a burden-sharing lever. However, the absence of serious US participation in the force was a major factor limiting its credibility and effectiveness.

The leaders gave political support to a smaller group of allies—a coalition of the willing of sorts—that intended to provide new military assistance to local forces in Egypt and Syria combatting ISIL. While none of the allies involved intended to put "boots on the ground," several of the European allies, Canada, and the United States already had begun providing lethal military capabilities as well as humanitarian assistance.

While the external challenges to allied security were the headline grabbers, the leaders took a series of steps intended to address the internal alliance issues that grew out of the perpetual burden-sharing issue. NATO had recommended that allies spend at least 2 percent of their gross domestic product on defense. Only the United States, United Kingdom, Estonia, and Greece were currently spending at or over that level, and in the context of Europe's recession and a perception of diminishing threats to European security, governments had found it politically difficult to increase defense spending.

In Wales, the allies pledged to try to meet this goal over the next decade. This qualified commitment was perhaps of dubious value, but allied leaders also agreed to increase defense investment and military/industrial cooperation, both seen as critical to future European defense efforts. They also pledged to measure national contributions in terms of military output—not only how much is spent, but also whether or not it is spent productively. What countries actually produce in capabilities is in many ways much more important than the 2 percent goal, but such measures are not nearly as simple a measure of commitment to the alliance.

On paper, the summit agreements were impressive, and illustrated how the combination of Russian aggressive behavior and the threat from ISIL in Iraq had produced at least a veneer of allied cohesion and common purpose. At a time when pressure seemed to be growing[87] on the United States to remove its small force of residual nuclear weapons from European bases, the perception of a new Russian threat and President Vladimir Putin's implicit nuclear threats[88] in the context of the Ukraine crisis led the allies to observe that "As long as nuclear weapons exist, NATO will remain a nuclear alliance."[89] The appearance of unity did hide differences among the allies on how far sanctions against Russia can and should be pressed and about how significant defense improvements can be made at a time when European economies are still struggling to achieve even small growth margins.

On the leadership front, the UK's host Prime Minister David Cameron struck a strong chord before and at the summit. President Barack Obama sought to lead from the front, rather than from behind, and both the optics and the outcomes of the meeting suggested that American leadership facilitated a solid summit outcome. The meeting was the last for outgoing NATO Secretary General Anders Fogh Rasmussen, leaving behind as his principal legacy the Lisbon Strategic Concept. The allies welcomed his successor, former Norwegian Prime Minister Jens Stoltenberg, who would take on responsibility for guiding the alliance down the next difficult paths.

The real tests were yet to come. In the near term, few allies would find strong domestic support for substantial increases in defense spending unless the situations with Russia and ISIL increased threat perceptions dramatically. Whether Putin would back down in Ukraine to permit some kind of political settlement seemed uncertain. NATO's support for Ukraine combined with Putin's goal of, one way or the other, bringing Ukraine back into the Russian orbit could lead to a widened conflict in Central Europe. Would NATO unity stand up in such a case? In spite of these difficult questions, the Wales Summit made a clear statement in support of Ukraine, in opposition to ISIL, and in favor of strengthening the alliance. It at least set the stage for the next act in the struggles between "the West" and the opponents of the values and interests it represents.

Figure 8.2 President Obama greets NATO Secretary General Stoltenberg in May 2015 on Stoltenberg's first official visit to Washington as Secretary General.

The Minsk Accords

On September 5, as the NATO leaders wrapped up their summit, negotiations in Minsk, Belarus, facilitated by the Organization for Security and Cooperation in Europe, amongst representatives of Ukraine, Russia, and the Russian-supported separatists, reached an agreement on a ceasefire intended to lead to a peace settlement. But fighting continued over the coming months, and the accord collapsed in January 2015,[90] leading to a new set of negotiations.

The new talks in Minsk included Germany and France, bringing some Western clout into the talks to help balance Russia's position, which naturally supported the separatist authorities representing the Donetsk Peoples Republic and the Luhansk Peoples Republic: both entities had been self-proclaimed by separatist leaders in May 2014. These talks produced a new ceasefire accord on February 12, announced by the leaders of France (President François Hollande), Germany (Chancellor Angela Merkel), Russia (President Vladimir Putin), and Ukraine (President Petro Poroshenko). The accord differed little from the September "Minsk 1," and the chance that the ceasefire would lead to a political settlement was just as uncertain.[91]

The shaky ceasefire continued through mid-2015, with more-or-less constant skirmishes along the ceasefire lines and counter claims of responsibility. What didn't change was the continued assistance being provided by Moscow to the separatists, including both Russian troops and weapons finding their way into the separatist positions. Even when Russian soldiers were taken prisoner by Ukraine, Moscow claimed that any Russian soldiers in Ukraine were there of their own volition, volunteering while on leave from the regular Russian units. Those claims were rejected not only by the government of Ukraine, but also by NATO and EU governments. NATO Supreme Allied Commander Breedlove was outspoken about Russian involvement in testimony before the US Senate Armed Services Committee, saying:

> In Ukraine, Russia has supplied their proxies with heavy weapons, training and mentoring, command and control, artillery fire support, and tactical-and operational-level air defense. Russia has transferred many pieces of military equipment into Ukraine, including tanks, armored personnel carriers, heavy artillery pieces, and other military vehicles.
>
> What we have seen over the course of the fight, was that when the Russian proxy offensive ran into trouble, Russian forces intervened directly to "right the course."[92]

Breedlove's statement was welcomed by the committee chairman, Senator John McCain, who was a leading proponent of the United States providing lethal arms to Ukraine to help it defend itself. McCain observed that "Nothing we have done has succeeded in deterring Putin's aggression and halt his slow-motion annexation of eastern Ukraine ... The Ukrainian people aren't asking for U.S. troops. They're simply asking for the right tools to defend themselves and their country."[93]

In June, the United States and NATO continued to implement the commitments made in Wales. For its part, the United States announced that it would be pre-positioning military equipment, including tanks and artillery, in seven European states, including those closest to Russia's border. Ash Carter, US Secretary of Defense, in Europe for NATO meetings, announced in Tallinn, Estonia, that "the Baltic states—Estonia, Lithuania, Latvia—as well as Bulgaria, Romania and Poland agreed to host elements of the military equipment. Some of the equipment would also be located in Germany."[94]

The equipment stored in each country would, at a minimum, support an army company (about 150 soldiers) and at a maximum a battalion (about 750 soldiers). In total, according to Carter, "We will temporarily stage one armored brigade combat team's vehicles and associated equipment in countries in central and eastern Europe."[95] In addition, the United States committed additional support for NATO's new High Readiness Joint Task Force.

Following Carter's announcement, a meeting of NATO Defense Ministers on June 25 announced good progress on the Readiness Plan agreed in Wales. They announced that NATO's Response Force was on the way to becoming larger and more capable: "It will be on a higher level of readiness, more responsive and more interoperable."[96] In addition, the ministers announced that the interim Very High Readiness Joint Task Force (VJTF), led by Germany, the Netherlands, and Norway, had become operational, and that a VJTF brigade led by Spain would be available to respond on short notice to "any contingency" in 2016.

In sum, the allied military response to Russia's confrontational policies was not overly dramatic, but did pay attention both to the need to enhance deterrence of any additional Russian adventurism and reassurance for allies that felt most threatened. It was designed to show strength without adding fuel to the crisis with Russia, which in any case immediately condemned the NATO decisions. Earlier in the month, President Putin had dismissed Western concerns about Russian intentions, telling an interviewer that "I think that only an insane person and only in a dream can imagine that Russia would suddenly attack NATO."[97]

How effective the reassurance might be, however, was called into question by the release of a public opinion poll[98] that found most European allied publics reluctant to envision using military force to defend other NATO states. According to the survey:

> Going forward, most NATO members are willing to provide economic aid to Ukraine and offer it NATO membership. But they generally shy away from sending arms to Kyiv or escalating economic sanctions against Moscow. And at least half in Germany, France and Italy are unwilling to use military force to defend other NATO allies [to say nothing of Ukraine] against Russian aggression.[99]

Public opinion, of course, does not reflect government commitments, and all NATO governments remain committed to NATO's Article 5 collective defense pledge. However, such weak levels of support for NATO and, it must be said, EU allies, suggest why it is so difficult to win public and parliamentary support for increased defense efforts. Particularly at a time of very narrow fiscal margins available for discretionary spending, there is no desire to use military force if any other avenue is available. Perhaps for many Europeans, the turbulent situation with Greece, and the potential threats to the future of both the Euro and the European Union itself, seemed a more imminent threat to their future well-being. And the challenge of dealing with the constant flow of sea-born refugees trying to escape the ongoing conflicts in the Middle East and North Africa was also more pressing.

Meanwhile, with the EU facing the decision of whether or not to continue sanctions against Russia, some member state officials, for example in Greece and Hungary, expressed reluctance to continue the measures. When the EU foreign ministers met on June 22, however, they agreed to continue the sanctions until at least the end of January 2016.[100]

Transatlantic alliance in crisis

A decade that started with considerable promise came to its mid-point with many dark clouds hanging over transatlantic security. The US withdrawal from Iraq had been followed by the emergence of the Islamic State (ISIL) threat, guided by a radical Islamic philosophy and facilitated by former Sunni military leaders from Saddam Hussein's military. Not only did ISIL threaten Iraq, it also spread to other vulnerable states in the region, including war-torn Syria and chaotic post-Gaddafi Libya. While the ISIL threat was not one that fell into NATO's mission set, it nonetheless posed a direct threat to the Western value-system that both NATO and the EU represent.

The declared conclusion of the US and NATO combat mission in Afghanistan at the end of 2014 satisfied the goal set by US President Obama. The residual US and coalition forces left behind in operation "Resolute Support" were to serve training and counter-terrorism missions. But the government of Afghanistan's ability to maintain control and deal with the still-viral Taliban on its own remained in question, even as the Trump administration in 2019 sought to negotiate a "peace" deal with the Taliban that would reportedly draw down US troops even further.

The hope that relations with Russia could be "re-set" were dashed by the events in Ukraine that led Russia to annex the Crimea region and to support the separatist movements in the Ukrainian cities Donetsk and Luhansk. Neither Russia nor the West necessarily wanted "a new cold war," but Russia's aggression against Ukraine, combined with provocative actions by Russian military aircraft all around Europe and President Putin's invocation of nuclear threats against Western states, was impossible for NATO and EU nations to ignore.

At the same time, the West faced some internal challenges, including the drift of Turkey away from democracy and its Western moorings, the illiberal tendencies in many NATO/EU states, the decision by the United Kingdom to leave the European Union (Brexit), and the persistent burden-sharing problem. All these issues persisted and were joined by a major crisis of confidence for the transatlantic alliance with the election in November 2016 of Donald J. Trump as the president of the United States.

Turkey's drift away from the West

As one of the countries that have long-struggled with NATO's value-driven preconditions, Turkey today is most in danger of violating them. This development is particularly threatening because Turkey has become a pivotal player on NATO's southeastern flank and the bridge between Brussels, the Middle East, and Islam. Ankara is also an important participant in the fight against international terrorism and has accepted the largest number of refugees from Syria, Iraq, Afghanistan, and Africa (more than four million registered and perhaps several hundred thousand non-registered by 2019).[101]

The secular, pro-Western state that dates to Atatürk's reforms starting with the Constitution of 1924 was substantially modified by an April 2017 national referendum called by President Recep Tayyip Erdoğan. Its popular approval by a small margin gives considerably more power to the presidency at the expense of the parliament and judiciary, and this referendum is seen by many as the first step toward creation of a Putin-style regime under Erdoğan's control.

Turkey's shifting external alignments

As a member of NATO since 1952, Turkey should value Western ideals and, indeed, millions of its citizens do. However, President Erdoğan is pursuing a different agenda that calls into question its commitment to the West and suggests that Turkey may be moving toward new positions both domestically and internationally that could estrange the nation from the transatlantic community.

NATO has relied on Turkey as an outpost for Western principles in an area surrounded by contending beliefs and undemocratic governments. With a military ranking second only to the United States in numbers of military personnel, Turkey historically has been a key NATO contributor. But, Turkey's interest in participating in NATO has waned in recent years and little progress has been registered in its lengthy EU-entry negotiations, largely frozen since 2018.

Ever since the EU accession talks began, there were those in the EU that believed Turkey could never qualify for membership. Most recently, the

Turkey–EU relationship has been driven largely by the refugee crisis. Having seen very limited returns from the deal, President Erdoğan threatened to withdraw Turkey's EU accession bid. In March 2019, the European Parliament, in a non-binding vote, called for suspension of the negotiations altogether.[102]

Meanwhile, Ankara has actively pursued closer working relationships with Russia and Islamic nations such as Iran. Frustrations with the stalled EU negotiations have served as one of the motivations—or excuses—for Erdoğan to pursue closer ties with Russia. Poking a thumb in NATO's eye, Turkey reached an agreement with Moscow in July 2017 to purchase as well as co-produce a major Russian S-400 anti-aircraft defense missile system. This decision ultimately became a major source of tension between Turkey and the United States as the Trump administration in 2019 informed Ankara that acquisition of the system would call into question the previously agreed Turkish participation in the US F-35 fighter jet program and purchase of the fighters. President Erdoğan on balance seems to be transitioning from Atatürk's 1924 secularism toward a kind of Sunni-Islam-fueled nationalism, seeking to retrieve some of the Ottoman Empire's former stature in the Islamic world. This perceived drift away from the West is deeply rooted in domestic Turkish politics. Ethnic (Turkmen vs. Kurdish) and party tensions have been rising for several years, leading to a failed *coup d'état* against the Erdoğan government, the subsequent purges, and a constitutional referendum designed to deepen his and his party's control of the nation as well as its Islamization.

President Erdoğan's proposed 2016 constitutional referendum allegedly intended to address concerns about terrorism (there were more than ten major explosions in large Turkish cities in 2016), the economy, and supposed government weakness, but was clearly designed to enhance his control of national decision-making. The proposed constitutional reforms had already failed in the parliament, so Erdoğan sought to give the changes democratic legitimacy through the referendum. It won a narrow 51.4 percent to 48.6 percent victory. That slim win, combined with allegations of election fraud and disproportionate media coverage of the "Yes" camp, suggested that Erdoğan was less than beloved by his people and was trying to use the referendum—a supposed instrument of democracy—to strengthen his grip on power.

The passed constitutional changes gave Erdoğan and his political party, the Justice and Development Party (AKP), an even more dominant place in Turkish governance. By drawing power away from the parliament, allowing closer relationships between the office of the president and the majority party, severely limiting the office of prime minister, and making the president the sole spokesman for the national government, Erdoğan was able to consolidate his power. The abilities given by the referendum would allow Erdoğan to remain in power until 2029—a disturbing prospect considering his ever-increasing tendency toward authoritarian rule.

The apparent move toward a more authoritarian, illiberal government structure with power transferred to the executive is incompatible with the

Western ideals of democracy and the rule of law. Erdoğan's post-coup purges also threaten to weaken Turkey's military and thus the security of NATO. Many officers assigned to NATO were recalled and presumably many who returned to Turkey have ended up in jail, including as much as a third of Turkey's officer corps. Some officers on NATO duty sought asylum in NATO countries to escape that fate.

In the foreseeable future, it would be nearly impossible to resume EU accession negotiations unless Erdoğan shifts dramatically back toward open democracy, and there is no sign he is so disposed. However, so long as the EU is willing to pursue a strong economic partnership with Turkey, that may be enough from Erdoğan's perspective. One scholar had suggested that Ankara is now interested in economic partnerships with Western countries and organizations, but no longer wants to adhere to its political norms.[103] If so, is this compatible with Turkey's membership in NATO? How will the West reconcile its basic values with the political necessity of sustaining, at a minimum, partnership with Erdoğan's regime?

At a time when the West is facing both external threats and internal challenges, Turkey is moving progressively from being a vitally important geostrategic partner nation to a liability and potentially a threat itself. The Turkish case is different from all other cases of illiberal advances among Western democracies. Perhaps, as has happened in Turkey's past, it will come out of this undemocratic period with restoration of Western-style democracy. From a strategic perspective, Turkey has been the tip of the West's spear in the Middle East. But the drift that President Erdoğan is piloting away from Western democratic norms not only is creating divisions among NATO allies but also suggests that Turkey could be the first NATO ally to leave the alliance, perhaps even allying with Russia. This would be a huge loss to NATO's strategic position in the region as well as to the West's demonstration of the validity of its political model.

Illiberal political trends

In the decade 2010–2019, populist radical right parties in continental Europe came to represent a formidable challenge to the liberal transatlantic order. One expert has defined populism as a political tactic that assumes that "good people" are betrayed by an "evil elite."[104] Ironically, populist parties may be led by the very elites they decry, as is suggested by Donald Trump's populist following in the United States. This specific brand of populism that has risen in Europe has been called the "populist radical right (PRR)" by Dutch political scientist Cas Mudde.[105]

The reality is that, at this point, centrist political forces have not yet found the silver bullet to deal with the surge in populist radical right movements. Their strength has grown from the refugee crisis on top of a general malaise created by social, economic, and governance issues.

At the end of the Cold War, Western countries breathed a sigh of relief. Some observers suggested that liberal democracy had finally demonstrated that it was the inevitable wave of the future, capable of withstanding all future threats. But new challenges soon replaced such optimism.

No single event or political, economic, or military development was responsible for what happened over the next three decades. Part of the failure of Western powers was believing their political system could be forcefully transplanted into countries whose existing systems had been banished but which had no historical experience with or traditions of democracy. The Iraq and Afghanistan conflicts became part and parcel of a war on terrorism and drained the West not only of resources but also of confidence in the future. The Arab Spring gave reason for optimism concerning the overthrow of autocratic regimes in the Middle East, but the optimism was short-lived as, in most cases, more liberal structures failed to take root.

The Great Recession of 2007–2008, caused by the collapse of a speculative bubble, had already undermined optimism in the future. When Western countries mounted recoveries, the benefits largely flowed to the already wealthy rather than to average citizens. In the United States, Vermont's Senator Bernie Sanders emerged to lead the populist protest of the concentration of wealth in "one percent" of the population and to campaign for the Democratic presidential nomination. But the malaise also created openings for parties and movements on the far right that were not committed to the values and political systems of the West. Those movements were aided and abetted by Russia's Vladimir Putin, who was determined to try to re-establish Russia as a major power, and even to retrieve regions lost when the Soviet Union disbanded.

While radical right populist parties have achieved major successes in some nations and faltered in others, the overall trend in Western nations has been increased support for these movements. Across the continent, these parties have employed the same main tactics to appeal to disillusioned populations: demonizing the elite class, promising extreme transformations of establishment policies, and capitalizing on the immigration crisis by inciting fear and xenophobia.

The steep rise of radical right populism in the United Kingdom culminated in the Brexit crisis (discussed later in this chapter), and the appointment of Boris Johnson, leader of the Conservative Party, as prime minister. In Germany, the right-wing group Alternative for Germany overcame the cautious anti-Nazi sentiments of the nation to win seats in every state parliament and become the largest opposition party.

The rise of the far-right party Vox in Spain has been considered especially surprising, considering that, since the end of Francisco Franco's dictatorship, only one seat had been won by a far-right candidate (in 1979).

Sweden, too, despite having welcomed more asylum seekers per capita than any other European country and reportedly showing the most positive attitudes toward migrants, saw an uptick in support for the anti-immigration Sweden Democrats. The party won about 18 percent of the vote in 2018, a significant increase from the country's prior general election.

Even in France, a country in which the far-right National Front Party leader Marine Le Pen suffered a resounding defeat to centrist-liberal candidate Emmanuel Macron in their 2017 presidential election, radical right populism continued to grow. After rebranding the National Front into the National Rally, Le Pen's party managed to win more seats than any other in France during the 2019 elections for European Parliament.[106]

These trends are incredibly troubling considering the authoritarian route populist parties tend to take once in power. This combination is already exemplified by the two nations where populist agendas have been most successful. In Hungary and Poland radical right populist leaders have grossly amplified authoritarian rule. Viktor Orbán, head of the Hungarian Fidesz party, altered the constitution after gaining a two-thirds governmental majority in 2014 and effectively consolidated all elements of the state in the context of the 2020 pandemic. Meanwhile, in 2015 the Polish Law and Justice party completely overturned the country's judicial bodies in order to change the constitution.

As is suggested by a joint report by the Center for American Progress and the American Enterprise Institute, "the threat of authoritarian populism will not recede unless a new generation of political leaders offers a credible agenda for improving people's lives that is more appealing to the public than the populist alternative."[107] Otherwise, liberal Western systems, the foundation of the transatlantic partnership, remain in imminent danger.

Brexit's shock

The 2016 referendum forcing the UK to begin negotiations to leave the European Union—a process known as "Brexit"—suggests that many Brits still see a wide cultural, political, and economic channel between themselves and "the Europeans."[108]

The 2016 referendum favoring by a close margin British departure from the European Union was a shock to British politics and to the European Union, but it also created uncertainties affecting transatlantic relations, international affairs, and the future of the West more generally. As the first of two 2016 quakes that rattled the West, Brexit reflected perhaps the growing power of populist sentiment and rejection of globalism and distance regulation/governance. Brexit turned out to be a warning that neither traditional assumptions nor professional opinion polls could be completely trusted in this new era. Applauded and supported by Vladimir Putin, neo-nationalist and populist politicians in Europe, including France's Marine Le Pen and then-US presidential candidate Donald Trump, the outcome raised questions about how the overall strength and importance of the EU would be affected and whether Britain's role in the world would be diminished.

On Thursday, June 23, 2016, millions of British voters went to the polls to determine whether the United Kingdom was to remain a member of the European Union. Most opponents and proponents of departing the EU may both have believed that leaving would be rejected, especially based on polls. Pollsters across the board, from Huffington Post Pollsters to a YouGov poll conducted on election day, overwhelmingly predicted that "Remain" would triumph over the xenophobic, anti-immigration Vote Leave campaign. These projections, reassuring to most believers in liberal democracy and Britain's role in Europe constituted, as *The New York Times* claimed, "yet another failure" in the realm of election prediction.[109]

Confident forecasts of a victory for Remain went out the window as the results flowed in during the early hours of June 24. By only 3.78 percent—just over one million votes—Leave had won. Across the English Channel and across the Atlantic, committed liberal democratic supporters and European Union fans watched in awe as Prime Minister David Cameron resigned his post to Theresa May, who promised to spearhead British departure from the EU. Making a long story short, May was unable to negotiate a deal with the EU that would pass parliament, despite commanding a majority in the body, and stepped down from party leadership and her position as prime minister in May 2019.[110]

The Brexit vote to leave the EU was one of the most important victories for illiberal political movements in Europe. While the UK's leading populist radical right party—UKIP—did not win control or even direct participation in government, it nonetheless scared the hell out of the Conservatives and led them down the road to a disastrous consequence and Cameron to political oblivion.

British departure from the EU, on balance, would be a net loss for the EU. The UK has frequently been a drag on some of the more integrative approaches favored by continental EU members, but it has brought British common-sense, practical solutions, and Atlanticist and global perspectives to the table that have made the EU a more formidable union. This is to say nothing of the fact that a significant part of the EU's economic and financial strength will no longer be under the EU's collective roof. In 2015, the UK's share of the EU's Gross Domestic Product was 17.5 percent, second only to Germany among EU members. The UK's contribution to the EU budget in that year was over 15 percent of the total.

In terms of strategic military impact, the fact that the UK will remain a leading member of NATO will take some of the sting out of the impact of Brexit on European security. However, to the extent that the EU aspires to develop independent military cooperation on the European level—something old made new again by Donald Trump's unreliable leadership of the alliance—the British departure will handicap any future efforts in this direction. This prospect could be mitigated should the UK and the EU negotiate a post-Brexit bilateral defense cooperation agreement, but it will be hard to compensate fully for the absence of British capabilities, leadership, and perspectives in the EU mix.

The bottom line is that Brexit will weaken the EU in many ways. As one commentator observed in the wake of the referendum, "Brexit will harm the EU's cohesion, confidence and international reputation. The biggest consequence of all, therefore, is that Brexit will undermine the liberal political and economic order for which Britain, the EU and their allies and friends around the world stand."[111]

Brexit, without question, weakens the West. Although in leaving the EU the UK is not leaving the West and will not necessarily adopt illiberal policies simply because it is no longer a member of the pro-Western EU club, ultimately, weakening the EU amounts to weakening the West. Brexit is a gift to Russia's President Putin who favors and promotes anything that divides or takes away from the West's key institutions: NATO and the EU. And, this blow to the West was followed in 2016 by the Trump political tsunami in the United States.

The Trump disruption

The second major 2016 shock for transatlantic relations came in the United States with the Republican nomination and then electoral victory of Donald Trump. Trump raised concerns throughout the campaign as someone who played on the fears of Americans concerning both terrorism and their own financial well-being, blaming not only the administration in power but also the system of government and international commitments for which he claimed the Obama administration and the Democratic Party stood. This quintessential populist campaign had much in common with the approaches of European radical right populist parties.

Candidate Trump blamed "bad" international trade deals for the loss of manufacturing jobs in the United States. His style and approach ran roughshod over the more traditional Republicans against whom he contended the primaries, and then turned enough swing states in the general election to win the presidency, despite receiving close to three million fewer votes than his opponent, Hillary Clinton.

During the campaign, Trump displayed his disdain for the European Union and for NATO as well, calling the transatlantic alliance "obsolete" and claiming that low levels of European defense spending meant that the Europeans had not been "paying their dues."[112] In one stunning attack on NATO, he suggested that the United States should not be willing to come to the defense of an ally that had not been spending enough on defense—this despite the collective defense commitment (Article 5) of the 1949 North Atlantic Treaty, a commitment that every American president since 1949 had unconditionally reaffirmed.

If Brexit was a shock for transatlantic relations, the election of Trump was a tsunami, arguably jeopardizing nearly 70 years of transatlantic commitments, political assumptions and security cooperation. It also gave rise to speculation in Europe about the possibility of an independent German nuclear deterrent, or an EU one, and renewed talk of a "European army," but, realistically, these are not necessarily more likely even despite the uncertainties created by President Trump.[113]

Candidate Trump rejected most trade arrangements made in recent years or anticipated in the future as "unfair" to the United States and "bad deals," including the North American Free Trade Area (NAFTA), which he vowed to renegotiate, and the Trans-Pacific Partnership, from which he withdrew the United States after becoming president. Negotiations for a potential free trade accord between the United States and Europe—the Transatlantic Trade and Investment Partnership (TTIP)—were put in limbo. But it was his attitude toward NATO that most directly assaulted the values and interests that define the West.[114]

President Trump

US allies were somewhat relieved when President Trump did not initially repeat the threat to abandon the US collective defense commitment even though he did not abandon demands for more allied defense spending. When Trump nominated retired General James Mattis as Secretary of Defense, the allies interpreted the selection as a possible sign of a return to orthodoxy.

On his inaugural visit to NATO headquarters, Secretary Mattis delivered a hybrid model of Trump's NATO policy. Mattis essentially said the allies must increase defense spending and that failure to do so could have consequences. At a Brussels press conference on February 15, Mattis said, "America will meet its responsibilities, but if your nations do not want to see America moderate its commitment to the alliance, each of your capitals needs to show its support for our common defense."[115]

Prior to the Mattis visit to Brussels, Trump had met with British Prime Minister Theresa May. The two appeared to hit it off, and May even said that Trump had given "strong support" to NATO. Candidate Trump had endorsed the UK's departure from the EU, which British voters had favored narrowly in a June 2016 referendum, and May was intent on carrying out that mandate. That, combined with the UK's position as one of the few NATO countries that was already meeting NATO's agreed 2014 goal of spending at least 2 percent of Gross Domestic Product (GDP) on defense by 2024, had set up the two leaders for a successful meeting.

The same could not be said of the circumstances surrounding Trump's first meeting with German Chancellor Angela Merkel. As the leader of the EU's political and economic powerhouse, Merkel also represented, in Trump's eyes, the leading "free rider" on American defense efforts. The Trump–Merkel discussion on March 17 concluded with a press conference that put the awkward relationship on full view. After avoiding the traditional handshake with Merkel in the Oval Office photo opportunity, Trump declared in the press conference: "I reiterated to Chancellor Merkel my strong support for NATO as well as the need for our NATO allies to pay their fair share for the cost of defense. Many nations owe vast sums of money from past years, and it is very unfair to the United States. These nations must pay what they owe."[116]

The suggestion that Germany and other allies owed past dues to the alliance, or even to the United States, reflected once again Trump's lack of understanding of how NATO works, or even for what the alliance stands. Allies do not contribute to the alliance by paying dues, other than providing their share of funds to support common programs like NATO infrastructure, including NATO headquarters in Brussels. The main "contribution" made by each ally is the money spent on their own defense efforts. There is no question that many allies have not spent as much on defense since the end of the Cold War, or even throughout the history of the alliance, as the United States would have liked. But the notion of allies owing "past dues" was completely inconsistent with the terms of the North Atlantic Treaty and the allies' practice over the last 70 years.

Finally, Trump's attitude toward NATO cannot be divorced from his peculiar perspective on Russia and its president, Vladimir Putin. Trump studiously avoided critiquing either Russia or President Putin. That fact, combined with the ongoing investigations of links between the Trump campaign and Russia's clandestine efforts to influence the outcome of the US elections in Trump's favor, cast a continuing cloud over Trump's approach to NATO. How can allies put their trust in an American president who seems conflicted about one of the most important threats to many NATO nations and to Western interests and values more generally?

Against this backdrop, a NATO summit meeting was scheduled for May 24–25, as a highlight of Trump's first international trip as president. The NATO allies were collectively holding their breath in expectation of more Trump bombast. But Trump's new national security advisor, the well-respected General H. R. McMaster who had replaced discredited Trump nominee retired General Michael Flynn, offered reassurance. Prior to Trump's departure from Washington, McMaster said, "President Trump understands that America first does not mean America alone ... To the contrary, prioritizing American interests means strengthening alliances and partnerships that help us extend our influence and improve the security of the American people."[117]

As the date for President Donald Trump's arrival in Brussels neared, Trump's White House remained upside-down with controversy while, in Brussels, allies worried about how to deal with the unpredictable yet demanding American president. The controversies swirled around issues of interest to NATO, including charges of Trump's collusion with Russia to affect the presidential election and a Trump dump of classified information into the laps of Russian Foreign Minister Sergei Lavrov and Russia's reputed spymaster Ambassador to the United States, Sergey Kislyak.

By the time Trump arrived in Brussels, internal consultations among the allies and with Secretary General Jens Stoltenberg had produced a strategy designed to please the American president while defending against his possible assaults on the alliance and individual allies. The strategy included limiting the time available for formal presentations (to avoid boring Trump) and not preparing a final "declaration" to avoid potential battles over contentious issues, like burden-sharing and Russia relations.

The visit to the sparkling new NATO headquarters began with dedication of displays at the entrance intended to commemorate the fall of the Berlin Wall and the 9/11 attacks on the United States. In Trump's remarks, after asking for a moment of silence for the victims of the terrorist attack in Manchester, England earlier in the week, and condemning terrorists, he launched a critique of defense spending levels of NATO members. His burden-sharing remarks did not come as a surprise. The big question was whether he would clarify his position on the American commitment to collective defense. According to press reports, "Mr. Trump offered a vague promise to 'never forsake the friends that stood by our side' in the aftermath of the Sept. 11 attacks—a pledge that White House officials later said amounted to an affirmation of mutual defense."[118] This unclear statement was hardly the ringing endorsement for which the European allies had hoped.

The weak affirmation of collective defense was made even more telling by the fact that, once again, Trump chose not to challenge Russia on its aggression against Ukraine and threats to NATO allies. He focused instead almost entirely on the terrorism and refugee issues. As if to add an exclamation mark to his hard line on underperforming allies, he at one point pushed his way to the front of the gathering of leaders, physically brushing aside Dusko Markovic, the Prime Minister of Montenegro, scheduled to become NATO's newest member on June 5, 2017. The great irony, or the explanation, if one is inclined toward conspiratorial thinking, for the rude behavior (replayed all over social media) was that Markovic had led his country through a successful bid to join NATO in the face of strong overt and clandestine Russian opposition.

Before Trump left Brussels, the alliance announced that NATO, as an organization, would formally join the anti-ISIS coalition (all members were already contributing to the effort in one form or another). To demonstrate that they were listening to Trump's burden-sharing complaints, the allies agreed to develop annual national plans for how they intend to meet the 2014 defense investment pledge, covering cash, capabilities, and contributions. With the summit in the rearview mirror, more turmoil lay ahead for the alliance as well as for President Trump. The most important consequence of the summit and the G-7 meeting that followed was the reaction of German Chancellor Angela Merkel to her interactions with Trump. In a campaign appearance after the meetings, Merkel said the days when Europe could rely on others was "over to a certain extent."[119] Merkel's comment, made in the context of the British exit from the EU, Trump's demands on NATO, and his calling German automakers "very bad," suggest that Trump handed Vladimir Putin an important victory in his campaign to split the Western alliance.

Ironically, within weeks Trump was headed to Europe again, this time for a summit of the G-20, a gathering of the world's leading economic powers, including a much-anticipated bilateral meeting with Russia's Putin. On his way to the summit in Hamburg, Germany, hosted by Chancellor Angela Merkel, the White House scheduled a stop in Warsaw, Poland, for the president to make a major speech before a very friendly audience. The Warsaw visit was hosted by the Polish government led by Trump's soul-mate populist radical right party, Law and Justice, which bussed in enthusiastic supporters from outside Warsaw.

Trump's speech, delivered in front of the historic Uprising Monument at Krasinski Square, praised the Polish people's sense of nation and courage to defend it against a long history of assaults.[120] Trump made a clear assertion of America's support for NATO collective defense: "I would point out that the United States has demonstrated not merely with words but with its actions that we stand firmly behind Article 5, the mutual defense commitment." At the same time, he bragged inaccurately that it was his insistence that had produced increases in NATO defense spending (increases that had been long planned following Russia's aggression against Ukraine). In addition, he claimed to be supporting "Western values" and said that they were strengthened by "the bonds of culture, faith and tradition that make us who we are" and weakened by "the steady creep of government bureaucracy." His remarks sounded to some more like his political platform than the openness and inclusivity that most see as hallmarks of liberal democracy.

Trump moved on to a less welcoming reception in Hamburg, where thousands were waiting to protest not just Trump but what they saw as the wealth and control represented by the G-20. In Hamburg, Trump found himself on the outside looking in on issues of climate change and multilateral trade issues, as the other Western leaders had pretty much decided to move on without the usual US lead. Trump's focus was far more on his meeting with Putin than with leaders of allied countries. US officials after the meeting claimed that Trump had raised the issue of Russian meddling in the US elections, and that the two leaders had agreed to disagree. The Russian side, however, suggested that Trump had accepted Putin's denial of culpability—a denial that ran counter to what the entire US intelligence community had long-since concluded.

It was subsequently revealed that Trump also met with Putin for a post-dinner conversation that lasted as much as one hour. There was no American record of the meeting (other than Trump's recollection that it was just an exchange of "pleasantries" and adoption) because the only other person in the discussion was Putin's interpreter, and no American one—thought by most observers to be a significant diplomatic and national security mistake.

Questions about US leadership of the West persisted into 2018, as the allies waited in various degrees of dread for Trump to turn up at the summit scheduled to be held in Brussels in July. US, Canadian, and European officials had worked diligently prior to the summit—as is the usual case—to prepare a communiqué that would make a positive response to Trump's burden-sharing demands while at the same time moving the alliance ahead to meet the challenges it faced. The summit was marked by more Trump criticism of allied defense spending including false accusations that spending had declined, and that Germany was under Moscow's control, given its reliance on Russian energy supplies.[121]

The general reaction among allied officials when Trump left Brussels for a summit with President Putin in Helsinki was that they could once again be thankful that the alliance had survived another summit with Trump. The sense of relief did not last long, however, as Trump's meeting with Putin produced more bombshells. First, the continued warmth of Trump toward Putin contrasted sharply with the harsh attitudes taken toward US allies. Second, in a press conference at the conclusion of the private meetings between the two leaders, Trump suggested he believed Putin's claim that Russia had not interfered in the 2016 US elections, accepting Putin's word over the very specific conclusions of the US intelligence community that Russia had not only sought to disrupt the elections but also to promote Trump's election.

As 2019 approached, bringing with it the 70th anniversary on April 4 of NATO's founding, the allies came up with a plan designed to avoid a Trump catastrophe: the actual April 4 anniversary would be marked by a meeting of foreign ministers in Washington. A December 2019 summit would be held in London. At every opportunity, Trump continued his off-hand critique of the allies along with his persistent praise for virtually every despotic leader he met. Surely, this didn't enhance the US image as the leader of Western democracies. At the same time, NATO Secretary General Jens Stoltenberg followed a deliberate strategy of continuously complimenting allies for their accomplishments, particularly those who had increased defense spending, urging them to do more, and praising Trump for having produced whatever progress had been achieved. In recognition of his wise leadership, and as an apparent message to Trump, Stoltenberg was invited to address a joint session of the US Congress—the first head of an international organization ever to do so.[122]

Is the US abdicating leadership of the West?

President Donald Trump quickly became widely seen in Europe and by his numerous critics in the United States as having abdicated American leadership of the West. When German Chancellor Angela Merkel traveled to Washington in March 2016 to visit Trump, one headline blared "The Leader of the Free World Meets Donald Trump."[123] This perception of abdication was based partly on Trump's persistent refusal to criticize Vladimir Putin for his kleptocratic foreign policy, annexation of Crimea, and aggression against Ukraine.

It was solidified by Trump's meetings with NATO and G-7 leaders in Europe in late May and then additionally confirmed when Trump announced he would pull the United States out of the Paris climate agreement (which incidentally gave China the opportunity to claim that it was now the "responsible" international leader on climate issues). The question then became whether Merkel's Germany would be able to provide the leadership that the West and its predominant institutions—NATO and the European Union—need. The answer, most likely, was no.

The European allies certainly could do more for their own defense, and part of this could come from concerting efforts, reducing duplication, sharing missions, and other practical cooperative steps. But an effective European alternative to NATO would likely cost far more than what they are currently able to produce for their contributions to NATO. This is to say nothing of the new complications resulting from the British decision to leave the European Union. Some might see this British move as facilitating EU military cooperation, but it takes more away in potential capabilities than it adds in the ease of making political decisions.

In some respects, Trump may have succeeded beyond his wildest imagination in his Europe/NATO policies. He boasted he had made the European allies do things that no other American president has done. And, to be honest, he helped unite the Europeans. Unfortunately, he largely united them against the United States, rather than behind it. The result may include more European spending on defense, but a much less cooperative transatlantic relationship, which could be disastrous for US efforts to gain international support for its policies. Would America's European allies volunteer to invoke Article 5, as they did on 9/11, in response to a future terrorist attack if Trump's policies undercut trust in and sympathy for the United States?

The Trump impact on transatlantic relations also gave new life to proposals for intensified European defense cooperation. Some of them were arguably fanciful—like the suggestion for a European aircraft carrier,[124] but some were very positive, if more modest. Challenged by Brexit and uncertainty concerning future American policy toward the alliance, members of the EU took several steps to strengthen their security and defense cooperation.[125] In 2018, EU members worked on a myriad of projects, from the already-established Common Security and Defence Policy (CSDP), the Military Planning and Conduct Capability (MPCC), the Coordinated Annual Review on Defence (CARD), the European Defence Fund (EDF), and the Capability Development Plan (CDP) to signing a second Joint Declaration in July to ensure continued EU–NATO coordination. This wide range of initiatives aimed to strengthen European military planning structures, improve civilian crisis management, and boost defense investment throughout the continent. The process sought to demonstrate a serious European approach to defense, given Trump's criticism, as well as to continue building a foundation for more intense future cooperation.

The EU's major project of 2018 was building Permanent Structured Cooperation (PESCO), introducing a total of 34 defense projects that year to fill a wide range of military capability deficits. Considering land, sea, air, space, and cyber threats, PESCO members agreed to develop radio navigation employing space assets, a military space surveillance network, an unmanned ground system, autonomous maritime systems for mine countermeasures, the Eurodrone, an upgraded Tiger Mark III attack helicopter, cyber rapid response teams, a high atmosphere airship platform, a medical command, a counter Chemical, Biological, Radiological and Nuclear Defence Battalion (CBRN) surveillance system, and military co-basing.

Meanwhile, the advent of the Trump presidency produced a dramatic shift in global opinion of the United States. According to the well-respected Pew survey published in June 2017, "The sharp decline in how much global publics trust the US president on the world stage is especially pronounced among some of America's closest allies in Europe and Asia, as well as neighboring Mexico and Canada. Across the 37 nations polled, Trump got higher marks than Obama in only two countries: Russia and Israel."[126]

The decision of the Trump administration to abandon the Joint Comprehensive Plan of Action (JCPOA) with Iran that had been negotiated during the Obama administration added more fuel to the transatlantic fire.[127] The accord had been designed to halt Iran's movement toward producing nuclear weapons in exchange for lifting some of the Western sanctions that were devastating Iran's economy. Most European governments saw the accord as imperfect but better than no agreement at all. Before the accord was negotiated, many Europeans believed it inevitable that Iran would become a nuclear weapons state, particularly if it perceived itself as vulnerable to attack by the United States and US regional allies Saudi Arabia and Israel. Moreover, Iran's diplomacy in Europe was quite successful in pleading the case against

Table 8.2 *Some key developments (January 2009–May 2020)*

Jan 2009	Barack Obama entered office as President of the United States
March 2009	French President Nicolas Sarkozy returned France to NATO's Integrated Command Structure
Dec 2009	President Obama announced the United States would "surge" 30,000 additional troops to Afghanistan, with the goal to begin withdrawal by July 2011
Nov 2010	New NATO strategic concept "Active Engagement, Modern Defence" issued
March 2011	UNSC approved Resolution 1973 on Libya; NATO subsequently took control of international military actions against Libyan dictator Muammar Gaddafi's forces.
Nov 2011	Obama administration officials said the United States was "pivoting" or "rebalancing" its foreign policy strategy toward the Asia/Pacific Region

Table 8.2 *(Continued)*

Feb 2014	Confrontation between Ukrainian protestors and police in Kiev's Independence Square turned violent, leading to the ouster of President Yanukovych
March 2014	A referendum organized by pro-Russia Crimean authorities allegedly approved Russian annexation of Crimea, followed by its incorporation into Russia.
Sept 2014	At summit in Wales, NATO leaders responded to provocative Russian actions and pledged increases in defense spending
July 2015	The Joint Comprehensive Plan of Action (JCPOA) among Iran, China, France, Germany, Russia, the United Kingdom, the United States, and the European Union set limits on Iran's nuclear activities in exchange for reduced sanctions
Nov 2016	Donald Trump was elected President of the United States, causing widespread uncertainty over the fate of the transatlantic relationship
May 2017	President Trump at a NATO summit in Brussels chastised NATO leaders for not paying their fair share of alliance costs
May 2018	President Trump announced US withdrawal from the JCPOA and re-imposed sanctions on Iran lifted under the deal
July 2018	At a summit meeting in Brussels, President Trump made false claims that allies were indebted to United States and that defense spending had been declining
July 2018	President Trump, meeting with Russian President Putin in Helsinki, Finland, suggested that, despite US intelligence conclusions to the contrary, he saw no reason that Russia would have interfered in the 2016 US election
	The EU agreed to delay Brexit to give the UK additional time to decide terms under which it would leave
May 2019	The Senate Armed Services Committee approved a defense authorization that would make it tougher for President Donald Trump to pull the United States out of NATO
Aug 2019	The United States withdrew from the INF Treaty with Russia claiming Russian violation of the terms of the treaty
Nov 2019	French President Macron said NATO was experiencing "brain death" because of a lack of US strategic coordination and leadership
Dec 2019	The allies met at the summit in London to celebrate NATO's 70th anniversary after having postponed a session on the actual birthday of April 4
Jan 2020	The UK formally began the process of leaving the EU
March 2020	A global pandemic stunned European and American health systems and economies, raising questions about whether transatlantic cooperation would be strengthened or weakened

US abandonment of the accord. And, in addition to their strategic concerns, EU members had economic interests in resuming more normal economic relations with Iran, which became more difficult when the United States began re-imposing sanctions.

It is ironic that President Trump in so many ways assaulted the closest American allies while saying virtually nothing critical about America's leading geopolitical adversary: Russia. On balance, by 2020 Donald Trump had done more to weaken American leadership of the West and to put American interests at grave risk than even his most severe critics might have anticipated before his inauguration.

In the next chapter, this analysis turns to a review of the external threats and internal challenges to the West and the responses that might be required from NATO and the European Union.

Questions for discussion

1. What were some practical differences between President George Bush's relationship with NATO countries and President Obama's?
2. What were the most important accomplishments reflected in the 2010 Lisbon Strategic Concept?
3. How would you rate NATO's intervention in Libya? What did the mission accomplish? What were its failures?
4. What arguments favored the US policy of "pivoting" toward Asia? What were the downsides of the approach?
5. This chapter includes descriptions of several scholarly opinions about the results of NATO enlargement and its impact on Russian behavior. Which of these views do you find the most convincing and why?
6. How important is Turkey to the Western alliance?
7. Will British exit from the EU damage Western security? Will it undermine NATO?
8. Has the Trump presidency irreparably damaged transatlantic relations? If not, why? If so, can the damage be repaired, and how?

Notes

1 For discussion of the causes and consequences of the recession, see: "World Economic Outlook, Crisis and Recovery," International Monetary Fund, April 2009. www.imf.org/external/pubs/ft/weo/2009/01/pdf/text.pdf [accessed June 12, 2015].
2 Jeff Zeleny and Nicholas Kulish, "Obama, in Berlin, Calls for Renewal of Ties With Allies," *The New York Times*, July 25, 2008. www.nytimes.com/2008/07/25/us/politics/25obama.html?ref=politics&_r=0 [accessed June 8, 2015].

3   Ryan Evans, "An Admiral in the Storm: Stavridis on Leadership and Civility," *War on the Rocks*, January 25, 2015. http://warontherocks.com/2015/01/an-admiral-in-the-storm-stavridis-on-leadership-and-civility/ [accessed July 22, 2015].

4   Barack Obama, "Remarks by the President in Address to the Nation on the Way Forward in Afghanistan and Pakistan, December 1, 2009. www.white-house.gov/the-press-office/remarks-president-address-nation-way-forward-afghanistan-and-pakistan [accessed June 12, 2015].

5   Howard LaFranchi, "NATO Countries Pledge 7,000 More Troops for Afghanistan," *The Christian Science Monitor*, December 4, 2009. www.csmonitor.com/USA/Foreign-Policy/2009/1204/p02s05–usfp.html.

6   "NATO and Russia Agree to Move Partnership Forward," North Atlantic Treaty Organization, December 4, 2009. www.nato.int/cps/en/natohq/news_59970.htm [accessed June 12, 2015].

7   "NATO Military Committee Concludes Two Days Meetings in Brussels," North Atlantic Treaty Organization, January 27, 2010, www.nato.int/ims/news/2010/n100127e.html [accessed June 12, 2015].

8   Slobodan Lekic, "NATO, Russia Boost Military Ties in Afghan War," Associated Press, January 27, 2010. www.boston.com/news/world/europe/articles/2010/01/27/nato_kazakhstan_agree_on_afghan_supply_route/ [accessed June 12, 2015].

9   "NATO 2020: Assured Security; Dynamic Engagement, Analysis and Recommendations of the Group of Experts on a New Strategic Concept for NATO," North Atlantic Treaty Organization, May 17, 2010. www.nato.int/nato_static_fl2014/assets/pdf/pdf_2010_05/20100517_100517_expertsreport.pdf [accessed June 12, 2015].

10 Jens Ringsmose and Sten Rynning, "Introduction: Taking Stock of NATO's New Strategic Concept," *NATO's New Strategic Concept: A Comprehensive Assessment, DIIS Report 2011:02*, Copenhagen: Danish Institute for International Studies, 2011, p. 13. www.diis.dk/files/media/publications/import/extra/rp2011-02-nato_web_2.pdf [accessed June 12, 2015].

11 Ringsmose and Rynning, "Introduction," 13–14.

12 The full text of the concept can be found at: www.nato.int/nato_static_fl2014/assets/pdf/pdf_publications/20120214_strategic-concept-2010–eng.pdf [accessed June 15, 2015].

13 For an analysis of the first stages of post-Cold War collective defense thinking see my 1995 report to Congress subsequently republished by the NDU Press: Stanley R. Sloan, *NATO's Future: Beyond Collective Defense* (Washington, D.C.: National Defense University Press, 1996).

14 "Strategic Concept For the Defence and Security of The Members of the North Atlantic Treaty Organisation," (hereafter referred to as "SC2010"). Adopted by Heads of State and Government in Lisbon, November 19, 2010. para. 4. a. Paragraph 16 also illustrates the effective merger of Article 5 and 4 under the collective defense rubric: "Defense and Deterrence. The greatest responsibility of the Alliance is to protect and defend our territory and our populations against attack, as set out in Article 5 of the Washington Treaty. The Alliance does not consider any country to be its adversary. However, no one should doubt NATO's resolve if the security of any of its members were to be threatened."

15 See, for example, Stanley Sloan and Heiko Borchert, "Europe, U.S. Must Rebalance Soft, Hard Power," *Defense News*, September 8–15, 2003.

16 For one such approach combined with a skeptical European view of the future of NATO and transatlantic cooperation more generally see Stanley Sloan and Peter van Ham, *What Future for NATO?*, Centre for European Reform, London, October 2002.

17 SC2010, para. 4. b.

18 SC2010, para. 21.

19 A copy of the resolution can be found at: www.icc-cpi.int/NR/rdonlyres/081A9013-B03D-4859-9D61-5D0B0F2F5EFA/0/1970Eng.pdf [accessed June 18, 2015].

20 A copy of the resolution can be found at: www.nato.int/nato_static/assets/pdf/pdf_2011_03/20110927_110311-UNSCR-1973.pdf [accessed June 17, 2015].

21 Other members of the coalition had their own names for the operation, including: Opération Harmattan for France; Operation Ellamy for the United Kingdom; and Operation Mobile for Canada.

22 Operation Unified Protector Final Mission Stats, North Atlantic Treaty Organization, November 2, 2011. www.nato.int/nato_static/assets/pdf/pdf_2011_11/20111108_111107factsheet_up_factsfigures_en.pdf [accessed June 18, 2015].

23 John F. Burns, "British Military Expands Links to French Ally," *The New York Times*, November 2, 2010. www.nytimes.com/2010/11/03/world/europe/03britain.html?_r=0 [accessed June 18, 2015].

24 Lawrence F. Kaplan, "Open Wide: How Libya Revealed the Huge Gap Between U.S. and European Military Might, *The New Republic*, April 26, 2011. www.newrepublic.com/article/crossings/87377/libya-nato-military-power-europe-us [accessed June 18, 2015].

25 Kaplan, "Open Wide."

26 Steven Erlanger, "Libya's Dark Lesson for NATO," *The New York Times*, September 3, 2011, www.nytimes.com/2011/09/04/sunday-review/what-libyas-lessons-mean-for-nato.html [accessed June 18, 2015].

27 Ivo H. Daalder and James G. Stavridis, "The Right Way to Run an Intervention," *Foreign Affairs*, March/April 2012. www.foreignaffairs.com/articles/libya/2012-02-02/natos-victory-libya [accessed June 23, 2015].

28 Robert M. Gates, "The Security and Defense Agenda (Future of NATO)," Transcript of Speech, Department of Defense, Brussels, June 10, 2011. www.defense.gov/speeches/speech.aspx?speechid=1581 [accessed June 19, 2015].

29 Gates, "The Security and Defense Agenda."

30 Gates, "The Security and Defense Agenda."

31 "Pivot to the Pacific? The Obama Administration's 'Rebalancing' Toward Asia," CRS Report R42448, March 28, 2012, 2. www.fas.org/sgp/crs/natsec/R42448.pdf [accessed June 20, 2015].

32 European Defense Agency, "Defense Data 2013," 2015, 2. http://issuu.com/europeandefenceagency/docs/eda_defence_data_2013_web/1?e=4763412/12106343 [accessed June 20, 2015].

33 Christian Mölling, "Trends Within the European Union," in *The Implications of Military Spending Cuts for NATO's Largest Members*, ed. Clara Marina O'Donnell,

Center on the United States and Europe, The Brookings Institution, July 2012, 6. www.brookings.edu/~/media/research/files/papers/2012/7/military%20spend ing%20nato%20odonnell/military%20spending%20nato%20odonnell%20pdf [accessed June 20, 2015].

34 See, for example, one of the most active proponents of this view: Sarwar Kashmeri, "Nato Needs a Leadership Rethink to Remain Relevant," *The Guardian*, May 20, 2012. www.theguardian.com/commentisfree/cifamerica/2012/may/20/ nato-leadership-rethink-sarwar-kashmeri [accessed June 23, 2015].

35 "Chicago Summit Declaration Issued by the Heads of State and Government participating in the meeting of the North Atlantic Council in Chicago on 20 May 2012," North Atlantic Treaty Organization, May 20, 2012. www.nato.int/ cps/en/SID-404A88D3-574689CB/natolive/official_texts_87593.htm?mode= pressrelease [accessed June 23, 2015].

36 "Chicago Summit Declaration," para. 5.

37 "Deterrence and Defence Posture Review," North Atlantic Treaty Organization, May 20, 2012. www.nato.int/cps/en/SID-404A88D3-574689CB/natolive/ official_texts_87597.htm?mode=pressrelease [accessed June 23, 2015].

38 "Deterrence and Defence Posture Review," para. 26.

39 See discussion of the Obama approach to missile defense in Europe in Chapter 7.

40 "Deterrence and Defence Posture Review," para.21.

41 "Chicago Summit Declaration," para. 39.

42 Members of the group are: Canada, France, Germany, Italy, Japan, Russia (sus- pended in 2014), United Kingdom, United States, and the European Union.

43 Steve Gutterman, "Putin Flexes Muscle in Shunning U.S.-hosted G8 talks," *Reuters*, May 10, 2012. www.reuters.com/article/2012/05/10/us-russia-putin- usa-idUSBRE8491DY20120510 [accessed June 24, 2015].

44 "Chicago Summit Declaration," para 35.

45 "Summit Declaration on Defence Capabilities: Toward NATO Forces 2020," North Atlantic Treaty Organization, May 20, 2012. www.nato.int/cps/en/SID- 404A88D3-574689CB/natolive/official_texts_87594.htm?mode=pressrelease [accessed June 24, 2015].

46 "Summit Declaration on Defence Capabilities," para. 1.

47 The Eurozone includes all members of the European Union that have adopted the Euro as their currency.

48 The Mediterranean Dialogue currently includes the following non-NATO Mediterranean states: Algeria, Egypt, Israel, Jordan, Mauritania, Morocco and Tunisia.

49 The Istanbul Cooperation Initiative invited six Gulf Cooperation Council states to join in this partnership framework. Bahrain, Qatar, Kuwait and the United Arab Emirates have joined. Saudi Arabia and Oman reportedly have also shown an interest in the Initiative.

50 NATO's partners across the globe are: Afghanistan, Australia, Iraq, Japan, the Republic of Korea, Mongolia, New Zealand, and Pakistan.

51 "Australia-NATO Joint Political Declaration," North Atlantic Treaty Organization, June 12, 2012. www.nato.int/cps/en/natohq/official_texts_94097.htm?selected Locale=en [accessed June 24, 2015].

52 "Chicago Summit Declaration," para 56.

53 The mission, initiated in 2004 after the Baltic States had joined NATO, was a symbol of collective defense against potential Russian threats.

54 Will Englund and Kathy Lally, "Ukraine, Under Pressure From Russia, Puts Brakes on E.U. Deal," *The Washington Post*, November 21, 2013. www.washingtonpost.com/world/europe/ukraine-under-pressure-from-russia-puts-brakes-on-eu-deal/2013/11/21/46c50796-52c9-11e3-9ee6-2580086d8254_story.html [accessed June 25, 2015].

55 James Marson, Alan Cullison and Alexander Kolyandr, "Ukraine President Viktor Yanukovych Driven From Power," *The Wall Street Journal*, February 23, 2014. www.wsj.com/articles/SB10001424052702304914204579398561953855036 [accessed June 25, 2015].

56 Matt Babiak, "Russian Insider Says Putin Openly Planned Invasion of Ukraine Since 2003," *EuroMaidan Press*, November 25, 2014. http://euromaidanpress.com/2014/11/25/russian-insider-says-putin-planning-invasion-of-ukraine-since-2003/ [accessed July 13, 2015].

57 Adam Taylor, "To Understand Crimea, Take a Look Back at its Complicated History," *The Washington Post*, February 27, 2014. www.washingtonpost.com/blogs/worldviews/wp/2014/02/27/to-understand-crimea-take-a-look-back-at-its-complicated-history/ [accessed June 25, 2015].

58 Full text of the "Treaty of Friendship, Cooperation and Partnership between the Russian Federation and Ukraine," http://kiev1.org/en/text-dogovora-13.html [accessed June 26, 2015].

59 Steven Woehrel, "Ukraine: Current Issues and U.S. Policy," Congressional Research Service Report RL33460, February 12, 2015, p. 2. www.fas.org/sgp/crs/row/RL33460.pdf [accessed June 26, 2015].

60 Budapest Memorandums on Security Assurances, 1994, Primary Sources, Council on Foreign Relations, December 5, 1994 www.cfr.org/nonproliferation-arms-control-and-disarmament/budapest-memorandums-security-assurances-1994/p32484 [accessed July 7, 2015].

61 "Statement by NATO Foreign Ministers," North Atlantic Treaty Organization, April 1, 2014. www.nato.int/cps/en/natohq/news_108501.htm [accessed June 26, 2015].

62 "Ukraine and Russia Sanctions," U.S. Department of State www.state.gov/e/eb/tfs/spi/ukrainerussia/ [accessed June 26, 2015].

63 "EU Sanctions Against Russia Over Ukraine Crisis," European Union Highlights http://europa.eu/newsroom/highlights/special-coverage/eu_sanctions/index_en.htm [accessed June 26, 2015].

64 John J. Mearsheimer, "Why the Ukraine Crisis is the West's Fault: The Liberal Delusions That Provoked Putin," *Foreign Affairs*, September/October 2014. www.foreignaffairs.com/articles/russia-fsu/2014-08-18/why-ukraine-crisis-west-s-fault [accessed June 26, 2015].

65 Mearsheimer, "Why the Ukraine Crisis is the West's Fault."

66 Stephen F. Cohen, "Cold War Again: Who's Responsible?," *The Nation*, April 1, 2014. www.thenation.com/article/179119/cold-war-again-whos-responsible [accessed June 26, 2015].

67 Sean Kay, "NATO Revived? Not So Fast," www.warontherocks.com, March 6, 2014. http://warontherocks.com/2014/03/nato-revived-not-so-fast/ [accessed June 26, 2015].

68 For a well-focused debate between Mearsheimer and two critics, see: Michael McFaul, Stephen Sestanovich and John J. Mearsheimer, "Faulty Powers: Who Started the Ukraine Crisis?," *Foreign Affairs*, November/December 2014. www.foreignaffairs.com/articles/eastern-europe-caucasus/2014-10-17/faulty-powers [accessed June 27, 2015].

69 Michael Rühle, "NATO Enlargement and Russia: Myths and Realities," *NATO Review*, July 2014. www.nato.int/docu/review/2014/Russia-Ukraine-Nato-crisis/Nato-enlargement-Russia/EN/index.htm [accessed June 26, 2015].

70 Anne Applebaum, "The Myth of Russian Humiliation," *The Washington Post*, October 17, 2014. www.washingtonpost.com/opinions/anne-applebaum-nato-pays-a-heavy-price-for-giving-russia-too-much-credita-true-achievement-under-threat/2014/10/17/5b3a6f2a-5617-11e4-809b-8cc0a295c773_story.html [accessed June 26, 2015].

71 Applebaum, "The Myth of Russian Humiliation."

72 McFaul, Sestanovich, and Mearsheimer, "Faulty Powers."

73 McFaul, Sestanovich, and Mearsheimer, "Faulty Powers."

74 "Conscious Uncoupling," *The Economist*, April 5, 2014. www.economist.com/news/briefing/21600111-reducing-europes-dependence-russian-gas-possiblebut-it-will-take-time-money-and-sustained [accessed June 28, 2015].

75 For a graphic illustration of the heavy dependence of many European countries on Russian energy sources see: "How Much Europe Depends on Russian Energy," *The New York Times*, updated September 2, 2014. www.nytimes.com/interactive/2014/03/21/world/europe/how-much-europe-depends-on-russian-energy.html?_r=0 [accessed June 30, 2015].

76 "Conscious Uncoupling."

77 Tomas Hirst, "France Could Sell Those Russian Mistral Warships to China," *Business Insider*, May 11, 2015. www.businessinsider.com/france-could-sell-those-russian-mistral-warships-to-china-2015-5 [accessed July 1, 2015].

78 Andrea Thomas, "German Ex-Chancellor Schröder Celebrates Birthday With Russia's Putin," *The Wall Street Journal*, April 29, 2014. www.wsj.com/articles/SB10001424052702304163604579531301211746032 [accessed June 30, 2015].

79 Peter Baker, Alan Cowell and James Kanter, "Coordinated Sanctions Aim at Russia's Ability to Tap its Oil Reserves," *The New York Times*, July 29, 2014. www.nytimes.com/2014/07/30/world/europe/european-sanctions-russia.html [accessed June 30, 2015].

80 Baker, Cowell, and Kanter, "Coordinated Sanctions."

81 Anders Fogh Rasmussen and Philip M. Breedlove, "A NATO for a Dangerous World," *The Wall Street Journal*, August 17, 2014. www.wsj.com/articles/anders-fogh-rasmussen-and-philip-m-breedlove-a-nato-for-a-dangerous-world-1408317653 [accessed June 30, 2015].

82 John Deni, "What NATO Needs to Do in the Wake of the Ukraine Crisis," *Defense One*, July 22, 2014. www.defenseone.com/ideas/2014/07/what-nato-needs-do-wake-ukraine-crisis/89282/?oref=search_deni [accessed June 30, 2015].

83 Margateta Pagano, "Land For Gas: Merkel and Putin Discussed Secret Deal Could End Ukraine Crisis," *The Independent*, July 31, 2014. www.independent.co.uk/news/world/europe/land-for-gas-secret-german-deal-could-end-ukraine-crisis-9638764.html [accessed June 30, 2015].

84 "The Wales Declaration on the Transatlantic Bond," North Atlantic Treaty Organization, September 5, 2014. www.nato.int/cps/en/natohq/official_texts_112985.htm?selectedLocale=en [accessed June 30, 2015].

85 "Wales Summit Declaration Issued by the Heads of State and Government participating in the meeting of the North Atlantic Council in Wales," North Atlantic Treaty Organization, September 5, 2014. www.nato.int/cps/en/natohq/official_texts_112964.htm?selectedLocale=en [accessed June 30, 2015].

86 Gareth Jones, "Four NATO Allies Deny Ukraine Statement on Providing Arms," *Reuters*, September 7, 2014. www.reuters.com/article/2014/09/07/us-ukraine-crisis-nato-arms-idUSKBN0H20E820140907 [accessed June 30, 2015].

87 Julian Borger, "New Push to Remove Tactical Nuclear Weapons from Europe," *The Guardian*, February 3, 2012. www.theguardian.com/world/julian-borger-global-security-blog/2012/feb/03/nuclear-weapons-tactical [accessed June 30, 2015].

88 Greg Botelho and Laura Smith-Spark, "Putin: You Better Not Come After a Nuclear-Armed Russia," *CNN*, August 30, 2014. www.cnn.com/2014/08/29/world/europe/ukraine-crisis/ [accessed June 30, 2015].

89 "Wales Summit Declaration."

90 Rick Lyman and Andrew E. Kramer, 'War is Exploding Anew in Ukraine; Rebels Vow More,' *The New York Times*, January 23, 2015. http://nyti.ms/1yCOtc7 [accessed July 1, 2015].

91 "Ukraine Crisis: Leaders Agree Peace Roadmap," BBC, February 12, 2015. www.bbc.com/news/world-europe-31435812 [accessed July 1, 2015].

92 General Philip Breedlove, "Senate Armed Services Committee Opening Statement by General Phil Breedlove, Commander, U.S. European Command," U.S. European Command, April 30, 2015. www.eucom.mil/media-library/article/33031/senate-armed-services-committee-opening-statement-by-general-phil-breedlove-commander-u-s-european [accessed July 1, 2015].

93 John Vandiver, "Breedlove: More Assets Needed to Counter Russia in Ukraine," *Stars and Stripes*, April 30, 2015. www.stripes.com/news/breedlove-more-assets-needed-to-counter-russia-in-ukraine-1.343378 [accessed July 1, 2015].

94 "US to Position Tanks, Arms in 7 European Nations," *Voice of America*, June 23, 2015. www.voanews.com/content/carter-us-will-not-rely-on-cold-war-playbook-with-russia/2833572.html [accessed July 1, 2015].

95 "US to Position Tanks, Arms in 7 European Nations."

96 "Statement by NATO Defence Ministers," North Atlantic Treaty Organization, June 25, 2015. www.nato.int/cps/en/natohq/news_121133.htm [accessed July 1, 2015].

97 Jack Sommers, "Vladimir Putin Says 'Only An Insane Person' Would Think Russia Would Attack Nato," *The Huffington Post UK*, June 6, 2015. www.huffingtonpost.co.uk/2015/06/06/vladimir-putin-russia-nato_n_7525546.html [accessed July 1, 2015].

98 Katie Simmons, Bruce Stokes, and Jacob Poushter, "NATO Publics Blame Russia for Ukrainian Crisis, But Reluctant to Provide Military Aid," Pew Research Center, June 10, 2015. www.pewglobal.org/2015/06/10/1-nato-public-opinion-wary-of-russia-leary-of-action-on-ukraine/ [accessed July 1, 2015].

99   Simmons, Stokes, and Poushter, "NATO Publics Blame Russia for Ukrainian Crisis".

100   Laurence Norman, "EU Extends Economic Sanctions on Russia Until End of January," *The Wall Street Journal*, June 22, 2015. www.wsj.com/articles/eu-extends-economic-sanctions-on-russia-until-end-of-january-1434960823 [accessed July 1, 2015].

101   Alan Makovsky, "Turley's Refugee Dilemma," Center for American Progress, March 13, 2019. www.americanprogress.org/issues/security/reports/2019/03/13/467183/turkeys-refugee-dilemma/ [accessed April 19, 2020].

102   Gilbert Reilhac, "EU Parliament Calls for Freeze on Turkey's Membership Talks," *Reuters*, March 13, 2019. www.reuters.com/article/us-eu-turkey/eu-parliament-calls-for-freeze-on-turkeys-membership-talks-idUSKCN1QU2LD_[accessed June 22, 2019].

103   Middle East Institute, "Turkey's Relations with the E.U., MEI VantagePoint," filmed June 1, 2017, Youtube video, 19:54, published June 6, 2017, www.youtube.com/watch?v=ZhmnQ1YHau4 [accessed April 27, 2020].

104   K. A. Hawkins, *Venezuela's Chavismo and Populism in Comparative Perspective* (Cambridge: Cambridge University Press, 2010).

105   C. Mudde, *Populist Radical Right Parties in Europe* (Cambridge: Cambridge University Press, 2007).

106   "Europe and Right-Wing Nationalism: A Country-by-Country Guide," *BBC*, May 24, 2019. www.bbc.com/news/world-europe-36130006 [accessed August 8, 2019].

107   Matt Brown, Dalibor Rohac, and Carolyn Kenny, "Europe's Populist Challenge," Center for American Progress, May 10, 2018. www.americanprogress.org/issues/democracy/reports/2018/05/10/450430/europes-populist-challenge/ [accessed August 6, 2019].

108   See 71–3 for discussion of the UK's struggle with the question of joining the process of European integration.

109   Nate Cohn, "Why the Surprise Over 'Brexit'? Don't Blame the Polls," *The New York Times*, June 24, 2016. www.nytimes.com/2016/06/25/upshot/why-the-surprise-over-brexit-dont-blame-the-polls.html [accessed October 7, 2017].

110   "Text: British Prime Minister Theresa May Announces Her Resignation," *Reuters*, May 24, 2019. www.reuters.com/article/us-britain-eu-may-text/text-british-prime-minister-theresa-may-announces-her-resignation-idUSKCN1SU0YH [accessed June 22, 2019].

111   Tony Barber, "Five Consequences of the UK's Exit from the EU," *Financial Times*, June 24, 2016. www.ft.com/content/b1a2d66e-3715–11e6–9a05–82a9b15a8ee7 [accessed July 23, 2017].

112   W. J. Hennigan, "President Trump Says NATO Allies Owe the U.S. Money. He's Wrong," *Time*, July 11, 2018. https://time.com/5335111/donald-trump-nato-spending-facts/ [accessed August 9, 2019].

113   This chapter is based in part on analysis originally presented in: Stanley R. Sloan, "Policy Series: Donald Trump and NATO: Historic Alliance Meets A-historic President," H-Diplo International Security Studies Forum, June 8, 2017. https://issforum.org/roundtables/policy/1-5am-nato [accessed October 8, 2017].

114   For a more detailed examination of Trump's attitudes toward NATO before and during the 2016 election campaign and during his presidency, see: Stanley R.

Sloan, *Transatlantic Traumas: Has Illiberalism Brought the West to the Brink of Collapse?* (Manchester: Manchester University Press, 2018).

115 Dan Lamothe and Michael Birnbaum, "Defense Secretary Mattis Issues New Ultimatum to NATO Allies on Defense Spending," *The Washington Post*, February 15, 2017. www.washingtonpost.com/news/checkpoint/wp/2017/02/15/mattis-trumps-defense-secretary-issues-ultimatum-to-nato-allies-on-defense-spending/?utm_term=.268c36fd75b5 [accessed October 8, 2017].

116 Jeff Mason and Andreas Rinke, "In First Trump-Merkel Meeting, Awkward Body Language and a Quip," *Reuters*, March 17, 2017. www.reuters.com/article/us-usa-trump-germany-idUSKBN16O0FM [accessed October 8, 2017].

117 Noah Bierman, "Trump Prepares for First Overseas Trip, with Anti-Globalism at Bay," *Los Angeles Times*, May 15, 2017. www.latimes.com/politics/la-na-pol-trump-globalist-20170515-story.html [accessed October 8, 2017].

118 Michael D. Shear, Mark Landler, and James Kantermay, "In NATO Speech, Trump Is Vague about Mutual Defense Pledge," *The New York Times*, May 25, 2017. www.nytimes.com/2017/05/25/world/europe/donald-trump-eu-nato.html?hp&action=click&pgtype=Homepage&clickSource=story-heading&module=first-column-region&region=top-news&WT.nav=top-news [accessed October 8, 2017].

119 Henry Farrell, "Thanks to Trump, Germany Says It Can't Rely on the United States. What Does That Mean?" *The Washington Post*, May 28, 2017. www.washingtonpost.com/news/monkey-cage/wp/2017/05/28/thanks-to-trump-germany-says-it-cant-rely-on-america-what-does-that-mean/?utm_term=.def-364cdb312 [accessed October 8, 2017].

120 Donald J. Trump, "Remarks by President Trump to the People of Poland | July 6, 2017," *The White House*, July 6, 2017. www.whitehouse.gov/the-press-office/2017/07/06/remarks-president-trump-people-poland-july-6-2017 [accessed October 8, 2017].

121 www.factcheck.org/2018/07/trumps-false-claims-at-nato/ [accessed July 8, 2019].

122 www.nato.int/cps/en/natohq/news_165249.htm [accessed July 8, 2019].

123 James P. Rubin, "The Leader of the Free World Meets Donald Trump," *Politico.com*, March 16, 2017. www.politico.com/magazine/story/2017/03/the-leader-of-the-free-world-meets-donald-trump-214924 [accessed October 8, 2017].

124 Sebastian Sprenger, "The Strange Case of a 'European Aircraft Carrier'," *Defense News*, March 11, 2019. www.defensenews.com/global/europe/2019/03/11/the-strange-case-of-a-european-aircraft-carrier/ [accessed August 9, 2019].

125 For a thorough examination of the European initiatives, see Daniel Fiott, *Yearbook of European Security* (European Union Institute for Security Studies, 2019). www.iss.europa.eu/content/euiss-yearbook-european-security-2019 [accessed August 6, 2019].

126 Richard Wike, Bruce Stokes, Jacob Poushter, and Janell Fetterolf, "U.S. Image Suffers as Publics Around World Question Trump's Leadership," Pew Research Center, June 26, 2017. www.pewglobal.org/2017/06/26/u-s-image-suffers-as-publics-around-world-question-trumps-leadership/ [accessed August 16, 2017].

127 Zachary Laub, "What Is the Status of the Iran Nuclear Agreement?" Council on Foreign Relations, July 31, 2019. www.cfr.org/backgrounder/what-status-iran-nuclear-agreement [accessed August 12, 2019].

Part III

Defense of the West

9

External threats and internal challenges

In considering the future of transatlantic relations and "defense of the West," it is important to take into account not only the external threats that NATO and the EU will face but also the internal challenges confronting Western nations, which will affect their ability to deal effectively with those external threats. This chapter inventories the external threats and the internal challenges, while examining the interactive dynamic between the two categories and discussing the circumstances under which NATO and EU member states may, or may not, be successful in dealing with them.

External threats

During the Cold War, defining the threat to European security was a relatively straightforward exercise, even if shaping a response often required difficult negotiations among the allies. Today, while threats to the Western alliance may not seem as imminent as those posed by the Soviet Union once did, they are more complex, both in terms of the sources and the character of the threats.

Russia remains a threatening neighbor for most European democracies, as well as an existential and political threat to the United States. But this traditional challenge is joined by others including radical extremist terrorism, continued Middle Eastern turbulence, refugees flowing out of North Africa and the Middle East, and a more subtle and emerging threat from another major international power: China.

Among NATO and EU member states, the ones closest to Russia undoubtedly feel that their existence as free, democratic nations could be in jeopardy. For NATO and EU countries along Europe's southern rim, the new threats and their consequences emerging in North Africa and the Middle East have been judged increasingly as the priority concern, even if not posing an "existential" threat.

Threats as portrayed in NATO post-Cold War communiqués

Before examining contemporary threats, it might be useful to survey how "threats" have been perceived in major NATO documentation since the end of the Cold War. What threats has NATO—the United States, Canada, and the European allies—identified in the post-Cold War era?

The first post-Cold War Strategic Concept in 1991 argued that NATO would remain relevant given the "risks and challenges" still facing the allies, carefully avoiding the use of the word "threats"—a much stronger term that implicitly or explicitly would be linked to an "enemy." The word "threat" appeared only nine times in the document, and most of these were references to the fact that threats of the past had disappeared. The concept said that "the risks to Allied security that remain are multi-faceted in nature and multi-directional, which makes them hard to predict and assess." It noted that:

> Risks to Allied security are less likely to result from calculated aggression against the territory of the Allies, but rather from the adverse consequences of insta-bilities that may arise from the serious economic, social and political difficulties, including ethnic rivalries and territorial disputes, which are faced by many coun-tries in central and eastern Europe.[1]

It also suggested that "Alliance security interests can be affected by other risks of a wider nature, including proliferation of weapons of mass destruction, disruption of the flow of vital resources and actions of terrorism and sabotage." The term "risks" was definitely in vogue in the optimistic days of 1991, having overtaken the term "threats" by the end of the Cold War.

The 1999 concept preserved the "risks and challenges" language, as the allies were still debating the extent to which NATO was relevant to non-Article 5 issues. Following the 1991 example, "threat" showed up just nine times in this document.[2]

Yet, in 2010, the new strategic concept approved by the allies began to intimate growing concern, employing "threat" some 20 times. In the context of relations with Moscow, however, "threat" was used only to proclaim that NATO posed no threat to Russia. The term referenced primarily non-Russian or generic threats from proliferation of ballistic missile technology as well as: nuclear and other weapons-of-mass-destruction technologies; other types of new weapons technologies that could end up in the wrong hands; terrorism; instability beyond NATO's borders; cyber attacks; threats to vital communica-tion, transport and transit routes, and energy supplies; and environmental and resource constraints.

Throughout the two decades after the end of the Cold War and the dissolu-tion of the Soviet Union, the reluctance to use the term "threat," particularly with regard to Russia, reflected the strong desire to develop a partnership with

Russia that would hopefully help this major European country become a constructive member of the Euro-Atlantic and international communities.

By the time of the Wales Summit in September 2014, the 2010 concept still seemed like a good overall strategic framework for the allies, but some significant changes had occurred in the world that introduced some new threats to consider. Granted, it's a lengthy document, but the summit communiqué featured the term "threat" some 54 times.[3] Most of the instances have to do with ISIL, terrorism, and related topics, but the allies also chose to make several direct and indirect references to threats posed by Russia. The allies had moved from talking about "risks and challenges" toward calling a spade a spade. The threats, not risks, faced by the alliance specified in the words of the Wales Summit Declaration included (emphasis added):

- ... *Russia's pattern of disregard for international law* including ... use of military and other instruments to coerce neighbours. *This threatens the rules-based international order and challenges Euro-Atlantic security.*
- ... the specific *challenges posed by hybrid warfare threats*, where a wide range of overt and covert military, paramilitary, and civilian measures are employed in a highly integrated design.
- *Growing instability in our southern neighbourhood*, from the Middle East to North Africa, as well as transnational and multidimensional threats, are also challenging our security.
- *The so-called Islamic State of Iraq and the Levant (ISIL)* poses a grave threat to the Iraqi people, to the Syrian people, to the wider region, and to our nations.
- *Terrorism poses a direct threat* to the security of the citizens of NATO countries and to international stability and prosperity more broadly, and will remain a threat for the foreseeable future. It is a global threat that knows no border, nationality, or religion—a challenge that the international community must fight and tackle together.
- The threat to NATO populations, territory, and forces posed by the *proliferation of ballistic missiles* continues to increase and missile defence forms part of a broader response to counter it.
- The *proliferation of nuclear weapons and other weapons of mass destruction* (WMD), as well as their means of delivery, by states and non-state actors continues to present a threat to our populations, territory, and forces.
- *Cyber attacks* can reach a threshold that threatens national and Euro-Atlantic prosperity, security, and stability.

One particularly interesting aspect of the Wales inventory of "threats" was that the many paragraphs focused on Russia's aggressions featured very few uses of the term. This may have reflected diplomatic restraint, revealing the reluctance of many NATO members to risk destroying completely the bridge between Russia and the alliance.

One might have expected that after Donald Trump assumed the presidency with a very critical attitude toward NATO, the EU, and multilateral coop-eration in general, and a remarkably friendly approach to Russia's Vladimir Putin, NATO's threat assessments might have changed substantially as a result. But when the allies met at the summit in Brussels in July 2018, the threat statements still included a strong focus on Russia, their final communi-qué leading off with the assessment that "Russia's aggressive actions, includ-ing the threat and use of force to attain political goals, challenge the Alliance and are undermining Euro-Atlantic security and the rules-based international order."[4] The document went on to discuss not only the variety of threats posed by Russia but also other elements of "a dangerous, unpredictable, and fluid security environment," including the consequences of Middle Eastern instabil-ity, the ongoing crisis in Syria, and proliferation of weapons of mass destruc-tion and missile technology. The emerging China challenge did not appear in this communiqué.

Assessing the threats

Russia

By 2014, Russia had clearly become a revisionist power, seeking to change the Euro-Atlantic security system as it had evolved after the end of the Cold War. Whether the NATO allies and their enlargement decisions were partially to blame for Russia's revisionist behavior, or if the "humiliation" claimed by Russia was simply a cover for maintaining President Putin's domestic control and his expansionist desires, a clear Russian threat had emerged to the West's defense of the Euro-Atlantic security system. If this threat remains unaltered by future Russian actions, it will likely continue to be the primary driver for NATO and Western policies for many years to come.

In terms of defense decisions, the allies had already begun the process of building up capabilities along Russia's border with NATO to provide a minimal amount of reassurance to exposed allies and deterrence to Russian aggres-sion (see Chapter 8). The response was initially limited by differing threat perceptions in European countries and by the weakened condition of many EU nations. It was nonetheless clear that the alliance required a more coherent European response, politically and in terms of resources, and strong American leadership. Neither of these ingredients were guaranteed in the early stages of the response to Russia's challenges.

It was true that, for both reassurance and deterrence, the European allies would be called on to increase spending, as promised at Wales in 2014, and to begin investing in the task of rebuilding military establishments that had been shedding capabilities and credibility for more than two decades. At the same time, the United States would have to continue its process of reasserting leadership in the alliance. This would not mean abandoning a stronger focus on Asian security, but it would require both words and deeds acknowledging that US leadership remained critical to NATO's survival. While the Trump presidency, as discussed in Chapter 8, put unusually forceful pressure on the allies to do more, it failed to provide effective political leadership of the alliance, even as the United States improved its forces available to NATO.

The new Russian threat was a complex one and would require a complex response. Whether or not one accepted the term "hybrid" to describe Russia's military operations against Ukraine, the fact was that the Russian offensive against the Western security system included: covert introduction of military units and equipment in Ukraine; a persistent line of propaganda disclaiming involvement while placing blame on the adversary; extensive use of social media to influence perceptions of Russian intentions; overt and covert intervention in Western elections; selective disruption with cyber attacks; and the backing of large conventional military—including nuclear—capabilities.

Russia enjoyed a number of advantages in its revisionist strategy, including the following:

- Strong centralized control of the national government, active suppression of dissent, and fairly widespread domestic support for overcoming Russia's "humiliation" gave President Putin substantial flexibility in seeking changes to the European order.
- Support and admiration from the Russian Orthodox Church for Putin's advocacy for "traditional values" and Russian nationalism contributed to his domestic popularity and, to a certain extent, support in some EU and NATO countries.
- Putin's control of most print and broadcast media, as well as the Kremlin's increasing control of social media, helped create a steady propaganda message out of Moscow.
- Russian military forces enjoyed the benefit of proximity and tactical advantage over NATO forces in the Baltic region.
- The political and economic weakness and inbred corruption in Ukraine made Kiev a vulnerable target.
- European dependence on Russian oil and gas provided leverage for Russian diplomacy. Russia also benefitted from the fact that the West had come to rely on cooperation with Russia in many areas including the fact that Russia would remain an important player in European security affairs no matter how cooperative or uncooperative its leadership.
- Russia gained a new advantage with the election of Donald Trump as US president. Trump refused to criticize Putin and even seemed to welcome Russian interference in US elections.

But Russia also had some disadvantages:

- Russia's economy, which had been booming, was made vulnerable by a combination of unpredictable oil market pricing and the dislocations caused by Western sanctions.
- Russia's military, although having benefitted from significant investment over the past decade, remained less capable than sometimes imagined in the West.[5]
- Russian actions in Ukraine and various threats directed at NATO and EU nations had a solidifying effect on the West, supporting continued sanctions in spite of Western dependencies and the reluctance of some allies.
- Putin's nuclear saber-rattling[6] did not negate the fact that the West had a wide range of potential responses (considering those of France, the UK, and the United States) to any nuclear threats or attacks on the West—and Putin knew this.
- Russia had no reliable allies; Putin's "pivot" to Asia might bring short-term cooperation with China but also perhaps longer-term dependence and potential conflicts.[7]
- Russia's bold entry into the civil war in Syria may have enhanced Russia's influence in the region, but in the long run it could create serious burdens for Russia's troubled economy and further entangle Moscow in ongoing Middle Eastern crises.

How would NATO and the EU manage relations with Russia in view of these circumstances? It appeared that some balance would have to be struck between confrontation and accommodation—an updated version of the Harmel Report's formula from the 1960s. In the foreseeable future, Western countries would likely seek policies and actions that would reassure exposed allies and build up sufficient risks to limit Russian adventurism and meddling, while keeping the door open to near-term cooperation where there were mutual interests.

Conflict, instability, and ISIL in the Middle East and North Africa

NATO had already recognized and, to some extent, engaged in attempts to deal with threats emerging from the turbulent Middle East. NATO did not play a combat role in either of the Iraq wars but had helped train military officers for the new Iraqi government in Baghdad. NATO's role in Libya was much more central in the ousting of long-time authoritarian leader Muammar Gaddafi; NATO had provided support to anti-Gaddafi forces that were critical to him being overthrown and killed. While the operation itself represented a successful use of NATO infrastructure, it also revealed European political and military shortcomings and, in the end, sent Libya into a new chaotic stage of its history. The United States, of course, had been deeply engaged in the region, intervening in wars against "enemy" states (Saddam Hussein's Iraq, Gaddafi's Libya), and in support of more friendly regimes. Several European states (most notably the UK, France, and Italy) were in part motivated by historic ties to the region resulting from their colonial presence earlier in the twentieth century. Additionally, the European Union had developed both humanitarian assistance programs and associations with states in the region that were intended to foster peace and economic development.

Despite Western efforts in this region, turmoil continued to spiral out of control. Although there remained no peace in sight between Israel and the Palestinians, the focus shifted away from this formerly leading touchstone of Middle Eastern conflict to the new threat posed by ISIL. Meanwhile, the much hoped for democratic reform of the region growing out of the "Arab Spring" moved steadily toward a chaotic Middle Eastern Winter.

One of the immediate threats posed by ISIL's expansion in the region was a refugee crisis in the Mediterranean, as citizens of war-torn countries across the Middle East and North Africa sought to escape the fighting while finding safer homes and opportunities in Europe. The burden of dealing with this surge of asylum seekers fell first on the EU and NATO states along the northern rim of the Mediterranean. But as the numbers escalated, the EU recognized that it would have to take steps not only in response to the humanitarian aspects of the crisis but also with the threats to Europe's open border policies. On April 23, 2015, the EU Council issued a statement finding that "The situation in the Mediterranean is a tragedy." The Council pledged to "mobilise all efforts at its disposal to prevent further loss of life at sea and to tackle the root causes of the human emergency that we face, in cooperation with the countries of origin and transit." The EU states "decided to strengthen our presence at sea, to fight the traffickers, to prevent illegal migration flows and to reinforce internal solidarity and responsibility."[8]

President Obama, at the September 2014 NATO summit in Wales, managed to get a strong NATO consensus behind US policy to "degrade and destroy" ISIL, but the actual fighting fell outside NATO's mandate. It was a somewhat unusual case of the allies publishing a strong NATO statement against a threat without supporting collective action, under a NATO flag, to address it.

For the United States, ISIL represented a serious threat to the accomplishments of US forces and policies in Iraq. Some NATO allies, particularly the United Kingdom, shared that concern. Most NATO allies could join in seeing the bigger picture: ISIL not only represented a source of dramatic instability in the Middle East and North Africa but also a direct challenge to the values and interests on which membership in both NATO and the EU membership was founded. Moreover, ISIL spokesmen promised that, from their growing base of operations, they would carry their threat to those values and interests through terrorist attacks on the United States and Canada as well as on next-door Europe.

In some respects, the threats posed by Russia and ISIL converged in a somewhat unexpected manner, raising some difficult questions for the West. Russia deployed fighter bombers and troops to Syria to support the regime of

President Bashar al-Assad, which had been losing ground both to ISIL and a loose mix of other anti-regime forces. Syria had remained a key ally for Russia at the end of the Cold War, having been an important Middle Eastern ally for the Soviet Union since 1956 and providing access to a key naval base on the Mediterranean. Russia described its military support for Assad as intended to fight ISIL, but the missions of the deployed Russian forces made it clear that Russia was targeting Western-supported anti-Assad forces equally if not more than ISIL. The challenge for the United States and its allies was how to continue supporting "moderate" opponents of Assad and encourage Russia to train its guns on ISIL while not coming into accidental conflict with Russian forces.

When the Trump administration came to office in 2017, it went to work on the president's pledge to defeat ISIL, driving it out of all the territory it had occupied in the previous years. In the first month of the new administration, it issued a "Presidential Memorandum Plan to Defeat the Islamic State of Iraq and Syria."[9]

By mid-2019, ISIL's territorial control had been virtually eliminated by the US-led international coalition, formed under the leadership of US President Obama in 2014 and further enhanced by President Trump. But the goal held by its followers of continuing to challenge the West undoubtedly remained. The question became how the threat would present itself in the future, and whether Western nations and institutions would be prepared to counter it.

Terrorism

Terrorism, as a generic threat, played an important role in NATO's post-Cold War definitions of threats, particularly after the 9/11 attacks on the United States. Once again, the discussion came back to Western values and interests. Granted, "terrorism" can be in the eye of the beholder, just as a guerrilla fighter can be seen as a "freedom fighter" or a terrorist, depending on which side attracts one's sympathy. But in this case, terrorism is clearly a tactic being used to attack the ways and means of "the West." Western values were al-Qaeda's target when the group organized the 9/11 attacks. Terror became a tool used by ISIL in its attempts to destroy and disrupt Western society.

NATO took a direct part in responding to terrorist threats on the occasion of 9/11 (discussed in Chapter 7). Subsequently, allied cooperation continued, inside NATO committees, in cooperation with other organizations, and on a bilateral basis. When in 2016 the alliance created a new division for intelligence sharing, which would include intelligence on terrorism, Donald Trump claimed that it was all due to his initiative. However, the organizational changes had long been in the works and, as noted in Chapter 8, were not made in response to Trump's complaint.[10]

The Western response to terrorism has continued to include elements of both traditional military responses—to weaken the bases from which groups like ISIL and al-Qaeda mount their attacks—and internal security measures that are always trying to stay one step ahead of the terrorists. So long as ideologically or religiously based groups believe that their interests would best be served by undermining, or even destroying, the Western political and economic system, the West will face the challenge of counteracting those goals.

The Afghan Taliban

With the departure of most US and NATO forces, the government of Afghanistan was left largely to its own devices to try to maintain, or in some cases, establish, control of the country. The residual threat to the West was that the Afghan authorities might not be able to do so. In this case, not only would the lives and monies expended there by the United States and its coalition partners be wasted, but new threats could emerge if the Taliban provided refuge and bases to ISIL, al-Qaeda, or other anti-Western groups. One of the missions of the remaining US forces in Afghanistan was to conduct anti-terrorist operations, as well as to help train Afghan National Army forces. To the extent that the government of Afghanistan was not able to control its territory, the risk grew that US and NATO forces there would be insufficient for the tasks assigned, or that the United States and its allies would abandon the mission completely. This could produce a growing threat to Western interests in this region and more broadly.

The threats of nuclear weapons and ballistic missile proliferation

These were "generic" threats that presented themselves most immediately in the Middle Eastern region. NATO's response to these threat areas had been to support the Nuclear Non-Proliferation Regime as well as some modest steps by the United States to deploy an anti-missile defense system to Europe. The focus of this threat had for some time been on Iran. The potential for Iran to deploy strategic missile systems with nuclear warheads that could strike targets in Europe had been the primary rationale for NATO's plan to deploy a missile defense system. Russia, of course, looked at these plans as a threat to their offensive strategic strike capabilities, but NATO consistently argued that the planned system would do nothing to degrade Russia's weapons.[11]

The need for the system and financial support for it was temporarily diminished with negotiation of the Joint Comprehensive Plan of Action (JCPOA) that placed limits on Iran's nuclear program ensuring it remained aimed at peaceful purposes in exchange for lifting of Western sanctions. The future of the agreement was thrown into question when the Trump administration disavowed the accord, claiming that it did not limit Iran sufficiently to serve US interests.[12]

Some observers argued that Russia's nuclear threats aimed at European states already warranted NATO consideration of focusing missile defense systems on Russian capabilities as well as Iranian ones.[13] A shift by the allies toward focusing their anti-missile plans on Russian capabilities, however, would likely be opposed by many allies unless Russia took much more dramatic and threatening moves toward the West.

The Western charge that Russia violated the terms of the US-Soviet 1987 Intermediate-Range Nuclear Forces (INF) Treaty with deployment of a new missile system and the subsequent US announcement that it would leave the treaty opened an entirely new set of issues, including questions of whether a new missile competition would be the result and, if so, how divisive would shaping a response be for the NATO alliance.[14]

Cyber threats

Cyber threats fall into the same generic category as terrorism. The allies could face cyber attacks from almost any quarter, potentially disrupting communications, power grids, military and security systems, and banking systems. A targeted cyber attack could serve as the prelude to a military strike, or disrupt NATO's ability to react to one. After NATO-member Estonia—the alliance's most digitally dependent country—suffered a serious cyber attack in 2008, the alliance decided to establish a NATO Cooperative Cyber Defence Centre of Excellence in Tallinn. At the Wales Summit, the allies confirmed that cyber defense was part of the alliance's core task of collective defense, which, as noted in Chapter 8, included threats as well as attacks. In the future, NATO and the EU will have to be alert to defend against cyber attacks from Russian sources but also possibly from other quarters, including China and Middle Eastern terrorist organizations.

Information wars

While cyber warfare had become a collective defense concern for the alliance, ongoing information assaults from the alliance's leading challenger, Russia, posed more imminent, albeit political, threats.

Russian information warfare has been aimed at many targets. Some of the distortions and outright lies ("There are no Russian troops in Ukraine") were aimed at a domestic audience. While the Russian people apparently largely supported Putin's policies toward Ukraine, they, for the most part, seemed unaware of the fact that Russians were fighting and dying there.

But some of the disinformation campaigns, waged on social media as well as through more traditional outlets, were designed to influence audiences in the West. The primary targets included Russian-speaking populations in the Baltic States and elsewhere, as well as various pro-Moscow political forces around Europe. In addition to reporting inaccurately about events in Ukraine, the Russian propaganda machine played up the "humiliation" theme, which was intended to support the arguments of those in the West who believed NATO enlargement was to blame for the crisis, as well as to appeal to domestic Russian national pride.

The European Union in the spring of 2015 responded to the Russian campaign by deciding to mount a counter offensive of its own. The EU launched an Action Plan on Strategic Communications intended, according to Latvian Foreign Minister Edgars Rinkevics, to "help counter, in an improved manner, and more effectively, Russia's disinformation campaigns both in EU member states and neighboring countries."[15]

Ironically, acceleration of the Russian propaganda campaign came at a time when the ability of some traditional US information outlets that focused on Central and Eastern Europe were being cut back. Radio Free Europe, Radio Liberty, and the Voice of America had been key American "voices" directed at the Warsaw Pact countries during the Cold War, but had seen a decrease in funding as the United States sought, over several administrations, to develop more cooperative relations with Moscow. Russia's seizure of the Crimea and aggression against Ukraine may have reversed the trend, and these outlets saw some increased funding and growing audiences in and around Russia.[16]

NATO had for many years maintained a very active public affairs program, but the new threats from Russian disinformation posed challenges not seen since the end of the Cold War. Perhaps the most important messengers for the alliance were the Secretary General and the Supreme Allied Commander, Europe. Both top NATO officials made frequent public statements which were then very often spread by the press—and critiqued by the Kremlin.

The main strength of the West in dealing with Russian propaganda was that none of the official Western news outlets intentionally published deceptive information, but rather attempted to report facts while, at the same time, adding interpretations through a Western lens. It may also have been a key vulnerability, given Moscow's unabashed willingness to distort the truth. Given the fact that public and parliamentary opinion came into play in deciding Western responses to Russian policy, NATO, the EU, and member governments were required to counter Russian disinformation efforts with a constant flow of accurate, validated, and defensible information.

Before ISIL operational bases were virtually eliminated by the US-led coalition, ISIL also conducted very active information warfare against the West. The threat was different than that posed by Russia but was quite challenging in its own right. ISIL used information warfare to "advertise" its brutal killings as a terror tactic, intended to spread fear among populations that it sought to control, as well as those in the West that it simply hoped to disrupt.

Another aspect of ISIL information warfare was the extensive social media campaign to gain recruits among disaffected Muslims in Western countries. By 2015, the vast majority of these Western recruits, said to be in the thousands, had come from European countries, with less than 200 or so from the United States.[17] But in 2015 ISIL seemed increasingly to be seeking to develop assets in the United States and in Europe who would conduct "lone wolf" attacks in their home countries, rather than join the fighting in the Middle East. Because

ISIL aimed to undermine or destroy values and interests that were central to the political and economic systems of the United States and Europe, simple changes of Western policies would not be effective in countering this threat. The response therefore had to rely on trying to influence potential targets of ISIL propaganda with facts about ISIL's "real world" and with internationally coordinated police work that detected and prevented potential attacks and took potential terrorists out of circulation.

The Chinese challenge

At this point, the NATO allies have not agreed that China poses a threat to the alliance, although the spread of Chinese influence and power is now stirring debate about the question. The European allies have always been reluctant to bring consideration of Asian security issues formally under the NATO umbrella, even though the United States has historically urged them to regard Asian security challenges as potential threats to European security. The United States, as an Asian and European power, has usually found itself alone among NATO member states in dealing with Asian security challenges.

Now, however, Europeans increasingly recognize that Chinese influence is a growing economic, financial, political, and perhaps strategic factor in European affairs. Before Chinese President Xi Jinping visited several European countries early in 2019 to promote Beijing's Belt and Road Initiative,[18] polls suggested that he was facing significant European skepticism about his ability to provide international leadership. But, according to a Pew Research Poll, "lack of enthusiasm for Chinese leadership does not equate to concern about Beijing's power: A median of just 31% across the 10 European nations see China's power and influence as a major threat to their country, the lowest level of worry expressed across eight different threats tested."[19] Chinese support for European countries hard-hit by COVID-19 nonetheless won Beijing a significant public opinion boost in some European countries.[20]

There are, however, some Europeans who recognize the potential danger of an alliance between Russia and China that would provide a front against Western values and systems. One analyst has coined the term "Dragonbear" to capture the possible emergence of such an alliance that could eventually challenge the transatlantic community led by the United States and built around the EU and NATO. Velina Tchakarova argues, "The Dragonbear alliance is imminent due to mutual strategic interests, common strategic objectives as well as shared risks and threats perceptions."[21] Whether a transatlantic perception of a Chinese threat will eventually emerge remains an open question. Perhaps the first step in that direction was taken at the NATO London Summit in December 2019 when the leaders declared "We recognise that China's growing influence and international policies present both opportunities and challenges that we need to address together as an Alliance."[22]

Complex threat environment

What has been described in the paragraphs above constituted a complex and demanding threat environment.[23] It was one that targeted not just the "territory" of NATO and EU member states, but also their societal values, political systems, and economic interests. Also, the fact that environmental changes and the COVID-19 pandemic will pose serious threats to transatlantic security and well-being is not dealt with here. Even though such threats were recognized by NATO and were definitely on the EU agenda, the allies had not established the kind of comprehensive transatlantic cooperation on the non-military threats to security that may become increasingly important in the decades ahead.

Meanwhile, this set of threats was made even more difficult to manage by the fact that the Western community of nations—with NATO and EU at its institutional core—faced a difficult set of internal challenges. These were challenges to the values, well-being and political coherence of "the West," many of which could be managed but some of which could affect the West's ability to deal effectively with the external threats.

Internal challenges

For the purpose of this analysis, "internal challenges" are those with roots largely inside the West, even though such challenges, in some cases, interact importantly with external threats. Such challenges are handled only peripherally in official NATO and EU declarations, because they have much to do with internal affairs of the member states or relations among them. An inventory of some of those challenges and their implications follows.

Questions raised about American political leadership

The most significant internal challenge to the alliance, perhaps in its entire history, has been that posed by US President Donald Trump. But the questioning of US leadership did not begin with Trump.

As noted in Chapter 8, the Obama administration in 2012 decided that the United States needed to put increased emphasis and resources on US interests in East Asia. There was little objection among the European allies to the administration putting some special emphasis on China's growing power and the need for effective US relations with and presence in allied states in the region.

Some allies undoubtedly wondered whether the pivot/rebalancing was also a message to the European allies that they needed to get their act together. Did the administration believe that backing away from a leadership role in Europe would force the Europeans to fill the gap both in terms of leadership and resources, in the Middle East as well as in Europe? If so, this approach may have been based on an overly optimistic Obama administration view of the ability of the European Union to produce coherent and effective foreign and defense policies.

In these realms, Europe remained decisively a *Europe des états*, and the states still had too many differences among them to manage meaningful common policies on difficult security and defense issues. This new US approach came at a time of serious economic weakness in Europe, when there simply were neither political nor financial resources to support a confident European defense and security policy role. Additionally, threats in the Middle East and Europe were simultaneously taking dramatic turns for the worse.

Dysfunctional American political system

Related to the question of American leadership was the gridlock in the American domestic political system that seriously weakened the foundation on which American leadership rested. In fact, one of the most experienced and wise Washington hands, Leon Panetta, judged early in 2015 that dysfunction in Washington was the biggest threat to US security.[24] If the American political system is dysfunctional for the United States, it is also dysfunctional for the transatlantic alliance and the West.

The divide between President Obama and the Republican Party did not stop at the water's edge. The 2015 Munich Security Conference saw US Senate Republicans busily labeling Angela Merkel as an appeaser while senior US administration officials were trying to "lead from behind" the German chancellor (as some described the Obama administration's policy of letting allies take the lead, particularly during NATO's Libya mission).[25] Granted, the "water's edge" had been washed away by modern travel and communications, and politics were now global. But Washington's dysfunction certainly diminished US credibility, soft power, and leadership ability in NATO.

That erosion intensified with the election of the NATO-skeptic Donald Trump as president of the United States in 2016. The consequences of his election are discussed in detail in Chapter 8. The American trumpet for NATO had never been as uncertain in the history of the alliance as it became under Trump, and the uncertainty had a significant impact on the issues already facing the alliance—some of which had helped engender the Trump threat.[26]

Inadequate European defense spending and investment

As the history recorded in this volume demonstrates, the failure of the European allies to produce what Americans would consider reasonable contributions to the common defense has been a divisive influence on transatlantic relations from the very beginning. The Obama administration, particularly during the term in office of Robert Gates as its Secretary of Defense, sent strong warnings to the allies—documented earlier—that American patience was wearing thin. The Gates warnings came fully to life with Donald Trump.

Before Trump's assault on the alliance, the 2014 Wales Summit had put a clear focus on the need for quantitative and qualitative improvements in European defense spending but, sadly, as long-time NATO expert Larry Chalmer likes to observe, "rhetoric does not equal resources."[27] Calculations suggested that, during the economic crisis (roughly the period from 2008 to 2015), the downward path of European defense spending that began in 1990 had only accelerated. NATO data revealed that spending declined by close to 4 percent in 2014.[28]

Many promises were made in Wales, but failure to make progress would exacerbate burden-sharing tensions between the United States and Europe, and among European countries themselves.

In fact, the Wales commitments, given new urgency by the Trump message, did produce some steady increases in European defense efforts.[29] Whether they would be enough to satisfy Trump, or even more NATO-friendly US presidents in the future, remains an open question. The severe recession as a product of the 2020 COVID-19 pandemic could severely limit European defense spending for the foreseeable future.

European economic and political vulnerabilities

There is an intimate relationship between a struggling economy and ineffective political leadership. Economic growth not only increases prosperity and improves the population's well-being but also encourages optimism about the future and margins for creative and constructive political decisions. European economies were not only hit hard by the "great recession," but several EU states struggled to re-establish growth and reduce unemployment, which had skyrocketed in some EU members during the recession. As one who has observed the process of European integration from the 1970s on, it has always seemed clear to me that the process of developing European unity moved ahead more successfully when there were economic margins that supported investment in the future and stimulated political courage to move forward. Neither was a possibility in the period of 2008–2015.

As could have been predicted, Germany emerged from that recession most quickly and decisively, supporting the emergence of Chancellor Angela Merkel not only as the most influential voice in EU affairs but also in European political leadership more generally. Merkel found herself out in front on issues ranging from how to deal with Russia's belligerent Vladimir Putin, to seeking a solution to the Greek debt crisis. However, even Merkel had problems. She had to deal with influential fellow countrymen who had financial interests in accommodating Russia and with anti-American sentiment fed by spy scandals. Moreover, Merkel's Social Democratic partners were leaning toward a conciliatory approach to Moscow, making life even more difficult for the chancellor.

In spite of Merkel's leadership, Europe remained in an economically vulnerable position and with large questions about the future of the process of European integration. One of the looming issues was how the British departure from the EU would affect the union's future. The Greek debt crisis not only raised questions about whether Greece could remain in the 19-member Eurozone but about whether the Euro and the process of European integration could survive the disruption of the crisis over the long term.

While some American analysts and European protagonists would like to believe that "Europe" not only exists but will become more and more coherent as years go by, the evidence from the early years of the twenty-first century was that EU members had not yet shown the willingness to sacrifice sufficient national sovereignty to make a common currency work effectively, to say nothing of giving up control over defense and foreign policy to a central European authority. This remained the European reality in 2020. Its contours influenced assessments of the future of transatlantic relations and practical planning for that future.

Insufficient NATO–EU collaboration

One of the key sources of Western weakness was the inability of NATO and the EU to cooperate effectively with each other. From the early 2000s on, the NATO allies increasingly recognized that contemporary security challenges required "comprehensive approaches." As noted earlier in this volume, practical collaboration between NATO and the EU had been blocked particularly by one philosophical and one political factor.

The philosophical block came from the competing preferences for Eurocentric and Atlanticist approaches. This issue was not nearly as prominent as it was before France returned to NATO's military command structure and no longer served as a touchstone for French policy toward transatlantic relations, but it remained in the background and, to some extent, was fostered particularly by those who believed that cooperation in and with NATO could limit the autonomy of decision-making in the EU. Support for a more autonomous and united European Union grew even as prospects for such an outcome came into question.

The political block was a product of the continuing dispute between NATO members Greece and Turkey (not an EU member) over the status of Cyprus. Intransigence by Greece, Cyprus, and Turkey made it very difficult for the two organizations to address more than a few issues on which there could be joint action. The block to effective decision-making hindered efforts in Afghanistan and proved a very serious obstacle to cooperation in the Ukraine crisis. As one observer commented:

> The Ukraine crisis makes closer cooperation between NATO and the EU all the more necessary ... It is not only about improving the EU's security and the stabil-

ity of its Eastern neighbors. It is also about sharing increasingly scarce military and civilian capabilities at a time when the tools of hard and soft power are needed more than ever.[30]

By 2020, NATO/EU cooperation had improved, but much remained to be done. For continued progress, the allies needed to focus on the external threats to transatlantic security and values rather than on competing philosophies and organizational structures.

Internal European and transatlantic political challenges

Even before the issue of the Ukraine crisis in Russia's relations with the West, some questioned whether the main challenges to the West were outside or inside its member states. The deep economic recession and the accompanying increases in unemployment, particularly among young cohorts, weakened the political center in Europe and strengthened those parties advocating more radical approaches to European security.

In recent years, the connections between internal dissent and its external sources of support have been exposed. Russia's President Putin has mandated influence campaigns on social media and cyber attacks on Western infrastructure. His campaign has supported politicians on both sides of the Atlantic whose approach to transatlantic relations undermines the Western values on which the transatlantic alliance is based.

At the same time, radical Islamist terrorists have sought to achieve virtually the same objectives pursued by Moscow. Their goal has been to weaken Western societies and the faith of their citizens in Western values, systems, and leadership.

The Islamic State, through its aggressions in the Middle East and North Africa and terrorist attacks on Western targets, produced a flow of refugees seeking safety and a better future in Europe. This crisis destabilized the West and disrupted European unity, thus advancing some of the Islamic State's objectives.

There is little disagreement in the West about the need for effective counter-terrorist capabilities, across the range of threats. But the refugee challenge has produced no such consensus. Profound divisions have plagued European unity. Southern European states have had to bear the initial burdens of dealing with the refugees, while many northern European states have tried to avoid having to do so.

But there is another, more ideological, division. That division is between those in Europe and in the United States who believe that humanitarian instincts should govern responses to the refugee problem and those who believe that security and economic factors should be the key considerations. In any case, the disruptive Russian and terrorist-produced challenges provided fertile ground on which radical right populist politicians and parties have thrived.

These politicians have used the natural fear stirred by the external intrusions as a political tool to convince populations that they should be willing to accept "strong" leadership and limits on their individual and collective freedoms—the very freedoms that all NATO member states are committed to defend.

Very few transatlantic nations have escaped the surge in what has been called the "populist radical right."[31] This surge has given new life to a variety of right-wing political parties or candidates playing on otherwise legitimate popular fears and concerns, advocating simplistic, sloganeering political approaches that challenge the assumptions of established Western liberal democracy. Such politicians and parties have thrown around their political weight in several countries, exercising power in some, including the United States, Hungary, Poland, Switzerland, and Turkey.

These radical right populists share some common traits. In general, they:

- exacerbate fears of immigrants;
- promise "strong" leadership, undermining institutions and free press, and the rule of law;
- oppose or question both NATO and the EU;
- make cynical appeals to religion;
- admire Russian President Putin's leadership style.

These radical right "populist" politicians are using Western democratic systems and practices to try to turn them in illiberal directions. Today, many countries on both sides of the Atlantic are facing decisions about what kind of democracy they want. Is it liberal democracy, based on the North Atlantic Treaty's value statement and the values articulated by the European Union? Or is it what has been called "electoral democracy," and which one European leader proudly calls "illiberal democracy"? This seems to mean that elections are held, but the rule of law and individual liberties, like freedom of speech and the press, are limited. Decisions by NATO member states, including the United States, about which path to choose will have at least as much impact on the viability of the alliance as will decisions regarding levels of defense spending.

Dealing with these internal European political challenges was complicated by developments in the transatlantic relationship. Most importantly, the unauthorized release of secret US intelligence documents in 2015 revealing that the US National Security Agency had been spying on the German and other European governments, including Chancellor Merkel's private telephone conversations, outraged many Europeans and increased their level of distrust of the United States. The appreciation for the American role in World War II and even in the much more recent reunification of Germany— critically facilitated by American diplomacy—had faded. Differences over the Iraq war remained viral in some quarters, and in the former East Germany, as well as in some former Warsaw Pact countries, a certain romantic memory of the "predictable" days of communist control lingered.

With revelations of the National Security Agency spying, the well-respected Pew Surveys of public opinion reflected drops in favorable German opinion of the United States and confidence in President Obama—whose ratings had been sky-high prior to the leaked revelations.[32] At a critical time in transatlantic relations, the revelations that the United States had been conducting a variety of intelligence collection efforts against one of its closest allies—and that it had been caught—were particularly damaging. In any case, it was clear that the interaction between external threats and internal political dissonance posed a serious challenge to the West.

Once Donald Trump assumed the presidency in the United States, the spying scandal tended to disappear into the background as new sources of distrust emerged. Still, the overall impact has been to undermine positive impressions of the United States not only in Germany but all over Europe.

Western values and interests

Perhaps the future of the West comes down to a very fundamental choice: should the United States and its European partners acquiesce in Russia's geopolitical demands for a buffer zone between Putin's kleptocracy and the democratic West, as Donald Trump seemed inclined to do, or should they assert, with actions as well as words, the liberal values that they hoped would shape post-Cold War Europe? And what should the United States and its allies do about the threat posed by ISIL and other radical groups that are determined to attack the foundations of Western values and interests when there is little taste in Europe or the United States for participation in more Middle Eastern wars?

President Putin made it very clear: he does not accept the Western model that he says the United States, NATO, and the European Union tried to impose on Europe at a time of Russian weakness. He first made Georgia a battleground for this confrontation. He won. He then made the Crimea a battleground. He won there too. Some have said he has been winning in his war against a free and sovereign Ukraine. Will Belarus be his next target? Does the West care? If it does not, it raises the question of what the West stands for or believes in. It would seem that the transatlantic allies and their leading institutions—NATO and the EU—now must successfully defend the values and interests they claim to hold dear while not increasing the chances of a new and prolonged Cold War, or even a hot one.

In conclusion, while the external threats to the West are real—far more than "risks and challenges"—internal weaknesses could block Western democracies from working together to deal with them. If transatlantic solidarity fails, then the future of the West would be in doubt. The transatlantic community is more than ever dependent on the right choices being made on both sides of the Atlantic. The United States has not recently been inclined to ride in on its white horse to rescue the old continent. Perhaps the best answer will be a true rededication to transatlantic cooperation, stimulated by a sense of shared values and interests, to bring out the best on both sides of the Atlantic. But that may have to await new leadership in the United States.

Questions for discussion

1. Russia's ability to leverage its control of oil and gas supplies has given Putin an advantage with regard to the conflict in Ukraine. Do you think this ability to use the energy "weapon" threatens Europe with a new form of imperialism that should be countered by the United States and its European allies?
2. How much of the turmoil that arose in the Middle East was a direct result of US and European intervention? How much of the terrorism, revolution, and chaos could have and would have materialized without any external ventures from NATO countries?
3. Is friction between NATO and the EU inevitable and insurmountable, or are the stumbles experienced so far just expected bumps in the road to a more collaborative relationship?
4. From your reading in this chapter, which external threats and internal challenges have proven to be more immediate and menacing to the stability of the alliance?
5. What will be required for US–European relations to recover from the traumatic blows delivered by President Trump?

Notes

1   "The Alliance's New Strategic Concept," North Atlantic Treaty Organization, November 8, 1991. www.nato.int/cps/en/natolive/official_texts_23847.htm [accessed July 2, 2015].
2   "The Alliance's Strategic Concept," North Atlantic Treaty Organization, April 24, 1999. www.nato.int/cps/en/natolive/official_texts_27433.htm [accessed July 2, 2015].
3   "Wales Summit Declaration," North Atlantic Treaty Organization, September 5, 2014. www.nato.int/cps/en/natohq/official_texts_112964.htm [accessed July 2, 2015].
4   Brussels Summit Declaration, North Atlantic Treaty Organization, July 11, 2018. www.nato.int/cps/en/natohq/official_texts_156624.htm#68 [accessed July 14, 2019].
5   See an interesting analysis by Andrew S. Bowen, "Russia's Deceptively Weak Military," *The National Interest*, June 7, 2015. http://nationalinterest.org/feature/russias-deceptively-weak-military-13059 [accessed July 5, 2015].
6   Pavel K. Baev, "Apocalypse a Bit Later: The Meaning of Putin's Nuclear Threats," Brookings.edu, April 1, 2015. www.brookings.edu/blogs/order-from-chaos/posts/2015/04/01-putin-nuclear-threats-meaning [accessed July 5, 2015].

7   William Courtney, David Sedney, Kenneth Yalowitz, and Stephen Young, "How Durable is the China–Russia 'Friendship?'" *Reuters*, May 13, 2015. http://blogs. reuters.com/great-debate/2015/05/12/how-durable-are-china-russia-relations/ [accessed July 13, 2015].

8   "Special Meeting of the European Council, 23 April 2015—Statement," European Council Press Release, April 23, 2015. www.consilium.europa.eu/en/press/ pressreleases/2015/04/23-special-euco-statement/ [accessed July 6, 2015].

9   The White House, "Presidential Memorandum Plan to Defeat the Islamic State of Iraq and Syria," January 28, 2017. www.whitehouse.gov/presidential-actions/ presidential-memorandum-plan-defeat-islamic-state-iraq-syria/ [accessed July 14, 2019].

10 Louis Jacobson, "Donald Trump Wrong Again about NATO Increasing Terrorism Efforts 'Largely' Because of Him," *Politifact*, September 27, 2016. www.politi- fact.com/truth-o-meter/statements/2016/sep/27/donald-trump/donald-trump- wrong-again-about-nato-increasing-ter/ [accessed July 16, 2019].

11 Paul Sonne, "Russia Threatens NATO Over Missile Shield," *The Wall Street Journal*, April 16, 2015. www.wsj.com/articles/russia-threatens-nato-over-mis- sileshield-1429185058 [accessed July 6, 2015].

12 Paul K. Kerr and Kenneth Katzman, "Iran Nuclear Agreement and U.S. Exit," CRS Report R43333, July 20, 2018. https://fas.org/sgp/crs/nuke/R43333.pdf [accessed July 16, 2019].

13 Ian Armstrong, "The Lagging Architecture of NATO Missile Defense," *International Policy Digest*, July 6, 2015. www.internationalpolicydigest.org/2015/07/06/ thelagging-architecture-of-nato-missile-defense/ [accessed July 6, 2015].

14 Tom Nichols, "Mourning the INF Treaty: The United States Is Not Better for Withdrawing," *Foreign Affairs*, March 4, 2019. www.foreignaffairs.com/arti- cles/2019-03-04/mourning-inf-treaty [accessed July 16, 2019].

15 "Latvia's MFA: Action Plan on Strategic Communication Will Help Counter Russia's Disinformation Campaigns," *The Baltic Course*, June 28, 2015.

16 Jan Flemr, "Cold War Veteran Radio Free Europe is Back On Frontline Over Ukraine," AFP, October 2, 2014. www.businessinsider.com/afp-radio-free-europe- back-on-frontline-over-ukraine-2014-10 [accessed July 7, 2015].

17 Kevin Johnson, "ISIL's Sophisticated Recruiting Campaign Poses Persistent Threat in U.S.," *USA Today*, April 26, 2015. www.usatoday.com/story/news/ nation/2015/04/26/foreign-fighters-isil-fbi/26202741/ [accessed July 7, 2015].

18 Andrew Chatzky and James McBride, "China's Massive Belt and Road Initiative," Council on Foreign Relations, May 21, 2019. www.cfr.org/backgrounder/chinas- massive-belt-and-road-initiative [accessed July 26, 2019].

19 Kat Devlin and Christine Huang, "Few Europeans Confident in Xi as He Seeks to Extend Chinese Economic Influence in the Region," Pew Research Center, March 22, 2019. www.pewresearch.org/fact-tank/2019/03/22/few-europeans- confident-in-xi-as-he-seeks-to-extend-chinese-economic-influence-in-the-region/ [accessed July 19, 2019].

20 Francesco Bechis, "Polls Show Concerning Effect of Chinese Coronavirus Charm Offensive in Italy," Atlantic Council of the United States, April 17, 2020. https:// atlanticcouncil.org/blogs/new-atlanticist/polls-show-concerning-effect-of-chi- nese-coronavirus-charm-offensive-in-italy/ [accessed April 19, 2020].

21 Velina Tchakarova, "The Russia, China Alliance: What Does 'The Dragonbear' Aim to Achieve in Global Affairs?" Medium Corporation, November 24, 2016. https://medium.com/@vtchakarova/the-russia-china-alliance-what-does-the-dragonbear-aim-to-achieve-in-global-affairs-e09b1add1c4a [accessed July 19, 2019].

22 London Summit Declaration, North Atlantic Treaty Organization, December 4, 2019. www.nato.int/cps/en/natohq/official_texts_171584.htm [accessed April 19, 2020].

23 The threat environment, of course, could be described as including many other factors, including global warming, environmental degradation, pandemics, population growth, food and water shortages, extreme poverty, and so on. While these are critically important global issues, they generally fall outside the scope of this analysis of "defense of the West."

24 Nick Gass, "Leon Panetta Blasts 'Total Dysfunction in Washington'," *politico. com*, February 15, 2015. www.politico.com/story/2015/02/leon-panetta-blasts-totaldysfunction-in-washington-115217.html [accessed July 13, 2015].

25 Stephen Brown and Noah Barkin, "Merkel Defends Ukraine Arms Stance in Face of U.S. Criticism," *Reuters*, February 8, 2015. http://uk.reuters.com/article/2015/02/08/uk-ukraine-crisis-idUKKBN0LA13N20150208 [accessed July 13, 2015].

26 Borrowing here the biblical warning deployed frequently to call for clear and forceful leadership. One of the best-known references came from General Maxwell D. Taylor in his 1960 book critiquing US military strategy and efforts during the Cold War: Maxwell D. Taylor, *The Uncertain Trumpet* (New York: Harper & Row, 1960).

27 2015 remarks to an audience at the US National Defense University, as related by Chalmer to the author.

28 Andrew Chuter, "NATO Defense Spending Continues to Decline," *Defense News*, June 23, 2015. www.defensenews.com/story/defense/policy-budget/budget/2015/06/23/nato-reports-alliance-members-defense-spending-decline/29153965/ [accessed July 8, 2015].

29 See, for example, Jonathan Stearns, "U.S. Allies in Europe to Boost Defense Spending for Fourth Year," *Bloomberg.com*, June 25, 2019. hwww.bloomberg.com/news/articles/2019-06-25/u-s-allies-in-europe-to-boost-defense-spending-for-fourth-year [accessed July 18, 2019]. See also NATO's official 2019 statement on allied defense spending: NATO, "Defense Expenditures of NATO Countries (2012–2019)," COMMUNIQUE R/CP(2019)069, June 25, 2019. www.nato.int/nato_static_fl2014/assets/pdf/pdf_2019_06/20190625_PR2019-069-EN.pdf [accessed July 18, 2019].

30 Judy Dempsey, "Time to End the EU–NATO Standoff," Carnegie Europe, December 8, 2014. http://carnegieeurope.eu/strategiceurope/?fa=57423 [accessed July 8, 2015].

31 Cas Mudde, *Populist Radical Right Parties in Europe* (Cambridge: Cambridge University Press, 2007).

32 "Global Indicators Database, Germany, Opinion of the United States," June 2015. www.pewglobal.org/database/indicator/1/country/81/ [accessed July 10, 2015].

10

Can the West survive?

Transatlantic alliance at the heart of the West

The history of the transatlantic alliance, as reflected in these pages, includes many crises. Some, at the time, seemed to threaten the future of the transatlantic bargain that shapes the subtext of this volume. And yet, every time the clock struck midnight at the culmination of each crisis, the allies decided that cooperation in a transatlantic framework remained in their best interests.[1] No ally has left NATO. Until the British decided to leave the European Union, no member state had concluded its interests would be better served on the outside. Over the past seven decades, many countries have aspired to membership in one or both organizations, and most who have met the membership criteria have been admitted.

Of course, the transatlantic alliance does not solely constitute "the West." When the term is defined broadly, it certainly includes Eastern democracies such as Japan, South Korea, Australia, and New Zealand. The role of the United States as a global power provides linkage between the two regions, as well as multilateral security links including, importantly, the "Five Eyes" cooperative intelligence arrangement in which the United States, the United Kingdom, Canada, Australia, and New Zealand continue to share intelligence on global security concerns.

Ultimately, however, the members of NATO and the European Union represent the heart of the West, and thus the well-being of the transatlantic alliance is key to the survival of the West. Moreover, not all members of this core group have always met the high standards set in the North Atlantic Treaty and the several treaties that comprise the EU's constitution. Without the crucial element of American leadership to keep the transatlantic heart pumping, what we have known as "the West" would not exist.

The current crisis in the alliance did not start with Donald Trump, even though he certainly brought it to a head and made its potential consequences even more ominous. From an historical point of view, the fundamental crisis goes back to NATO's founding. The distribution of costs and benefits of the alliance has always been an issue. Because popular support for leaders of democratic states depends on the ability to deliver the level of security demanded by their constituents and at a price deemed reasonable by the voters, each member of the alliance tries to attain the level of security desired by citizens at the lowest possible cost. The value placed on defense and willingness to spend varies between countries, and, consequently, the alliance will be perpetually plagued by a "burden-sharing" problem that requires constant negotiations and adjustments of the burdens to find a balance of costs and benefits with which all the allies can live.

Burden-sharing is an issue among all the allies, but there is an especially dramatic push and pull between the United States and its allies. It is no accident that the first version of this book, written in the early 1980s, argued the case for rebalancing US and European NATO roles in a "*new* transatlantic bargain"—a term and concept that has been generously borrowed by others over the last three decades.[2]

If the fate of the West rests with its transatlantic core, liberal democrats should be very concerned about the future possibilities for the alliance. It is useful to recall that continuity, inertia, and resistance to change are powerful forces. Democracies, built on free, fair elections (the political requirement for consensus-building and adherence to process—usually referred to as the rule of law) can be slow to adopt and implement change. This process can be frustrating but occasionally is a blessing in disguise. If a political system—like the democratic ones of the United States and its European allies—is built on a solid constitutional foundation, major changes need to be considered seriously and tested before public opinion. The same should be true of alliances among democratic states.

That said, democracies that do not deal effectively with the concerns of the populace are vulnerable to pressure to give way to populist appeals and more radical change. As this volume has discussed, such pressures have troubled most of the transatlantic allies in recent years. Those pressures have been aided and abetted by politicians seeking to build their power through playing on popular fears and making promises of strong leadership to respond to those fears. At the same time, states with undemocratic political systems are increasingly taking advantage of the openness of liberal democratic systems, freedom of the press, and social media to undermine the democratic systems they see as threats to their more centralized and controlling systems of government.

Transatlantic futures

Below, I describe three general frameworks of potential futures for the transatlantic alliance. Several variables obviously come into play in such an exercise. I have already mentioned the importance of inertia and resistance to change.

These realities buy some time for decision-making, but that purchase is not necessarily a long-term guarantee.

In the case of the transatlantic alliance, assessment of the wide range of threats to the members of the EU and NATO is a good place to start, as the most primal instinct of both man and state is survival. The combination of external and internal threats surveyed in this volume will not likely disappear in the near term and can be assumed to present continuing challenges to the survival of both liberal democracy and the transatlantic alliance. The relative balance among these threats will continue to be a source of debate among experts, politicians, and citizens alike. The outcome of those discussions will influence how effectively the transatlantic allies respond to the threats.

The second level of assumptions concerns responses. The goal of the debates about threats presumably is to produce ways and means of protecting individual political systems, states, and the alliance against those threats. The availability of resources comes into play in this discussion. This part of the equation involves budget debates and resource allocations that reflect the popular perception of threats and societal needs or, at least, of the interests that have the greatest influence over such decisions. In all members of the transatlantic alliance, there is a tension between spending on defense to deal with military threats and spending on domestic needs to affect the well-being and sustainability of government and society. The decisions reached in each member state have direct and indirect effects on the alliance, which is why the burden-sharing debate is the most divisive issue among the allies and particularly between the strongest alliance member and its less-powerful but necessary partners.

This analysis therefore assumes that, despite inertia, the alliance is not necessarily locked into any particular future and allied governments will, in a certain range, have choices that affect the alliance's future. The allies will likely continue to seek to protect themselves against external and internal threats, and such decisions as they reach will be of major importance to how they individually allocate their resources. They will be required to find an acceptable balance of risks and responsibilities among them to ensure the alliance's continuation.

Against this backdrop, let's postulate for the sake of discussion three broad possibilities for the transatlantic alliance that the allies could imagine or aspire to over the next decade. The basic assumption of this exercise is that a healthy, functioning transatlantic relationship is a "good thing." For those who start from another assumption, the answers would undoubtedly be different. All three assume relative continuity in the threat environment: Russia still poses political and military challenges while its economy continues to weaken. The threat of terrorist attacks persists and concerns about Chinese power mix with opportunistic cooperative deals with this emerging Asian superpower. It is now clear that the UK is leaving the EU, but the consequences remain very dependent on how the departure is negotiated and managed. That said, these three broad scenarios present a range of perspectives on the future:

1. substantial continuity;
2. radical positive change;
3. radical negative change.

Substantial continuity

In this potential future, very little changes the trend lines that have been laid down by history. The United States remains committed to participate in the defense of Europe, deploy substantial numbers of troops, and retain military leadership of NATO with a senior American general serving as NATO's Supreme Allied Commander. Post-Trump administrations try to repair damage done to US leadership of the alliance without abandoning US burden-sharing concerns. All current allies remain in the alliance, despite some wavering (Turkey) and others experimenting with forms of democracy that do not conform to the values specified or implied in the North Atlantic Treaty. With the United Kingdom having abandoned its EU membership, the EU continues with some successes and some failures in attempts to give the Union a more substantial integrated military capability. The UK makes some cooperative military arrangements with its former EU partners while seeking a continued "special relationship," including intelligence sharing, with the United States. In this potential future, several allies spend around 2 percent of GDP on defense by 2024 as was agreed at the 2014 Wales summit, while others fall short.

Radical positive change

In this future, the goal of a more balanced transatlantic relationship comes more clearly into view. The United States remains committed to the alliance while supporting European efforts progressively to take on more responsibilities and burdens in the alliance. The members of the EU make substantial advances in coordinating and even integrating their defense establishments. A true European army under the control of a politically united Europe remains out of reach, but all EU members increasingly sacrifice bits of their national control of forces in a variety of pragmatic cooperative arrangements. The UK, despite its departure from the EU, commits to thorough defense cooperation with EU members, while remaining fully committed to NATO. Increased European spending on defense is accompanied by the revitalization of a European defense industry, with multinational firms and co-production arrangements setting up a healthy competition across the Atlantic whose sharp edges are moderated by stronger transatlantic defense industrial cooperation as well. The stronger European contribution to defense is acknowledged with alternating European and American Supreme Allied Commanders of NATO as a transition to a possible future in which Europeans routinely hold this post. The role of Secretary General—the political leader of the alliance—also alternates between prominent European and North American political leaders.

Radical negative change

This much darker future would see the United States essentially abandoning its transatlantic commitments and leadership roles while its European allies fall into disputes about how to maintain their security and provide new leadership. Such a scenario could be initiated by the reelection of Donald Trump to another four-year term as American president. In this hypothetical scenario, he continues the process of abandoning US international leadership in his second term, including in NATO, and decides to remove all US forces from Europe. Trump announces that he and Vladimir Putin have agreed that such a move would promote peace and security in Europe. In response, the European allies discuss seeking creating strong, integrated European defense structures to replace the transatlantic NATO one but find it too challenging politically and financially. Even the projection[3] made in 2019 by the International Institute for Strategic Studies that overwhelming financial commitments would be required of EU members to create a defense system as capable as that of NATO on their own turns out to be overly optimistic. Several EU countries suggest that the EU should follow the US lead and sign a peaceful relations accord with Russia in which both sides pledge to take no aggressive actions against the interests of the other. Even though some commentators immediately label this "the 21st century Munich," most European governments decide they have little choice. In addition, this move toward accommodation with Russia strengthens illiberal pro-Moscow parties throughout Europe and produces several national administrations that lean more toward fascist forms of governance than liberal democracy.

Variants

There are, of course, endless variants on the three scenarios. The continuity option could produce no forward movement and leave the alliance essentially where it was in 2020. Or, it could move more rapidly toward more radical positive change. The radical positive change scenario could, despite this analyst's skepticism, move rapidly toward a united Europe. Ironically, the same could happen in the case of American abandonment, although I doubt it. There are all kinds of dark scenarios that could be added to the negative variant. In some ways, it seems the positive possibilities are severely limited and the negative ones more open-ended.

What can history tell us about the future?

In theory, we pay attention to history in the hopes that it will help guide us to the future. George Santayana's wise saying, "Those who cannot remember the past are condemned to repeat it," is popular for a good reason. We do need to learn from history, even if it doesn't predictably repeat itself. And, as Timothy Sayle has remarked in an excellent new history of NATO's Cold War history, "If history is not repeating itself, do the policy papers and memorandums of conversation of post-Cold War NATO officials at least rhyme with the archival record?"[4]

In the case of transatlantic relations, two global conflicts in the last century led democratic leaders at the end of World War II to agree on some major international steps to try to avoid another repeat. The major creation was the United Nations, which was established with appreciation for the fact that the international structure attempted after World War I—the League of Nations—failed miserably, in part because the United States decided not to join. After World War II, as the United States emerged at the preeminent global power, it was clear that, to have any chance of succeeding, the support and leadership of the United States would be required.

At the same time that the United Nations was establishing itself as the international organization where states would attempt to manage a system of collective security, preventing war among its members, European democracies decided that their future security required some additional protection, given the European origins of both world wars. Those countries decided to develop regional cooperation to move past the conflicts that had devastated the continent and to build a system of political and economic cooperation. The result was the Western European Union to manage security relations and, subsequently, what we now know as the European Union, to promote all aspects of cooperation among European democracies. Wise leaders in the post-war American government recognized that US interests would best be served by helping the Europeans recover from the war and build economic cooperation among them. This recognition inspired the Marshall Plan of economic assistance that has since been recognized as the most generous and creative self-interested program that a victorious nation has ever mounted for devastated allies and enemies alike.

On the security side, however, the United States required urging from the Europeans to join them in providing for the common defense of the transatlantic area. The countries that the United States had joined to defeat Hitler's Germany were not confident that they could establish a stable internal European system and a defense against an expansionist Soviet Union on their own. They also did not believe that the United Nations, with the Soviet Union as one of its most powerful members, would suffice to meet their security requirements. They convinced the United States that it should, in its own interest, join in a mutual defense pact based on shared values and interests. The result was NATO.

The fact that this set of creative decisions produced systems of security and cooperation among the transatlantic democracies for over 70 years should not be forgotten—as Santayana's warning suggests. With all its imperfections and sources of disagreements, this system that still is supported institutionally primarily by NATO and the European Union makes its own case for preservation. Those who argue for major changes in the arrangement still bear the burden of proving that they have a better idea.

Disruptive forces

That said, while the seven-decade history is replete with examples of crises that resolved into evolutionary change and a substantial degree of continuity, recent years have seen a combination of disruptive forces that arguably have unsettled the transatlantic relationship and its institutions more than at any previous point in its history. The confluence of external and internal challenges and threat discussed in the previous chapter has produced serious doubt about the future of transatlantic relations. The external threat posed once by communist ideology and the associated power of the Soviet Union, after having seemingly disappeared at the end of the Cold War, has been succeeded by one from a dissatisfied and revisionist authoritarian Russian regime. The Russian threat to the West has been joined by one rooted in radical Islamist forces that are committed to undermining the West's perceived influence over their lives. Now, China is emerging as a new challenge: perhaps not yet a traditional threat but a growing power that is throwing its weight around—and not just in Asia. And, the explosive Middle East, including differences around relations with Iran, pose continuing threats.

At the same time, internal forces are disrupting usual patterns of politics and undermining traditional assumptions about democracy and transatlantic relationships. The radical right populist surge on both sides of the Atlantic has raised fundamental questions about the presumed preference of NATO and EU members for liberal democracy. That surge in part lent support to some very traditional British desires to keep UK sovereignty from being lost in the European unity movement, producing the Brexit disaster that is leading the UK out of the EU and perhaps even dividing the United Kingdom between those bits that like being in Europe and those that don't.

Finally, the most disruptive force of all has been the American presidency of Donald J. Trump. Trump refused to accept virtually all the political and strategic assumptions on which transatlantic political, economic, financial, and security relations have been based for 70 years. And, given the transatlantic alliance's heavy reliance on American leadership and involvement, Trump's lack of commitment has placed huge question marks over the West's future.

The future?

So, will history return to somewhat more reliable and familiar patterns, as suggested in the continuity model outlined above, or will the forces of disruption steer the transatlantic democracies in very different and potentially dangerous directions? The West is still composed, by definition, of democracies, and thus the people and governments of the member nations, especially the most powerful ones, will determine its direction. The ability of the people to decide their future is a basic and great quality shared by the democratic governments that comprise the transatlantic community. However, there remains the risk that the people may make choices that will not serve their or their descendants' interests well. The current collision between history and disruptive forces of change has posed a huge challenge to the United States, Canada, and their European allies. Future histories of the next decade of transatlantic relations will record the people's ultimate decisions and the success or failure of the attempts to manage the crisis.

Questions for discussion:

1. How would you define "the West?" How important do you think the transatlantic alliance is to the future of the West?
2. Why should the members of NATO want to keep the alliance alive and relevant? What role do values play in this equation?
3. How do external threats unite Western nations? How do such threats divide them?
4. How important is it for the NATO and EU member states to sustain political systems that support democracy, individual liberty, human rights, and the rule of law? How can failures to preserve liberal democratic values affect national security?
5. This chapter presents three possible scenarios for the next decade in transatlantic relations. Which one do you find most likely and why?
6. Will the factors of continuity in the history of transatlantic relations return to dominance in the next decade or will the disruptions of illiberal politics, Brexit, and Trump's presidency fundamentally alter basic assumptions of transatlantic relations and the West?

Notes

1   See, for example, Wallace J. Thies, *Why NATO Endures* (New York: Cambridge University Press, 2009), 207.
2   Stanley R. Sloan, *NATO's Future: Toward a New Transatlantic Bargain* (Washington, D.C.: National Defense University Press, 1985). I acknowledged in that work that the term "transatlantic bargain" had originated in Harlan Cleveland's *NATO: The Transatlantic Bargain* (New York: Harper & Row, 1970).
3   Douglas Barrie, Ben Barry, Dr Lucie Béraud-Sudreau, Henry Boyd, Nick Childs, and Dr Bastian Giegerich, "Defending Europe: Scenario-Based Capability Requirements for NATO's European Members," International Institute for Strategic Studies, April 2019.
4   Timothy Andrews Sayle, *Enduring Alliance: A History of NATO and the Postwar Global Order* (Ithaca: Cornell University Press, 2019), 245.

Appendix 1

The North Atlantic Treaty: Washington D.C.—April 4, 1949

The Parties to this Treaty reaffirm their faith in the purposes and principles of the Charter of the United Nations and their desire to live in peace with all peoples and all governments.

They are determined to safeguard the freedom, common heritage and civilisation of their peoples, founded on the principles of democracy, individual liberty and the rule of law. They seek to promote stability and well-being in the North Atlantic area.

They are resolved to unite their efforts for collective defence and for the preservation of peace and security. They therefore agree to this North Atlantic Treaty:

Article 1

The Parties undertake, as set forth in the Charter of the United Nations, to settle any international dispute in which they may be involved by peaceful means in such a manner that international peace and security and justice are not endangered, and to refrain in their international relations from the threat or use of force in any manner inconsistent with the purposes of the United Nations.

Article 2

The Parties will contribute toward the further development of peaceful and friendly international relations by strengthening their free institutions, by bringing about a better understanding of the principles upon which these institutions are founded, and by promoting conditions of stability and well-being. They will seek to eliminate conflict in their international economic policies and will encourage economic collaboration between any or all of them.

Article 3

In order more effectively to achieve the objectives of this Treaty, the Parties, separately and jointly, by means of continuous and effective self-help and mutual aid, will maintain and develop their individual and collective capacity to resist armed attack.

Article 4

The Parties will consult together whenever, in the opinion of any of them, the territorial integrity, political independence or security of any of the Parties is threatened.

Article 5

The Parties agree that an armed attack against one or more of them in Europe or North America shall be considered an attack against them all and consequently they agree that, if such an armed attack occurs, each of them, in exercise of the right of individual or collective self-defence recognised by Article 51 of the Charter of the United Nations, will assist the Party or Parties so attacked by taking forthwith, individually and in concert with the other Parties, such action as it deems necessary, including the use of armed force, to restore and maintain the security of the North Atlantic area.

Any such armed attack and all measures taken as a result thereof shall immediately be reported to the Security Council. Such measures shall be terminated when the Security Council has taken the measures necessary to restore and maintain international peace and security.

Article 6[1]

For the purpose of Article 5, an armed attack on one or more of the Parties is deemed to include an armed attack:

- on the territory of any of the Parties in Europe or North America, on the Algerian Departments of France,[2] on the territory of or on the Islands under the jurisdiction of any of the Parties in the North Atlantic area north of the Tropic of Cancer;
- on the forces, vessels, or aircraft of any of the Parties, when in or over these territories or any other area in Europe in which occupation forces of any of the Parties were stationed on the date when the Treaty entered into force or the Mediterranean Sea or the North Atlantic area north of the Tropic of Cancer.

Article 7

This Treaty does not affect, and shall not be interpreted as affecting in any way the rights and obligations under the Charter of the Parties which are members of the United Nations, or the primary responsibility of the Security Council for the maintenance of international peace and security.

Article 8

Each Party declares that none of the international engagements now in force between it and any other of the Parties or any third State is in conflict with the provisions of this Treaty, and undertakes not to enter into any international engagement in conflict with this Treaty.

Article 9

The Parties hereby establish a Council, on which each of them shall be represented, to consider matters concerning the implementation of this Treaty. The Council shall be so organised as to be able to meet promptly at any time. The Council shall set up such subsidiary bodies as may be necessary; in particular it shall establish immediately a defence committee which shall recommend measures for the implementation of Articles 3 and 5.

Article 10

The Parties may, by unanimous agreement, invite any other European State in a position to further the principles of this Treaty and to contribute to the security of the North Atlantic area to accede to this Treaty. Any State so invited may become a Party to the Treaty by depositing its instrument of accession with the government of the United States of America. The government of the United States of America will inform each of the Parties of the deposit of each such instrument of accession.

Article 11

This Treaty shall be ratified and its provisions carried out by the Parties in accordance with their respective constitutional processes. The instruments of ratification shall be deposited as soon as possible with the Government of the United States of America, which will notify all the other signatories of each deposit. The Treaty shall enter into force between the States which have ratified it as soon as the ratifications of the majority of the signatories, including the ratifications of Belgium, Canada, France, Luxembourg, the Netherlands, the United Kingdom and the United States, have been deposited and shall come into effect with respect to other States on the date of the deposit of their ratifications.[3]

Article 12

After the Treaty has been in force for ten years, or at any time thereafter, the Parties shall, if any of them so requests, consult together for the purpose of reviewing the Treaty, having regard for the factors then affecting peace and security in the North Atlantic area, including the development of universal as well as regional arrangements under the Charter of the United Nations for the maintenance of international peace and security.

Article 13

After the Treaty has been in force for twenty years, any Party may cease to be a Party one year after its notice of denunciation has been given to the Government of the United States of America, which will inform the governments of the other Parties of the deposit of each notice of denunciation.

Article 14

This Treaty, of which the English and French texts are equally authentic, shall be deposited in the archives of the Government of the United States of America. Duly certified copies will be transmitted by that Government to the Governments of other signatories.

Notes

1 The definition of the territories to which Article 5 applies was revised by Article 2 of the Protocol to the North Atlantic Treaty on the accession of Greece and Turkey signed on 22 October 1951.
2 On January 16, 1963, the North Atlantic Council noted that insofar as the former Algerian Departments of France were concerned, the relevant clauses of this Treaty had become inapplicable as from July 3, 1962.
3 The Treaty came into force on 24 August 1949, after the deposition of the ratifications of all signatory states.

Appendix 2

Strategic concept for the defence and security of the members of the North Atlantic Treaty Organization

Adopted by Heads of State and Government in Lisbon

Active engagement, modern defence

Preface

We, the Heads of State and Government of the NATO nations, are determined that NATO will continue to play its unique and essential role in ensuring our common defence and security. This Strategic Concept will guide the next phase in NATO's evolution, so that it continues to be effective in a changing world, against new threats, with new capabilities and new partners:

- It reconfirms the bond between our nations to defend one another against attack, including against new threats to the safety of our citizens.
- It commits the Alliance to prevent crises, manage conflicts and stabilize post-conflict situations, including by working more closely with our international partners, most importantly the United Nations and the European Union.
- It offers our partners around the globe more political engagement with the Alliance, and a substantial role in shaping the NATO-led operations to which they contribute.
- It commits NATO to the goal of creating the conditions for a world without nuclear weapons—but reconfirms that, as long as there are nuclear weapons in the world, NATO will remain a nuclear Alliance.
- It restates our firm commitment to keep the door to NATO open to all European democracies that meet the standards of membership, because enlargement contributes to our goal of a Europe whole, free and at peace.
- It commits NATO to continuous reform towards a more effective, efficient and flexible Alliance, so that our taxpayers get the most security for the money they invest in defence.

The citizens of our countries rely on NATO to defend Allied nations, to deploy robust military forces where and when required for our security, and to help promote common security with our partners around the globe. While the world is changing, NATO's essential mission will remain the same: to ensure that the Alliance remains an unparalleled community of freedom, peace, security and shared values.

Core tasks and principles

1. NATO's fundamental and enduring purpose is to safeguard the freedom and security of all its members by political and military means. Today, the Alliance remains an essential source of stability in an unpredictable world.

2. NATO member states form a unique community of values, committed to the principles of individual liberty, democracy, human rights and the rule of law. The Alliance is firmly committed to the purposes and principles of the Charter of the United Nations, and to the Washington Treaty, which affirms the primary responsibility of the Security Council for the maintenance of international peace and security.

3. The political and military bonds between Europe and North America have been forged in NATO since the Alliance was founded in 1949; the transatlantic link remains as strong, and as important to the preservation of Euro-Atlantic peace and security, as ever. The security of NATO members on both sides of the Atlantic is indivisible. We will continue to defend it together, on the basis of solidarity, shared purpose and fair burden-sharing.

4. The modern security environment contains a broad and evolving set of challenges to the security of NATO's territory and populations. In order to assure their security, the Alliance must and will continue fulfilling effectively three essential core tasks, all of which contribute to safeguarding Alliance members, and always in accordance with international law:

   a. **Collective defence.** NATO members will always assist each other against attack, in accordance with Article 5 of the Washington Treaty. That commitment remains firm and binding. NATO will deter and defend against any threat of aggression, and against emerging security challenges where they threaten the fundamental security of individual Allies or the Alliance as a whole.

   b. **Crisis management.** NATO has a unique and robust set of political and military capabilities to address the full spectrum of crises—before, during and after conflicts. NATO will actively employ an appropriate mix of those political and military tools to help manage developing crises that have the potential to affect Alliance security, before they escalate into conflicts; to stop ongoing conflicts where they affect Alliance security; and to help consolidate stability in post-conflict situations where that contributes to Euro-Atlantic security.

c. **Cooperative security.** The Alliance is affected by, and can affect, political and security developments beyond its borders. The Alliance will engage actively to enhance international security, through partnership with relevant countries and other international organisations; by contributing actively to arms control, nonproliferation and disarmament; and by keeping the door to membership in the Alliance open to all European democracies that meet NATO's standards.

5. NATO remains the unique and essential transatlantic forum for consultations on all matters that affect the territorial integrity, political independence and security of its members, as set out in Article 4 of the Washington Treaty. Any security issue of interest to any Ally can be brought to the NATO table, to share information, exchange views and, where appropriate, forge common approaches.

6. In order to carry out the full range of NATO missions as effectively and efficiently as possible, Allies will engage in a continuous process of reform, modernisation and transformation.

The security environment

7. Today, the Euro-Atlantic area is at peace and the threat of a conventional attack against NATO territory is low. That is an historic success for the policies of robust defence, Euro-Atlantic integration and active partnership that have guided NATO for more than half a century.

8. However, the conventional threat cannot be ignored. Many regions and countries around the world are witnessing the acquisition of substantial, modern military capabilities with consequences for international stability and Euro-Atlantic security that are difficult to predict. This includes the proliferation of ballistic missiles, which poses a real and growing threat to the Euro-Atlantic area.

9. The proliferation of nuclear weapons and other weapons of mass destruction, and their means of delivery, threatens incalculable consequences for global stability and prosperity. During the next decade, proliferation will be most acute in some of the world's most volatile regions.

10. Terrorism poses a direct threat to the security of the citizens of NATO countries, and to international stability and prosperity more broadly. Extremist groups continue to spread to, and in, areas of strategic importance to the Alliance, and modern technology increases the threat and potential impact of terrorist attacks, in particular if terrorists were to acquire nuclear, chemical, biological or radiological capabilities.

11. Instability or conflict beyond NATO borders can directly threaten Alliance security, including by fostering extremism, terrorism, and trans-national illegal activities such as trafficking in arms, narcotics and people.

12. Cyber attacks are becoming more frequent, more organised and more costly in the damage that they inflict on government administrations, businesses, economies and potentially also transportation and supply networks and other critical infrastructure; they can reach a threshold that threatens national and Euro-Atlantic prosperity, security and stability. Foreign militaries and intelligence services, organised criminals, terrorist and/or extremist groups can each be the source of such attacks.

13. All countries are increasingly reliant on the vital communication, transport and transit routes on which international trade, energy security and prosperity depend. They require greater international efforts to ensure their resilience against attack or disruption. Some NATO countries will become more dependent on foreign energy suppliers and in some cases, on foreign energy supply and distribution networks for their energy needs. As a larger share of world consumption is transported across the globe, energy supplies are increasingly exposed to disruption.

14. A number of significant technology-related trends—including the development of laser weapons, electronic warfare and technologies that impede access to space—appear poised to have major global effects that will impact on NATO military planning and operations.

15. Key environmental and resource constraints, including health risks, climate change, water scarcity and increasing energy needs will further shape the future security environment in areas of concern to NATO and have the potential to significantly affect NATO planning and operations.

Defence and deterrence

16. The greatest responsibility of the Alliance is to protect and defend our territory and our populations against attack, as set out in Article 5 of the Washington Treaty. The Alliance does not consider any country to be its adversary. However, no one should doubt NATO's resolve if the security of any of its members were to be threatened.

17. Deterrence, based on an appropriate mix of nuclear and conventional capabilities, remains a core element of our overall strategy. The circumstances in which any use of nuclear weapons might have to be contemplated are extremely remote. As long as nuclear weapons exist, NATO will remain a nuclear alliance.

18. The supreme guarantee of the security of the Allies is provided by the strategic nuclear forces of the Alliance, particularly those of the United States; the independent strategic nuclear forces of the United Kingdom and France, which have a deterrent role of their own, contribute to the overall deterrence and security of the Allies.

19. We will ensure that NATO has the full range of capabilities necessary to deter and defend against any threat to the safety and security of our populations. Therefore, we will:
    - maintain an appropriate mix of nuclear and conventional forces;
    - maintain the ability to sustain concurrent major joint operations and several smaller operations for collective defence and crisis response, including at strategic distance;
    - develop and maintain robust, mobile and deployable conventional forces to carry out both our Article 5 responsibilities and the Alliance's expeditionary operations, including with the NATO Response Force;
    - carry out the necessary training, exercises, contingency planning and information exchange for assuring our defence against the full range of conventional and emerging security challenges, and provide appropriate visible assurance and reinforcement for all Allies;
    - ensure the broadest possible participation of Allies in collective defence planning on nuclear roles, in peacetime basing of nuclear forces, and in command, control and consultation arrangements;
    - develop the capability to defend our populations and territories against ballistic missile attack as a core element of our collective defence, which contributes to the indivisible security of the Alliance. We will actively seek cooperation on missile defence with Russia and other Euro-Atlantic partners;
    - further develop NATO's capacity to defend against the threat of chemical, biological, radiological and nuclear weapons of mass destruction;
    - develop further our ability to prevent, detect, defend against and recover from cyber-attacks, including by using the NATO planning process to enhance and coordinate national cyber-defence capabilities, bringing all NATO bodies under centralized cyber protection, and better integrating NATO cyber awareness, warning and response with member nations;
    - enhance the capacity to detect and defend against international terrorism, including through enhanced analysis of the threat, more consultations with our partners, and the development of appropriate military capabilities, including to help train local forces to fight terrorism themselves;
    - develop the capacity to contribute to energy security, including protection of critical energy infrastructure and transit areas and lines, cooperation with partners, and consultations among Allies on the basis of strategic assessments and contingency planning;
    - ensure that the Alliance is at the front edge in assessing the security impact of emerging technologies, and that military planning takes the potential threats into account;

- sustain the necessary levels of defence spending, so that our armed forces are sufficiently resourced;
- continue to review NATO's overall posture in deterring and defending against the full range of threats to the Alliance, taking into account changes to the evolving international security environment.

Security through crisis management

20. Crises and conflicts beyond NATO's borders can pose a direct threat to the security of Alliance territory and populations. NATO will therefore engage, where possible and when necessary, to prevent crises, manage crises, stabilize post-conflict situations and support reconstruction.
21. The lessons learned from NATO operations, in particular in Afghanistan and the Western Balkans, make it clear that a comprehensive political, civilian and military approach is necessary for effective crisis management. The Alliance will engage actively with other international actors before, during and after crises to encourage collaborative analysis, planning and conduct of activities on the ground, in order to maximise coherence and effectiveness of the overall international effort.
22. The best way to manage conflicts is to prevent them from happening. NATO will continually monitor and analyse the international environment to anticipate crises and, where appropriate, take active steps to prevent them from becoming larger conflicts.
23. Where conflict prevention proves unsuccessful, NATO will be prepared and capable to manage ongoing hostilities. NATO has unique conflict management capacities, including the unparalleled capability to deploy and sustain robust military forces in the field. NATO-led operations have demonstrated the indispensable contribution the Alliance can make to international conflict management efforts.
24. Even when conflict comes to an end, the international community must often provide continued support, to create the conditions for lasting stability. NATO will be prepared and capable to contribute to stabilisation and reconstruction, in close cooperation and consultation wherever possible with other relevant international actors.
25. To be effective across the crisis management spectrum, we will:
    - enhance intelligence sharing within NATO, to better predict when crises might occur, and how they can best be prevented;
    - further develop doctrine and military capabilities for expeditionary operations, including counterinsurgency, stabilization and reconstruction operations;
    - form an appropriate but modest civilian crisis management capability to interface more effectively with civilian partners, building on the lessons learned from NATO-led operations. This capability may also

be used to plan, employ and coordinate civilian activities until conditions allow for the transfer of those responsibilities and tasks to other actors;

- enhance integrated civilian-military planning throughout the crisis spectrum,
- develop the capability to train and develop local forces in crisis zones, so that local authorities are able, as quickly as possible, to maintain security without international assistance;
- identify and train civilian specialists from member states, made available for rapid deployment by Allies for selected missions, able to work alongside our military personnel and civilian specialists from partner countries and institutions;
- broaden and intensify the political consultations among Allies, and with partners, both on a regular basis and in dealing with all stages of a crisis—before, during and after.

Promoting international security through cooperation

Arms Control, Disarmament, and Non-Proliferation

26. NATO seeks its security at the lowest possible level of forces. Arms control, disarmament and non-proliferation contribute to peace, security and stability, and should ensure undiminished security for all Alliance members. We will continue to play our part in reinforcing arms control and in promoting disarmament of both conventional weapons and weapons of mass destruction, as well as non-proliferation efforts:

- We are resolved to seek a safer world for all and to create the conditions for a world without nuclear weapons in accordance with the goals of the Nuclear Non-Proliferation Treaty, in a way that promotes international stability, and is based on the principle of undiminished security for all.
- With the changes in the security environment since the end of the Cold War, we have dramatically reduced the number of nuclear weapons stationed in Europe and our reliance on nuclear weapons in NATO strategy. We will seek to create the conditions for further reductions in the future.
- In any future reductions, our aim should be to seek Russian agreement to increase transparency on its nuclear weapons in Europe and relocate these weapons away from the territory of NATO members. Any further steps must take into account the disparity with the greater Russian stockpiles of short-range nuclear weapons.
- We are committed to conventional arms control, which provides predictability, transparency and a means to keep armaments at the lowest possible level for stability. We will work to strengthen the con-

ventional arms control regime in Europe on the basis of reciprocity, transparency and host-nation consent.
- We will explore ways for our political means and military capabilities to contribute to international efforts to fight proliferation.
- National decisions regarding arms control and disarmament may have an impact on the security of all Alliance members. We are committed to maintain, and develop as necessary, appropriate consultations among Allies on these issues.

Open door

27.   NATO's enlargement has contributed substantially to the security of Allies; the prospect of further enlargement and the spirit of cooperative security have advanced stability in Europe more broadly. Our goal of a Europe whole and free, and sharing common values, would be best served by the eventual integration of all European countries that so desire into Euro-Atlantic structures.
- The door to NATO membership remains fully open to all European democracies which share the values of our Alliance, which are willing and able to assume the responsibilities and obligations of membership, and whose inclusion can contribute to common security and stability.

Partnerships

28.   The promotion of Euro-Atlantic security is best assured through a wide network of partner relationships with countries and organisations around the globe. These partnerships make a concrete and valued contribution to the success of NATO's fundamental tasks.
29.   Dialogue and cooperation with partners can make a concrete contribution to enhancing international security, to defending the values on which our Alliance is based, to NATO's operations, and to preparing interested nations for membership of NATO. These relationships will be based on reciprocity, mutual benefit and mutual respect.
30.   We will enhance our partnerships through flexible formats that bring NATO and partners together—across and beyond existing frameworks:
- We are prepared to develop political dialogue and practical cooperation with any nations and relevant organisations across the globe that share our interest in peaceful international relations.
- We will be open to consultation with any partner country on security issues of common concern.
- We will give our operational partners a structural role in shaping strategy and decisions on NATO-led missions to which they contribute.
- We will further develop our existing partnerships while preserving their specificity.

31. Cooperation between NATO and the United Nations continues to make a substantial contribution to security in operations around the world. The Alliance aims to deepen political dialogue and practical cooperation with the UN, as set out in the UN-NATO Declaration signed in 2008. including through:
    - enhanced liaison between the two Headquarters;
    - more regular political consultation; and
    - enhanced practical cooperation in managing crises where both organisations are engaged.

32. An active and effective European Union contributes to the overall security of the Euro-Atlantic area. Therefore the EU is a unique and essential partner for NATO. The two organisations share a majority of members, and all members of both organisations share common values. NATO recognizes the importance of a stronger and more capable European defence. We welcome the entry into force of the Lisbon Treaty, which provides a framework for strengthening the EU's capacities to address common security challenges. Non-EU Allies make a significant contribution to these efforts. For the strategic partnership between NATO and the EU, their fullest involvement in these efforts is essential. NATO and the EU can and should play complementary and mutually reinforcing roles in supporting international peace and security. We are determined to make our contribution to create more favourable circumstances through which we will:
    - fully strengthen the strategic partnership with the EU, in the spirit of full mutual openness, transparency, complementarity and respect for the autonomy and institutional integrity of both organisations;
    - enhance our practical cooperation in operations throughout the crisis spectrum, from coordinated planning to mutual support in the field;
    - broaden our political consultations to include all issues of common concern, in order to share assessments and perspectives;
    - cooperate more fully in capability development, to minimise duplication and maximise cost-effectiveness.

33. NATO–Russia cooperation is of strategic importance as it contributes to creating a common space of peace, stability and security. NATO poses no threat to Russia. On the contrary: we want to see a true strategic partnership between NATO and Russia, and we will act accordingly, with the expectation of reciprocity from Russia.

34. The NATO–Russia relationship is based upon the goals, principles and commitments of the NATO-Russia Founding Act and the Rome Declaration, especially regarding the respect of democratic principles and the sovereignty, independence and territorial integrity of all states in the Euro-Atlantic area. Notwithstanding differences on particular issues, we remain convinced that the security of NATO and Russia is intertwined and that a strong and constructive partnership based on mutual confi-

dence, transparency and predictability can best serve our security. We are determined to:

- enhance the political consultations and practical cooperation with Russia in areas of shared interests, including missile defence, counter-terrorism, counter-narcotics, counter-piracy and the promotion of wider international security;
- use the full potential of the NATO-Russia Council for dialogue and joint action with Russia.

35. The Euro-Atlantic Partnership Council and Partnership for Peace are central to our vision of Europe whole, free and in peace. We are firmly committed to the development of friendly and cooperative relations with all countries of the Mediterranean, and we intend to further develop the Mediterranean Dialogue in the coming years. We attach great importance to peace and stability in the Gulf region, and we intend to strengthen our cooperation in the Istanbul Cooperation Initiative. We will aim to:

- enhance consultations and practical military cooperation with our partners in the Euro-Atlantic Partnership Council;
- continue and develop the partnerships with Ukraine and Georgia within the NATO-Ukraine and NATO-Georgia Commissions, based on the NATO decision at the Bucharest Summit 2008, and taking into account the Euro-Atlantic orientation or aspiration of each of the countries;
- facilitate the Euro-Atlantic integration of the Western Balkans, with the aim to ensure lasting peace and stability based on democratic values, regional cooperation and good neighbourly relations;
- deepen the cooperation with current members of the Mediterranean Dialogue and be open to the inclusion in the Mediterranean Dialogue of other countries of the region;
- develop a deeper security partnership with our Gulf partners and remain ready to welcome new partners in the Istanbul Cooperation Initiative.

Reform and transformation

36. Unique in history, NATO is a security Alliance that fields military forces able to operate together in any environment; that can control operations anywhere through its integrated military command structure; and that has at its disposal core capabilities that few Allies could afford individually.

37. NATO must have sufficient resources—financial, military and human— to carry out its missions, which are essential to the security of Alliance populations and territory. Those resources must, however, be used in the most efficient and effective way possible. We will:

- maximise the deployability of our forces, and their capacity to sustain operations in the field, including by undertaking focused efforts to meet NATO's usability targets;
- ensure the maximum coherence in defence planning, to reduce unnecessary duplication, and to focus our capability development on modern requirements;
- develop and operate capabilities jointly, for reasons of cost effectiveness and as a manifestation of solidarity;
- preserve and strengthen the common capabilities, standards, structures and funding that bind us together;
- engage in a process of continual reform, to streamline structures, improve working methods and maximise efficiency.

An alliance for the 21st century

38. We, the political leaders of NATO, are determined to continue renewal of our Alliance so that it is fit for purpose in addressing the 21st Century security challenges. We are firmly committed to preserve its effectiveness as the globe's most successful political-military Alliance. Our Alliance thrives as a source of hope because it is based on common values of individual liberty, democracy, human rights and the rule of law, and because our common essential and enduring purpose is to safeguard the freedom and security of its members. These values and objectives are universal and perpetual, and we are determined to defend them through unity, solidarity, strength and resolve.

[Agreed at Lisbon, Portugal, November 19–20, 2010]

Select bibliography

For basic NATO information go to the NATO web site at www.nato.int for information on current developments and historical documentation. European Union information, including a chronology of developments from 1945 to the present day, is on the Europa website at http://europa.eu/about-eu/eu-history/index_en.htm. On many of the topics covered in this volume, the Congressional Research Service produces and updates objective and non-partisan reports. Most CRS reports can now be accessed directly at https://crsreports.congress.gov/ as well as at some other sites, including: http://fas.org/sgp/crs/index.html. The bibliography does not include any references to specific CRS reports as they can now be found via internet search for most topics. The London Centre for European Reform produces excellent analyses of issues affecting the process of European integration. Other very useful websites include that of the EU Institute for Security Studies, at www.iss.europa.eu/ where the Chaillot Papers are located; the Atlantic Council of the United States, at www.atlantic-council.org/, the International Relations and Security Network (Zurich), at www.isn.ethz.ch/, and the author's Atlantic Community Initiative, at www.AtlanticCommunity.org, where a "living history" of the Atlantic Community that supplements the information in this volume can be found.

Acheson, Dean. *Present at the Creation: My Years in the State Department*. New York: W. W. Norton, 1969.

Asmus, Ronald D., Richard L. Kugler, and F. Stephen Larrabee. "Building a New NATO." *Foreign Affairs*, September–October 1993, 28–40.

Balladur, Edouard. *For a Union of the West between Europe and the United States*. Stanford: Hoover Institution, 2009.

Bannerman, Edward, Steven Everts, Heather Grabbe, Charles Grant, and Alasdair Murray. *Europe after September 11th*. London: Centre for European Reform, 2001.

Barrie, Douglas, Ben Barry, Lucie Béraud-Sudreau, Henry Boyd, Nick Childs, and Bastian Giegerich. *Defending Europe: Scenario-Based Capability Requirements for NATO's European Members*. London: International Institute for Strategic Studies, 2019.

Becker, Jordan, "Accidental Rivals? EU Fiscal Rules, NATO, and Transatlantic Burden-Sharing," *Journal of Peace Research*, May 2019.

Binnendijk, Hans and Gina Cordero, eds. *Transforming NATO: An NDU Anthology.* Washington, D.C.: Center for Technology and National Security, National Defense University, 2008.

Boxhoorn, Bram, Niklaas Hoekstra, and Rob de Wijk, eds. *NATO after Kosovo.* Breda, the Netherlands: Royal Netherlands Military Academy, 2000.

Braun, Aurel, ed. *NATO-Russia Relations in the Twenty-First Century.* Abingdon: Routledge, 2008.

Brenner, Michael. *Terms of Engagement: The United States and the European Security Identity.* The Washington Papers no. 176. Center for Strategic and International Studies. Westport: Praeger, 1998.

Buchan, Alistair. *NATO in the 1960s: The Implications of Interdependence.* New York: Praeger, 1963.

Burrows, Mathew and Frances G. Burwell. *Europe in 2022: Alternative Futures.* Washington: Atlantic Council of the United States, 2017.

Bush, George and Brent Scowcroft. *A World Transformed.* New York: Knopf, 1998.

Cleveland, Harlan. *NATO: The Transatlantic Bargain.* New York: Harper & Row, 1970.

Coffey, Luke. "Keeping America Safe: Why U.S. Bases in Europe Remain Vital," Heritage Foundation Special Report #111 on National Security and Defense, July 11, 2012.

Cook, Don. *Forging the Alliance.* New York: Arbor House, 1989.

Cottey, Andrew, ed. *The European Neutrals and NATO: Non-Alignment, Partnership, Membership?* London: Palgrave Macmillan, 2017.

Daalder, Ivo H. *Getting to Dayton: The Making of America's Bosnia Policy.* Washington, D.C.: Brookings Institution Press, 2000.

Daalder, Ivo H. and James Goldgeier. "Global NATO," *Foreign Affairs*, September/ October 2006.

Daalder, Ivo H. and James G. Stavridis. "The Right Way to Run an Intervention," *Foreign Affairs*, March/April 2012.

Dahl, Ann-Sophie, ed. *Strategic Challenges in the Baltic Sea Region: Russia, Deterrence, and Reassurance.* Washington, D.C.: Georgetown University Press, 2018.

de Wijk, Rob. *NATO on the Brink of the New Millennium: The Battle for Consensus.* London: Brassey's, 1997.

Dean, Jonathan. *Watershed in Europe: Dismantling the East-West Military Confrontation.* Lexington: Lexington Books, 1987.

Deni, John R. *Alliance Management and Maintenance: Restructuring NATO for the 21st Century.* Aldershot: Ashgate, 2007.

——*Rotational Deployments vs. Forward Stationing: How Can the Army Achieve Assurance and Deterrence Efficiently and Effectively.* Carlisle: Strategic Studies Institute and U.S. Army War College Press, 2017.

Diesen, Glenn, *EU and NATO Relations with Russia: After the Collapse of the Soviet Union.* London: Routledge, 2015.

Drew, Nelson S. *NATO from Berlin to Bosnia: Trans-Atlantic Security in Transition.* Washington, D.C.: National Defense University Press, 1987.

Ducasse, Mark D., ed. *The Transatlantic Bargain.* Rome: NATO Defense College, 2012.

Everts, Steven, Lawrence Freedman, Charles Grant, François Heisbourg, Daniel Keohane, and Michael O'Hanlon. *A European Way of War.* London: Centre for European Reform, 2004.

Fiott, Daniel. *Yearbook of European Security, 2019*. Paris: European Union Institute for Security Studies (EUISS), 2019.

Freedman, Lawrence. *The Future of War: A History*. New York: Public Affairs, 2017.

Friend, Julius. *The Long Presidency: France in the Mitterrand Years, 1981–1995*. Boulder: Westview, 1998.

Genscher, Hans Dietrich. *Rebuilding a House Divided*. New York: Broadway Books, 1998.

Gnesotto, Nicole, ed. *EU Security and Defence Policy: The First Five Years (1999–2004)*. Paris: Institute for Security Studies, 2004.

Goldgeier, James M. *Not Whether but When: The U.S. Decision to Enlarge NATO*. Washington, D.C.: Brookings Institution Press, 1999.

Goodman, Elliot R. *The Fate of the Atlantic Community*. New York: Praeger, 1975.

Gordon, Phillip H. and James B. Steinberg. *NATO Enlargement: Moving Forward*. Washington, D.C.: Brookings Institution Press, 2001.

Gow, James. *Triumph of the Lack of Will: International Diplomacy and the Yugoslav War*. New York: Columbia University Press, 1997.

Grant, Charles. *Is Europe Doomed to Fail as a Power?* London: Centre for European Reform, 2009.

Halle, Louis J. *The Cold War as History*. New York: Harper & Row, 1967.

Harrison, Michael M. *The Reluctant Ally: France and Atlantic Security*. Baltimore: The Johns Hopkins University Press, 1981.

Hendrickson, Ryan C. *Diplomacy and War at NATO: The Secretary General and Military Action after the Cold War*. Columbia: University of Missouri Press, 2006.

Hill, Roger. *Political Consultation in NATO*. Toronto: Canadian Institute of International Affairs, 1978.

Hillson, Joel R., *Stepping Up: Burden Sharing by NATO'S Newest Members*. Carlisle Barracks: U.S. Army War College Press, November 2014.

——*The Relevance of the North Atlantic Treaty Organization for the United States in the 21st Century*. Carlisle: Strategic Studies Institute and U.S. Army War College Press, 2018.

Hodes, Cyrus and Mark Sedra. *The Search for Security in Post-Taliban Afghanistan*. Abingdon: Routledge for the International Institute for Strategic Studies, 2007.

Hoffman, Stanley. "The Crisis in the West." *New York Review of Books*, July 17, 1980.

Holbrooke, Richard. *To End a War*. New York: Random House, 1998.

Howorth, Jolyon. *Security and Defence Policy in the European Union*. New York: Palgrave Macmillan, 2007.

Ireland, Timothy P. *Creating the Entangling Alliance: The Origins of the North Atlantic Treaty Organization*. Westport: Greenwood, 1981.

Jalali, Ali A. "Afghanistan: Regaining Momentum," *Parameters* 37(4) (Winter 2007): 5(15).

Joffe, Josef. *The Limited Partnership: Europe, the United States and the Burdens of Alliance*. Cambridge, Mass.: Ballinger, 1987.

Johnston, Seth Allen. *How NATO Adapts: Strategy and Organization in the Atlantic Alliance Since 1950*. Baltimore: Johns Hopkins University Press, 2017.

Jones, Seth G. *Counterinsurgency in Afghanistan: RAND Counterinsurgency Study—Volume 4*. Arlington: RAND Corporation, 2008.

Kagan, Robert. *Of Paradise and Power: America and Europe in the New World Order*. New York: Knopf, 2003.

Kamp, Karl-Heinz and David Yost, eds. *NATO and 21st Century Deterrence*. Rome: NATO College Research Directorate, May 2009.

Kaplan, Lawrence S., ed. *American Historians and the Atlantic Alliance*. Kent, Ohio: Kent State University Press, 1991.

——*The Long Entanglement: NATO's First Fifty Years*. Westport: Praeger, 1999.

——*NATO 1948: The Birth of the Transatlantic Alliance*. Lanham: Rowman & Littlefield, 2007.

——*NATO and the United States: The Enduring Alliance*. New York: Twayne, 1994.

——*NATO before the Korean War: April 1949–1950*. Kent, Ohio: Kent State University Press, 2013.

——*NATO Divided, NATO United: The Evolution of an Alliance*. Westport: Praeger, 2004.

——*The United States and NATO: The Formative Years*. Lexington: University Press of Kentucky, 1984.

Kaplan, Lawrence S. and Robert W. Clawson, eds. *NATO after Thirty Years*. Wilmington: Scholarly Resources, 1981.

Kashmeri, Sarwar. *NATO 2.0: Reboot or Delete?* Washington, D.C.: Potomac Books, 2011.

Kay, Sean. *NATO and the Future of European Security*. Lanham: Rowman & Littlefield, 1998.

Kelleher, Catherine. *The Future of European Security*. Washington, D.C.: Brookings Institution Press, 1995.

Korski, Daniel. *Afghanistan: Europe's Forgotten War* (Policy Paper). European Council on Foreign Relations, 2008.

Larson, Jeffrey A. and Kurt J. Klingenberger, eds. *Controlling Non-Strategic Nuclear Weapons: Obstacles and Opportunities*. Colorado Springs: USAF Institute for National Security Studies, 2001.

Leurdijk, Dick A. *The United Nations and NATO in Former Yugoslavia: Partners in International Cooperation*. The Hague: Netherlands Atlantic Commission, 1994.

Lindley-French, Julian. *The North Atlantic Treaty Organization: The Enduring Alliance*. London: Routledge, 2015.

Lundestad, Geir, ed. *Just Another Major Crisis? The United States and Europe since 2000*. London: Oxford, 2008.

Lunn, Simon. *Burdensharing in NATO*. London: Royal Institute of International Affairs, 1983.

——*The Modernization of NATO's Long-Range Theater Nuclear Forces*. Report prepared for the US House Committee on Foreign Affairs. Washington, D.C.: Congressional Research Service, Library of Congress, 1981.

Lute, Douglas and Nicholas Burns. *NATO at 70: Alliance in Crisis*. Cambridge: Belfer Center for Science and International Affairs, 2019.

McFaul, Michael, Stephen Sestanovich, and John J. Mearsheimer. "Faulty Powers: Who Started the Ukraine Crisis?" *Foreign Affairs*, November/December 2014.

Menon, Anand. "Empowering Paradise? The ESDP at Ten," *International Affairs* 85(2) (2009), 227–46.

Michel, Leo G. "Defense Transformation à la française and U.S. Interests." *Strategic Forum* No. 233, Institute for National Strategic Studies, National Defense University, September 2008.

Moens, Alexander. "American Diplomacy and German Unification." *Survival* (November–December 1991), 531–45.

Molenaar, Arnout. *[Dis]Organising European Security*. The Hague: Netherlands Atlantic Association, 2007.

Moore, Rebecca R. and Damon Coletta, ed. *NATO's Return to Europe: Engaging Ukraine, Russia, and Beyond*. Washington, D.C.: Georgetown University Press, 2017.

Myers, Kenneth A., ed. *NATO—The Next Thirty Years: The Changing Political, Economic, and Military Setting*. Boulder: Westview, 1980.

Norris, Pippa and Ronald Inglehart. *Cultural Backlash: Trump, Brexit and Authoritarian Populism*. Cambridge: Cambridge University Press, 2019.

North Atlantic Treaty Organization, Afghanistan Report 2009. Brussels: NATO Public Diplomacy Division, 2009.

Nye, Joseph S. *The Paradox of American Power: Why the World's Only Superpower Can't Go It Alone*. Oxford: Oxford University Press, 2002.

O'Hanlon, Michael. "NATO's Limits: A New Security Architecture for Eastern Europe," *Survival*, October–November 2017, p. 7–24.

Olsen, John Andreas, ed. *NATO and the North Atlantic: Revitalising Collective Defence*. London: Routledge, 2017.

Osgood, Robert. *NATO: The Entangling Alliance*. Chicago: University of Chicago Press, 1962.

Papacosma, S. Victor, Sean Kay, and Mark R. Rubin, eds. *NATO after Fifty Years*. Wilmington: Scholarly Resources, 2001.

Petersson, Magnus, *NATO and the Crisis in the International Order: The Atlantic Alliance and Its Enemies*. London: Routledge, 2018.

Polyakova, Alina and Benjamin Hadad. "Europe Alone: What Comes After the Transatlantic Alliance?" *Foreign Affairs*, July/August 2019.

Pond, Elizabeth. *The Rebirth of Europe*. Washington, D.C.: Brookings Institution Press, 1999.

Quinlan, Michael. *European Defense Cooperation: Asset or Threat to NATO?* Washington, D.C.: Woodrow Wilson Center Press, 2001.

Raj, Christopher S. *American Military in Europe*. New Delhi: ABC Publishing House, 1983.

Reyn, Sebastian. *Allies or Aliens? George W. Bush and the Transatlantic Crisis in Historical Perspective*. The Hague: Netherlands Atlantic Commission, 2004.

Risso, Linda, ed. *NATO at 70: A Historiographical Approach*. London: Routledge, 2019.

Roth, William V. Jr. *NATO in the 21st Century*. Brussels: North Atlantic Assembly, September 1998.

Rühle, Michael. "Imagining NATO 2011," *NATO Review* (autumn 2001), 18–21.

——"NATO enlargement and Russia: Myths and Realities," *NATO Review* (July 2014).

Rutten, Maartje, ed. *From St. Malo to Nice, European Defence: Core Documents*. Chaillot Paper no. 47. Paris: Western European Union Institute for Security Studies, 2001.

Rynning, Sten. *NATO in Afghanistan: The Liberal Disconnect*. Stanford: Stanford University Press, 2012.

——*NATO Renewed: The Power and Purpose of Transatlantic Cooperation*. New York: Palgrave Macmillan. 2005.

Sayle, Timothy Andrews, *Enduring Alliance: A History of NATO and the Postwar Global Order*. Ithaca: Cornell University Press, 2019.

Schweigler, Gebhard. "A Wider Atlantic?" *Foreign Policy* (September–October 2001), 87–88.

Serfaty, Simon. *Architects of Delusion: Europe, America and the Iraq War.* Philadelphia: University of Pennsylvania Press, 2008.

——*The Vital Partnership: Power and Order, American and Europe beyond Iraq.* Lanham: Rowman & Littlefield, 2007.

Simmons, Katie, Bruce Stokes, and Jacob Poushter. "NATO Publics Blame Russia for Ukrainian Crisis, but Reluctant to Provide Military Aid; In Russia, Anti-Western Views and Support for Putin Surge," Pew Research Center, June 10, 2015.

Simon, Jeffrey. *Roadmap to NATO Accession: Preparing for Membership.* Washington, D.C.: Institute for National Strategic Studies, National Defense University, October 2001.

Sloan, Stanley R. *Defense of the West: NATO, the European Union and the Transatlantic Bargain.* Manchester: Manchester University Press, 2016.

——ed. *NATO in the 1990s.* Washington, D.C.: Pergamon-Brassey's, 1989.

——*NATO, the European Union, and the Atlantic Community: The Transatlantic Bargain Challenged.* Lanham: Rowman & Littlefield, 2005.

——*NATO's Future: Beyond Collective Defense.* Washington, D.C.: National Defense University Press, 1996.

——*NATO's Future: Toward a New Transatlantic Bargain.* Washington, D.C.: National Defense University Press, 1985.

——*Permanent Alliance? NATO and the Transatlantic Bargain from Truman to Obama.* New York: Continuum Books, 2010.

——*Transatlantic Traumas: Has Illiberalism Brought the West to the Brink of Collapse?* Manchester: Manchester University Press, 2018.

——*The United States and European Defence.* Chaillot Paper no. 36. Paris: Western European Union Institute for Security Studies, 2000.

Sperling, James and Mark Webber. "NATO: from Kosovo to Kabul (Report)," *International Affairs* 85(3) (May 2009), 491(21).

Stuart, Douglas and William Tow. *The Limits of Alliance: NATO Out-of-Area Problems since 1949.* Baltimore: The Johns Hopkins University Press, 1990.

Szabo, Stephen F. *The Diplomacy of German Unification.* New York: St. Martin's, 1992.

Thies, Walter J. *Friendly Rivals: Bargaining and Burden-Shifting in NATO.* Armonk: Sharpe, 2003.

——*Why NATO Endures.* New York: Cambridge University Press, 2009.

Toje, Asle. *America, the EU and Strategic Culture: Renegotiating the Transatlantic Bargain.* Abingdon: Routledge, 2008.

Treverton, Gregory R., ed. *The Shape of the New Europe.* New York: Council on Foreign Relations, 1992.

US Government. Department of State. *Foreign Relations of the United States* (series).

US Senate Committee on Foreign Relations. Subcommittee on European Affairs. *NATO at 40.* Report prepared by the Congressional Research Service, Library of Congress, May 1989 (includes extensive annotated bibliography).

Van Eeckelen, Willem. *Debating European Security, 1948–1998.* The Hague: Sdu Publishers, 1998.

——*From Words to Deeds: The Continuing Debate on European Security.* Brussels: Centre for European Policy Studies, 2006.

Van Heuven, Marten and Gregory F. Treverton. *Europe and America: How Will the United States Adjust to the New Partnership?* Santa Monica: Rand, 1998.

Walt, Stephen, "NATO Isn't What You Think It Is," *Foreign Policy*, July 26, 2018.

Whitmore, Steven J. and John R. Deni. *NATO Missile Defense and the European Phased Adaptive Approach: The Implications of Burden Sharing and the Underappreciated Role of the U.S. Army.* Carlisle Barracks: United States Army War College Press, 2013.

Williams, Phil. *The Senate and U.S. Troops in Europe.* London: Macmillan, 1985.

Yost, David S. *NATO Transformed: The Alliance's New Roles in International Security.* Washington, D.C.: United States Institute of Peace Press, 1998.

——*NATO's Balancing Act.* Washington, D.C.: United States Institute of Peace Press, 2014.

Zelikow, Philip and Condoleezza Rice. *Germany Unified and Europe Transformed: A Study in Statecraft.* Cambridge, Mass.: Harvard University Press, 1995.

Zoellick, Robert B. "The Lessons of German Unification," *The National Interest* (fall 2000), 17–28.

About the author

Stanley R. Sloan is a Visiting Scholar in Political Science at Middlebury College, a Non-resident Senior Fellow in the Scowcroft Center of the Atlantic Council of the United States, and an Associate Fellow at the Austrian Institute for European and Security Policy. He has been a member of the Middlebury Winter Term Faculty for over 15 years and is the founding Director of the Atlantic Community Initiative. In 2016, he was invited to join the Dūcō experts consulting group. He has served as a Woodrow Wilson Foundation Visiting Fellow and a member of the Fulbright Specialists Program.

Before retiring from 32 years of government service, he was the Senior Specialist in International Security Policy at the Congressional Research Service (CRS) of the Library of Congress, where he previously served as head of the Office of Senior Specialists, division specialist in US alliance relations, and head of the Europe/Middle East/Africa section. Prior to joining CRS, he was a commissioned officer in the US Air Force and held several analytical and research management positions at the Central Intelligence Agency, including Deputy National Intelligence Officer for Western Europe. In 1973, he served as a member of the US Delegation to Negotiations on Mutual and Balanced Force Reductions.

He has published hundreds of CRS Reports for Congress, as well as journal articles, book chapters, and opinion editorials in major US and European publications on international security topics, US foreign policy, and European security. Stan lectures widely on international security topics in the United States and Europe and testified in September 2018 before the Senate Foreign Relations Committee on NATO and US interests.

His books and monographs include *Transatlantic Traumas: Has Illiberalism Brought the West to the Brink of Collapse?* (2018); the predecessor to this volume, *Defense of the West: NATO, the European Union and the Transatlantic Bargain* (2016); *Permanent Alliance? NATO and the Transatlantic Bargain from Truman to Obama* (2010); *NATO's Future: Toward a New Transatlantic Bargain* (1985); *NATO in the 1990s* (1989); *NATO's Future: Beyond Collective Defense* (1995); *The U.S. Role in the Twenty-First Century World: Toward a New Consensus* (1997); *The United States and European Defence* (2000); *NATO and Transatlantic Relations in the 21st Century: Crisis, Continuity or Change?* (2002); *The Use of U.S. Power: Implications for U.S. Interests* (2004) (coauthor); and *NATO, the European Union, and the Atlantic Community: The Transatlantic Bargain Challenged*

(2005). He was rapporteur and study director for the North Atlantic Assembly's report on "NATO in the 1990s" (1988) and "NATO in the 21st Century" (1998).

Sloan received his B.A. from the University of Maine and his Masters in International Affairs from the Columbia University School of International Affairs; he completed all but his dissertation for a Ph.D. at the School of International Service, American University; and is a distinguished graduate of the USAF Officers Training School. In 2005, he was named an Honorary Ancien of the NATO Defense College, where he continues to lecture on a regular basis.

Index

Abkhazia 108, 232–34, 270
ABM Treaty (Anti-Ballistic Missile
    Treaty) 226
Acheson, Dean 9, 27–29, 35, 362
Achilles, Theodore 40
ACO *see* NATO, Allied Command
    Operations
ACT *see* NATO, Allied Command
    Transformation
Adenauer, Konrad 29, 38, 45, 56
ad hoc coalitions 144, 151, 185, 262
Afghanistan 7, 11–13, 61, 186, 189,
    204–10, 212–23, 236–37,
    242–45, 248–49, 253, 256–57,
    259–61, 265–71, 273, 289–90,
    306, 325, 364–66
  Afghan National Army (ANA) 207,
      209, 213–14, 219, 325
  Afghan National Army Air Corps 214
  Afghan National Police 212
  Afghan National Security Forces
      (ANSF) 270
  casualty differentials 218
  drug problem 213
  International Institute for Strategic
      Studies analysis 212
  International Security Assistance
      Force (ISAF) 179, 192, 205–10,
      213–16, 236–37, 257, 260,
      270–71, 273
  national caveats 207, 216–17
  non-governmental organizations
      (NGOs) 207, 211
  Operation Enduring Freedom (OEF)
      205, 208, 214
  Operation Resolute Support 289
  Provincial Reconstruction Teams
      (PRTs) 206–7, 211, 216, 248
  Soviet invasion of 90
  Taliban 74, 184, 186, 204–5,
      208–15, 218–19, 242–43, 249,
      256, 288–89, 325–26
  terrorist attacks on the United States
      and 16, 98, 186
"agonizing reappraisal" 16, 40, 44
Airborne Warning and Control System
    (AWACS) 186, 195
al-Assad, Bashar 324
Albania 14, 47, 126, 133, 142, 163,
    177, 194–95, 242, 246–47, 272
Albright, Madeleine 123, 165–66, 257
ANSF *see* Afghanistan, Afghan National
    Security Forces
al-Qaeda 8, 145, 183, 186, 204–5,
    208–10, 218, 222, 226, 242–43,
    325
Arab Spring 293, 323
arms control 13, 69–70, 81, 85, 87,
    175, 228, 251, 258, 353, 357–58
  agreements 61, 69–70, 152
  conventional 108, 357
Ashcroft, John 123–24
Asmus, Ronald D. 112, 118, 224, 247,
    250
Aspin, Les 111
Atatürk's reforms 290–91

Atlantic Community 17, 50, 72, 105, 362, 364, 367, 369
Atlanticist and Europeanist approaches 236
Attlee, Clement R. 20
Australia 216, 247, 271, 339
Austria 96, 108, 164, 168, 193, 246, 272
authoritarianism 9, 13, 90, 103, 174, 204, 279, 291, 294, 366
AWACS *see* Airborne Warning and Control System
"axis of evil" 187
Azerbaijan 247, 272

Baker, James A. 174, 198
Balkans 105–6, 131, 133, 136, 138, 141, 145, 148, 150–51, 163, 173, 178
Baltic States 125, 127, 194, 225, 228, 267–68, 273, 283–84, 288, 309, 326
Bartholomew, Reginald 158
Barzini, Luigi 72–73
Belarus 154, 229, 233, 272, 287, 335
Belgium 18, 21, 34, 41, 45, 70, 76, 82, 196, 199–200, 235–36, 242
Benelux 21
Benghazi 262
Berlin, Germany 22, 43, 85, 139, 162–63, 179, 198, 242, 247, 251, 254
Berlin 1996 Ministerial and Accord 140, 179, 236
Berlin Group 179
"Berlin plus" 192, 237
Berlin Wall 8, 78–79, 83, 103–5, 119, 173, 204, 278, 299
Bevin, Ernest 9, 20–21
Biden, Joseph 120–22, 124
Biegen, Steve 122
bin Laden, Osama 131, 184, 214
Binnendijk, Hans 113
Blair, Tony 145–46, 164–66, 182–83, 196, 199–200, 203, 223, 234–36
Bolton, John 245
Boniface, Pascal 55
Bonn Agreement of 2001, 205, 210–11

Bosnia 108, 111, 115–16, 129, 132–39, 141, 150–51, 158, 163, 173–74, 176, 179, 236
Brandt, Willy 56, 74, 280
Breedlove, Philip M. 281–82, 287
Brexit 290, 294–96, 302, 346
Brookings Institution enlargement study 194
Brussels, Belgium 41–42, 81–82, 114–17, 177–78, 180–81, 184, 187, 206, 235–36, 248, 251, 297–98, 304, 306–7, 366–67
Brussels Treaty 21–22, 26, 33, 35, 45–46, 139
Brzezinski, Ian 122
Brzezinski, Zbigniew 230
Bucharest Summit 231, 242, 271, 360
Bulgaria 14, 47, 126, 177, 192, 194, 242, 246–47, 272, 280, 288
Burns, R. Nicholas 186, 200, 236
Bush, George H. W. 110, 134–35, 152, 174, 182, 217
    administration of 110–11, 115, 134, 157, 160, 166
Bush, George W. 92, 94, 183–84, 193, 198–200, 223, 231, 237–38, 240, 242–43, 245, 253–54
    administration of 110–11, 134, 157, 160, 182, 184, 186–97, 199–201, 203–5, 214–15, 222–23, 226, 230–31, 234, 236–37
Byrd, Robert 124–25, 178

Cameron, David 281, 285, 295
Canada 6–7, 9–10, 15–16, 18, 22, 26, 87, 206–7, 215–16, 218, 303, 307–8, 346
Capability Development Plan (CDP) 302
Carter, Ash 288
Carter, Jimmy 60–61, 68, 70, 96
    administration of 61, 87
Caucasus 229
CDP *see* Capability Development Plan
Central Europe 5, 10, 15, 25–27, 74, 81, 83, 104, 109, 111, 114, 119–20, 123
CFE *see* Conventional Forces in Europe negotiations/treaty

Chaillot Paper 180, 252, 367
Chalmer, Larry 331
Chechnya 127, 204, 228
Cheney, Dick 111, 158
China 140, 142, 145, 148, 202,
    246–47, 262–63, 277, 302, 304,
    320, 322, 326, 328–29, 337–38
  Belt and Road Initiative 328
Chirac, Jacques 120, 140, 155, 165,
    190, 198–99
Christopher, Warren 113, 135
Churchill, Winston 20
CJTF *see* Combined Joint Task Force
Clark, Wesley K. 143, 145
Cleveland, Harlan 3, 18, 54, 56, 80–81,
    363
Clinton, Bill 110–13, 116–19, 121,
    135, 140, 144, 161, 173, 175–76,
    182, 200
  administration of 111, 114–15,
    120–21, 135–36, 139, 144,
    146, 158, 161, 163, 175, 178,
    181, 183
Clinton, Hillary 296
Cohen, William 120, 170–71
Cold War 4–14, 16, 18, 22–24, 32–42,
    46–99, 103, 105–10, 127, 133,
    152, 155–57, 178–79, 204, 226,
    228–29, 276–77, 317–18, 327,
    337–38
  post-Cold War 91, 101, 104–222,
    224, 226–60, 262, 264–302,
    304, 306, 308, 310, 312, 318
collective security 15, 17, 344
Collective Security Treaty Organization
    (CSTO) 233
Combined Joint Task Force (CJTF) 132,
    139, 141, 161–63, 176, 245
Committee of Three ("wise men") on
    Non-military Cooperation 57
Committee to Expand NATO 118
common values 4, 9, 84, 91, 127, 203,
    347, 358–59, 361
Commonwealth of Independent States
    233
comprehensive approaches 207, 248,
    261, 265, 332
Conference on Security and Cooperation
    in Europe (CSCE) 60, 78, 81, 104,
    106–7, 134, 173, 175

Congressional Research Service (CRS)
    122–23, 175–77, 179–81, 212,
    216, 246, 248, 251, 362, 365,
    367, 369
Connally, Tom 32
Contact Group 142, 179
Conventional Forces in Europe
    negotiations/treaty (CFE) 108–9,
    153, 251
Convention on General Relations
    between the Federal Republic
    of Germany, France, the United
    Kingdom, and the United States 35
Convention on the Presence of Foreign
    Forces in the Federal Republic of
    Germany 45
cooperative security 148, 258, 271,
    353, 358
COPS *see* European Union, Political and
    Security Committee
COPSI *see* European Union, Interim
    Political and Security Committee
Council of Europe 279
Council on Foreign Relations 309, 313,
    337
COVID-19 pandemic 304, 328–29,
    331, 337
Craddock, Bantz J. 255
Crimea 5, 94, 228–29, 274–77,
    279–80, 283–84, 289, 301, 304,
    327, 335
crisis management 12, 115, 160,
    235, 258, 260–62, 302, 352,
    355–56
Croatia 14, 133, 137, 177, 195, 242,
    267, 272
CRS *see* Congressional Research
    Service
CSCE *see* Conference on Security and
    Cooperation in Europe
CSTO *see* Collective Security Treaty
    Organization
Cuban Missile Crisis 53, 277
cyber attacks 284, 318–19, 321, 326,
    333, 354
Cyprus 34, 260, 272, 332
Czechoslovakia 47, 130
Czech Republic (Czechia) 7, 13–14, 112,
    119, 123–24, 166, 173, 175–77,
    191–94, 220–21, 225, 227

Daalder, Ivo 178–79, 264, 307, 363
Daesh (ISIL, ISIS) 8, 254
    see also Islamic State
Davis, Lynn 113
Dayton (Ohio) Bosnia peace
    negotiations 137, 139, 178, 363
DCI *see* NATO, Defense Capabilities
    Initiative
Dean, Jonathan 60
Declaration Inviting Italy and the Federal
    Republic of Germany to Accede to
    the Brussels Treaty 45–46
Declaration on Atlantic Relations 80
Declaration on Mutual and Balanced
    Force Reductions 59, 79
defense and détente combination 58
de Gaulle, Charles 43, 51–55, 57, 63,
    72–73, 77, 79, 140, 164, 190,
    201
democracy 9–10, 84, 105, 107–9,
    111–13, 122–24, 127–28, 130,
    175–76, 194, 202–3, 290–93,
    334, 340, 345
    illiberal 334
Dempsey, Judy 250–51, 338
Deni, John R. 310, 363, 368
Denmark 18, 45, 77, 216, 218, 247,
    272, 282
"deputies proposal" 162
deterrence 7, 10–11, 64–69, 71, 83,
    85, 95, 97, 106–7, 268, 270, 320,
    354, 356, 363
Dien Bien Phu 52
Distinctive Partnership, NATO-Ukraine
    Charter on 229
Dobbins, James 158
Dole, Robert 118
Donetsk 275, 279, 287, 289
DPC *see* NATO, Defense Planning
    Committee
Dragonbear 328
Drew, Nelson 176
Drozdiak, William 178
D-SACEUR *see* NATO, Deputy Supreme
    Allied Commander Europe
dual-capable aircraft 153, 155
dual-track decision 68–69, 79
Dulles, John Foster 38–41, 44–45, 47
dysfunctional American political system
    330

Eagleburger, Lawrence 111
EAPC *see* NATO, Euro-Atlantic
    Partnership Council
Eastern Europe 14–15, 98, 103, 106–7,
    110–11, 114, 117, 123, 128, 130,
    327, 333
East Germany 47, 56
    former 334
EC *see* European Communit(y)(ies)
economic sanctions on Russia 312
EDA *see* European Union, European
    Defense Agency
EDC *see* European Defense Community
Eden, Anthony 45, 47
EDF *see* European Union, European
    Defense Fund
EEC *see* European Economic Community
Egypt 285, 308
Eikenberry, Carl 212
Eisenhower, Dwight D. 29–30, 33,
    38–39, 44, 47, 57, 81
    administration of 38, 40, 43, 62–63,
    81, 152
enduring alliance 18, 346, 365–66
entangling alliance 23, 35–36, 364, 366
EPC *see* European Political Cooperation
Erdoğan, Recep Tayyip 290–92
ESDI *see* European Security and Defense
    Identity
ESDP *see* European Union, European
    Security and Defense Policy
Estonia 192, 194, 225, 233, 242,
    246–47, 251, 272, 275, 282, 285,
    288
EU *see* European Union
EURATOM *see* European Atomic Energy
    Community
Euro 159, 164, 214, 289, 308, 332
Euro-Atlantic area 17, 117, 126, 148,
    190, 270–71, 353, 359
Euro-Atlantic community 9, 234, 353,
    360
Euro-Atlantic Disaster Response
    Coordination Center 116
Euro-Atlantic security 171, 229, 258,
    260, 271–72, 284, 319–20,
    352–53, 358
Euro-corps 166, 236
Europe, defense of 6, 23, 25, 29, 32, 66,
    342

European army 28, 41, 167, 169, 297, 342

European Atomic Energy Community (EURATOM) 6, 77

European brigade 78

European Coal and Steel Community (ECSC) 6, 33, 76

European Communit(y)(ies) (EC) 25, 51, 53, 73, 77–80, 134, 157, 159, 240

European defense 32, 38, 40, 44, 72, 78, 154, 156, 160, 164, 180, 183

European Defense Community (EDC) 6, 10, 28, 33–35, 37–44, 48, 71–72, 76, 95, 129

European defense cooperation 7, 55, 78, 106, 157, 181, 235–36, 244, 252, 366

European Economic Community (EEC) 6, 53, 72, 76, 79–80

European monetary union 147

European pillar 25, 56, 72, 133, 157–59, 163, 235, 238, 263

European Political Cooperation (EPC) 51, 77–78

European Security and Defense Identity (ESDI) 133, 139, 146, 156, 161–63, 165, 167, 169

European Union (EU) 6–7, 13–14, 151, 154–59, 161, 163–67, 169–74, 202–3, 229–30, 234–38, 240–41, 251–52, 260–61, 271–75, 280–81, 294–96, 302, 307–8, 367, 369

Action Plan on Strategic Communications 327

Capabilities Commitment Conference 168

Capability Development Plan 302

Commission 157, 169

Commissioner for External Relations and European Neighbourhood Policy 241

Constitution 200, 235

Coordinated Annual Review on Defence 302

Council of Ministers 168–69, 179, 241, 248, 288, 337

defense dimension 157, 169, 203

European Defense Agency (EDA) 267, 307

European Defense Fund (EDF) 302

European Security and Defense Planning System 171

European Security and Defense Policy (ESDP) 151, 155–56, 164–65, 168–71, 173, 182–83, 234–35, 238–39, 241, 244, 251

Eurozone 271, 308

External Action Service 241

High Representative for the Common Foreign and Security Policy 163, 238–39, 241, 251

Interim Political and Security Committee (IPSC or COPSI) 170

Military Committee 168, 172

Military Planning and Conduct Capability (MPCC) 302

Military Staff 168, 236

Parliament 28, 238, 291, 294

Permanent Structured Cooperation (PESCO) 302–3

Political and Security Committee (PSC or COPS) 168, 170–71, 239

relationship to NATO 8, 168, 171, 234–37, 332–33

relations with Turkey 235, 312

Single European Act 181

Europe des patries 53

"evil empire" 70

external threats and internal challenges 8, 292, 305, 317–37

Federal Republic of Germany 7, 25, 35, 41, 44–47, 51–52, 55, 74–76, 82, 103

Federal Republic of Yugoslavia 141

Finland 168, 193, 246, 272, 304

Fischer, Joschka 198

Five Eyes 339

Flanagan, Stephen 113

flexible response strategy 10–11, 51, 62, 64–67, 71, 79–80, 129, 152–53

Flynn, Michael 298

Ford, Gerald 60, 67, 182

Former Yugoslav Republic 5, 7, 103, 105, 115, 120, 133, 141, 151, 178, 365

Founding Act on Mutual Relations, Cooperation and Security between NATO and the Russian Federation 13, 128

Four-Power and Nine-Power
    Conferences 44–45
France 21, 26–27, 29, 33–36, 40–45,
    50–55, 73–74, 76, 78–80,
    138–43, 148–49, 179–81, 190,
    196–201, 235, 241–43, 262–63,
    280–81, 287–88, 307–8
  Africa and 42, 52, 93
  Algeria and 42, 52
  Communist Party 43
  departure from NATO's integrated
      command structure 10, 53–54,
      64, 80, 129
  directorate concept 52
  Fifth Republic 51
  force de frappe 52, 55
  Fouchet initiative 53
  Fourth Republic 42–43, 51–52
  Germany, concern about 25–26, 28,
      39, 42–43
  global role 52
  Indochina and 43, 52
  National Assembly 26, 28, 41, 44,
      47–48
  nuclear role 52, 54–55, 63, 154–55,
      354
  return to NATO integrated command
      structure 161, 203, 238, 254,
      303
Franco, Francisco 293
Frasure, Robert 176
Freedman, Lawrence 363
Fried, Daniel 117

Gaddafi, Muammar 262–63, 265, 303,
    322
Gates, Robert M. 216, 249, 265–66,
    268, 307, 330–31
GDR *see* German Democratic
    Republic
geography as a source of transatlantic
    differences 86–87, 89
Georgia 14, 109, 175, 195, 228–34,
    242, 247, 250–51, 270–72,
    276–77, 284
German Democratic Republic (GDR)
    56, 103
Germany 14, 24–29, 32–33, 41–48,
    50–52, 55–56, 73–76, 78, 82,
    179, 196–200, 203, 205–8,

    217–18, 235, 242–43, 248–49,
    262–63, 287–88, 300–301
  Afghanistan and 186, 217
  Alternative for Germany 293
  Christian Democrats 56, 203
  constraints on military capabilities
      and roles 26–29
  Ostpolitik 56, 280
  reunification of 29, 50, 74, 76,
      103–4, 110, 128, 217, 334
  Social Democrats 29, 56
  United States, relations with 203
Goldgeier, James M. 111, 117, 119,
    175, 177, 364
Goodpaster, Andrew J. 47
Gorazde 136
Gorbachev, Mikhail 62, 70, 97, 110,
    130, 134, 153
Gore, Al 126
"Great Recession" 253, 271, 293, 331
Greece 14–15, 34–35, 45, 51, 77, 84,
    144, 194–95, 199, 282, 285, 289,
    331–32
GWOT *see* terrorism, Global War on
    Terror

Haekerrup, Hans 176
Haltzel, Michael 122
Hamburg G-20 Summit 300
Harmel, Pierre 56–57, 59, 106
Harmel Report and formula 10, 13, 51,
    56–59, 61–62, 69, 79–80, 106–7,
    129, 322
Havel, Vaclav 112, 192, 246
Helms, Jesse 113, 121, 123–24
Helsinki Final Act 15, 81, 106–7, 278
Helsinki Headline Goals 167
Helsinki Summit, Trump/Putin 301, 304
history, relevance of 36
  as source of transatlantic differences 88
Hitler, Adolf 20, 344
Hoffman, Stanley 90, 99
Holbrooke, Richard 117, 137, 179
Hollande, François 50, 280, 287
Holocaust Memorial Museum 112
Hoover, Herbert 31
Horn, Gyula 104
Hungary 7, 13–14, 112, 119–20,
    123–24, 130, 166, 173–77,
    193–94, 289, 294

Hunter, Robert 169
Hussein, Saddam 98, 131, 187, 190,
    195, 197, 199, 205, 214, 243,
    247
Hutchison, Kay Bailey 122
hybrid warfare 319, 321

Iceland 18, 45, 59, 166, 170, 181, 220,
    247, 272
ideology as a source of transatlantic
    differences 91–92
IFOR *see* Implementation Force
illiberalism 313, 343, 367, 369
Implementation Force (IFOR) 128, 137,
    141, 163
Indian King and blind men fable 8, 16,
    18–19
Indian Ocean 93
Indochina 27, 37–38, 42–43, 52
Intermediate-Range Nuclear Forces
    (INF) Treaty 71, 79, 304, 337
internal European and transatlantic
    political challenges 333
International Criminal Court 182
IPSC *see* European Union, Interim
    Political and Security Committee
Iran 89, 187, 200, 226–27, 269, 277,
    291, 303–5, 325, 345
    Joint Comprehensive Plan of Action
        (JCPOA) 304, 313, 337
Iraq 7, 187, 190–92, 195–202, 204–6,
    214–15, 218–22, 235–37, 244,
    246–47, 253–54, 256, 265–66,
    289–90, 323–24
    Afghanistan link 293
    coalition members 198, 246
    invasion of Kuwait 12
    war divisive for transatlantic relations
        190, 195–96, 236, 243–44, 251
    war in 196–98, 231, 235, 253, 322,
        334, 367
Ireland 25, 36, 77, 168, 193, 272, 364
ISAF *see* Afghanistan, International
    Security Assistance Force; NATO,
    International Security Assistance
    Force
Islamic State (Daesh/ISIL/ISIS) 8, 254,
    256, 264, 284–86, 289, 291, 319,
    322–25, 327–28, 333, 335, 337
Ismay, Hastings (Lord) 33, 47

Istanbul Cooperation Initiative 271,
    308, 360
Istanbul (Turkey) Summit 196, 206
Italy 32, 34, 40, 45–46, 57, 63, 70, 76,
    82, 120, 179, 194, 196–97
Ivanov, Sergei 198

Jackson-Nunn Amendment 96
Jalali, Ali A. 212
JCPOA *see* Joint Comprehensive Plan of
    Action
Jinping, Xi 328
Johnson, Boris 293
Johnson, Lyndon B. 54, 63, 75, 95
Joint Comprehensive Plan of Action
    (JCPOA) 303–4, 325
Joulwan, George 162

Kaliningrad 227
Kaplan, Lawrence S. 3, 18, 23, 36, 43,
    49, 177, 246
Karzai, Hamid 205, 211–12, 268
Kay, Sean 18, 36, 156, 180, 246, 250,
    277, 309, 366
Kazakhstan 154, 233, 272
Kennan, George 124
Kennedy, John F. 63, 95, 277
Kislyak, Sergey 298
Kissinger, Henry 61, 67, 80–82, 252
Korean War 26–27, 31, 267, 308, 365
Kosovo 115–16, 129, 132, 141–46,
    148–51, 163, 166, 173–74, 179,
    186, 191, 363, 367
Kosovo Liberation Army 143
Kruzel, Joseph 111, 113, 176
Kugler, Richard L. 112, 118, 176, 249,
    362
Kuwait 12, 131, 308
Kyl, Jon 122, 124
Kyrgyzstan 233, 272

Lake, Tony 111, 175
Lange, Halvard 57
Larrabee, F. Stephen 112, 118, 176,
    362
Latvia 192, 194, 202, 225, 242,
    246–47, 272, 275, 282, 288, 327
Lavrov, Sergei 298
League of Nations 15, 20, 22, 119, 344
Leahy, Patrick 124

Le Pen, Marine 294
liberal democracy 6, 123, 293, 295,
     300, 334, 340–41, 343, 345
Libya 262–65, 268–69, 289, 303, 305,
     307, 322
Lieberman, Joseph 124
Lisbon (Portugal) force goals 33–34,
     37, 48
Lisbon Strategic Concept 269–71, 286,
     305
Lithuania 126, 192, 194, 202, 225,
     242, 246–47, 272, 275, 282, 288
London Declaration on a Transformed
     North Atlantic Alliance 104, 129,
     153, 173, 175, 180
London/Paris agreements 47, 74
Lott, Trent 124
Lugar, Richard G. 112–13, 122, 187,
     245
Luhansk 275, 279, 287, 289
Luxembourg 18, 21, 34, 41, 45, 76,
     134, 199–200, 235, 242, 251

Maastricht (the Netherlands) EC
     Summit/Treaty 158–61, 163, 173
McCain, John 287
McChrystal, Stanley A. 219
McClellan, John 32
Macedonia 116, 126, 141, 194–95,
     246–47
McFaul, Michael 278–79
McMaster, H. R. 298
Macmillan, Harold 63
McNamara, Robert 64
Macron, Emmanuel 294, 304
Madrid (Spain) NATO Summit 119–21
Maidan Nezalezhosti 273, 279
Malaysian Air Airlines, flight MH17
     shot down 280
Mansfield, Mike and the "Mansfield
     Resolutions" 95–96
Markovic, Dusko 299
Marshall, George C. 21
Marshall Plan 6, 21, 33, 76, 344
Martino, Gaetano 57
Marxist critique of capitalism 91–92
Mattis, James 297
May, Theresa 295, 297
MBFR *see* Mutual and Balanced Force
     Reductions

Mearsheimer, John J. 278
Medvedev, Dmitry 227–28, 233–34,
     270
Mendes-France, Pierre 41–42
Merkel, Angela 247, 255, 263, 280,
     282, 287, 297–302, 310, 331–32,
     334, 338
Middle East 78, 80, 238, 244, 267–69,
     289–90, 292–93, 317, 319–20,
     322–27, 330, 333, 335–36
Mikulski, Barbara 123–24
Milosevic, Slobodan 141–44, 148
Minsk Accords 287
Mitterrand, François 104, 154, 175,
     180, 364
MLF *see* nuclear strategy, Multilateral
     Force
Moldova 109, 229, 272
Molotov, V. M. 42
Monnet, Jean 28
Mons (Belgium) 115, 236
Montenegro 14, 135, 272, 299
Morgenthau, Hans J. 4–5, 18
Morocco 308
Moynihan, Patrick 124
MPCC *see* European Union, Military
     Planning and Conduct Capability
Mullen, Mike 215, 249
Munich Security Conference 217, 330
Mutual and Balanced Force Reductions
     (MBFR) 59–60, 79, 81, 106, 108,
     369
Mutual Security Act(s) of 1953, 1954, 40

NAA *see* North Atlantic Assembly
NAC *see* NATO, North Atlantic Council
NACC *see* NATO, North Atlantic
     Cooperation Council
NAFTA *see* North American Free Trade
     Area
NATO (North Atlantic Treaty
     Organization) 5–18, 33–36, 53–59,
     61–69, 103–83, 185–90, 192–93,
     200–206, 212–21, 232–37,
     241–51, 254–73, 275–79,
     281–85, 295–300, 302–12,
     320–30, 341–46, 351–61, 363–67
     1991 strategic concept 12, 104,
     129–32, 137, 154–55, 158,
     173, 259, 318

1999 strategic concept 145–47, 149, 155, 172–73, 179, 185, 206, 258–59, 318

2010 strategic concept 145, 255, 257, 268, 283, 303, 305, 318–19, 353

adaptation 10, 129, 139, 155, 162, 172, 174, 188

Afghanistan and 248–49

alliance theory 4

Allied Command Channel 133

Allied Command Europe 133, 221

Allied Command Operations (ACO) 221

Allied Command Transformation (ACT) 220–21, 238

allied commitments reports 96

authoritarian regimes, tendencies, in 9, 291, 294

burden-sharing and 5–6, 48, 50, 94–99, 216, 218, 265–67, 282, 285, 299, 301, 330–31, 340–42, 364–65, 368

collective defense and 10–11, 15–17, 129–31, 147, 165, 167, 179, 181, 257–60, 282–84, 296–97, 299–300, 306, 326, 355

consensus in 144, 160, 162, 170, 172, 188, 193, 196, 206, 257–58, 323

Cooperative Cyber Defence Centre of Excellence 326

crisis management and 12, 115, 129, 146, 158, 160, 235, 258, 260–62, 352, 356

Defense Capabilities Initiative (DCI) 147, 166, 171, 180, 189, 221

Defense Planning Committee (DPC) 180, 196

Deputy Supreme Allied Commander Europe (D-SACEUR) 140, 162, 171–72, 179

détente and 10, 51, 56–61, 69, 93–94, 106–7, 129

Deterrence and Defense Posture Review 269–70, 308

Euro-Atlantic Partnership Council (EAPC) 15, 115–16, 173, 271–72, 360

Europeanization of 139, 161

European Union and 8, 168, 171, 200, 203, 234–37, 252, 254, 258, 260–61, 263, 265, 332–33

former Soviet republics and 5, 10, 110, 125, 127, 195, 202–3, 225, 228–29, 233–34, 247

Greece-Turkey issue and 34, 260, 332

habits of consultation, cooperation 13, 57, 138, 151, 260

Integrated Command Structure (ICS) 35, 76, 140, 194, 303

International Security Assistance Force (ISAF) 205–11, 213–19, 236–37, 257, 260, 267, 271, 273

see also Afghanistan, International Security Assistance Force

international staff 59

Iraq and 7, 12, 187, 190–92, 195–96, 198–99, 202–4, 206, 214, 229, 231, 235–37, 322–23

Long-Term Study 133

MC 48, 1954 strategy including nuclear weapons 47, 62, 64

Mediterranean and 34, 93, 106, 140, 185, 195, 262, 271, 308, 323–24, 360

Middle East and 93, 223, 244, 256, 267–69, 283, 289–90, 292–93, 317, 319–20, 322–24

Military Committee 11, 47, 168, 171–72

military headquarters in Mons 236

missile defense and 91, 183, 193, 223, 226–28, 258, 268–70, 325

multiple-hatting procedure 140, 162

new strategic concept for 7, 306

non-collective defense and 12, 124, 137, 139, 148–50, 318

North Africa and 244, 289, 317, 319, 322–23, 333

North Atlantic Cooperation Council (NACC) 110–11, 114–15, 175

North Atlantic Council (NAC) 9, 11, 33, 56–57, 59, 170–71, 175, 178–81, 184–85, 224–25, 242, 245, 248–49, 257, 308

Nuclear Planning Group (NPG) 64–65, 153

NATO (North Atlantic Treaty
Organization) (*cont.*)
Planning and Review Process (PARP)
115
post-Cold War role 13, 15, 104,
106–7, 109–11, 119, 125–26,
132–33, 140, 152, 154–55, 162
Provincial Reconstruction Teams
(PRTs) 207, 211, 216
Russia and 7, 123, 128, 223, 232,
257, 275, 306, 359
Secretary General 33, 109, 223–24,
239, 251, 255, 257, 286, 298,
327, 342
Senior Political Committee 58
Standing Naval Forces 185
terrorism and 16–17, 131–32,
183–95, 198, 205, 207, 210,
242–43, 245, 270, 273, 289–90,
318–19, 323–26, 353–54
Ukraine and 229, 231, 271, 275–76,
284
NATO enlargement 111–13, 116–18,
121–27, 177–78, 192–94, 223,
225–26, 231, 244, 246, 276,
278–79
debate in US Senate 128, 177–78
issue of 111, 118, 127, 177, 225, 277
Madrid summit and 173
Membership Action Plan (MAP) 126,
146, 194
nuclear weapons and 128, 225–26,
351
Prague Summit and 192
process of 127, 177, 229, 244
Russia and 276, 310, 326, 366
Study on 117, 121, 173, 177, 194
NATO Parliamentary Assembly (NPA)
125, 147, 167, 180–81, 245
NATO Participation Act of 1994 118
Netherlands 18, 21, 41, 45, 70, 76,
82, 197, 201, 205, 207, 217–18,
235
Nine-Power and Four-Power
Conferences 44–45
Nixon, Richard M. 60, 67, 95–96, 182
Nixon administration 75, 96
Nixon Doctrine 96
North American Free Trade Area
(NAFTA) 297

North Atlantic Assembly (NAA) (now
named "NATO Parliamentary
Assembly") 112, 125, 164, 176,
178, 366, 370
see also NATO Parliamentary
Assembly
North Atlantic Treaty 3–4, 8–9, 11–12,
14–16, 18–19, 21–27, 31–35,
45–46, 95–96, 118–19, 129–30,
184–85, 244–45, 259, 347,
349–50, 352–54
(Article 4) 12, 150, 258–59, 283,
348
(Article 5) 16, 123, 147, 149–50,
186, 188–89, 204, 258
mandate 8–9, 12, 130, 147, 150,
259–60, 323
non-Article 5, 124, 137, 139,
147–50, 189, 318
preamble 9, 84
text 347
North Korea 10, 26, 129, 187
North Macedonia 14, 272
Norway 18, 45, 57, 107, 166, 288
NPA *see* NATO Parliamentary Assembly
NPG *see* NATO, Nuclear Planning Group
nuclear strategy 50, 62, 64–65, 152
extended deterrence 66–69, 71
flexible response 71, 79–80, 129,
152–53
massive retaliation 10, 44, 62, 64,
152
MC 48, 47, 62, 64
Multilateral Force (MLF) 63
no-first-use 154
PD-59, 87
nuclear weapons 10–11, 38, 41, 44,
47–48, 62–66, 71, 74, 85, 149,
151–54, 225–26, 351, 354–55,
357

Obama, Barack 219, 227, 231, 238,
250, 253–54, 256, 264, 268,
285–86, 303, 305–6, 308, 367,
369
administration 209, 213, 218–20,
227, 264, 266, 269–71, 278,
296, 303, 307, 329–30
OEEC *see* Organization for European
Economic Cooperation

Open Skies 57
Operation Deliberate Force 136, 173
Operation Eagle Eye 141
Operation Odyssey Dawn 262
Operation Unified Protector 262–63
Orange Revolution 230, 242, 276
Orbán, Viktor 294
Organization for European Economic
 Cooperation (OEEC) 6
Organization for Security and
 Cooperation in Europe (OSCE)
 15–16, 107–8, 141, 148, 230,
 233, 248, 251, 272, 277, 287
OSCE *see* Organization for Security and
 Cooperation in Europe
Ottawa (Canada) Declaration 55

Pakistan 209–10, 308
Palmerston, John Temple (Lord) 3
Paris climate agreement 302
Paris Club 198
PARP *see* NATO, Planning and Review
 Process
Partnership Coordination Cell 115
Partnership for Peace (PFP) 13, 15,
 105, 113–16, 126, 133, 173, 177,
 271–72, 360
peace dividend 23, 108, 147, 156, 159,
 173
Pearl Harbor 88
Pearson, Lester 47, 57
Permanent Joint Council (PJC) 128,
 224–25
Perry, William and the "Perry
 Principles" 118
Persian Gulf 78, 97
PESCO *see* European Union, Permanent
 Structured Cooperation
Petersberg tasks 159–60, 163
PFP *see* Partnership for Peace
pivot US defense priorities 269, 271,
 303, 329
Platform on European Security Interests
 78
Pleven, René and the "Pleven Plan" 28,
 33
Poland 13–14, 112, 120, 123–24,
 173, 175–77, 193–94, 196–97,
 225, 227, 229, 267–68, 273, 275,
 282–84

Pompidou, Georges 73, 110
Poos, Jacques 134
Portugal 18, 33, 77, 84, 115, 197, 247,
 257, 272, 361
Powell, Colin 151, 182, 198–99
Prague (Czech Republic) Summit 2002,
 191–92, 194–95, 220–21, 242,
 249–50
Protocol on the Termination of the
 Occupation Regime in the Federal
 Republic of Germany 45–46
Protocol to the North Atlantic Treaty
 on the Accession of the Federal
 Republic of Germany 46
PRTs *see* Afghanistan, Provincial
 Reconstruction Teams; NATO,
 Provincial Reconstruction Teams
PSC *see* European Union, Political and
 Security Committee
Putin, Vladimir 223–25, 228–29, 244,
 269–70, 273–74, 276, 278–80,
 283, 286, 298, 300–301, 308–11,
 321–22, 335–36

radical right populism 300, 333–34, 345
Ralston, Joseph 186, 255
Rasmussen, Anders Fogh 255, 257,
 281, 285
Reagan, Ronald 70, 79
 administration of 61, 70, 87, 90, 92,
 182
refugee crisis 323, 333
Reykjavik (Iceland), signal, declaration
 59, 170, 181, 220, 249
Rice, Condoleezza 201, 237
Rinkevics, Edgars 327
RMA *see* United States, Revolution in
 Military Affairs
Robertson, George 167, 170, 185, 196,
 223–25, 235
Romania 14, 120, 126, 192, 194, 225,
 231, 242, 246–47, 272, 275
Rome (Italy) Declaration 110, 181, 359
Rome Treaties 6, 53, 76–77, 79
Roosevelt, Franklin 20, 22
Rose Revolution 232
Rosner, Jeremy D. 121–23, 125, 224
Roth, William V. 120–22, 125, 164,
 178, 181, 366
Rühe, Volker 112

Rühle, Michael 277, 310
Rumsfeld, Donald 182, 204, 237, 249
Russia 7–8, 10–11, 13, 15–17, 108–11,
    122–24, 126–28, 193–94, 204,
    223–34, 244–46, 250, 269–70,
    273–89, 291–93, 298–99, 303–5,
    308–10, 317–28, 359–60
  aggression 64, 152, 254, 256, 270,
    278–79, 282–84, 287–89,
    299–301, 319–20, 327
  Balkans and 16, 133, 148
  borders, concerns about 128, 225,
    233, 288, 320
  Chechnya and 127, 343
  Conventional Forces in Europe (CFE)
    and 251
  dissatisfied 127
  domination 269
  energy/gas 230–31, 279–80, 301,
    310
  Georgia and 232, 250
  humiliated 278
  information warfare 326–27
  isolation of 277
  Kaliningrad enclave 227
  missile defense and 123, 193, 223,
    226–28, 269–70, 325
  NATO, relations with 224, 234, 242,
    333, 360
  NATO enlargement and 5, 113,
    123–24, 127, 178, 231, 244,
    276–77, 305, 326
  revisionist agenda 267, 278, 320–21
  support for illiberalism 321
  Syria and 274, 322–24
  threats 14, 285, 320–21, 345
  Ukraine and 250, 254, 256, 273–75,
    281–82, 284, 287–88, 304,
    309, 320, 322, 326

Saakashvili, Mikheil 232
SACEUR *see* Supreme Allied
    Commander, Europe
Saint-Malo (France) Declaration
    165–67, 173, 181
SALT *see* Strategic Arms Limitation
    Talks
Sanders, Bernie 293
Sarajevo (Bosnia and Herzegovina) 50,
    136, 176, 236

Sarkozy, Nicolas 50, 140, 203, 238,
    254–55, 303
Sayle, Timothy 343
Scheffer, Jaap de Hoop 199, 225, 235,
    239, 251, 255
Schmidt, Helmut 66
Schroeder, Gerhard 165, 190, 198, 280
Schuman, Robert 26, 28–29, 33
Scowcroft, Brent 157, 160, 174
Security Identity, European 180
Serbia 129, 133, 135–37, 141–43,
    147–50, 163, 166, 173, 272
SFOR *see* Stabilization Force (SFOR), in
    Bosnia
Shalikashvili, John 113
Slovakia 14, 126, 177, 192, 194, 225,
    242, 246–47, 272
Slovenia 14, 120, 125–26, 133, 177,
    192, 194, 225, 242, 246, 272
Smith, Gordon 124
Smith, Robert 124
Solana, Javier 163–64, 167, 170,
    238–39, 251
Sommer, Theo 241
South Ossetia 108, 232–34, 270
Soviet Union 5, 20, 26–27, 44, 47–48,
    55, 57–59, 61–62, 66–71, 74,
    78–79, 85, 89–94, 97–98, 103–4,
    106–11, 126–30, 132–33,
    152–54, 277–78
Spaak, Paul-Henri 41
Spain 14, 32, 51, 77, 110, 116, 119,
    196, 198–99, 288, 293
Spofford, Charles 28–29
Srebrenica (Yugoslavia) peacekeeping
    disaster 136
Stabilization Force (SFOR), in Bosnia
    137, 141, 163, 237
Stalin, Joseph 20, 39
Stavridis, James G. 255, 264, 281,
    363
Stevens, David 122
Stockholm (Sweden) Accord on
    Confidence and Security Building
    Measures and Disarmament 106
Stoltenberg, Jens 286, 301
Strasbourg/Kehl Summit 248, 255
Strategic Arms Limitation Talks (SALT)
    61, 66, 82
  SALT II treaty 61, 70

Supreme Allied Commander, Europe
(SACEUR) 31–32, 38, 47, 64, 113,
115, 139, 162, 186, 255–56, 264
Sweden 106, 168, 193, 246, 272, 293
Syria 254, 277, 284–85, 289–90,
319–20, 322–24, 337

Taft, Robert 31–32
Taft IV, William 157
Tajikistan 108, 233, 272
Talbot, Strobe 111, 113, 117, 128
Taylor, Maxwell D. 338
Tchakarova, Velina 328
terrorism 131–32, 183–89, 191–92,
195, 220, 223, 243, 245–46, 296,
299, 318–19, 324, 326, 353
attacks 91, 98, 186, 188, 193–94,
220, 223, 241, 245, 299, 302
Global War on Terror (GWOT) 94,
205, 247
radical Islamist 83, 131–32, 152,
183–84, 186, 191, 270,
324–25, 333, 353–54
threats 131, 187, 324
Test Ban Treaty 53
Thatcher, Margaret 104
threat perceptions 147, 268, 328
threats 11, 41–42, 48, 67–68, 94,
130–32, 147–50, 184–85,
222–23, 226–27, 258–60,
285, 289–90, 292–94, 317–20,
322–30, 340–41, 345–47, 353,
355–56
cyber 259, 303, 326
new 83, 149, 152, 253, 257, 317,
319, 323, 325, 327, 351
"three Ds" 158, 166–67
"three Is" 167
Tito, Josip Broz 133
transatlantic bargain 3–4, 6–8, 16–18,
20–21, 31–32, 35, 37–49, 51–52,
79–80, 83, 151–52, 155–56, 346,
363, 367, 369
Transatlantic Trade and Investment
Partnership (TTIP) 297
Trans-Pacific Partnership 297
Treaty of Amsterdam 163
Treaty of Dunkirk 21
Treaty of Washington *see* North Atlantic
Treaty

Treaty on Conventional Armed Forces
in Europe 108, 130, 232
Tripartite Agreement on the Exercise of
Retained Rights in Germany 45
Tripartite Joint Intelligence Operations
Center 209
Truman, Harry 20, 22, 31, 367, 369
administration of 7, 9, 21–22, 24,
28, 32–33, 35, 38
Truman Doctrine 21, 27–28
Trump, Donald J. 290, 292, 295–305,
312–13, 320–21, 324, 329–31,
335, 339, 343, 345
administration of 289, 291, 298,
303, 305, 321, 324–25, 346
approach to Europe/NATO 297–99,
302, 312, 324, 330–31
disruption 296, 301
influence of Putin and Russia
298–301, 304, 320–21, 335,
343
TTIP *see* Transatlantic Trade and
Investment Partnership
Turkey 14–15, 34–35, 166, 172,
194–96, 240, 247, 260, 272, 277,
290–92, 332, 334
Tymoshenko, Yulia 273

Ukraine 8, 10–11, 14, 228–32, 242,
247, 250, 271–84, 286–89,
299–301, 309, 311, 321–22,
326–27, 336–37
Crimea 231, 274, 309
crisis 18, 281–82, 285, 309–11,
332–33, 365, 367
destabilize 276
distinctive partner 284
divided 230
eastern 287
former Soviet republic 5, 195
government of 273, 287
Orange Revolution 230, 242, 276
regions of Donetsk and Luhansk 275,
289
Russia and 229–30, 280, 309
UN *see* United Nations
United Kingdom 18, 20–21, 25–26,
45–46, 52–53, 55, 63, 70–74, 80,
91–92, 144–45, 147–49, 153–54,
164, 307–8

Afghanistan role 185, 205, 215,
    217–18, 243
Commonwealth and 25, 72–73, 185
Conservative Party 293
Europe and 25, 46, 71–73, 77, 164,
    290, 293, 295, 297, 342, 345
global role 7, 25, 37, 72
Northern Ireland and 131
nuclear role 53–54, 63, 154, 354
parliament 9, 295
United States, special relationship
    with 25, 72–73, 203, 342
United Nations (UN) 136–38, 142,
    146–48, 205, 208, 229, 233, 243,
    248, 259, 261, 344, 347–52
mandate issues 134, 137–38, 142,
    148–49, 190, 196–97, 206,
    208, 210, 216, 234
Security Council 135, 142, 148, 196,
    259, 278, 348–49, 352
UNPROFOR (Protection Force)
    134–36
United States 3–7, 12–18, 24–29,
    35–53, 61–66, 69–76, 87–99,
    118–29, 131–45, 147–58,
    160–67, 179–92, 194–205,
    212–23, 232–47, 261–67,
    272–85, 296–305, 320–25,
    333–40
Balkans and 123, 134, 136, 138, 151
Democratic Party 296
Department of Defense 45, 160
Department of State 27, 111, 113,
    236
Europe, relations with 85–99, 158,
    164, 166, 169, 171, 192, 200,
    202–3, 234–38, 241
France, relations with 24–27, 29,
    40–44, 50–55, 139–40, 143,
    160, 162, 200, 203, 235, 238,
    241, 243
global role 92, 94, 97, 160, 339, 344
hegemony 120, 145, 190, 197, 200
International Criminal Court 182
Joint Chiefs of Staff 162, 215
Kyoto Protocol and 182
missile defense 63, 91, 183, 193, 223,
    226–28, 250, 268, 308, 325
National Security Agency (NSA)
    334–35

National Security Council 39, 47,
    117, 245
"National Security Strategy of the
    United States" 191, 246
"new look" approach to defense
    strategy 38, 41, 47, 63
nuclear weapons in Europe 6, 10, 38,
    41, 47, 85, 95, 152–55, 225,
    285, 357
presence and role in Europe 14, 22,
    27–29, 32, 62, 80, 95–96, 157,
    187, 264
Republican Party 296, 330
Revolution in Military Affairs (RMA)
    94, 166, 239
Russia, relations with 111, 113,
    118, 123–24, 226–28, 231,
    270, 275–76, 278–79, 281–82,
    298–301, 304–5
Soviet Union, relations with 21, 53,
    58, 60–62, 67–70, 89–92, 97,
    128, 153, 326
unilateralism 17, 81, 151, 190–91,
    197–98, 200, 239–40
vulnerability, attitudes toward
    90–91, 99
"war on terrorism" 94, 184, 187,
    189, 193–94, 205, 273, 293
"yes, but" approach to European
    defense cooperation 157, 171,
    180
United States Congress 6–7, 20–25,
    27–28, 31–32, 39–40, 96,
    117–19, 121, 176–79, 264, 266,
    365, 367, 369
burden-sharing and 48, 50, 96, 187
Great Debate 31
House of Representatives 6, 117, 195
NATO enlargement and 112–13,
    117–25, 177–78, 195, 246
Senate ix, 6, 22–23, 31–32, 35,
    70, 96, 99, 118–21, 123–25,
    177–78
Senate Committee on Armed Services
    121, 177
Senate Committee on Foreign
    Relations 120, 122, 124
Senate NATO Observer Group
    121–22, 177–79
Senate Resolution 8, 31–32

"war powers" and 32
UNPROFOR *see* United Nations,
  UNPROFOR
Uzbekistan 233, 247, 272

Vandenberg, Arthur H. 20, 22
Vandenberg Resolution 21–22
Vershbow, Alexander 117
Vietnam War 31, 43, 88, 93, 95, 267

Walesa, Lech 112
Wales Summit Declaration 281, 283,
  286, 311, 319, 326, 331, 336, 342
Warner, John 123–25
Warsaw Pact 5, 59, 62, 64–65, 81, 83,
  85, 103–4, 106–7, 109–10, 113,
  126–28, 130, 173, 176
Warsaw (Poland) 81, 116, 300
  Bill Clinton's comments in 117
  Donald J. Trump speech in 300
  George W. Bush speech in 193
Washington (D.C.) Summit 145–46,
  149, 166, 191, 221
Washington Treaty *see* North Atlantic
  Treaty
weapons of mass destruction 3, 8, 11,
  17, 131, 226, 318–20, 353, 357
Wellstone, Paul 124, 178
the West 3, 44, 99, 282, 286, 293, 317,
  324, 329, 339, 346

Western ideals 290
  of democracy 292
Western model 335
Western values 289, 300, 324, 328,
  333, 335
Western weakness 332
Western European Union (WEU) 46,
  78–79, 132, 134, 139, 157, 159,
  161–63, 165, 167, 169
West Germany 24–25, 32, 34–35, 45,
  47, 52, 70, 73–76, 82, 95,
  103–4
WEU *see* Western European Union
Wherry, Kenneth 31
Wherry resolution 31–32
Wilson, Charles 39
Wilson, Woodrow 20, 119
Woerner, Manfred 104, 109, 174
Wolfowitz, Paul 195, 198

Yanukovych, Viktor 228, 273–74, 280,
  304
Year of Europe 51
Yeltsin, Boris 118–19, 223
Yugoslavia 133–34, 141–43, 178,
  364
Yushchenko, Viktor 230

Zapatero, Jose Luis Rodriguez 198
zero option proposal 70